Do you know what you need to know about:

—The differing personality characteristics of various dog breeds

—The physical and mental stages of a dog's development

—The arguments for and against spaying

—The normal dog lifespan

—The prevention and treatment of neuroses that a dog may pick up

—Dangers of environmental pollution that threaten a dog

—The vast and varied assortment of illnesses and accidents that a dog may suffer

—All the other knowledge that should be mastered to fulfill your responsibility and ensure your dog's health and happiness

You will find everything at your fingertips, arranged for easy reading and instant reference in this most valuable of all guides.

"When we finished the book, we could only wonder why it has taken so long to make such information available to the layman. Dr. Vine's book isn't just good, nor simply really good. It's the best!"
                                                            —Dog Fancy *Magazine*

"The finest, most authoritative and up-to-date book on dog care . . . a *must* for every dog owner!"
                                            —*Cecily R. Collins, breeder, exhibitor*

Books by
Louis L. Vine, D.V.M.

*Common Sense Book
of Complete Cat Care*

The Total Dog Book

Available from
WARNER BOOKS

THE TOTAL DOG BOOK

by Louis L. Vine, D.V.M.

The Breeders' and Pet Owners' Complete Guide
To Better Dog Care

Edited by Norma C. Scofield

WARNER BOOKS

A Warner Communications Company

WARNER BOOKS EDITION

Copyright © 1971, 1977 *by Louis L. Vine.*
All rights reserved.

This Warner Books Edition is published by
arrangement with the author

Warner Books, Inc
666 Fifth Avenue
New York, N.Y. 10103

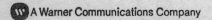 A Warner Communications Company

Printed in the United States of America

First Warner Books Printing: *February, 1984*

10 9 8 7 6 5

Tenderly dedicated to

FLORENCE

and to

THE VETERINARIAN

(21 Doctors in 1)

In the treatment of human beings, there are 21 men, each specializing in a different field of medicine, to take a person from prenatal days to post-mortem. And yet, there is *one* man who must be obstetrician - pediatrician - orthodontist - exodontist - endocrinologist - internist - orthopedist - surgeon - psychiatrist - psychologist - urologist - gynecologist - neurologist-neurosurgeon - psychoanalyst - metabolist - dietitian - cardiologist - roentgenologist - geriatrist - pathologist to take a dog through his span of life.

He is, of course, your *veterinarian*.

—Adapted from *The Italian Greyhound*

VETERINARIAN

We think of him as someone who
Attends to dogs and cats;
Prescribes a little medicine
And gives them loving pats.

Who keeps them from distemper and
From rabies when they stray,
And boards our precious animals
The weeks we go away.

But seldom do we realize when
We pay his little fee
How hard he has to study for
His medical degree,
His knowledge of our horses and
Our cows and hogs and sheep,
And how he serves in peace and war.

And who is there to estimate
His everlasting worth
As he devotes his life to all
God's animals on earth?

—JAMES J. METCALFE

Contents

Part Two

AN OUNCE OF PREVENTION

Part Three

GOOD, BAD, OR INDIFFERENT BEHAVIOR

Part Five

BREEDING

Part Six

QUESTIONS AND ANSWERS

Part Seven

APPENDIX: UP-TO-DATE DEVELOPMENTS

PREFACE

During the course of the centuries a quiet revolution has occurred in the relationship between man and his dog. In the beginning dogs served as man's slaves. They provided a cheap form of labor that liberated man from certain drudgeries. They also acted as man's protectors. But how the roles have reversed! The dog has become the pet—the privileged and protected member of the family. Man now serves and protects his dogs.

With the changing relationship between man and dog, the functions of the veterinarian are being transformed. The veterinarian can no longer limit himself solely to safeguarding the physical health of the family pet; he must become involved in the mental health of the pet's family. This trend is so interchangeable that many psychologists believe that in the near future veterinarians will become members of mental-hygiene teams. Highly charged emotional currents are characteristic of the relationship between a dog and his master. The veterinarian is witness to the complex dynamics of personality—the interplay between the pet and his human family. Pets mirror and localize man's emotional illnesses. They serve as therapeutic agents and aids for emotional health.

To people with problems a pet can mean the difference between sickness and health, between despair and a will to live. A famous psychiatrist once said, "I have found that the therapeutic value in the companionship of a pet is ofttimes better medicine than can be found in a bottle or a pill." There is an increasing use of pets in mental and physical therapy. The life of an aged person can become a monotonous and lonely ritual. Often the companionship of a dog will add new dimensions to that life. It is heartening to see a single puppy lift the spirits of an entire retirement home. The same holds true for shut-ins. People, old and young alike, with chronic illnesses seem to thrive on the companionship of a dog.

Troubled children, too, profit immeasurably from having a pet. With the mentally disturbed, animals often succeed where humans fail. A chronic introvert can possibly be brought out of his shell with animal companionship. Not uncommonly, when society has all but given up on a juvenile delinquent, the responsibility of caring for a pet has wrought almost miraculous change. Through their understanding and instinctive love, dogs are able to reach youngsters whose lives are lacking in love and genuine friendship. Through looking after a pet, the youngster learns that he is needed and accepted by at least one living creature. By learning to accept love from an animal a youngster can go on to affectionate loving relationships with humans.

Emotional disorders in children can be prevented by pets. If the youngster succeeds in teaching his dog, he will have learned a great deal about controlling himself. The dog learns from his master, and the boy learns about himself from his dog. A pet enlarges the scope of a child's experience in ways both happy and sad. Even the crises and sufferings that a boy may share with a pet can provide important growth and learning experiences. When the dog is seriously ill, or injured, the child knows extreme anxiety and distress. The death of a pet can be a rehearsal, on a small scale, of the suffering we all have to face in the death of a loved one. Through this experience a child can develop sympathy for living things and a compassion for pets in distress which may transmit itself into sympathetic understanding of the emotional suffering of humans.

If at all possible, every child should be raised with a pet. The sharing of love and understanding with a dog is real life in capsule form. To form a loving friendship with a dog is an invaluable prelude to warm relationships with people—and the child gains an insight into the happiness, the sadness, and the realities he will be facing in his upcoming life.

L.L.V.

INTRODUCTION

In writing about dogs I am really writing about people. Through my thirty-three years of caring for dogs I have been able to see into the private lives of most of their so-called masters. I have seen people make incredible sacrifices for their dogs, and I have seen them make fools of themselves. I have seen lonely people find rewarding companionship, and I have seen selfish people abandon their dogs because they would not be inconvenienced. I have seen dogs pampered with dyed hair and painted toenails, and I have seen them appallingly mutilated through superstitions.

Although there are many dogs in my life—and I sincerely believe that dogs are wonderful people—I should like to make one point clear. There are also real people in my life. I like people. Some of my best friends are people. But the longer I think upon it, the more convinced I am that dogs aren't just dogs. They are people too. At least they think they are, and I'm not so sure that they aren't right. Certainly dogs are the only animals who would rather be with humans than with their own species. They will desert other dogs to be with their masters, and they will even fight packs of dogs or other animals to protect their human families. So many of their problems are so similar to those of humans too—physical ailments, emotional problems, psychosomatic illnesses, and even personality clashes. Psychiatry, geriatrics, and plastic surgery for cosmetic purposes are not limited to the two-footed animal. Not many years ago the veterinarian was known as a horse doctor; today he has to be physician, surgeon, psychoanalyst, babysitter, and whittler at the roots of superstitions.

However, your dog, despite all his human qualities, and because ability to talk is not one of them, is wholly dependent on your knowledge and understanding of him as his means of communication with you. Because you are his world, he desires above all to be known and understood—to be as much a part of your love and life as possible. His reason for being is to serve you, to comfort you, and my reason for writing this book is to help him fulfill his destiny—*to help you raise your dog to be a healthy, happy, and well-adjusted individual who will in return help to make you a contented and well-adjusted dog owner.* With this aim I have tried to keep technical details and medical phraseology at a minimum and have concentrated on your dog in terms of common-sense knowledge in everyday language.

In communicating emotions, the dog's tail is the barometer of his ups and downs. And here again, in his emotional fluctuations, there is a significant parallel with humans. Through close association pets acquire many of their owners' likes and dislikes and personality traits. Unfortunately some of these characteristics are undesirable. We are seeing more and more nervous and neurotic dogs in our veterinary clinics as the human race becomes more neurosis-ridden. I don't mean to imply that all bad habits in the dog come from humans. Canine playmates are often mischievous and bad-habit mates (chasing cars, for instance, can be learned from a buddy), and some dogs are emotionally disturbed by heredity or from birth. Nonetheless, the main responsibility for each dog's behavior rests with his owner. Each dog expects his master to guide him through life in good health, and in return he gives the ultimate in love, loyalty, and lifelong affection.

The early recognition and detection of any physical, emotional, or mental abnormality in your dog is paramount in the maintenance of his health. There is no one better qualified than you, his master, to know when he is not feeling well. Any deviation from a habit or any abnormal manifestation is a signal for you to look for reasons. *This book can serve as a guide to the health and well-being of your pet as well as to the symptoms and treatment of the ailments and diseases he is subject to.* It is not meant to be used for diagnoses and treatment, but is meant to guide you in knowing when you should get your dog to your veterinarian—usually as soon as possible. Even the most competent veterinarian benefits immeasurably in the treatment of your pet from your help in getting the patient to him during the earliest stages of any illness.

Research is progressing rapidly in all eighteen veterinary colleges in the United States and in schools throughout the world. Research is also being conducted on a large scale in the larger drug and dog-food company laboratories. The pooling of this knowledge through seminars, articles, conventions, etcetera, is rapidly improving the standards of available veterinary medical treatment.

Veterinary medicine is also benefiting greatly from the advancement of medical research in human fields. The way I look at it, if it's good enough for human beings, it's all right to use on my canine friends.

With the advancement of drugs and techniques, animals who not long ago were considered hopeless are now being saved as daily routine in any good veterinary hospital.

As a result of the tremendous strides in veterinary research, the United States is in the midst of a remarkable revolution in veterinary medicine. Service in an animal hospital is now comparable to that given in the most modern human hospital. In response to demands for better medical treatment for pets, small-animal hospitals in the country are increasing nine times as fast as hospitals for humans. Today there are more than 4,000 small-animal hospitals where you will find the latest equipment. You will find air-conditioned kennels with piped-in music to soothe the nerves of homesick patients. There are cages with piped-in oxygen for the pet who is in shock or is having difficulty breathing. Most good veterinary clinics have a blood bank stocked for any emergency—and attendants on duty around the clock. Veterinarians employ the full range of medical knowledge, such as intravenous anesthetics and feeding, tranquilizers, antibiotics, and blood analysis. The latest in laboratory diagnostic equipment is available: heart ailments can be diagnosed with the EKG (electrocardiograph) machine; brain and spinal diseases can be diagnosed with the EEG (electroencephalograph) machine. The latest surgical procedures are being performed as routine practice. Even open-heart surgery is becoming more common, as well as other refined types of surgical operations. Canine dentistry has progressed to where the veterinarian uses high-frequency dental units to remove tartar from the teeth, and extractions of decayed and infected teeth and the care of sore gums are routine in most veterinary hospitals.

Specialization is growing apace in veterinary medicine, with many veterinarians devoting their time solely to surgery, radiology, heart diseases, eye diseases, and various other aspects of canine and feline medicine.

With the revolution in veterinary research and medicine, many dogs are living longer, and the fairly new field of geriatrics is gaining prominence. It is now possible to treat heart, liver, kidney diseases, rheumatism, and arthritis in aging dogs. Many of the patients are brought back to health so that they can enjoy added years of life and give added years of joy to their owners and companions. Most veterinarians oppose euthanasia, or mercy killing, unless the animal is hopelessly and totally ill. In the past it was the easy way out to destroy the dog; today most veterinarians will work tirelessly in the attempt to save your pet.

For your dog's well-being and your peace of mind you must both have confidence in your veterinarian and his staff. And by cooperating with your veterinarian you both can receive the full benefit of their knowledge, ability, and skills.

Today more than 55 percent of all American families own some kind of pet. There are over 25 million dogs in the United States. These dogs are a valued part of our families and fill the void in many lonely lives. It is to these faithful companions and protectors that I dedicate this book.

Part One

A DOG IS A DOG IS A . .

1 SELECTING A PUPPY

Since dogs come in all sizes, shapes, colors, hair lengths, and temperaments—and prices—choosing a puppy for the first time and while flying blind can sometimes be an almost soul-shattering experience. Although some knowledge of basic breed characteristics is helpful, actually no breed is smartest, cleanest, most affectionate, or best with children. Most dogs are what their masters make them, and most of all they require love, effort, time, and patience.

There are more than 150 kinds of purebred dogs alone, to say nothing of the mongrels and crossbreeds. More than one-third of the families in America own dogs, about 8 million of which are purebred. But whether purebred or of mixed parentage, each dog is as pure a friend as any man can have.

No two dogs are alike in personality, and each breed has its special characteristics. In buying a purebred there is a reasonable guarantee that the puppy will grow up to resemble his parents and the rest of his breed in temperament as well as in looks and size. In spite of the popular belief, the mongrel has no edge on the purebred in health and intelligence. Although all dogs are subject to the same diseases and ailments, actually far more purebreds survive than mongrels because most breeders strive to eliminate hereditary diseases and congenital defects. But the heart of the mongrel dog is as big as that of any purebred, and when he is properly cared for he returns just as much devotion.

Dogs vary in intelligence much as do their owners—genius or moron, smart or dumb. Intelligence is developed with training, although some dogs are born with native intelligence and reasoning power. Also, as with humans, no one dog and no one breed is perfect. We all have our faults.

All dogs came from two common ancestors millions of years ago. Even though they have changed in shape and size through the centuries, some breeds claim the wolf as their ancestor, while the rest claim the jackal. Collies, with their weather-resistant coats and their endurance and cleverness, were selected to be bred as herd dogs. The northern dogs, such as the husky, chowchow, and Samoyed, all with their heavy coats and curled tails to protect their noses while sleeping in the cold and their powerful build, were bred to be sled and draft animals. Terrier dogs, powerful little animals, were bred to catch rats and badgers, by farmers and hunters in the British Isles. The guard dogs, on the other hand, come from the Greek and Roman arenas, and the bull mastiffs are their ancestors. They were large and stout-hearted and often had to fight lions in the arena.

BREEDS

Some breeds are born to be cuddly, some are aristocratic and don't want much handling, some want to be just hunters, and others want to be guardians. Still others just want to be carefree and lovable. And each dog varies in each breed.

In deciding which breed to pick, besides considering size, color, and type of coat, there are breed temperament characteristics which are quite dependable.

For example, the hunting breeds are usually happiest when they have lots of room in which to run about freely, exposed to the elements where there are birds and rabbits to chase. If they are kept confined to a house for long periods, they become edgy and rambunctious. However, many bird dogs, setters, and pointers become wonderful companions as well as fine hunters. It is not true that making a pet out of a hunting dog ruins him as a hunter. It all depends on the love and attention the owner gives the dog. Each owner makes his dog what he is.

Chihuahuas, Pomeranians, and Pekingese usually tend to be high-strung and nervous and are more compatible with adults. Beagles and other hound breeds are easy to handle. Cocker spaniels are a little temperamental, although lovable. Boxers, English bulldogs, setters, and pointers are usually good-natured.

Some breeds are more high-strung than others, mostly because of inherited characteristics which occasionally can be altered with proper environment and training. Mostly, what the dog is depends on his training and on the person who owns him. Dogs are adaptable, and they adjust to their environment whether it is an apartment in New York City or a farm in Kansas.

In choosing a breed, consider the climate in which you live. The short-faced breeds, such as the bulldog, are not likely to survive a very hot climate. Dogs with long, heavy coats are troublesome where there are not distinct seasonal changes so that they can shed their coats. In subtropical or tropical climates I would recommend short-coated dogs with long-nosed heads. In cold climates the chowchow, spitz, Samoyed, Norwegian elkhound, and Newfoundland seem to thrive best.

In some breeds the cropping of ears and the docking of tails is done to uphold the looks of the breed. If you choose such a breed, you should have it done. It is not cruel, and the surgery is performed under general anesthetic. Those who don't approve of ear cropping and tail docking should not pick such a breed.

In determining which breed to choose, go through some of the good books especially created for this purpose and containing pictures and detailed descriptions of the various breeds. You can't always depend on the salesmanship of a breeder or pet-shop owner.

BARGAIN PUPPY, GOOD SPECIMEN OR GOOD PEDIGREE

The price of a dog depends on breed, sex, age, and how close he is to the standards of perfection of his breed. A bargain puppy may have a minor flaw which will keep him out of the show ring, but as long as he is suited in personality to a family, he will be perfect as a pet and companion.

It is best to have a combination of a good specimen with an excellent pedigree. By good specimen I mean a dog that looks like the standard of the breed—the better the conformation, the more perfect he will be. In other words, I would always pick the good specimen with a fairly good ancestry (good sire and good dam) over one with a champion-studded pedigree but not necessarily a perfect specimen himself. The novice buyer cannot expect to walk into a kennel or pet shop and buy a champion. Development of champions takes generations of selective breeding.

Many show dogs are as lovable and intelligent as any ordinary pet. As a matter of fact, a show dog should be both a superb and a lovable dog. You can have both qualities in the same animal.

TEMPERAMENT, DISPOSITION, AND INTELLIGENCE

Temperament, disposition, stability, and trainability should be looked into and discussed before getting any dog of any breed. Although one dog may be more difficult to train than another, certain breed characteristics can be depended on. Each dog varies in temperament according to how he is bred and to the happiness or unhappiness of his childhood. Puppies who have had early handling and patient rearing usually have the best chance for a good relationship with humans.

Select a well-developed, outgoing puppy. Don't choose a puppy who hides in corners, who is shy and retiring, unless you are deliberately choosing a dog with emotional problems and are willing to give him a great deal of love and attention to keep him from being a misfit. Some people take on such dogs as a personal challenge, and with tender loving care some of the dogs become well-adjusted pets. As a rule, however, it is best to pass up a neurotic and shy dog, as he may be temperamental, as well as dangerous.

Watching a puppy play is helpful in determining temperament and certain emotional traits. A good temperament usually manifests itself in curiosity, friendliness, and playfulness.

Some people think that the puppy who opens his eyes first will be the healthiest and smartest of the litter. Others believe that the puppy who gets out of the nest first will be the most intelligent. Other firsts are the first to play and the most fearless. Although all these opinions have some merit, they are not always entirely accurate. When I personally pick a dog from a litter, I choose the one that is the most friendly and most desirous of affection. As I constantly reiterate, to me temperament is the outstanding quality of all.

SEX

The female has the advantage. She is more easily trained and housebroken, more sanitary, more sensitive to children and their needs, and better-behaved in the house.

Of course, she does have her heat periods, disturbing both the household and the neighborhood. If she is not spayed, the twice-a-year job of keeping her confined for 3 weeks should be considered. For those who wish to raise a litter or two, the bitch can be spayed afterward.

The male, when he gets the call of the wild during certain seasons, will stray from home in search of a companion. He may stay away two or three days and return home quite beaten up. During the period of courting he will indulge in several fights to establish himself as the leading contender for the affection of the female who is the center of all the attention.

Some aggressive males will fight for any reason to assert themselves. If there are several large aggressive dogs in the neighborhood, I don't advise getting a large male dog, as there will be many fights—both dogs and people—and it will be easy to lose a friend or a neighbor.

More and more people are having their male dogs castrated to keep them at home and to counteract their aggressiveness. Castrated males make excellent pets and are similar to spayed females in affection. If the situation requires it, I heartily endorse the castration of male dogs—much to the dismay of my Samsonian male friends who think that depriving the male of his rightful hormones is a crime against nature.

The decision between female and male is strictly a matter of preference. Females are inclined to be more gentle with children, less damaging inside and outside, and less apt to roam. Males, on the other hand, are inclined to be more aggressive and are usually better watchdogs.

LONG-HAIRED OR SHORT-HAIRED

Short-coated breeds shed as much as long-coated breeds. Although with long-haired breeds, long hairs are more noticeable, short hairs also must be picked out of carpets and upholstery.

In apartments short-haired breeds shed a little hair all year round. Long-haired breeds shed mostly in the spring and fall. But frequent brushing and grooming will remove most of the loose dead hair and prevent it from being a nuisance in any breed. Any breed can adapt to indoor living so long as the house is not overheated.

If a breed is desired that can be kept outdoors summer and winter, a long-coated one is probably preferable. A short-coated breed, properly housed, can live outdoors in unheated but dry and draftless quarters, although if the weather tends to get very cold, a heated kennel should be provided.

Some breeds don't shed under normal conditions, and that is one of the reasons the poodle has become such a favorite. So too the Kerry blue terrier. When they do shed, it signifies some kind of metabolic disturbance. But such breeds require professional grooming every 6 to 8 weeks, and this should be taken into consideration. The old English sheep dog and the Afghan hound require daily brushing and combing to keep their coats in good condition.

COLOR

Some dogs change color when they get older; for example, the silver poodle is born black and starts changing at 6 to 8 weeks. Bedlington terriers and Kerry blues change from black to gray. Weimaraner puppies are sometimes born with stripes which change as they get older. Dalmatians are usually born pure white. To test a young Dalmatian to see how his spots will appear, wet him down, and the pigmentation will show on his skin.

SIZE

In determining size, whether one lives in the city or the country, in a small apartment or a house, is looking for a lap dog or a field companion, are all matters to be taken into consideration. However, large dogs do adapt to apartment living.

Certainly the small toy breeds readily adapt to restricted quarters, require little exercise, are easily carried about and are efficient burglar alarms. But some of the large breeds are well disciplined, need less exercise and are less inclined to damage furniture and draperies than are some of the smaller more excitable breds. If a large dog is taken out three times a day, with the normal amount of time for playing and romping, he can easily be maintained in a small area. It depends entirely on the dog's temperament.

For the king-sized dogs, such as the Great Dane, Irish wolfhound, Great Pyrenees, Newfoundland, and St. Bernard, I advise the owner to have plenty of room.

A minor consideration is food bills. The larger the dog is, the more he will eat. But once a dog is mature—even the Great Dane or the St. Bernard—he doesn't eat that much more food in proportion to his size than the medium-sized dog. Of course, in the growing stage, the first year of his life, he does pack away huge quantities.

AGE

There is a widely held belief that if one wants a friendly and satisfactory puppy, it should be taken directly from the mother's breast right into the home. This is not necessarily so, as many mature dogs adapt beautifully to a new environment and many stray dogs stick around long enough to become devoted family members.

There are many who prefer to buy an older dog because they feel that bad dispositions and serious faults are often hidden by puppy charm.

The psychologists with animal behavior in mind say that the ideal age for getting a puppy is about 8 weeks. But if there are young children in the house, an older puppy, 3 months and up, is better, because a puppy any younger is not strong enough to repel rough handling. If there is someone in the family who has a fear of dogs, then it is best to buy a puppy as young as possible. As the dog grows the fearful person will more easily adjust to it.

There are disadvantages in picking a very young puppy. Because of the diseases and parasites the puppy is prone to, the new owner must be certain that the puppy has received adequate immunity from his mother's colostrum (first milk) or from inoculations; the very young puppy is destructive of furniture, rugs, and clothing; and the younger the puppy, the more exasperating is the housebreaking process.

Although 8 to 12 weeks of age is when most puppies are sold, some people who don't want to go through the early puppy trials and tribulations enjoy a retired brood bitch or a stud who is no longer in demand. A dog who has been retired from the show ring can also adjust to a new owner if the dog is of a normal and healthy temperament. Older dogs can make good pets.

Even though, in my opinion, 8 to 12 weeks is the best time to get a puppy, age doesn't really matter if you can determine that he is lovable and affectionate. Half-grown or grown dogs deserve a chance at human companionship. The adage that you can't teach an old dog new tricks is not necessarily correct.

THE HUMAN FAMILY

In deciding to get a puppy, make sure that the entire family will give affection to this bundle of love, and that the little tyke will receive daily care, feeding, grooming, training, cleaning, and control.

Whether your family would live easier with a docile pet or a boisterous and playful one is also a consideration. But no matter which, you should choose a puppy who is wide awake, responds promptly when called, exhibits a friendly disposition, and is easygoing.

Nervous pets make nervous people more nervous. Such people should have calm, easygoing dogs to help allay their tensions and show them how to relax and enjoy life.

Children and Puppies

Children and dogs just naturally go together. Although there is no one breed that is better for children than others, the toy or small breeds are not generally considered especially good with children. They sometimes have shorter tempers and are apt to snap and growl at children when handled roughly. The breeds preferring adults to young children include Pomeranian, Chihuahua, Yorkshire terriers, Maltese terrier, and Pekingese.

If there are a lot of boys in the family, a boxer, Dalmatian, or one of the terrier breeds might be considered. If there are young children 2 to 6 years of age, a collie or similar breed would be excellent, since their herding instinct makes them fine babysitters and they are large and easygoing enough to put up with manhandling.

A very young child will tend to maul a poppy with loving hands, and a very small puppy can be injured. But one of the large breeds can frighten a child by unintentionally knocking him down, which can easily spoil the relationship between the two. For toddlers I recommend one of the smaller breeds, such as spaniel, basset, Scotty or schnauzer.

It is up to the parents to teach children how to handle a new puppy, such as picking it up with both hands so that the hindquarters are supported and not dangling. Children should be taught not to bother the dog while he is eating, as even the most even-tempered dog will growl and may bite someone who interferes with his dinner.

Children should be taught to respect the rights of the dog. Some rules the tot should be instructed in at the beginning are:

—Never attempt to take away food or a bone while the dog is eating.

—Never disturb a sleeping dog.

—Never attempt to take a toy or other valued object away from a dog.

—Don't attempt to take a puppy away from a nursing bitch.

—Never allow a child to play with a tiny puppy, as he may be too rough with it.

—Children should be taught not to play with or chase strange dogs.

When a child's own dog bites him, it is usually because the child is tormenting the dog.

I should like to explode two fallacies about dogs and children:

—Children do *not* get pinworms or any other worms from dogs.

—Children are *not* susceptible to distemper or any other viral diseases of dogs.

In the main, children and dogs adapt well to one another and form a close bond of love. Most dogs will not harm children, seeming to realize their tenderness.

CHOOSING A HEALTHY PUPPY

The small breeds are not necessarily weaker or sicklier than the larger breeds. There are many small breeds which are tough and sturdy and make equally good pets in the country or the city.

In choosing a healthy puppy:

—The eyes should be clear, bright, and free from matter. There should be no scars or light spots on the cornea.

—Avoid the puppy who is extra-plump or extra-large. Pay more attention to the puppy who is neither fat nor thin and has a well-porportioned body. A potbelly usually means parasites.

—The puppy's nose and ears should be clean and with no signs of discharge. If he shakes his head a lot, look into his ears to see if he has ear mites or any other infestation.

—The skin should be clean and with no rough spots. Constant scratching is a sign of parasites. The hair coat should be fluffy, glossy, and slightly oily. Any hair loss, either generalized or in spots, should be avoided, as the puppy may have mange, fungus, or ringworm, or be heavily infested with lice.

—The small baby teeth should be bright and clean. The mouth should have a clean smell, and the color of the gums should be light pink. A pale or white color signifies anemia and is usually due to a heavy infestation of parasites. Heavy hookworm infestation can cause death in young puppies.

—Be sure to ascertain if the puppy has diarrhea or stools that contain mucus or blood. These conditions usually signify a heavy parasite population or the ever-present and dangerous disease, coccidiosis.

—The bone structure should be solid, and without curvature or bumps in the legs, which can indicate rickets. Beware if the puppy is still-legged or lame.

—In choosing a puppy in a breed where deafness is a tendency, be careful. The breeds predisposed to deafness are usually of white or blue-brown color, such as white bull terrier, Dalmatian, blue merle collie, Sheltie, white Great Dane, and white boxer. Be sure to test these puppies for deafness, or have your veterinarian do so.

—Another indication of a dog's health is his behavior. Shyness sometimes indicates sickness. Usually a healthy puppy is lively and hungry.

The suggestions I have made are mainly for the health and well-being of the puppy. I am not qualified to give advice on the finer show points. This should be left to the judgment of the potential dog owner and the advice of an expert in the show-dog field.

GETTING A DOG FROM A KENNEL OR PET SHOP

It is wise to check the kennel or pet shop and observe the sanitation and the way the dogs are kept. If there are any sick dogs with diarrhea, coughing, or eye or nose discharge, stay away!

Most conscientious breeders will stand behind their dogs, and if a puppy shows any signs of sickness within two weeks after purchase, they will usually assume the medical expenses or replace the puppy with a healthy one or refund the purchase price.

When going to a kennel, it is a good idea, if possible, to see the dam and the stud, as often you can get a good insight into conformity and temperament from the parents.

The object of most breeders is to develop a friendly, intelligent, mild-tempered pet rather than a high-strung, nervous, barking, snapping animal that is detrimental to society.

I would insist on buying a dog on the approval of a veterinarian. Be suspicious if this request is refused.

The dog buyer should be wary of "cut-rate" or "bargain" puppies. Most breeders and owners of pet shops are honest, but unfortunately there are some "horse-traders." There are puppy factories which buy and sell puppies unscrupulously. But most breeders go by the letter of the rulebook and abide by all the regulations necessary to maintain and sell healthy puppies.

CHOOSING THE BEST OF A LITTER

It is always difficult, even for an expert, to choose the best in a litter. Although, even at a tender age, there are many distinctive qualities to be noted in picking out a desirable puppy, there are points that cannot be checked out in a puppy that is very young.

—Color can be deceptive, as puppies in the nest are usually darker than they will ultimately be. Small white marks on the chest often disappear in a few weeks.

—Some puppies that are born small may soon catch up with their litter mates and by the time they are adults surpass them in weight and bone structure.

—Heads differ widely, and so it is necessary to know what the breed considers desirable.

—In some breeds a pointed nose is wanted, while in others it will exile the dog from the show ring.

—If the puppy has a badly roached back or bowed legs, the defect will magnify with age.

—An excellent puppy at 8 weeks can develop faults by the time he is one year to 18 months of age. However, this is not common.

A PUPPY AS A SECOND DOG

Because jealousy is one of the strongest of all canine emotions, when you already have a dog at home there is bound to be some animosity toward the new stranger in the house. The old dog will feel that his universe is being threatened, and so he should get first preference in everything and not be made to feel that he is being shoved into the background.

The dogs should be fed in separate rooms, as the new puppy will eat many more times a day than the older dog requires. The older dog should be given a tiny bit of food every time the young dog is fed so that his feelings will not be hurt.

There may be some growling and a wrestling match occasionally, but rarely will an older dog injure a young puppy. He may slap him down occasionally. I've never heard of an older dog killing a puppy that comes into the household. Let the two of them work it out for themselves; the older one will likely be the boss.

AFTER YOU HAVE PICKED YOUR PUPPY

It is wise to take your new puppy to a veterinarian within 24 hours. If there is any abnormality present, the veterinarian will discover it; and he will give advice on immunization procedure from adolescence through adulthood.

MAN'S RESPONSIBILITIES

Remember, you are taking on at least a 10-year project, and it is up to you to see that the puppy has proper care, exercise, and grooming, day by day. In turn he will devote all his life and loyalty to you. It is one of man's most enjoyable privileges, keeping a dog.

Fortunately most dog owners are careful not to allow their pets to offend their neighbors. Most do all in their power to prevent their pets from becoming nuisances, and from barking, whining or howling unnecessarily. Anyone who allows his dog to dig up his neighbor's garden is not cognizant of his responsibilities and is abusing the rights and privileges of having a pet.

2 PUPPY CARE AND TRAINING

The formula for raising a healthy puppy is to start him off right and follow through with a good management program, which should involve the following factors: (1) proper housing; (2) proper sanitation; (3) proper nutrition; (4) control of parasites and disease; (5) proper training.

Before taking a puppy home, you should receive all necessary information about past wormings and vaccinations. Get the name of the serum or vaccine that the puppy has received so that there will be no misunderstanding. Many puppies have become victims of distemper because their owners thought that when the puppy was vaccinated at the age of 6 weeks, he received immunization for life. Likewise, some people assume that if a puppy is wormed at 6 weeks, another worm checkup will not be necessary for a year or two.

The first 6 months of a puppy's life is the most dangerous period, as he is susceptible to anything and everything, and especially to diseases and parasites. I advise the new owner to take the puppy to a veterinarian within a day or two for a thorough checkup. If there is anything wrong—for example, a congenital defect or a disease—the puppy can usually be returned, with some form of remuneration. But most important, the good health of the puppy will be ensured, and a schedule will be set up for future vaccinations and wormings.

INTRODUCTION TO THE NEW HOME

The puppy will be lonesome for the companionship of his brothers and sisters and for the warmth of his mother's breast. He will want to be cuddled. He must be treated gently, and with a minimum of noise and confusion, as he gradually becomes acquainted with his new family. He is all yours, and you are all that he has. As a dog is man's best friend, so also is man a dog's best friend.

If possible, bring the puppy home early in the day so that by nighttime he will have checked out the house. When he first arrives, he should be given some warm milk, and then light and frequent feedings. A prime mistake of new dog owners is to put down a large bowl of food and let the puppy eat all he wants. Most puppies will gorge themselves right into extreme digestive disturbances. After being made to feel secure in his oral needs, and about where he is to eat, the puppy should be shown where he will sleep, where he will exercise and where he will eliminate. He should, of course, be confined to parts of the house not easily soiled.

The first 10 days are the most difficult, and since the dog is a creature of habit, he must be run on a fairly rigid schedule.

He wants to be taught, and his lessons should be repeated until he gets the point.

However, no advice that I can give, or that you read elsewhere, should be hard and fast, but should be something worked out between your dog and your family. As no two dogs and no two people are alike, you will have to adjust what you read to you and your dog.

The Bed

It is wise to give the puppy a bed of his own. It gives him a sense of ownership. For an overly boisterous or destructive puppy, a shipping crate can be used. As well as serving as a bed, it will keep him confined, and as most puppies will not soil their beds, it will help in housebreaking too.

The first night or so puppies tend to be homesick but will usually settle down if taken to bed with one of the family. Unless this is to be allowed every night, however, it should be done only as a last resort; the puppy will substitute the family member for his mother and will expect a human bed the rest of his life.

Some puppies will be content in their own bed with a hot-water bottle to cuddle, or a ticking clock, or an old shoe. In severe cases a baby aspirin or a wee bit of a sleeping pill will quiet the puppy and allow everyone a good night's sleep.

HOUSEBREAKING

Most puppies are a bit nervous at first and are liable to have an accident or two. Don't be upset; be gentle and patient. In housebreaking it is up to the owner to instruct, not to condemn. Teach the puppy properly, and he will respond graciously. Don't punish him unless you are sure that you are communicating with him—that he understands what you are trying to convey to him. The dog is the closest of all animals in communication with humans; he will understand if you are explicit enough.

The average dog takes 4 to 6 weeks for complete housebreaking, but there are problem dogs and problem cases. Patience, understanding, and a ready mop are requisites. The muscles which control the bladder and intestines develop with age. Give the puppy a chance—it takes time. Success in housebreaking depends on whether you, the dog owner, can be trained. Any failure in housebreaking is usually the owner's fault.

Age to Start

Even though progress is slower with puppies under several months of age, it is never too early to start. Housebreaking may take several weeks with a puppy acquired at 6 weeks of age. Less time is required for one at 3 months. And only a few days are needed for a puppy 6 months old. Don't expect too much before 12 weeks of age; but the earlier you start, the quicker the puppy will respond.

Responsibility

Although various members of the household may help, it is best for one person to be responsible for most of the training; otherwise everyone's job soon becomes no one's job.

Supervision

Housebreaking is not a part-time task; constant supervision is necessary. The puppy must be aired upon rising, once or twice after each meal, as often as possible during the day, and especially after playing and before retiring. Dogs usually prefer to eliminate outside, and the puppy must be kept out until he has completely relieved himself. He should be praised; and if he is given a tidbit each time, the association will soon make him eliminate quickly to get his reward.

Prevention

In forming habits, an ounce of prevention is worth many pounds of correction. Watch the puppy closely. An expectant look, running back and forth to the door, and scratching at it will all indicate his needs. This is the time to get him outdoors at once. Each accident inside prolongs the housebreaking process, both by breaking down the correct habit and by providing the puppy with a place inside that he will have a tendency to use.

Regularity

Feed the puppy on a regular schedule and take careful note of his habits. Bowel movements usually occur a short time after eating. Exercise the puppy after each meal and try to get him to eliminate before allowing him back inside the house. Take him to the same area over the same route; he has a strong association for previous odors. Try to take him out at regular intervals that he can rely on, and he will soon get into the swing of things.

Some puppies stay cleaner at night if fed lightly toward evening and not fed at all after about 8 P.M. Other puppies require a feeding right before bedtime—11 to 12 P.M.—in order to stay quiet during the night. The time for the last feeding can be experimented with, earlier or later, depending on the puppy's digestive system and his ability to contain his bowel movements until morning.

Confinement

Don't allow a puppy the complete run of the house and expect him to find his way to the door each time he has to eliminate. In the daytime he should be confined to a small area where there is a linoleum surface, such as the kitchen or utility room. At night he should be confined to a small area which is well covered with newspapers. As most dogs will not soil their bedding, an older puppy who persists in having a bowel movement during the night could be confined to a small sleeping box.

Discipline

The memory of the puppy is about 30 seconds long; if he is disciplined after that time, he will not realize what he has done wrong. Try to act as quickly as possible when he errs. Either catch him in the act or take him back to the bad deed and discipline him at the spot. As soon as he has been disciplined, he should be rushed outside to the area which he is to use for elimination.

Usually scolding is adequate to show the puppy the extent to which he has fallen into disfavor. He will want to avoid such scenes. Some puppies' feelings are badly hurt at being shamed. But too, most dogs love to be praised. Be lavish with praise and petting when indicated. If scolding doesn't work, most puppies will respond to the sound of a newspaper being slapped against a hand or the floor. Persistent offenders (assuming you are not at fault) may require spanking with a rolled-up newspaper.

47

Paper Training

Training to newspapers may be the wisest procedure in cold weather or for people who live in apartments. Several thicknesses of newspapers are spread out on the floor, preferably on tile or linoleum. All the principles of training described above are employed except that the puppy is placed on the papers instead of outside. It is surprising how soon the puppy will want to feel the newspapers under him before eliminating. Since dogs tend to return to their own odors, some people keep one soiled newspaper to entice the puppy to the same spot. Once he knows what the papers are for, he can be taken outside on papers until he gets the idea that he is to go outside, then the papers can be discarded. Be sure to scrub immediately all mistakes with a disinfectant and deodorant (such as chlorox, pine oil or lysol) to remove odors so that the pup will not return to the scene of the crime again.

There are some excellent commercial aids for training puppies to newspapers. They have the odor of urine, which draws the puppy to the spot. Although they are helpful, they are not the total answer.

Problem Dogs

There are some problem dogs who never seem to be housebroken. In reality the dog eventually housebreaks his owner so that the owner will take him out at regular intervals.

Some spoiled dogs refuse to be housebroken, in order to punish their owners.

For certain problem dogs the discipline has to involve a certain amount of physical pain, but it should never be severe.

There are some dogs who cannot be housebroken, but not because they don't want to be. Sometimes a puppy cannot control his bladder or bowels. A veterinarian should check to make sure that infection or parasites are not causing the incontinence.

Sometimes it helps to take the puppy out with older dogs, and through imitation he learns that he is to relieve himself outdoors.

When a puppy doesn't seem to be able to get the idea of housebreaking, it is best to confine him to the kitchen as much as possible and to leave his leash on him all the time. In this way you can immediately give him a slight tug at the collar, accentuated with a firm "No!" He will soon learn that each time he makes a mistake there will be a tug and a harsh word. Take him outdoors immediately, and when he eliminates praise him as if he had performed a marvelous deed.

Some General Facts about Housebreaking

During the first 2 to 3 weeks puppies urinate and defecate in response to licking by the mother. After 3 weeks they leave the nest to urinate and defecate. By 8 to 9 weeks they localize the functions in definite spots. Normally a puppy 8 to 12 weeks of age is expected to have a call of nature every 2 hours.

Clean up the mistake carefully and take the cloth with the odor on it outdoors to the spot designated for elimination. In this way you convey to the puppy what is wanted of him. Incidentally, when puppies urinate on rugs, wash the spot out with soap and water, and then club soda, which is an excellent detergent for urine spots. A turkish towel pressed to the spot for a few hours will dry it out.

In housebreaking, don't just put a puppy out; take him out, otherwise he'll forget why he's out, and you won't know if he actually performed. Cold rain or snow shouldn't stop either of you. The puppy has a thick enough coat to be insulated against the weather.

There are some dogs who in the beginning will not relieve themselves well on a lead and have to be turned loose. This modesty should be overcome if one lives where it is dangerous to allow a dog to run. It is better for him to be constipated until he is broken from such a habit than to be killed.

As a rule females are housebroken more easily. They relieve themselves more modestly and require less shrubbery and trees than males. The male is more anxious to roam—looking for adventure and sex.

To sum it all up, feeding on schedule, regular walks, and instant scolding will quickly housebreak a puppy.

FEEDING THE PUPPY

During the first 90 days after weaning there is particularly rapid growth in the puppy and therefore the need for a high amount of protein. The extra protein enables the puppy to cope better with emergencies in his early life, such as diseases and parasites.

Proper nourishment will help the puppy's body to develop immunity against parasites, diseases, and serious infections which strike early in life.

All puppies vary in food requirements. What may be sufficient for one may be famine for another. A weaning puppy should be fed at least 5 or 6 times a day. For the 3-month-old puppy frequent feeding is advocated. From 10 weeks on he should be fed 4 meals a day, up to 4 months. Three meals daily between 4 and 6 months should be fed and 2 meals a day between 6 months and a year. After 1 year of age most dogs require only one meal a day. However, this is arbitrary. Each dog should be fed according to his needs; and the type of food and its quality must be considered in determining how many times a day to feed.

The following is a typical feeding schedule for a medium-sized breed—30 to 50 pounds at maturity. It can be altered to suit small breeds or extra-large breeds by drawing comparisons:

Age	Weight	Feedings
2 months	6-8 pounds	*Morning* 5-6 tbsp. milk 3-4 tbsp. cereal or dog food *Noon* 1-2 heaping tsp. raw ground meat or commercial canned or dry *Afternoon* Repeat morning feeding *Evening* Repeat noon feeding *Bedtime* (late evening): 5-6 tbsp. milk
3 months	10-15 pounds	Increase amounts per feeding according to puppy's growth and capacity. Gradually eliminate afternoon and bedtime feedings

4 months	15-25 pounds	*Morning*
		½-1 cup milk
		4-8 tbsp. cereal or dog food
		Noon
		4-8 heaping tbsp. raw ground meat or commercial canned or dry food
		Evening
		4-8 tbsp. meat or dog food
		3-6 tbsp. cooked mashed vegetables or table scraps
6 months	25-30 pounds	*Morning*
		¾-1½ cups milk
		¾-1½ cups cereal or dog food
		Noon
		½-1 cup meal or dog food mixed with
		½-1 cup cereal or dry dog food
		Evening
		1-2 cups meat
		½-1 cup dog food
		½-1 cup vegetables or table scraps
8 months	about 30 pounds	*Morning*
		1½ cups milk
		toast, cereal, dog food, or dry dog food
		Evening
		2 cups meat
		cereal or toast
		vegetables or table scraps
9 months	30-40 pounds	*Morning*
		milk and cereal (2 cups each)
		Evening
		2 cups meat
		2 cups table scraps or dry dog food

10 months	40-50 pounds	*Morning*
		Milk or cereal or dog food if he will eat it. Some do not want the morning meal at this age
		Evening
		3 cups meat or dog food and vegetables or table scraps
12 months	maturity	Total amount of food—1-1½ lbs. per day:
		1½ cups meat
		1½ cups cereal or dry dog food
		1½ cups vegetables or table scraps

The delicate digestive system of a puppy at weaning frequently requires a soft, bland diet before a regular adult ration can be tolerated. Baby cereals and baby foods are excellent.

A safe rule for frequency is "demand feeding." But don't give the puppy all he wants, as he is sure to be a glutton. Feed him all that he will digest without upsetting him. Some puppies double their weight in 2 to 3 weeks, so the quantity has to be adjusted accordingly.

The amount of food that a puppy demands depends somewhat on breed, amount of exercise, and general condition. A general rule, although arbitrary, is ½ ounce of food per pound of dog weight, per day. The dog should be fed at regular times so that he can count on and look forward to his meals.

Small breeds need more food per pound of body weight than do the large breeds. When they see a St. Bernard or a Great Dane, most people shudder to think of the food bills. But be assured that the giants eat extremely large amounts of food only during the first year or year and a half of their growth. After they have reached maturity, they don't eat much more than a collie or German shepherd. The owner of a St. Bernard or a Great Dane will feed more to his puppy the first year of his life than he will for the next 2 years.

Raw meat is more easily digested than cooked meat. Too much fat is not good for a puppy, although small amounts should be an integral part of the diet. The puppy can have most kinds of meat, such as beef, lamb, and chicken. Meat products such as liver, tripe, and kidney are beneficial additives. Horse meat is too strong for some puppies and gives them diarrhea. Egg yolks are excellent, raw or cooked, but the whites are not beneficial, especially raw.

Throughout the first year of his life the puppy should have daily amounts of vitamins and minerals added to his food. These can be in powder, liquid, or tablet form.

The health of the puppy depends on the kinds of meals that he is given every day. Fortunately the days of haphazard feeding are over. A good puppy chow prepared by a commercial company provides a basic well-balanced diet, and such a food should make up the major part of the dog's diet.

Supplements

Puppies need variety in food as well as we do, and table scraps and leftovers are an excellent means of breaking up the monotony of the everyday diet. But they should be used as a supplement and not as the main part of the diet.

Vegetables are fine for puppies and are a good food supplement. Potatoes are not injurious, as is widely believed, and within proportion are an excellent supplement. Cake, candy, and other sweets are all right to give a puppy, within reason. And incidentally, candy does not cause worms.

With their tender gums and growing teeth, most puppies enjoy gnawing on objects such as human flesh, expensive shoes, and antique furniture. The addition of kibbled food to the daily ration or the occasional large bone can provide distraction and fine therapy for teeth and gums. It should be a large beef bone, preferably a knuckle. Beef bones are all right if they are of the large variety, but rib bones or T-bones are often injurious, as they tend to break off in sharp points and cause damage to the intestinal tract. Never give small bones, such as chicken, pork, veal, lamb, or rabbit; they are injurious to throats and intestines.

Some people put chicken bones into the pressure cooker, which thoroughly softens them. Bones prepared in this way will not harm the dog, and the nutritional benefits are excellent.

Loss of Appetite

If a puppy refuses a feeding, take the food away and try again in an hour or two. If he refuses more than 2 or 3 meals, a veterinarian should be consulted, as this is a sure sign that something is wrong. A puppy must not go more than 8 hours without food; he will dehydrate, weaken, and go into shock very quickly.

Sometimes a puppy will be distracted and would rather play than eat. Keep eating and play periods separate.

Most puppies gulp their food and seldom chew it. This has nothing to do with manners and is perfectly normal. Often a puppy will regurgitate his food and then eat it again. Don't stop him from doing this no matter how distasteful it may seem to you. This is his way of predigesting his food, and is an ancestral instinct.

The Finicky Eater

There are some cuties who will hold out for filet mignon no matter what entree you put in front of them. And of course there are those who contend that the puppy will be spoiled if he is given steaks and chops and presumably will not eat commercial dog food. This may be so, but a combination of the two becomes a palatable mixture for a finicky eater.

For the finicky eater, the master must experiment and compromise. Often a puppy develops tastes which don't jibe with what the owner has in mind, and there is a constant battle of wits until either the puppy or the owner wins. A compromise is the best solution.

It may be necessary to change the diet frequently. Sometimes mix palatable table scraps with a commercial food in varying proportions. Or let the puppy miss a meal or two so that he will appreciate something he doesn't really care for (he thinks).

Overfeeding

Dogs are the most delightful beggars in the world. They love to plead for food. Don't be taken in and break down every time the dog begs. Overfeeding will result in diarrhea, vomiting, and a noisy intestinal tract.

It is not healthy for a puppy to get overweight; it puts a strain on his growing bones. It is much easier to keep his diet down than to reduce him.

Overfeeding a puppy to get a large-sized dog is not the way to do it. His size may be changed slightly—bulgingly—

but heredity determines the final size of a dog and not the amount of food he is given.

Likewise, a toy-sized dog has to be bred from toy-sized parents and half-starving the dog will only make him sickly. Incidentally, the belief that feeding a puppy alcoholic beverages will stunt his growth, while widely held, has never been scientifically substantiated. (Fortunately, alcohol doesn't affect the growth rate of human creatures either.)

Don'ts

Don't allow a puppy to play or exercise strenuously immediately after eating. In some breeds, notably the Great Dane, the bloating can end in a ruptured stomach, which would be fatal.

Although a puppy should always have water handy, don't allow him to drink all he wants, especially after eating. Some puppies bloat up extensively.

Although milk is an excellent food, some puppies cannot properly assimilate it, and it gives them diarrhea. Buttermilk, however, is an excellent substitute for sweet milk and is desirable for puppies when they have a digestive upset. It restores the normal healthy bacteria to the intestinal tract during or after an illness, and it is an excellent additive during a siege of coccidiosis.

While a puppy is eating, it is best to leave him alone. And don't allow children near him. One of his ancestral instincts is to guard his food, and many a child has been bitten for getting too close to a feeding dog. Even the gentlest dog will defend his food.

Many a puppy has been poisoned by ingesting a foreign object. When you find the puppy eating something he's not supposed to, discipline him at once, and keep careful watch over him.

TEETHING

Beginning at the age of 4 months, the baby teeth (or milk teeth) fall out, allowing the adult teeth to push through the gums. By 7 to 8 months, if the baby teeth have not fallen out it is wise to have a veterinarian pull them. If they are left in, they can impede the permanent teeth and the puppy will be left with a double row of teeth or crooked teeth, which will hurt him cosmetically and in the show ring. The teeth should be taken out by a professional because if this is not done properly, they may break off at the roots and present complications in formation of the adult teeth.

Teething can cause the puppy to go off his feed, and there may be a slight diarrhea. The gums will be sore, and at such times a soft bland diet should be fed for a few days.

Most puppies like to chew on human flesh during the teething process, and it is judicious to teach them not to destroy too much of one's anatomy during this period.

TOYS

Hard-rubber toys, commercially prepared bones, and rawhide bones are fine for puppies to gnaw on, and they are soothing to sore gums and helpful in teething. Soft-rubber toys are taboo, as a puppy can quickly chew them up and the rubber that is swallowed can harm his intestinal tract.

Old neckties or several pairs of ladies' nylon hose tied together are safe and enjoyable for the puppy to play with. Toys amuse him and keep him from destroying the household.

GROOMING

Start the grooming program while the puppy is young and can be made to feel that grooming is a game. He will soon learn to look forward to being spruced up.

A soft brush is sufficient to keep most puppies in good condition. In a long-haired dog, a comb or wire brush will take care of the mats; and as he gets older a stiffer brush can be used.

In breeds that require trimming (Scotties, poodles, etc.) it is advisable to trim the heads and feet at an early age, for sanitary reasons and to get the puppy acclimated to the procedure. It must be done carefully and gently because if someone is rough during the first few trimmings, the puppy will become a problem dog and require tranquilizers for future trimmings.

It is a good idea to trim a puppy's nails also at an early age so that he will get used to it. Be careful about cutting them too close and making them bleed, since he will never forget the sharp pain. Try to make him believe that it is part of his play period—getting him to lie on his back or side. After the nails, the matted hair between toes and pads can also be cut. A puppy indoctrinated at an early age for this chore will be easy to cope with all his life. Some docile pets turn into tigers when someone attempts to trim their nails. This can usually be traced to an unhappy puppyhood experience.

Many people believe it is wrong to bathe a puppy under 6 months of age. This is not quite correct. In the summer a puppy can be bathed at an earlier age. But in cold weather one must keep the puppy from being exposed to cold and draft, as he is extremely susceptible to sore throats and colds. However, there are times when a puppy is so dirty that he needs a soap-and-water bath.

When a puppy is bathed for the first time, it must be done gently so as not to frighten him and make him forever afraid of water. Use cotton in each ear to keep out the water; and a little mineral oil or boric acid ointment in his eyes will avoid soap irritation. A mild baby soap or face soap should be used; strong flea soaps or harsh detergent soaps will dry the oils of skin and hair. After getting a good lather, rinse the puppy well, then dry him. After toweling a hair dryer can be used.

There are some excellent aerosol foam shampoos (dry shampoos) which produce suds that are lathered into the coat and skin without water. A towel is used to wipe off the excess suds. Although not quite so good as soap and water, the dry shampoos do take away a lot of dirt and can be used without worry during the winter months.

There are times when a sponge bath with a wet soapy cloth will do. Here again it should be a mild soap. Just rub the slightly damp cloth over the puppy's entire body and dry him thoroughly with towels.

For fleas or ticks, certain special puppy flea sprays and powders can be used. However, be careful of the strong flea dips used on adult dogs, as the puppy may absorb some through his skin or lick it, and it can prove fatal.

AILMENTS AND DISEASES

The commonest ailments of young puppies are vomiting and diarrhea. If a puppy vomits more than 2 or 3 times, one may well suspect that he has swallowed a foreign object. The puppy is curious by nature and will pick up and chew almost anything he comes upon. I have often had to surgically remove from puppies' stomachs or intestines such indigestible objects as golf balls, pins and needles, and razor blades, and on one occasion a diamond ring. A word of advice: if ever you are missing a small object and your puppy is vomiting, have his stomach X-rayed.

In a simple diarrhea, caused by overfeeding or teething, Kaopectate, Pepto-bismol, or bismuth (1 tsp. per 10 lbs. of puppy, 3 or 4 times a day) is soothing to the stomach and to the sensitive lining of the intestinal tract.

Intestinal parasites (worms), coccidiosis, or an infectious enteritis can be the cause of an intestinal upset, and if not treated in time can result in death.

Heavy infestation by fleas, lice, or ticks can produce anemia. Hookworms are especially serious; they suck the blood and lower the resistance to other diseases. There are efficient drugs for destroying hookworms in even very young puppies (see p. 304-305).

Coccidiosis is a disease which causes a chronic, insidious type of diarrhea. Severe cases show mucus and blood in the stools. The disease is increasing in frequency and is dangerous to the lives of puppies. Pet shops and kennels that don't practice proper sanitary procedures often spread it, as it is contagious from one puppy to another through contamination of the bowel movements.

Von Gierke syndrome, which is a condition in toy breeds, is characterized by sudden coma, shock, and occasionally convulsions. Chihuahuas are mostly affected; Yorkshire terriers, Maltese terriers, and other small breeds also can be affected.

The cause is not completely known, although there seems to be a relationship in that stress conditions in young puppies cause hypoglycemia—a lowered level of sugar in the blood.

It can happen suddenly, without warning. The puppy is found in a semi-comatose condition with the usual signs of shock, such as pale gums and tongue, and dilated and unfocused eyes. The animal sometimes screams in pain.

Immediate attention is required to save the puppy. Karo syrup, molasses, or any other form of sugar should be poured slowly into the puppy's mouth. Stimulants, such as brandy, and warmth should be provided.

Any predisposing factor that causes lack of appetite, and no food for over 8 hours, can produce the syndrome (a puppy cannot go over 8 hours without food or water). Young toy puppies that are handled much or become exhausted are prone to this disorder. After an accident, illness, or any traumatic experience, force-feed the puppy with broth or eggnog.

58

Rickets is a condition of puppies caused by a deficiency of the minerals calcium and phosphorus. The minerals are helped in absorption by the presence of vitamins A and D.

Symptoms of rickets are bowed legs with large knots of bone at the leg joints. There are also knots of bone on the ribs. It is diagnostic to see a puppy with his toes spread in an awkward position and his legs bent at his carpal (wrist) joints.

Although any breed is susceptible to rickets, it is usually seen in fast-growing breeds, such as the Great Dane and German shepherds.

A deficiency of vitamins and minerals will also keep a puppy's ears from standing erect in such breeds as the boxer, Doberman, and Great Dane.

If a puppy does a lot of hiccupping, fear not. This is normal—spasms of the diaphragmatic muscle which occur at various times in the growing period. There is no pathological significance.

Signs of a Sick Puppy

—Vomiting
—Diarrhea
—Loss of appetite
—Lethargy, lassitude, listlessness
—Coughing
—Running eyes and nose
—High fever

Safety Rules for Puppies

—Give only large beef-knuckle bones
—Keep dangerous objects off the floor and out of reach
—Never, never worm a sick puppy
—Children should not be allowed to maul a young puppy
—Don't allow a puppy freedom of the outdoors if there is any danger from automobiles

EXERCISE, BEHAVIOR, TRAINING

Exercise

Overfeeding and insufficient exercise are the principal causes of fat, lazy, sluggish puppies; and this goes for adult dogs too. The dog's body is geared for running and playing, and both are necessary for his well-being. Lack of exercise can bring on all kinds of digestive disorders and physical and mental sluggishness. Playing with other dogs and humans provides physical and emotional gratification. A long walk with your puppy, besides being physically beneficial to both of you, is pleasing to his ego.

A puppy should be taken out every 2 hours, if possible, but at least 3 times a day. Walking with your dog should be a period of enjoyment as well as serious training for his future well-being. The earlier you leash-train him, the better. Teach him to walk a few steps in front of you, not constantly pulling on the leash.

I don't advise leashing or tying a puppy outdoors by himself for a long time. He may become entangled in the leash or rope and injure himself. An outdoor pen or a fenced-in area is desirable so he can have some freedom on his own and be outdoors when the weather permits. Some shelter should be provided in case of rain or on hot sunny days for shade. He should also have an ever-present pan of water. Some dogs prefer to be with humans and don't wish to stay outside by themselves. They should not be kept outside if they don't wish to stay, and certainly not in wet or cold weather, especially if they are toy or small puppies.

Leash Training. A certain amount of psychology is needed in teaching the puppy to be towed along with a leash attached to his neck. Don't expect the puppy to walk along at your side the first time. Invariably he will fight and tug and pull.

The first step is to teach the puppy to wear a collar. Any time after 6 weeks of age a light collar can be put on him. He will not like it and will scratch at it and try to get it off but will soon resign himself to his fate.

Allow him to get used to the collar for a week or so, and then attach a short length of rope to the collar and let him play with it and drag it around the house. Occasionally pick up the rope and hold it so that he knows you have control of his collar. At first he will pull and tug and try to go in every direction. Don't jerk it, and he will soon realize that nothing drastic will happen to him when you hold the rope. He will get to like your playing with him—catching the rope.

The next step is to teach him to walk with you without getting under your feet. Repeat the lesson 2 or 3 times a day;

just before mealtime is preferrable because he will get a reward when it's over.

Behavior

There is an old saying, like master, like dog, and a disobedient or neurotic dog is often the result of poor training. There is a ring of truth to the statement that neurotic dogs are the result of neurotic owners. However, I don't wish to imply that all neurotic dogs have emotionally unstable owners.

Puppies are great imitators, and a shy or timid dog is often reflecting those tendencies of his owner. Also, it is well to choose a puppy's companions wisely. If there are any with bad faults, keep the puppy away as you would keep a child away from a juvenile delinquent.

Good kennel owners give their puppies daily individual care. It has been proved that dogs that are raised in isolation with no human contact develop emotional imbalances that interfere with normal development.

Infantile autism, commonly called kennelitis, is often seen in dogs left in kennels without human love. It is characterized by excessive shyness and introspection and is brought on more by environment than by heredity. Some of these dogs become fearful of everyone but their owners and develop fear-biting.

There is also a tendency for this to happen when a puppy receives too much love and affection from one person. The puppy becomes so attached to the person that he growls at or bites anyone else. Such puppies don't have enough contact with the outside world and distrust the human race.

I advise all dog owners to take their puppies with them on trips around town so that the puppies can see all shapes and sizes of human beings. It will show them that people are not out to harm them—that many people love dogs and will stop and compliment and pat them. A puppy should make friends with strangers, up to a point.

Most destructive dogs do their bad deeds out of boredom. They are not necessarily juvenile delinquents if they chew and destroy things. This is part of the development stage in normal, healthy puppies. Before leaving a puppy alone in the house, it is a good idea to take him for a long walk—tire him out—so he will nap while you are out. This also works well when taking a puppy on a car trip.

Often I'm asked which breed is best for training. Although we see more poodles and German shepherds in obedience trials today, this doesn't necessarily mean that they are the smartest and most trainable. It just means that there are more of them. There is much convincing evidence that every breed is capable of doing well in obedience training, and that no one breed has a monopoly on brains. There are no "stupid" dogs. It is up to each owner to bring out his dog's inherent intelligence.

Each puppy is an individual in mentality and adaptability, and each master must supply the supervision that is needed to mold the development of the puppy's character and disposition. Some puppies are bold and some are shy, but the majority seem to be undecided which way they are going to develop.

Teaching the puppy his name is one of the first things to concentrate on. Pick a simple-sounding name and use it as much as possible every time you talk to him and with every command. He soon will learn that the word is his. When you call him and he comes to you, praise him, pat his head, and give him a tidbit. He should associate his name with something pleasant.

Start the training gently and tenderly and with much patience. Treat him as you would a child, with sympathy and understanding. Lavish upon him all the love that he deserves, and also the discipline that he deserves when he does wrong.

Don't be harsh with him. Yelling, cussing, kicking, and beating will not hurry up his training and more likely will deter him from the one and only desire in life, to please you, his loving master.

Don't expect miracles overnight. The puppy learns by repetition, and you must develop communication for complete and worthwhile training. Talk to him, explain to him and show him what you want. If he can't seem to learn something, teach him something else that he can do. He wants to learn, but we all have our limitations. Once you start teaching him something, keep repeating it until he understands completely.

The first rule in training is to make all lessons brief and interesting so that the puppy will not become bored.

In a training program rewards and discipline should be

given immediately. Be lavish in your praise; it is important to the dog's ego to be complimented. Usually a disgusted voice is discipline enough. If something more forceful is needed, a rolled-up newspaper should be sufficient. Most dog trainers say the hands should never be used in punishment; and I certainly don't advise striking a dog on the head or backbone, as these are delicate areas. A light thump on the fanny or the sides will get the point across.

Dogs don't understand words as words. They associate certain sounds with certain commands and get to learn what they must do when they hear the sounds. Actually, I have a number of patients who do seem to understand words and whose owners have to spell out certain words that they don't want the dogs to hear.

There are some basic commands that every puppy should be taught; these are discussed in Chapter 10. The most important command for the dog to understand is "No!" You have to make him know you mean it. "Quiet" should also be taught early in his life—and he should stop his noise immediately.

Training Rules—

—The best time for training the puppy is before he is fed, so that he will be looking forward to the reward of a good meal.

—For a satisfactory training program the puppy should have complete confidence in you.

—Never train a puppy while you are in a bad mood or have lost control of your emotions. Especially don't lose patience and kick a puppy in anger or throw things at him. He is still a babe in arms and cannot be expected to grasp everything at once.

—Allow only one member of the family to teach him commands and tricks. Once he has learned them all thoroughly, then others can help.

—Always talk to a dog before you approach him. This goes for any dog. Let him know you are his friend.

—Don't confuse a puppy by giving him inconsistent commands.

—Don't punish the dog with a training lead or other training object, or he will become fearful of training.

—Don't allow the training periods to get so long that the puppy becomes tired or bored.

—A puppy should never be picked up by his ears—as one of our Presidents found out, much to his chagrin.

3 ADOLESCENCE AND PUBERTY

MAN-DOG AGE EQUIVALENTS

The old theory that one year in the life of the dog is equivalent to 7 years in the life of man has been abandoned, and the new scale of equivalents shown below is now recognized. Thus, for example, a 6-month-old dog is comparable to a 10-year-old child, and a year-old dog to a 15-year-old child. After his first 2 years the dog's life proceeds more slowly relative to man's and each canine year is like 4 human years. Thus a 10-year-old dog compares to a man of 56, and a dog who reaches 21 can be said to celebrate his "centennial."

Man's Age	Dog's Age
10 years	6 months
13	8
14	10
15	12
20	18
24	2 years
32	4
40	6
48	8
56	10
64	12
72	14
80	16
88	18
96	20
100	21

MENTAL MATURATION

It is useless to be impatient with the mental development of a puppy—to expect so much of him that you become upset when he is not winning in the show ring at 6 months to a year of age. As has been noted, a 6- to 12-month-old puppy is comparable to a 10- to 15-year-old child—and puppies are as inconsistent as teenagers are. As to training for the show ring, one should not expect much of a puppy until he is at least 1 year of age. The small breeds mature faster, while the larger breeds sometimes are not fully mature until they are 2 years old.

As with children, there are precocious dogs who mature sooner and perform many tricks or obedience tasks at an early age.

It is normal for the adolescent dog to occasionally perform bad deeds—destroying articles, overturning garbage cans, bringing home various and sundry belongings of the neighbors'. Presently I'm having a problem with my young Irish setter. One of the first tricks I taught her was to fetch my morning newspaper from the driveway. She is so eager to please that she presents me not only with my own paper but usually with the papers from eight or ten of my neighbors' driveways.

I agree with the obedience-class concept of allowing puppies to enroll at 6 months of age. But they should not be expected to graduate *cum laude* at this age, and it is wise to repeat the obedience course 6 months later to refresh their memories.

Astute breeders believe that the best dogs of the breed are those who are late developers. Many an ugly duckling at the age of one turns into a champion or other magnificent specimen by the time he is 2 or 3. Puppies go through a development pattern, both mentally and physically, similar to children's.

PHYSICAL MATURATION

The puppy's body does not mature proportionally. The head reaches full growth ahead of the body. It would be unusual for the dog to be in complete proportion before 18 months of age.

Puppies go through a gawky stage during adolescence in which some breeds appear to be all legs, their gait is dreadful, and the body seems to be out of proportion. It is during this period that the fast-growing breeds (e.g., German shepherd) are most vulnerable to hip dysplasia; the body and heavy muscles produce an awkward gait. Also during this period most structural faults can be noticed, such as cow hock or paddling, two conditions that may improve with maturity.

Adolescent dogs will not be fat if left to their own exercise devices and choice of food. A 15-month-old dog is comparable to a teenager in growth stage. Most teenagers are tall and lean, and most adolescent dogs are also lean if not fed at too fast a rate by owners who want large dogs. Overfeeding is not conducive to proper growth of bones and muscles. Although exercise in an adolescent dog is desirable for development, the real conformity of his bone structure will not be reached until he is mature.

The owner must be patient during the physical and mental maturation period. There is no reason to rush the dog, and it is best not to interfere with nature's processes.

PUBERTY

The age from 5 months to 12 months is a most unattractive period because the dog has lost his puppy fat and appears to be all legs and neck. He barks more. He is becoming rougher. He is shedding his hair—his soft baby hair—and beginning to get his normal adult coat.

As he nears adulthood changes take place almost daily. Once he stops growing in height he begins broadening out, becoming firm to the touch. During this period food requirements are high both in quantity and in quality.

Puberty in the female occurs when she has her first heat period. The average female comes into heat at 8 months of age, but in the smaller breeds she can come any time after 6 months. The average age is between 7 and 10 months in most breeds, and thereafter she will go into season about every 6 months.

The first official day of the heat cycle is marked by a bloody discharge. Normal heat periods are 3 weeks. Don't trust the dog by herself for one second during this time. There are doggy panties available at pet shops to keep the discharge controlled, and there are sprays and pills that help deodorize the female in heat, but don't trust any of these devices to eliminate the danger of a male's taking advantage of her. She should be put in solitary confinement. Many accidents have happened even when the fortress was thought to be impregnable. If the facilities in the home are not adequate or if she causes too much disturbance, she should be put in a boarding kennel.

SPAYING

A question I am asked at least once daily is, "Should we spay our bitch, and if so, when?" Unequivocally I say that anyone who has a female pet whom he doesn't wish to breed should by all means have her spayed, and almost the younger the better.

There are many good reasons for spaying a bitch. The heat periods are upsetting to the dog as well as to the owner. When the bitch comes into heat, she is nervous and fretful. There are emotional changes during the 3-week period, and she is high-strung in her behavior toward her human companions and the male dogs flirting for her attention.

Spaying eliminates the nuisance factor of male dogs congregating and the attendant problems. "Cherchez la femme" has inspired many dog fights and untold damage to property. Also, when male dogs gather in packs, rabies epidemics are often started.

I don't advocate the spaying of all female dogs. There are many potential brood matrons who have such good temperament and fine conformation that they should be mated to perpetuate their desirable qualities. However, any dog that is not to be used for breeding should be spayed. There is no risk in the operation if it is performed by a qualified veterinarian, and it is relatively inexpensive for the many years of enjoyment that will accrue from it.

Other Reasons for Spaying

—It helps to keep the dog population from getting out of hand.

—In most states it is against the law to allow a female dog in heat to roam at will.

—It prevents dogs with congenital defects from propagating the defects (see p. 327 ff.).

—Shy, timid, or aggressive females should be spayed to keep them from perpetuating their bad temperaments.

—Dogs should be spayed to prevent foreseeable whelping problems.

—Spaying is useful in dogs who have irregular heat cycles and false pregnancies.

—Spaying controls all types of female problems, such as cystic ovaries, metritis, pyometra, and nymphomania, especially if done at an early age, preferably before she reaches her first birthday.

—Spaying is indicated for vaginal tumors and vaginal prolapse.

—Some bitches in heat become very nervous and undergo a change in personality from quiet and friendly to excitable and biting. These "frustrated" females should indeed be spayed.

—In working dogs, such as Seeing Eye, spaying is indicated.

—Guard dogs used in the services and for police and guard work should be spayed so that their heat periods will not disrupt their training and performance.

—There are certain skin problems caused by sexual abnormalities (e.g., homosexual dogs who show both male and female genital organs) based on hormonal problems which spaying sometimes clears up.

When to Spay

Since every dog owner and veterinarian seems to have his own opinion about the proper age at which to spay a bitch, whatever I say will surely be contradicted.

I advise spaying right before the age of sexual maturity, which is between 5 and 7 months of age. By this time the dog has enough of her female characteristics to be properly endowed. And I definitely advise spaying a pet before 1 year of age, because these dogs rarely develop mammary tumors later in life.

Some people advise waiting until after the first heat period, or until the bitch has had one litter of puppies, claiming that this will help her later in life. If she is being spayed after her heat period, it is best to schedule the surgery between her periods—2 or 3 months after the cycle.

There is a common belief that the bitch should have two heats before being spayed. This belief is based on the false premise that the ovaries mature one at a time—one during each heat period. There is no truth to this; both ovaries enlarge, mature and secrete their hormones at each heat period. The bitch works on both cylinders at all times.

68

When Not to Spay

Unless absolutely necessary, a bitch should never be spayed while she is in her heat cycle. It is a dangerous risk, because all the blood vessels are in a state of dilation.

A nursing bitch should never be spayed. It is best to wait a month or two after she has weaned her puppies so that her breasts and uterus will have returned to their normal size and condition.

Disadvantages

The spayed female is ineligible to compete in the show ring, and of course she can never have puppies.

Personality and Disposition

There are many who believe that spaying a dog will change her personality and disposition. Nothing could be further from the truth. With proper training and handling there should be no effects from the hormonal changes incident to spaying. Spayed females don't become mean because of the operation; if a spayed female is mean, she would have taken on such a disposition regardless of the operation.

Most Seeing Eye dogs are spayed females. They are a concrete example that intelligence, devotion, and performance are not affected by the spaying process and that dogs don't have to become obese or lose willingness or spirit after spaying.

Obesity

It is commonly believed that spaying a dog will increase her body weight. This is not necessarily so, as obesity is related to food intake, exercise, and hormonal control. It is best to start the bitch on female hormones within 6 months after the operation. The lost hormones (estrogens, which can be taken in pill form) will be replenished, and she will retain her girlish figure. The estrogens should be administered with the advice of a veterinarian; too large a dosage may give a false heat period.

SPAYING TECHNIQUES

The ovaries are the organs which bring the bitch into heat when the follicles which mature every 6 months secrete their hormones into the blood stream, causing physical evidence of estrus.

Normal Spaying

The normal spaying process necessitates complete removal of the ovaries, after which there will be cessation of the estrus cycles. If even the slightest part of an ovary is allowed to remain, the bitch will continue to come into heat at varying intervals.

Complete Spaying

I do a complete hysterectomy routinely in every spaying operation, and I believe that most veterinary surgeons agree it is the proper procedure. Both ovaries and the uterus are completely removed. This makes the bitch immune from metritis and other female infections as she gets older.

Incomplete Spaying (Tubal Ligation)

Some request just tying off the Fallopian tubes, which connect the ovaries to the uterus. They don't want their animal pregnant, but they object to removal of the ovaries in the belief that it affects the animal's personality.

Of course, the animal continues to come into heat twice a year, causing the same problems she did before her "operation." After several heat periods, generally these people request a complete hysterectomy.

Medicinal Spaying

Several years ago an injectable anti-heat drug was introduced into veterinary medicine. One injection kept a dog from coming into heat for a period of 6 months, and it was thought to be the answer to spaying. It was widely accepted, and thousands upon thousands of dogs were injected.

However, many dogs developed the female infection called endometritis, and some dogs never came into heat after their original injection. Much valuable breeding stock was involved, and many hysterectomies were necessary because of the female infection which resulted. The drug has been proved by the FDA in Washington to produce sterility and other undesirable effects in the female dog, and the government removed the drug from the market (for general use).

A birth control pill, OVABAN, is effective in shortening or eliminating heat periods. However, I would advise it only on a temporary basis, and not the entire life of the bitch. Surgery is the only completely satisfactory method.

CASTRATION

There are many people who don't approve of castration; they feel that the castrated male is not a "whole" dog. Actually he is similar to the spayed female in that he will stay at home, and his main object in life will be the pleasure and love of his human family. The loss of his sexual instinct changes his personality only in that he becomes sweeter and more lovable.

I don't advocate castrating all male dogs, but if a dog is not to be used in breeding, castration slows him down, and his life will henceforth revolve around his family.

Reasons for Castration

—In the presence of a congenital defect, such as cleft palate, harelip, or hip dysplasia, castration is indicated.

—There are some dogs who masturbate a great deal— "making love" to pillows, people's legs, and furniture. This is common in adolescence; however, if it continues into adulthood, dogs who seem to be oversexed are prime subjects for castration.

—There is a skin problem in the male dog which occurs because his bisexual organs develop in the testicles tumors that excrete female hormones, and this changes his appearance. He has large nipples and other female characteristics. To clear up the chronic skin problems exhibited by loss of hair, continual scratching, and dark-pigmented bare spots, castration is the only cure.

—There are some dogs who roam because they are lonely. Castration will keep them at home.

—For a vicious, aggressive male I recommend castration—or else increase your liability insurance policy. There is a common fallacy that castration turns a male dog vicious. Although inwardly he may be peeved at his owner for having had the operation performed, there is absolutely no change in aggressiveness or viciousness because of the operation. If anything, castration turns a dog into a gentler and less aggressive animal.

The Operation

Castration is a relatively simple operation with complete recovery in 2 to 3 days. Following the operation there is about a 30-day period of emotional and physical changes which are gradual. The end results are good.

Obesity

As with female dogs, alteration of male dogs doesn't necessarily mean that they will get unsightly and overweight. The addition of male hormones to the diet, in pill form, will replace any hormones needed to maintain a normal healthy metabolism. The dogs need not get fat; any obesity is the fault of the owners. With adequate exercise and proper amounts of food these dogs can maintain their sleek and muscular appearance.

OBESITY AND DIETING IN THE GROWN DOG

With the advent of soft and easy living, some of our dogs are losing their girlish or boyish figures, and I am daily seeing in my clinic dogs of many breeds who are fat almost to the point of obesity. The breeds I most often see overweight are cocker spaniels, dachshunds, beagles, and small terriers. Dogs that are allowed plenty of exercise will keep trim all their lives. Dogs that just lie around all day become obese. Dogs are meant to be active.

As mentioned before, there are many spayed females who are overweight, and this is due to a variety of causes. Castrated males are likewise prone to obesity. But there is no need for either to become overweight. With the use of hormones these dogs can remain slim and active.

Some breeds seem to have an underactive thyroid (hypothyroid) which makes them overweight, sluggish, and rather uninterested in any form of exercise. A veterinarian will likely put such an animal on thyroid drugs to stimulate the metabolism to burn up the excess fat.

When an animal is gaining too much weight, the amount of carbohydrates must be lowered and higher-protein food (eggs, meat, fish) given to cut down on the caloric intake. The diet should be at least one-half protein and then some of the essentials. The purpose of a reducing diet is to cause a gradual loss in body weight without serious side effects. The dog should have ample amounts of all nutrients needed by his body.

For extreme obesity there is a prescription diet called RD (reducing diet). Scientifically prepared, it gives a complete, well-balanced diet, satisfies hunger, and yet reduces weight.

In any reducing program there will be no significant loss in weight for at least 2 weeks—the time it takes for the dog's body to use up excess fluid.

Dieting will not work if the dog is not allowed exercise. It may be necessary to force him to exercise. Just putting him outdoors doesn't always work; some dogs just find a comfortable spot and lie down.

A recent survey reveals some very interesting facts regarding overweight dogs.

—Females are more commonly obese than males.

—Incidence rises sharply in both sexes toward middle age, and tends to decrease after 12 years.

—Obesity is more prevalent in dogs fed on biscuits, meal, tablescraps or prepared foods, less in those fed canned products.

—Incidence is higher among dogs owned by obese people than by those owned by persons of more normal physique, also among dogs owned by middle-aged or elderly persons.

—Thirty-one per cent of those persons owning obese dogs considered them to be normal in weight.

Diet Pills

I have known people to put their dogs on the same diet pills that they themselves take. Some of these drugs contain benzedrine to kill the appetite and stimulate the metabolism. They should be given only on the advice of a veterinarian, as they can be harmful if the dog has any history of heart or circulatory disease.

Quality, not quantity, in food is important in keeping the dog's weight at a proper level, and exercise is a very important ingredient.

4 THE OLD DOG: GERIATRICS

Today dogs, like people, are living longer. Veterinary medicine has progressed to the point where dogs, once considered old at 8 to 10 years, now are living 18 to 20 years.

The small breeds generally have a longer life span than the large breeds; for example, terriers live longer than Great Danes.

As the dog gets old and feeble he may cause some inconvenience such as a wet rug once in a while, or he may have to be carried up and down stairs, or special care may have to be taken with his diet, but these things are a small price to pay for all his years of love and loyalty. It is up to the master to take good care of him in his old age, keep him from undue suffering and let him live the last enjoyable years of his life with the people he loves.

WHY DOGS ARE LIVING LONGER

—Balanced nutrition in commercial foods
—Advances in veterinary medicine
—Improved vaccines for prevention of diseases
—Improved techniques for management of diseases
—Advances in parasite control
—Dog owners are more aware of proper care and control of their pets for long survival
—More strenuous leash laws, keeping pets from traffic hazards, dog fights, and wild packs

GENERAL CARE

The older dog should be kept in a warm place, free from drafts, because with advancing age he becomes more susceptible to diseases and colds, and his old, brittle bones are more sensitive to cold weather. Conversely he is also more sensitive to hot weather and should be kept in a cool, shaded area, or better still, in an air-conditioned house to keep his respiration and heart from being taxed by heat and humidity.

Extra consideration should be given, such as drying him thoroughly after a bath or after exposure to rain or snow. The hair and skin seem to dry with age, and medicated baths to help relieve irritation and parasites are in order. Fleas seem to thrive on the older dog, and as well as their being a health hazard the dog's life becomes untenable if he has to scratch and bite all the time.

A feeble dog's bed should be as comfortable as possible with added rugs or foam pillows. He should have an extra bed or two around the house for his napping convenience.

NUTRITION

After middle age dogs need less energy and therefore less food. Quality, not quantity, should be the watchword. It is best to give the older dog more frequent and smaller meals because of his failing ability to assimilate food; small amounts are more easily digested. And he may not be able to digest the greasy, fatty foods he once did, or the same number of bones.

When the dog reaches 10 to 12 years of age, his nutritional requirements change because of the changing body processes and of course the decrease in exercise. In general, more meat and more diet supplements such as vitamins are needed, and fewer starchy foods and carbohydrates. Instead of being fed all he wants, he should be given limited amounts of fully nourishing food each day. He can still be given tidbits, but not many fattening delicacies. Any extra fat and tissue on the older dog hastens his deterioration and puts added stress on his weakening organs.

Vitamins

If the dog becomes thin or his coat becomes dry and brittle, it indicates that his diet needs some changes. Such things as milk, eggs, rice pudding, and other cereals may be added to his diet to help maintain his weight. Vitamins are beneficial to the aging dog (and people), even though they may not live up to all the claims implied in such names as "youth pills" and "cell rejuvenation" vitamins.

Vitamin E is generally regarded as the old-age vitamin. It has been credited with increasing the life span, improving skin and coat, and improving fertility and sexual stamina. It can be found in wheat-germ cereal and wheat-germ oil.

Hormones

As the dog gets older and feebler and his muscles weaker, hormones (male hormones for the male dog and female hormones for the female) will help muscle tone and general metabolism and contribute to overall well-being.

Vitamin-hormone preparations are available in wafer, liquid, or powder form which can be added to the dog's food, and they indeed help to maintain and prolong the activity of all the vital body functions in the aging animal. I endorse the normal use of hormones in an old dog, but only on the advice of a veterinarian, as misuse will upset the balance of nature and can cause untoward consequences.

Obesity

Sometimes obesity is due to heredity, but dogs who love to eat are the ones who are prone to overweight in their old age. It is during middle age that they begin showing signs of an overfat condition.

Once a dog is overweight it is difficult to reduce him. It is much easier and healthier to prevent the condition. Overweight predisposes the older dog to heart trouble, constipation, skin infection, and general lethargy. Overfeeding is one of the greatest causes of a shortened life.

Watch the weight of the dog after middle age. Each dog requires a different amount of food to maintain his weight and health, and his diet should be adjusted to his general activity and his emotional condition (e.g., high-strung dogs usually require more food than lethargic dogs).

The Digestive Tract

—As the dog gets older he cannot assimilate the foods he did during his earlier years. Fried, greasy, spicy, and salty foods should be eliminated from his diet.

—Any sudden change in diet will upset his digestion.

—He is prone to constipation and diarrhea.

—Flatulence is a common ailment in older dogs, and it is best treated by eliminating gas-producing foods, such as vegetables, liver, and other organ foods, from the diet. Charcoal tablets are helpful in reducing gas in the intestinal tract.

—Chicken, lamb, and beef seem to be the foods most easily digested by the aging dog.

—A bland diet of cereals and starchy foods is easily digestible for the older dog with intestinal-tract trouble.

EXERCISE

When the dog gets older, he takes longer rests in between his play and exercise periods. This is normal and as it should be. He should not be made to overexercise lest he strain his heart. Unless he is terribly overweight, he will usually exercise sufficiently to keep in good health. He should be allowed to rest when he wants to.

When out for a walk, if he slows down, breathes harder and faster or pants excessively, he should either be carried back home or rested for a while; he has had enough exercise. Exercise is good for an older dog but in a mild form.

BEHAVIORAL CHANGES

A dog quickly becomes fixed in his habits and is easily upset by change. In his old age especially, he is geared to his daily routine, and any deviation may annoy him. He may become irritable and snap occasionally. Be patient with these old folks and remember the days when they did everything they could to please. If the irritability increases, the dog should have a physical checkup; pain, as from an abscessed tooth, can be responsible for the personality change.

The dog is happiest when he is in his own home, and when nursing is necessary, if possible take care of him there under the guidance of a veterinarian. He will respond better to treatment at home.

Jealousy is a strong canine emotion, and if a younger dog is brought into the house, the old pet should be shown preference and love (see p. 42).

When introducing a kitten into the household, be careful. Introduce it gradually; in an old dog jealousy can easily get the upper hand, and he might hurt or destroy the kitten.

When an older dog is involved, I advise getting a kitten rather than a grown cat; both will adjust easier.

PHYSICAL CHANGES

With age, the hair around the muzzle begins to whiten. The nerves and muscles of the hind legs are first to show signs of deterioration. The muscles may shake, as there is a gradual weakening of the legs. Sometimes there is a partial paralysis of the rear legs due to arthritis of the spine, and sometimes this weakness is due to a generalized arthritis or rheumatism.

Then the vital organs—heart, liver, kidneys—begin to show loss of efficient function. General stress and the wear and tear of living cause this aging. If any vital organ is damaged or diseased, there will be a general deterioration in the function and structure of the organ, and the life of the animal will be shortened.

It is up to the owner to have periodic checkups—I advise at least every 6 months in the aging dog—which can prolong the life of the pet. The veterinarian can discover in time what may be necessary to keep the animal healthy and alive. In future years we shall see more and more 20-year-old dogs.

Loss of Hearing

One of the first senile changes is loss of hearing—usually before sight and smell. The dog will have difficulty detecting the direction of sounds. In city traffic it is best not to let an old dog run loose; he might not hear or see an approaching automobile. As he deafens he will hear higher-pitched sounds, such as whistles, more clearly than voice commands.

As his hearing fails be sure to have your veterinarian check him; sometimes, with proper treatment and care, hearing can be prolonged. There may be a heavy coating of wax plugging the ear canal, worsening his deafness; or ear mites or other infection may be causing a loss of hearing.

As he deafens he will rely more on his sight and smell. He may watch his master more closely and stay at his side. As he gets older he doesn't want to be far away from the "one person in his life."

Following deafness, eyesight usually begins to fail. The dog will come to rely more and more on his old, established surroundings. He will not want to be disturbed.

With the dimming of vision there will be a bluish-gray color in his eyes. In a dimly lighted room he will bump into objects. He may hesitate to walk in unfamiliar surroundings. Cataracts are usually the cause. Cataract eye surgery is practical and often gives good results. Many a blind dog has had his eyesight thus restored.

As his eyesight lessens don't allow the dog outside by himself: he might stumble in front of a car. Keep his food and water in the same spot—also his bed—and give him extra amounts of affection, something that he can feel and understand.

A totally blind dog can get along surprisingly well as long as he is with his family in a familiar environment.

AILMENTS AND DISEASES

Periodic examinations by a veterinarian will detect many ailments and diseases in the earliest stages, and proper treatment can be instituted. By urine, blood, and clinical diagnoses many diseases can be apprehended. The old dog has less resistance to ailments and diseases, and his recovery time is slower.

Signs in an old dog that warrant veterinarian supervision:

1. Increased respiration with shortness of breath (heart trouble)

2. Coughing (congestive heart failure)

3. Fainting spells, sudden collapse, or paralysis (heart, cerebral stroke)

4. Increased thirst and urination (nephritis)

5. Halitosis (bad teeth or gums)

6. Urine odor from mouth (which could mean uremia)

Old dogs have many of the sicknesses that plague their old masters—kidney and heart diseases, liver and pancreatic ailments, cancerous tumors. Cancer is common in the older dog, and the tumors enlarge with advancing age.

There is no reason to believe that an old dog cannot be operated on, especially with newer techniques in anesthesia. Of course, surgery in an old dog does have a certain risk factor, but if necessary to relieve pain or to increase life, I advise giving permission. Rely on the discretion of your veterinarian; he will guide you through these trying years. The dog need not suffer undue pain from fear of surgery.

Constipation

Constipation is a fairly common ailment in older dogs because of lack of exercise and changes in metabolism. It is a simple condition to prevent but can lead to many problems in the older dog if not heeded.

Mild and gentle exercise, and frequent outings on the grass, will help elimination. Such foods as bran cereal, liver, and vegetables have a laxative effect and should be added to an old dog's diet. Too many bones or dry foods impede elimination.

If a laxative is needed, milk of magnesia (1-2 tbsp. or 2-6 tablets) is both gentle and effective. I don't advise mineral oil; it retards absorption of foods from the digestive tract. If necessary, a mild enema may be given to an older dog. It is necessary to keep the bowels moving daily for complete freedom from complications.

Retention of bowel contents and urine predisposes to kidney and liver ailments. Retention can cause a toxic condition of the liver and kidneys and a general bloated feeling with ensuing ill health.

In older male dogs the prostate gland, located right beneath the rectum, often becomes enlarged and causes constipation. In this condition defecation is painful. A veterinarian can easily massage the gland and relieve the constipation.

When a dog's abdomen enlarges abnormally, the first thing to think of is constipation, with ensuing gas formation in the intestinal tract. Other causes of abdominal enlargement are tumorous masses, or dropsical conditions due to congestive heart failure.

If ever there is blood in the bowel movements, a veterinarian should examine the dog internally to see if there are any growths inside the rectum.

The Teeth

As previously mentioned, proper nutrition will keep the dog in good health; but if he has badly worn or broken teeth, with consequent gum infection, he cannot eat properly and his health will be endangered.

The teeth of old dogs need regular attention. Tartar and loose and defective teeth should be removed; they can lead to serious infections of the teeth and gums.

When the dog consistently rubs his paw along the side of his mouth or drops his food while trying to eat, he is trying to tell his master that he has a sore tooth. Close observation and regular checkups will reveal any conditions that should be treated.

Pyorrhea is a condition of the gums that causes loosening of the teeth and soft, spongy gums, with accompanying putrid odor. The veterinarian can clean the dog's teeth, treat his gums and keep his mouth in excellent shape.

There is an old saying that when the teeth go, the rest will soon follow. The best way to avoid problems is to keep the dog's teeth clean throughout his life. This can be done by rubbing salt and soda solution, or tooth powder, on the dog's gums and teeth at weekly intervals.

Chronic sniffling and sneezing in old dogs may result from infection in the tooth roots.

Rheumatism and Arthritis

Stiffness in the hindquarters is an early sign of approaching old age. Although it can be caused by constipation, it usually signifies rheumatism or arthritis. Also, an overweight dog has more trouble moving about—the heavier his body, the more weight for his wobbly old legs.

After lying in one spot for a long period, he tends to have trouble getting up. Sometimes he will have to be helped, but once on his feet and he has warmed up a little, his legs and joints seem to work smoothly enough.

Sleeping in warm quarters is helpful in rheumatism and arthritis. The quarters should be arranged so that the dog doesn't have to walk up and down stairs; his tired old legs should be given as much consideration as possible.

Rheumatism is a lameness or stiffness due to muscular spasms. It is usually the result of an animal's lying on damp, cold surfaces. Therefore, in preventing rheumatism, a nice soft bed in a warm area free from drafts is advisable.

Rheumatism, in simple cases, can be helped by aspirin and heat—electric heating pads, hot-water bottles, or infrared bulbs. There is nothing better for old muscles and bones than heat.

Arthritis is a more severe problem because the bones and joints are affected. It is a chronic ailment and more painful and has crippled many a dog and human.

There is no known cure, but such drugs as aspirin, butazolidine, and cortisone preparations can maintain the dog free from pain and enable him to lead a happy life.

Arthritis can be caused by infected teeth or kidneys excreting their poisons into the blood stream, ending up in the joints. Therefore, keeping other parts of the body in good health may prevent arthritis. Actually any chronic infection is capable of stimulating arthritis in the dog.

Lameness and stiffness can be simply due to long toenails. Long toenails can cause the dog to stumble and fall, injuring his fragile bones. Extra-long toenails will cause his paws, weakening with age, to spread even farther apart. The condition is easily remedied by periodic nail clipping.

Calluses

Calluses are usually due to old age and lying on hard surfaces. They are a thickening of the skin at the elbows of the front legs and the hocks of the hind legs. I advise blankets and mattresses for older dogs, as any irritation may produce sores. Baby oil, vaseline, or lanolin applied to the calluses will keep them soft and prevent infection.

Warts

Old-age warts are tiny, round, hard, benign growths that are seen on older dogs. Sometimes there are just a few, but they can soon multiply so that a dog has as many as a hundred on his body. When they irritate the dog and he bites and scratches them, ulcerated areas can develop.

Many different medications have been tried. The simple remedy of castor oil on the wart daily may be helpful. Dry ice and salicylic acid have been successful in drying up warts. I have known people to take scissors and cut warts off, but there is profuse bleeding and I don't advise this procedure.

A veterinarian can remove warts with electric cautery under local anesthetic. I advise surgery only if the warts begin growing or are in a vital area, as on an eyelid, between the toes, or on the flaps of the ears.

Constantly observe the older dog for detection of small tumors. It is when tumors first appear that they respond most easily to surgery. Unfortunately they are usually neglected until they become large and the chances for survival are slimmer.

In unspayed females tumors are especially common in the breasts. If bitches are spayed before the age of one, mammary tumors are much less common. Spaying can be done at any age without complications and may help prevent further growth of tumors or female infections.

Mammary tumors grow markedly after heat periods because of the female hormones in the blood stream, and many veterinarians treat the tumors with male hormones. At best the male hormones may slow the growth of the tumors but will not cure them. To prevent further growth, complete hysterectomy may be the only answer. A mammary tumor should be removed as soon as it is discovered; any delay will let it continue to grow and spread to the point where surgical intervention may be impossible if other organs are affected.

It is best to do a hysterectomy on an old bitch while she is in relatively good condition and her chances for survival are greatest. Hormonal treatment of infected female organs, although practiced widely, does not give complete cure, and surgical intervention is eventually required.

In old male dogs a common site for tumors is around the anus. These tumors can be controlled somewhat with female-hormone injections, but surgery is the only complete answer. The tumors are usually cancerous and spread rapidly, sometimes infiltrating the inner recesses of the rectum, in which case they are inoperable.

Male dogs can develop tumors of the testicles, and if there is any enlargement, a veterinarian should be consulted; immediate removal can prevent a malignancy from spreading into the internal recesses of the body.

In boxers we see benign tumors of the gums which sometimes interfere with eating, as they often get larger than the teeth. The tumors have to be removed surgically. Occasionally they go into a cancerous condition, attacking both gums and jawbone with fatal results.

Old dogs are susceptible to tiny growths on the eyelids which cause irritation when they press against the eyeball and the cornea. The irritation causes a discharge, and the animal constantly blinks. In chronic cases ulceration and opaqueness of the eyeball result. Surgical removal of the growth is easily performed.

Cancerous growths can be found in vital organs—lungs, liver, digestive organs—and some breeds are quite susceptible to skin cancers, the boxer being more commonly affected. Any lump or growth should be examined by a veterinarian; early surgery can often avoid tragedy.

Female Irregularities

As the female arrives at the age of 8 to 10 years her heat cycles may take on an irregular appearance both in frequency and in the physical discharge.

She may have periods only once every year or two, or she may have periods every 2 or 3 months.

She may have "silent heat periods," with little or no discharge, only a slight swelling of the vulva, and only an occasional visit by a neighboring male dog. It is a blow to her feminine ego that she is losing her sex appeal.

On the other hand, she may have a profuse discharge which may be due to a prolonged heat period or possibly an infection of the uterus which produces an excessive bloody-looking, purulent discharge.

At times the cervix closes, which prevents the discharge from being expelled. This is a source of trouble, with resultant large abdomen accompanied by fever and pain. Unless early diagnosis of pyometra is made and a complete hysterectomy done, the dog may die.

Many owners of old bitches complain that male dogs are constantly in pursuit. Actually the male dogs are smelling the infected discharge emanating from the uterus. If this seems to be happening, the bitch should be gotten to a veterinarian as quickly as possible. Surgery may save her life.

Prostatitis

Old male dogs commonly suffer from prostatitis, which is an enlargement of the prostate gland that gives rise to painful symptoms. The dog may appear stiff-legged, walk awkwardly and show fever with pain. The enlarged prostate presses against the rectum, causing constipation. It also causes pressure on the urethra, with partial closure and with pain

84

upon urination. There will be frequent stops at bushes, but merely a dribble appears when the dog attempts to urinate.

By rectal examination the veterinarian can determine the condition of the prostate and massage it to help reduce the size. He can also note if there are growths or abscesses. Female hormones are used to reduce the size of the prostate.

One of the predisposing causes of prostatitis in an older dog is being stimulated by a female in heat. It is obvious, but not to him, that he is too old for this kind of running around. If prostatitis becomes chronic, I advise castration, which will allow a shrinkage of the prostate gland without any further trouble.

Hernia

Perineal hernia, which is the most common, is a rupture of the tissues around the rectum. It is usually seen in male dogs and is caused by chronic constipation. The dog strains to defecate, with eventual breakdown of the tissues surrounding the rectum. An enlarged prostate also predisposes old dogs to perineal hernia. Surgery is possible. Castration also seems to help, since it reduces the size of the prostate.

The Kidneys

As the dog gets older he may lose partial control of his bladder. This may be due to the normal aging process or it may be caused by a specific disease, such as nephritis, cystitis, prostatitis, or possibly stones in the bladder. Kidney diseases occur in about 76 percent of dogs over 8 to 9 years of age.

As the dog ages there is gradual degeneration of the kidney tissue with a lessening of the kidney function, which is so vital for life. The general symptoms of chronic kidney conditions are loss of weight, intermittent vomiting, bad breath, difficulty in walking, walking with a hunched-up back, frequent urination, and excessive water drinking. With the appearance of any of the symptoms a veterinarian should be consulted for a urinalysis. There is also a blood test—B.U.N.—which is used to check kidney function.

In an old spayed female, dribbling of the urine can be controlled rather easily with female hormones. If a male starts losing control, male hormones are helpful.

If there is blood in the urine, stones (calculi) in the kidneys or bladder can be suspected. Surgical removal of stones is a simple process in the modern veterinary hospital.

Sometimes the kidneys deteriorate to such a low point that uremia develops. It is aggravated when other conditions such as liver ailments and heart problems occur at the same time. The gums show ulceration and sores. Often there will be the odor of urine on the dog's breath. This shows that the animal is dangerously ill.

One of the commonest kidney infections seen in older dogs today is nephritis. The cause is still unknown. Kidney damage caused by various diseases, and especially leptospirosis, is blamed.

Kidney disease is kept under control by adjusting the diet to reduce certain proteins and by providing more water. An older dog should be expected to consume 2 to 3 times the amount of water of a younger dog, as his kidneys require it. This will involve more frequent urination, and so he should be taken outdoors more often, especially as his urinary control may not be as good as it once was. Having to wet inside the house is embarrassing to an old friend.

Diet should include all forms of liquids, such as broth, buttermilk, and fruit juices. Other excellent foods are dairy products, including cooked eggs, cereals such as oatmeal, certain types of vegetables, and any type of syrup. There are fine prescription diets for kidney diseases obtainable at most veterinary hospitals. It is a low-protein but high-quality-protein diet which is easily assimilated by an old dog without stress on the kidneys. The high protein of animal meats seems to be detrimental to diseased kidneys. Be sure to avoid any such foods as ham, bacon, and highly spiced tidbits, and any foods with salt. Remember: don't overwork the plumbing.

Shock

Any stress condition, traumatic condition, or even surgery or anesthesia can produce shock in an old animal. This is why the veterinarian is cautious about advising surgery on an old dog. However, with the improvement in anesthetics and with blood tranfusions and oxygen infusions, many older dogs can be prevented from going into shock.

With any blood loss, transfusions are primary in saving the animal and in preventing shock. Antibiotics are also useful in preventing shock. During any stress condition the veterinarian will usually administer cortisone in small doses.

For many years it was thought that older dogs were not susceptible to the virus of distemper. But it has been found that booster shots are necessary because old dogs have a mild form of distemper characterized by hair loss, apathy, weight loss, and poor appetite. Distemper in an old dog shows complications in the brain, with neurological damage. There are certain laboratory tests which can confirm any suspicion of distemper.

Old dogs are also susceptible to liver diseases, which can be diagnosed by laboratory tests.

Chronic asthma and bronchitis are also seen. The dog needs help in dilation of the bronchial tubes to allow him to breathe more easily.

Heart Disease

Clinical heart disease is found in about 10 percent of the canine population. Many of these animals develop congestive heart failure. With the advances in veterinary medicine and the advent of adequate drug therapy and controlled diet, many of these dogs are helped in reducing the effects of heart failure, and they live many happy and useful years.

Some symptoms of heart trouble are tiring easily, short breath, and panting upon the slightest exertion. Sometimes there are fainting spells, periodic coughing spells, and even convulsive spasms of the body. The veterinarian, with the stethoscope and electrocardiograph, can confirm any suspicions of heart trouble.

The veterinarian probably will digitalize the dog's heart to strengthen the muscles and then prescribe heart pills. In the treatment of heart patients there is often dropsy—an accumulation of fluid in the abdominal cavity—accompanied by coughing, another symptom of congestive heart failure. There are drugs to relieve the coughing and diuretics to help pass the excessive fluid from the body. The fluid develops not only in the abdominal cavity but also in the lung tissues and causes the coughing. Getting at the cause of the cough, strengthening the heart muscle, and reducing the fluid in the body are all paramount in treatment.

Excessive exercise and excitement from such things as visiting neighbors, grooming, and bathing should be limited. If any excitement is expected, either put the dog in a quiet place or give him a tranquilizer. Any emotional excitement is bad for the heart patient.

The heart patient suffers greatly in hot weather or high humidity. In areas where there are high temperatures, take a heart patient out only early in the morning and late at night. Getting a heart patient through a hot summer is difficult; complete rest in an air-conditioned room is helpful.

Weight and diet control are important in the treatment of heart conditions. Excess fat around the heart and its blood vessels reduces the chances of survival. There are some basic rules in feeding the heart patient. First is low salt. Highly seasoned or spicy foods must be avoided. Certain vegetables, including celery, spinach, turnips, and artichokes, should be avoided. Cheese and milk are not good. Salt butter and margarine are not acceptable.

Low-sodium diets are essential in preventing hypertension in heart patients. There are prescription diets (HD), but there are also many foods that the owner can either mix in with the prescription diet or use alone when the dog refuses the prescription diet. The heart patient requires smaller amounts of protein but of higher quality. The special diets are minimal in sodium and help keep the body free from water retention.

Lemon, lime, honey, and maple syrup make the prescription diets more palatable. Rice, macaroni, puffed wheat, and spaghetti are excellent fillers with fresh meat and vegetables. Vegetable shortening can be added to the diet to make the food more palatable and to help the dog's coat. Any type of fruit is acceptable. Asparagus, green beans, tomatoes, and lettuce are good. Baby foods, beef and chicken broths, and organ foods should be avoided because they contain salt.

As for exercise, the dog usually knows when he has had enough, so don't force him to run and play. Moderate exercise is the answer for the heart patient.

Parasites

An old dog is susceptible to worms, so during his checkup every 6 months, he should be checked for intestinal parasites. These can be debilitating to an old dog. The commonest parasite in the old dog is the tapeworm. However whipworms and hookworms are also possible.

A mild, gentle worm medicine should be used in the older dog so as not to disturb his sensitive intestinal tract.

EUTHANASIA, OR "PUTTING THE DOG TO SLEEP"

Euthanasia—a quiet and easy death. The right to end the suffering of a loved one, human or otherwise, has long been argued. When it comes to dogs, the practice is so general that few people do more than murmur a conventional "I'm sorry," when told of a friend having put his pet to sleep.

I am constantly asked, "What would you do if it were your dog, Dr. Vine?" The question haunts me, as do the faces of the doomed dogs and the tragedy in the eyes of those who love their dogs and must make the decision. To those who have decreed a quiet and easy death rather than a life of suffering when such suffering is inevitable, let me say that if it were my dog I would do the same. I can say no more than that.

Unfortunately some people make the decision hastily or cold-bloodedly with the feeling that they can always buy another dog. How wrong they are! Each dog is an entity just as each person is. It is heartbreaking when these people—and there are more of them than you might suppose—thrust a sick animal at me and say, "Put him out of his misery." It is their misery that they are so anxious to get rid of and not the dog's. Many of these dogs, with proper care and treatment, could have many more happy years of life. As long as life exists, is it not dearer by far than death, to a dog no less than to a man? Any way you look at it, it is a solemn question—to take or not to take a life. Yet a lot of people play God with no thought except to rid themselves of an animal that has become a burden to them.

Others to whom a dog is a beloved friend, a dear companion, and everything that is loyal and loving suffer dreadfully when confronted with such a decision. These are people who have a special kinship with their dogs. Always such people will do everything in their power to save the lives of their dogs. After all, a dog can lead a good existence with one leg amputated; with the sight gone from an eye or the hearing from an ear; with a cranky heart, or even a toothless jaw. I know this is so; I have treated them. What such a dog requires is just a little more love, a little more care, and more thoughtfulness than the average healthy dog needs. These

89

dogs don't feel sorry for themselves, as people are prone to do. They have a lot of life left in them and can manage quite well. So long as they are near their loved ones and are not suffering, I don't advise euthanasia.

However, I firmly believe that any animal that is diseased beyond all hope and without any relief from suffering should be allowed out of his misery. There are many cases that cannot be benefited; in cancerous conditions and other incurable diseases the decision should definitely be to put the animal to sleep.

I put to sleep several dogs a week in my clinic. These animals have a need for departing from this world. They are suffering, with no hope of cure, and so I help the owners make the decision. It is the decision I least enjoy in my practice; however, there are some people who cannot make the decision themselves, and so they ask my guidance.

The two questions I ask myself are: Is the dog undergoing undue suffering that cannot be relieved? Is the dog enjoying life? If the answers are obviously unfavorable, then I wholeheartedly advise euthanasia, which is literally going to sleep while the lethal dose is injected into a vein. There is no pain, no struggle, and the dog has no knowledge of what is happening. He is calm and quiet to the end, and the drug is almost instantaneous in action. Many animals are put to sleep with their owners holding them in their arms.

I still all too vividly recall an incident that happened when I was a yearling doctor just out of veterinary school. It taught me that although dogs do queer things when they are emotionally disturbed, human beings do even queerer things.

Of course, it is none of my business how individuals behave in their private lives, but when their reactions affect animals, then I feel that it is my business. In my early years of practice I was too inexperienced to protect a particular dog from his distraught owners. The case still bothers me.

A couple came to me to have their dog put to sleep. I was surprised to see the animal in good health and relatively young. I asked them why they wanted such a pretty dog destroyed. They said it was none of my business, and they would stay there until I did it. I tried to get them to give the dog to me, but they were determined to go through with the execution. So I did it as quickly as I knew how. The second the little dog lay still, the woman darted forward, grabbed it up and hugged it passionately to her breast, covering it with kisses. The man's eyes were blinded with tears, and his cheeks were wet. For a moment I had the insane notion that they would tear the dog in two, so violently did they struggle for possession of the body. After a bit they calmed down. "We're getting a divorce," the man said, "and neither one of us could give up the dog. We made up our minds that if we couldn't have it, then no one could."

The sacrifice to a selfish love lay motionless between the two emotionally disturbed people. Throughout these past twenty-six years I have been upset at both owners of the dog for being so selfish and at myself for acceding to their foolish demand.

GETTING ANOTHER DOG

Usually grieving owners claim that they will not replace their dogs. I know that it hurts to bring a new puppy into the house while mourning for the other, but I try to reason that the loss of a dog should not prevent getting another—and the sooner the better.

MacKinlay Kantor, Pulitzer-prize-winning author, worded his sentiments beautifully in a letter to a friend after the loss of his dog:

"Some silly folks cry and beat their breasts and yell, 'I will never have another dog.' Can you imagine anything more absurd? It is like saying, 'I owned a supreme friend. He gave me laughter, courage, tenderness, power. He gave me all those things and more—yet now he is gone. Therefore, I want never to have another friend.' You do not get another dog to replace the old one. No dog can ever replace another. But one dog can take over the responsibilities and duties of another. Dogs have a keen sense of fitness and propriety."

I agree with Kantor. One soon can learn to love another dog; maybe not in the same way, but all dogs are individuals, and they all have their own wonderful ways and become an integral part of the family. It is unreasonable to say that you will not have another dog because some day he will die. Just look forward to the 10 to 12 years that he will give you happiness, love, and loyalty.

I quote a poem that was written by a good friend of mine, Ina Forbus, for her four Scotties that departed over a period of years.

Dear God, I ask for these small friends
A wide green path for eager feet
That daily raced on cool green grass
And were not used to city streets.
And could You please give them a creek
Around the bend of which adventures lie
And let them chase a rabbit up the hill and down;
They'll never catch him but it's fun to try.
Just one more thing, Dear Father, I would ask:
LET ME BE GREETED AT THE OUTER DOOR
BY ALL THE MADLY WAGGING TAILS AND
LOVING EYES OF MY DEAR FOUR.

Part Two

AN OUNCE OF PREVENTION

5 NUTRITION: CAVIAR OR DOG CHOW?

The pets in this country are well nourished. Many of our dogs eat better than their masters. But with animals, as with humans, malnutrition problems more often result from excessive feeding than from lack of nutrients, and some people kill their dogs with kindness by overfeeding. The overfed house pet becomes lazy, shiftless, and a poor watchdog. He has bad breath, sheds his coat constantly, is disobedient because of overindulgence, and in general is not a credit to his master.

In my clinic I see many illnesses that arise from dietary problems other than deficiencies. Some of the ills are due to improper feeding, overfeeding, and feeding too frequently. It is necessary to regulate diet to each individual dog—and that is the theme of this chapter. Each dog should be fed according to his needs and to his likes and dislikes. No diet that I might give can pertain to every dog, and this chapter is for the exception rather than for the average dog.

The commercial dog-food companies have made it economical to feed the average dog, and the average dog is quite happy with and grateful for the well-balanced and palatable foods. The commercial foods are the result of years of careful research, and they contain all the ingredients for well-balanced diets. They relieve the dog owner of the burden of figuring out a good nutritional program.

Dog owners who consider themselves smarter than the nutritionists employed by the dog-food companies and who try to improve on the fine commercial offerings often end up unbalancing them. Although I am firmly convinced of the humanness of animals and of their love for "people" food, table scraps and tidbits should not form more than one-third of the basic commercial dog-food diet.

The dog's two main pleasures in life are eating and pleasing his master.

CALORIES

Calories are a measurement of energy, and every bit of activity in an animal requires energy. Calories are fuel for the body the same as gas is for the automobile. Also, calories are required to keep the body temperature normal.

Active dogs need more calories than pet dogs who cat-nap all day. The dog's temperament affects his caloric requirements; a high-strung dog requires more calories than a placid, easygoing animal. More calories are required in cold weather. During gestation and lactation the bitch needs more calories. Growing puppies require about twice as many calories as adult dogs. A small dog requires more calories per pound of body weight than a large dog. A 2-pound dog requires about 64 calories per pound of body weight, while a 22-pound dog requires 34 calories. The larger the dog, the less his caloric requirement per pound of body weight.

Fats furnish more than double the calories per gram that carbohydrates or proteins do. The calories of fats and carbohydrates should be used for energy, and the calories of proteins should be used for tissue building and maintenance of body functions. Most good commercial dog foods ensure a balance of calories and require no supplementation for the normal, healthy dog.

A MAINTENANCE DIET

A maintenance diet is one which researchers have found to be the food intake required to keep an animal in good health under normal circumstances. The animal will neither gain nor lose weight, nor will he develop a deficiency disease. Some animal diseases have a direct relationship to poor diet because of the weakened condition of the dog.

THE WELL-BALANCED DIET

Primarily the dog is a carnivorous animal, and in the wild state he not only eats meat but eats the entire animal. In devouring the whole prey he is assured a well-balanced diet, with muscle and organ foods and roughage.

Today's house pet has little need or urge to roam for his food, and any nutritional deficiencies are our fault, not his.

The definition of a well-balanced diet can be a good commercial dog food—dry or canned—with first-class proteins added if necessary (milk, eggs, meat, fish, cheese). It consists of foods which contain the correct proportions of proteins, fats, carbohydrates, vitamins, and minerals. Carbohydrates make up most of the energy, as they are the major source of calories. Foods must provide energy and nutrients for growth and maintenance. However, I want to emphasize that most dogs do perfectly well for their entire lives with a diet consisting of nothing else but a good commercially prepared dog food.

ESSENTIAL NUTRIENTS

Carbohydrates

These are usually in the form of starch and are the major part of the dog's diet—at least 70 percent of it. Carbohydrates provide energy, and if there are not enough in the diet the dog will use up proteins for energy. Carbohydrates are the most economical portion of the diet and are provided by cereals and sugars. Cereals, such as corn flakes, shredded wheat, oatmeal, and bread, are an excellent form of carbohydrates. Sugars are not provided in the commercial dog foods, and candies or other sweets in moderate amounts are not harmful to the dog.

Proteins

Proteins are necessary for growth and for development and maintenance of body tissue. Most commercial dog foods contain at least 20 percent protein. Puppies, lactating bitches, and convalescing dogs all need extra amounts, which can be found in eggs, milk, cheese, meat, soy beans, and fish.

Dogs with hookworm infestation, anemia, rickets, or skin disorders, and those emaciated from disease, need extra-high-quality protein.

Fats

Fat is another part of the well-balanced diet—5 to 10 percent. It is a source of energy, and it keeps the skin and hair in good condition. Dry, scaly skin is usually due to a fat-deficient diet.

Dry commercial foods are sometimes low in fat because of

the possibility of rancidity, and so the addition of fat (but not more than 20 percent for the normal dog) is recommended.

City dogs who live in warm apartments are prone to dry coats and skin and generally need fat supplements. Vegetable oil (e.g., corn oil) is a good fat additive.

The more active a dog, the more fat will be needed to support the body weight and energy demands. Working and hunting dogs generally need more fat added to their diets.

Fats add to the palatability of foods for dogs and are also important in that some vitamins cannot be utilized by the body if fat is not present. There are two sources of fat: animal (lard, butter, beef tallow) and vegetable (corn oil, soybean oil).

Roughage

Roughage is the bulk without which there would be constipation problems. Although most commercial foods contain adequate roughage, for dogs with chronic constipation and with anal-gland problems I advise adding wheat-bran cereal to the diet. Roughage consists of bran and other cereals and plants.

Vitamins and Minerals

There are usually enough vitamins and minerals in the commercial dog foods for the average adult dog, but for lactating bitches, growing puppies, and older dogs, I feel, extra amounts should be added to the diet. Foods which give extra amounts are liver, eggs, and some plant foods.

VITAMIN OVERFEEDING

Because of the availability of high-potency supplements at low prices, some people give extra amounts of vitamins, believing that if a little helps, a lot is even better. Fortunately the healthy adult dog will eliminate the extra amounts without harmful effects, but there can be problems.

The most commonly overused and most dangerous is vitamin D. It is found in oils such as fish-liver, and because it is oil-soluble it is difficult for the body to eliminate. Any slight excess is eliminated through the kidneys, but in excessive amounts calcium build-up is dangerous to the kidneys as well as to the bones as it can cause them to mineralize.

Overfeeding of vitamin A has not been proved harmful but is still in question. Vitamins B and E are not generally considered harmful in excessive amounts.

DEFICIENCIES

Since commercial dog foods are so well balanced, we seldom see deficiencies. Since liver contains the greatest amount of natural essential vitamins, I advise feeding it once or twice a week, raw or slightly boiled.

Vitamin A deficiency results in weak and running and infected eyes. Old-time folk advised an egg a day for treatment of eye trouble, and we now know that it was the high vitamin A content of the yolk which was responsible for the curative powers. Raw egg is not advisable; the white interferes with the normal digestive processes. Other symptoms of vitamin A deficiency are poor appetite and growth, and skin lesions.

Vitamin B_1 (thiamine) deficiency results in loss of appetite, nervousness, or convulsions and other neurological symptoms. Brewers' yeast is an excellent source of vitamin B_1, as are wholegrain cereals, nuts, legumes, liver, pork, egg yolk, milk, and green vegetables.

Vitamin B_2 (riboflavin) deficiency usually results in diarrhea, ulceration of the gums, and watery, bloodshot eyes. Good sources of vitamin B_2 are yeast, wheat germ, liver, meat, fish, poultry, eggs, milk, legumes, fruits, and green vegetables.

A deficiency of nicotinic acid (niacin) is responsible for ulcerated mouth and black tongue, which corresponds to pellagra in humans. Before the advent of well-balanced commercial diets, when corn formed the major part of the diet, it was much more prevalent. However, some not so fortunate humans and dogs in poverty-stricken areas still get it. Niacin is found in the same foods as vitamin B_2 except milk, eggs, fruits, and green vegetables.

Vitamin E is said to aid in fertility and reproduction, and is beneficial to skin and hair. It is present in egg yolks, wheat-germ oil, and green leaves.

Vitamin D is essential to bone formation and ricket prevention in puppies.

An All-Meat Diet

Feeding an all-meat diet, with nothing else, will eventually cause a mineral deficiency exhibiting itself in hair loss and red and irritated skin, especially under the armpits and in the groin. A calcium deficiency will develop in a puppy or a lactating bitch fed only meat.

Older dogs on all-meat diets usually develop kidney diseases from the high concentration of protein. Too much protein in the diet can cause a chronic irritation of the intestines, similar to colitis in humans, with a dark and foul-smelling diarrhea.

For dogs who eat nothing but meat, we must add vitamins, minerals, and oils. I would try to give them organ foods, such as liver or kidney, which are very nutritious.

The label "all meat" on commercial canned foods is prohibited unless the food contains only muscle meat. Most of the so-called meats have been whole carcasses of animals that include lungs, liver, spleen, brains, stomach, intestines, and other organs. Under the new regulations these will be labeled "meat by-products."

Raw Eggs

The reason eggs are erroneously considered harmful by some people is that the raw egg white contains an enzyme, avidin, which will destroy a B-complex vitamin, biotin. Actually, any harmful effects would be noticed only if the dog were fed excessive amounts of raw eggs, i.e., 6-12 a day. An occasional raw egg will not harm a dog as the biotin is quickly replaced by additional food consumed. In fact, in emergency feeding, raw eggs in their entirety have saved many a dog's life.

In cooking eggs, the avidin in the egg white is destroyed, which is why cooked eggs are advised.

Ailments and/or symptoms involved with an excessive amount of raw eggs could be diarrhea, vomiting, and an ambiguous skin problem (dry, itchy skin).

Signs of Nutritional Deficiencies

—Dry, scaly skin
—Excessive shedding
—Stunted growth

—Running eyes
—Rickets (bent legs)
—Black tongue and mouth ulceration
—Infertility
—Nervous disorders
—Anemia

Bad Habits Caused by Deficiencies

The eating of horse manure indicates a craving for cereal; the dog is seeking the undigested particles of cereal in the manure. By adding certain types of cereal, such as corn meal, to his food, the habit can be cured. Discipline will also be required to help cure the habit after the nutritional deficiency has been remedied.

Coprophagy (eating one's own droppings) is usually a symptom of a lack of vitamins and minerals, from the incomplete digestion of meat. It can also be caused by worms in the digestive tract. (For complete discussion see p. 166.)

When a dog constantly licks upholstery, carpets, and table legs the owner should suspect a nutritional deficiency. There should be a complete review of the dog's feeding program, and the addition of vitamins and minerals will probably be required.

BONES

Although bones have no nutritional value, they are excellent for growing puppies to distract them from destroying household effects; and as well as providing hours of pleasure and freedom from boredom, they exercise the gums and help keep the teeth free from tartar. I advise giving a pet at least one large bone a week.

Bones do supply a small amount of calcium and phosphorus. However, I would rather rely on commercial bone meal for mineral supplements.

The only bones that should be given are large beef bones, preferably knuckle bones, and shank bones of lamb or pork. Bones of chicken, rabbit, and fish, and small bones of lamb, pork, or veal, should never be given to a dog. They tend to splinter and can scratch the throat and the sensitive lining of the stomach and intestines.

With bones, as with everything else, use common sense. Too many bones will cause impacted bowels or will cause the stools to become dry and chalky, with the necessity of laxatives and enemas. White stools can also indicate a liver or pancreatic condition, and if this condition continues after the elimination of bones, the dog should be checked by a veterinarian.

Some people cook chicken bones or other bones in the pressure cooker, which makes them digestible. They are also a fine food if meat has been left on them.

Some dogs cannot digest bones in any form and vomit them. For dogs who have problems with bones, dog biscuits serve many of the same purposes and don't have the constipating effect of too many bones.

VARIETY AND PALATABILITY

Like humans, dogs get bored with the same food day in and day out. To keep a pet interested in his food, I recommend varying the diet a bit. About every 5th day he can be fed an entirely different food—either kibble, meal, or canned. Or the same basic commercial food can be used and another food added, such as liver, meat, or table scraps. Any products which are high in protein, such as meat, eggs, milk, fish, or cheese, are enjoyed by most dogs and make a meal quite palatable.

I believe a dog should have some fresh meat at least once a week. Organ foods, such as liver, kidney, sweetbreads, lungs, brains, tripe, and giblets, are nutritious and furnish vitamins and minerals.

The diet can also be varied by adding such flavors as bacon fat, chicken broth, onions, and garlic. But a great deal of fat may cause a digestive upset.

Foods mixed with hot water are favored by dogs in cold weather; the hot water seems to bring out the flavor.

Although vegetables are not an essential part of the dog's diet, let him have vegetables if he enjoys them. They will not give him much nourishment but will give him vitamins, minerals, and roughage (they are a good laxative for some dogs).

THE FINICKY EATER

Many generations of dogs have lived on nothing but commercial foods and been maintained in fine health. However, in my practice of veterinary medicine I deal with a lot of pet dogs who demand specially prepared foods and get them.

As with people, some dogs will not eat the food presented to them, and food has to be prepared to their liking. Most of us do spoil our dogs. As each dog is an individual, his feeding program has to be individual and geared to his activity, temperament, and likes and dislikes. I am not in favor of starving a dog into eating the food his master thinks he should eat. I believe a compromise should be worked out with the dog and that the master should endeavor to find the food that the dog likes most. The basic diet should be 75 percent or more of his meal, and then the little extras that the dog especially enjoys should be incorporated into it, up to 25 percent of the total.

There are many exotic foods that dogs eat because their human families eat them. To allay any doubts: I don't know of any food we eat that will harm a dog. Of course, once he tastes some gourmet morsel he may become addicted to it and subsequently be finicky.

Although the training experts maintain that it is not proper to feed dogs scraps at the table, each person must work this out with his dog. Our main concern is with health, and so long as the dog is not overfed to the point where he has digestive problems, I say spoil him. That is each owner's prerogative.

There is an expression that finicky eaters are not born but made. But whenever a dog refuses food for more than 24 hours, it is a warning that something is wrong. Loss of appetite is one of the earliest symptoms of most ailments and diseases and of worms.

Vitamin B is especially helpful in stimulating the appetite of a finicky eater. Or a little syrup on his food may tempt him. Malted-milk tablets appeal to some dogs. Canned fish is mouthwatering to some.

Most dogs are interested in the food their human family eats, and some finicky eaters will eat dog food if they think it is from the master's plate—if he makes believe he is eating it. Planning the diet of the finicky eater so that he eats a little each time his human family eats works in some cases.

Emotionally disturbed dogs can usually be coaxed into eating with a soothing voice, and they love to be hand-fed.

Another way to get a finicky eater to clean up his plate is to bring a strange animal into the house. Most dogs will eat their food to keep it from another animal.

Some finicky eaters go on hunger strikes because they are angry with their master, don't like the food offered, or are overfed and lazy. A long run out in the woods may stimulate a dog with a sluggish appetite.

It is advisable to throw out uneaten food and not leave it to become soggy and unpalatable. Always feed freshly prepared food.

SALT REQUIREMENTS OF DOGS

The average diet for dogs (a well balanced commercial dog food) contains enough salt to satisfy all of the sodium needs of his body. Unless advised by your veterinarian, do not add any extra amounts of salt to the diet. Salt helps to maintain proper fluid balance within the body; an excess can cause a strain on the kidneys. In older dogs with a heart problem a sodium-free diet is advisable. Old dogs that receive excessive salt can develop fluid accumulation around the heart and within the body tissues.

A normal amount of salt is necessary for production of stomach acids. Higher levels of salt will increase the water intake but it is wrong to add salt to the diet to make a dog drink more water. He might drink more water to flush out his kidneys but it is doing irreparable damage to the kidney tissue.

SPECIAL DIETS

The brood bitch needs extra amounts of proteins, vitamins, and minerals to maintain herself and to provide ample nutrients for the normal development of her litter. From the 4th week of pregnancy until the puppies are weaned—about 10 weeks—the bitch needs high-quality proteins.

The first 90 days after weaning, puppies must have extra amounts of food for their rapid growth and to allow their bodies to produce the antibodies that make them resistant to diseases. A puppy in poor health will not get ample immunity from vaccines.

Puppies require twice as much food per pound of body weight as adult dogs. However, because of their small stomachs they cannot digest much food at a time and hence need frequent feedings in small amounts.

A high-strung dog needs more food than his lethargic peer. He uses up much more energy than the docile pet who lies

103

around all day. The active dog doesn't necessarily need more meat or protein. Protein provides for growth and tissue building. Starches, carbohydrates, and fats are needed because they supply energy.

Some dogs have flatulence with certain foods. Foods high in meat and eggs often will cause gas to form in the intestinal tract. Boxers have the most trouble. Charcoal tablets are effective in reducing the amount of gas. More roughage in the diet (more dry food or kibble) may also be helpful.

Certain dogs have food allergies which may be manifested in digestive disturbances (vomiting or diarrhea) or in skin problems. It is a challenge to find out just what the dog is allergic to, and there is a procedure of eliminating one food at a time until the culprit is found (see p. 234).

Occasionally I find dogs whose digestive system cannot tolerate "people food" and upon eating tablescraps will become ill at both ends of their body. These dogs do perfectly well on commercial foods forever and forever.

Fattening Diet for Underweight Dogs

For a thin dog, or an active dog who needs to have his weight kept up, bread and milk are excellent additives. Most dogs like a little butter or sugar, also molasses or syrup, or raw egg yolk. Rice or grits soaked in chicken or beef gravy appeals to some dogs. Some dogs like rice pudding. Starchy foods and sweets are fine. Extra amounts of fat, within reason, may be added.

For working and hunting dogs, beef suet added to the diet is an excellent way to keep up weight. The diet should be varied according to the individual and his seasons of activity.

Bland Diet for Sick or Convalescing Dogs

Sick and convalescing dogs need a special bland diet to allow nature to heal the affected organs. The normal diet is too harsh and irritating to the stomach and intestines, and all commercial dog foods should be removed from the diet, especially horse meat. Milk is also taboo, as well as fried foods and bones.

The basic bland diet can be cooked rice, grits, noodles, or macaroni, added to chicken or beef broth, or flavored with lean beef, chicken, or lamb. Cooked cereals, such as Wheatena and Farina, are very good, as are Pablum and other baby cereals. All baby foods are acceptable. Cooked eggs are excellent. Buttermilk is recommended because it helps the normal intestinal bacteria to return to normal. Restore the dog to the regular diet gradually.

When an animal is running a fever, he often is very thirsty, but drinking large amounts of water usually results in vomiting. A good idea is to put a few ice cubes in a water dish, which will restrict the water to small amounts at a time.

FEEDING SUGGESTIONS

In the average adult dog it takes 18 hours for the food to pass through the digestive system, and therefore one meal a day is recommended.

Any sudden change in the dog's diet may cause a digestive upset, so when changing food, do so gradually. Add a little more of the new food each day and decrease the former food proportionally until the complete change is made.

During hot weather dogs will not eat as much food, and the fat content should be reduced. It is also best to feed late in the evening.

There is no difference in the nutritive value of beef or horse meat, but horse meat gives some dogs diarrhea.

It is best not to feed dogs raw pork, since they are just as prone to trichinosis as humans. Actually pork is not the best meat for dogs, because of the high fat content, and some dogs seem unable to tolerate it. Other meats to be avoided are those which are fried, smoked, spiced, or highly seasoned.

A watchdog who is on duty mainly at night when the master is asleep should not be fed later than 4 P.M., for with a full stomach he will become drowsy and sleep through his guarding chores. But a barking dog who keeps the neighbors awake at night should be fed late in the evening so that he will sleep most of the night.

A dog should not be fed within 3 hours of hunting or strenuous exercise. (Athletes never eat within 4 hours of a sporting event.) After hunting or other strenuous activity a dog should have a half-hour rest before being fed.

When taking a dog to a boarding kennel, advise the management of the brand of food the dog is used to. If he is an especially fussy dog, take his water dish and feeding pan along. If the dog is especially nervous about going to a kennel, give him a tranquilizer just before leaving, and he will adjust much more quickly.

When taking the dog from the hospital or kennel, let him quiet down for several hours before giving him anything to eat or drink, as overexcitement causes nausea.

FEEDING FALLACIES

There are many misconceptions about feeding dogs. Following are truths to replace some of the commonest fallacies:

—Different breeds don't need different foods. Chihuahuas eat exactly the same foods as Great Danes.

—It is not abnormal for a dog to gulp his food. The stomach takes care of the digestion.

—Dogs don't need to chew hard foods or bones to keep their teeth sound. A well-balanced diet will keep the teeth in good condition. Chewing bones does, however, help to keep the teeth tartar-free.

—Some think that feeding raw meat will make a dog mean and a better guard dog. Raw meat has nothing to do with it.

—Dogs don't need raw meat, but thrive on cooked or dried meat as well.

—Dogs can digest starch as well as humans, provided the starch is cooked. It is not harmful to feed a dog potatoes or other starches if these are in proportion to the rest of the diet.

—A normal amount of fat is not harmful to dogs; and working and hunting dogs need extra amounts.

—It is believed by many that candies and sweets are detrimental to the dog, that they give worms or ruin the teeth. Actually sugar is an important part of a dog's diet. Dental cavities are rare in dogs, and sugar plays no part. The only possible harmful effect is that sweets may spoil his appetite for his regular meals. Occasional sweets are good, and especially as rewards in a training program.

—Nor does milk cause worms. Worms are always caused by worm eggs, which don't stand a chance with pasteurization.

—The addition of garlic to the diet doesn't eliminate worms. It may, however, increase the palatability of a bland diet.

WHY DOGS EAT GRASS

When a dog has a digestive upset, he will eat long blades of grass. These irritate the lining of his intestines and cause

106

him to vomit and rid his stomach of excessive bile, as evidenced by yellow vomitus. At such times milk of magnesia is excellent. If the condition continues for more than a day, the dog should be checked by a veterinarian; it can signify worms or an intestinal infection.

IN SUMMARY

Each owner is responsible for how his dog looks—roly-poly or trim and sleek. Some people feed their animals as they themselves eat; usually a heavy person will have a heavy dog. If a dog is overweight, fats and carbohydrates should be kept at a minimum and proteins increased. Don't kill your dog with kindness! Overfeeding, incorrect feeding, and too frequent feeding are the greatest causes of shortened life in pets. The better the nutrition, the longer the dog will be a healthy specimen.

A good dry meal, kibble, or canned food, with first-class proteins added, such as milk, eggs, fish, and cheese for the finicky eater, will provide a well-balanced diet for the average pet, hunter, or show dog. As a result of careful research and testing most dog owners today can feed commercial foods and know that they contain all the ingredients of a well-balanced diet. But there is no perfect diet. Each dog has individual requirements which vary according to temperament, environment, and activity. Nature, through heredity, determines the size of the dog; extra feeding only brings on fatness.

The dangers of overzealousness in trying to prevent diet-deficiency ailments must not be overlooked. While feeding a growing dog an overabundance of high-protein foods with too-generous additions of vitamins and minerals enhances the growth rate, it also increases the bone growth to the point of often causing lameness in the fast-growing breeds. If you have questions or doubts, consult your veterinarian.

LOW-SODIUM DIETS FOR HEART DISEASE

Foods allowed: Beef, pork, veal, lamb, chicken, turkey, rabbit, fresh-water fish, salt-free cottage cheese, egg yolks. All fresh or frozen vegetables (except where salt is used in the freezing process) and all fresh fruit—raw or cooked. Tomatoes are especially good for keeping the urine acidic. Rice, macaroni, spaghetti, noodles can be used as fillers.

Foods to be avoided are: hearts, liver, kidney, ham, bacon, weiners, shellfish, baby foods, processed cheese and luncheon meats.

6 YEAR-ROUND CARE FOR COMFORT AND WELL-BEING

The house dog is the prisoner of his master, subject to his master's mode of living. The outside dog—the roamer—adapts himself, and his coat becomes thicker and longer to protect him from cold weather and snow, but the house dog is often the victim of overheating. His comfort and well-being depend on how well his master provides for his summerizing and winterizing with the change of seasons.

During their ancestral days dogs were forced to make adjustments to the climate, and they were able to withstand seasonal changes much better than today's pets. Only the hardiest dogs survived. Today's dogs have no need to race across ice packs or hot desert sands. They have lost their heavy undercoats and are physically more refined.

Since most of our pets stay indoors most of the time, in heated houses during the winter and in air-conditioned, low-humidity dwellings during the summer—contrary to what nature intended—we have to make various adjustments for them to help nature along. Today's dogs need special care with their skin, their undercoats, their haircuts. They have to be handled differently during each season. And that explains this chapter on the year-round care of the dog.

GENERAL GROOMING

Many people think that dog grooming is a mysterious art which takes a lot of time and professional training. Actually most of the tricks of a good grooming program can be learned in a short time. Because dogs enjoy the special attention they receive in grooming (along with discipline and training), regular grooming becomes established in the pet's mind and he looks forward to it. Grooming is essential to health and well-being.

Three types of hair coats have to be considered: (1)

short-haired, such as Dalmatian, dachshund, and beagle, which is relatively easy to keep well groomed; (2) long-haired, such as poodle and terrier, which needs trimming often; and (3) heavy-coated or shaggy, such as old English sheep dog and Afghan hound, which requires daily combing and brushing.

The aim of all good grooming is to have a full, glossy coat. It is much easier to prevent matted hair by frequent brushing than to try to restore a coat that is full of mats. Unless dogs such as the old English sheep dog and the Afghan hound are brushed and combed diligently, matted hair develops, and in extreme cases combing the mats becomes impossible and a complete clipping is necessary, much to the embarrassment of the dog. Incidentally, there are some excellent shampoos on the market which help untangle matted hair.

In many of the long-haired breeds it is recommended that the thick tufts of hair between the toes be carefully cut away, as is done with the poodle. This hair tends to ball up into felt-like mats, and it is a perfect landing place for burs, stickers, and foxtails, which are all painful and can cause lameness.

Long nails can cause foot problems. Any dog owner can become proficient in nail-clipping. If you cut too deeply and the quick bleeds, use alum powder or a styptic pencil to stop the bleeding. Clip the dew claws also.

In keeping the eyes clean, a mild salt-water solution applied with cotton or soft tissue is excellent.

The dog's mouth should be checked regularly. His teeth can be cleaned with a damp cloth dipped in salt and soda. When there is tartar, the veterinarian should be called on to remove it.

For removing tar or chewing gun from a dog's hair, nail-polish remover is excellent. Don't allow the solution onto the dog's skin, and wash the hair part immediately with soap and water.

BATHING

First comb out the hair until it is free of all mats or snarls, since soap will not rinse out of them. Apply petroleum jelly or mineral oil around the eyes to keep them free from soap. Put a big wad of cotton in each ear. Fill the tub with water up to the dog's knees and thoroughly soak him. Use luke-warm water. When you and the dog are both wet, apply a mild non-irritating shampoo and work the suds in com-

109

pletely, starting at the head and working back. Use your fingers to work the soap down to the skin, and don't neglect the ears or paws. Use a damp washcloth to clean the face. Rinse away the suds completely; incomplete rinsing will dull the coat and irritate the skin. After the water is drained from the tub, wrap the dog in a large bath towel and wipe off the excess water before he shakes. After he has shaken himself well, you can towel him dry or use a hair dryer. Don't let him get into a draft while he is drying. On a warm sunny day he can be taken out, but don't put him in an area where he will have access to dirt or gravel, for he may roll in it.

I would generally refrain from bathing a puppy under 3 months of age. However, if odor, dirt, or parasites necessitate a bath, then it is all right to go ahead if you are careful to avoid chilling the puppy. Wrap him in a towel and hand-dry him thoroughly before letting him run around in the house. To make sure he will avoid drafts or a chilling wind, don't allow him outdoors for at least 12 hours.

SHEDDING

During the wild days the long hours of summer sunlight activated the dog into shedding his heavy winter coat. Modern-day artificial conditions have the shedding cycle confused. With thermal control, air conditioning, and electric lighting, the indoor dog doesn't know at what time of the year to grow a new coat. Therefore some dogs shed their coats around the calendar.

Normally the dog sheds his undercoat when the weather gets hot. He gets rid of the dead hair and then grows a new coat. Cold fresh air aids nature in stimulating the circulation of the blood to the hair, which results in a glistening, shining coat.

During shedding usually the woolly undercoat comes out in rolls and chunks, and it is up to the owner to help nature along by combing out the loose hair every day. It should be removed with a wire brush or a blunt-toothed comb. Go right down to the skin with the brush or comb; the old hair will cling, causing mats, and any dead hair will cling. Undercoat left is liable to cause skin irritation. The undercoating is useful in winter but is unnecessary in summer. The long silky hair that is left keeps the dog looking beautiful and insulates him from the hot summer sun.

For short-haired dogs some people use brushes, and others

use hand gloves. A vacuum cleaner is excellent for pulling out the loose hair, and so is a hacksaw blade. Dogs who live in the house year round have a tendency to skin dryness and dandruff, which is why I recommend that wheat-germ oil, vegetable oil, or bacon or fat be added to the daily diet. Normally if all the loose hair is removed daily, the average dog will shed his entire coat in a couple of weeks. The quicker the old coat is removed, the sooner there is a shiny, healthy new hair glow.

SUMMERIZING

There are many fallacies regarding the "dog days" of July and August. Dog days originated in Egypt with Sirius, the Dog Star, which is visible during a 40-day period coinciding with sultry heat. It was assumed that because during this period the dog was irritable, hung his tongue far out, slobbered and sought eagerly for scarce water, it was an evil season. It was believed that the dog was possessed by devils, that his bite was poisonous and contained the rabies germ. Even today people believe that dogs are prone to madness during dog days. Rabies, however, is not seasonal; it is a year-round disease (see p. 284).

Dogs require proportionally more air for breathing than humans, and since the dog perspires through his tongue he is affected by the heat more quickly. After all, he wears almost the same coat winter and summer.

Actually dogs also perspire through the pads of their feet and slightly through their skin pores. But they perspire chiefly through their tongues; consequently in hot weather the dog pants more and tends to slobber. The more he pants, the more relief he feels.

Housing

During hot weather a favorite spot for the dog is a shady corner of the yard where he can dig a deep hole and lie against the cool earth. He also enjoys the basement of the house. If he is lucky enough to live with air conditioning, he enjoys the cool, dry air as much as does his owner.

The dog's house or sleeping quarters should be in a cool and shady spot. A shaded, screened-in porch is excellent. If the dog is to be outdoors, he must have a shady place.

Although puppies require a lot of fresh air, they should not

111

be exposed long during the heat of the day, as they are susceptible to heatstroke or sunstroke. Their runs should be protected by shade trees or canvas. Aluminum roofing is excellent, as it repels the rays of the sun.

Some dogs are especially susceptible to heatstroke—the short-nosed breeds, such as pug, Boston terrier, and English bull. They must have special care. They should be kept from direct sun, in a cool place, and not overexercised in the heat of the day.

Sanitation of kennel quarters during the summer is especially important because rubbish and debris attract flies and mosquitoes, which are a constant annoyance and irritation. By keeping the area around the dog's quarters clean and by spraying and disinfecting daily, the incidence of pests can be greatly reduced.

Diet

The dog eats less during hot weather. This is nature's way of protecting him from excessive heat. Most dogs prefer to eat late in the evening, when it is cooler.

Carbohydrates and starches should be limited during hot weather. The diet may be reduced by one half to one quarter. Less body heat is required, and the dog uses less energy.

Food should not be left out, as it will easily spoil. Dishes should be washed and disinfected daily.

Unlike humans, dogs don't need extra salt in the summer. They usually get enough salt from the commercial dog foods and table scraps.

In hot weather the dog should have free access to cool, clean water at all times. Allow him to drink as much as he wants—unless he is overheated, and then he will tend to drink too much and become nauseated.

Exercise

During hot weather the dog should be taken out only when it is coolest—in early morning or late evening.

Some dogs like to wade in water or swim. This is fine exercise, and a good way to cool off. However, if there is a wind or it is a slightly chilly day, dry the dog well after each swim.

The Summer Death Trap: The Car

Invariably, every summer many dogs are brought to me either dead or just about gone from heatstroke caused by leaving them too long in a car. *On hot days a car is a very dangerous place to leave a dog.* Park the car in the shade with the windows as wide open as is consistent with the dog's not being able to jump out, and be sure to check the dog's condition frequently.

Air-conditioned cars are a great help but dangerous when the motor is stopped and the air conditioning off. Some people go off for a "few minutes," only to find the dog in distress or dead upon their return.

The early signs of heat prostration are staggering, panting, and gasping. Put ice packs on the dog's head, pull his tongue forward so it doesn't choke him, and rush him to a veterinarian. If he is in bad shape, a spot of brandy or black coffee may be given as a stimulant (see p. 218).

Sometimes these animals can be saved, but unfortunately there is often brain damage, and with the ensuing complications they will not survive.

Clipping

In hot weather the dog should be kept especially clean and well-groomed. He likes being cool and refreshed too.

The subject of hair clipping is much discussed. I feel that moderation is the answer. I don't approve of shaving a dog's hair down to the skin; at least half an inch of hair should be left to protect him from the sun and from fleas, ticks, and lice.

Long-haired dogs may be more comfortable in the summer if their coats are thinned out or trimmed. But never shave a dog unless it is necessary for treatment of a skin disease.

Summer Skin Ailments

During hot weather dogs are subject to many more skin conditions because fungus is more in evidence, and fleas, ticks, and lice are more plentiful.

Fleas are the greatest cause of summer eczemas. A recent survey lists the flea as the cause of over 70 percent of summer skin problems. Prophylactic measures are the best means of preventing such problems—flea collars, flea sprays and powders, and periodic baths with a flea shampoo.

About 50 percent of all dogs are acutely sensitive to flea bites, and such dogs will itch and scratch incessantly from a single bite.

If lice, fleas, or ticks are present, brush the dog over a piece of white paper and crush the varmints when they fall. A good insecticide, either spray or powder, should be applied and brushed right down to the skin. When examining for ticks, look at the ears, loins, and between the toes. Use a tweezer or thumb and finger. Gradual pressure should be applied, otherwise the head will remain embedded. If the tick has a strong hold on the skin, a drop of turpentine or nail-polish remover will shock it sufficiently to release its hold. Then the tick should be burned or crushed.

For the dog who does a lot of running in the woods and consequently picks up many ticks, a good bedding of cedar shavings is an excellent way to reduce infestation, as the odor of cedar seems to discourage most parasites.

Flies worry the dog, since they bite and cause irritation. German shepherds and chows are especially sensitive to fly bites on the tips of their ears, and many have thick, scabby lesions because of it. Fly repellants, wax or tar on the ears, and medicated ointments are all helpful.

Mosquitoes are especially dangerous to the dog because they are the intermediate hosts of heartworms. When an infected mosquito sucks on a dog's blood and then bites another dog, the second dog will have adult heartworms within a few months. In mosquito-infested areas, if possible the dog should be kept in the house at night or in screened quarters.

Summer eczema is caused by fungus and by allergies to plants, grasses, pollens, and dust. That is why grooming every day is a must in hot weather.

A skin disease often seen in hot weather is "hot spots," which is a dermatitis characterized by itching skin and red and inflamed spots which exude moisture. Recovery is slow because the dog continually mutilates his skin with his tongue or by scratching with his dirty paws. The disease is also called weeping mange, but it has no connection with mange or ringworm. It is usually caused by fungus which the dog contracts from grass; it intensifies in severity by a secondary infection. Treatment consists in covering the area with medicated powders, surgical dressings, and ointments and lotions

114

that are soothing and healing and destroy the fungus infection.

Some dogs are sensitive to the sun and get sunburned. White dogs are more susceptible to the sun, parasites, allergies, and skin diseases than black-haired dogs. Short-haired dogs should not be left in the sun for long. The collie is especially susceptible to sun on his face and muzzle (see "collie nose," p. 267). Suntan lotion is helpful.

Mere hot weather causes itchy skin in some dogs. It is well to keep them out of direct sun and cool. Dirty skin intensifies skin problems. In warm weather, bathing every 2 weeks should be sufficient for the average house dog. Strong flea soaps and disinfectant soaps should be avoided. Combing with a metal stripping comb, getting at the undercoat, is helpful.

The Ears and Eyes

Ear infections seem to be more prevalent during the summer months, as the hot, moist condition that develops inside the ear canal is a great place for ear mites and fungus infections. The ears and eyes should be examined daily for dust and pollen.

Clean ears with cotton swabs dipped in alcohol or peroxide. Any black material in the canal is a sign that ear mites are present; after the ear has been cleaned, an ear-mite preparation should be inserted. Examine for ticks, as the ear is a favorite hiding place.

Summer Colds

Summer colds occur because warm days with chilly nights affect susceptible pets. A slight chill often leads to colds, tonsillitis, bronchitis, and other respiratory infections.

A word of caution regarding summer chill in puppies: Puppies can be playing happily in the sunshine one minute and almost immediately, with the disappearance of the sun, be shivering in a chilly wind. This is dangerous for the puppy; there easily develops a cold or more severe infection, such as pneumonia or distemper.

Spring is often dangerous because of the changeable weather. When putting out young dogs or toy breeds, see that they don't get cold, or provide a shelter into which they can retire if the weather should change.

Dry Nose

A dry nose during the hot summer is not necessarily a sign that the dog has a temperature. Such weather will usually keep the nose in a hot, dry condition but in fine health. Don't become concerned unless fever and lassitude are present.

Additional Summer Tips

When walking a dog on hot days, be wary of asphalt or tar. Either will cause a painful condition in the dog's pads. To remove such material from the pads, rub with pure lard or salad oil. Don't use turpentine or kerosene, these are irritating and can cause infected feet.

Many dogs are afraid of thunder and lightning and have hysterics during storms. Some actually go out of their heads. Many just need petting and to be with their owners. For others, heavy tranquilization and sedation is needed to calm them down.

It is amazing how most dogs can foretell summer storms long before they hit. Scientists believe that the dog's hearing is so acute that he can hear the high winds approaching miles away. ESP researchers believe that dogs can foretell approaching storms because of the sixth sense they possess.

Shipping a Dog in Summer

During the hot summer months the dog should travel mostly at night or early in the morning. This can be arranged with the airline or express company. Don't ship the dog on weekends or over holidays; he might have to stay in the crate several extra days. The crate should be wire or else have a lot of open ventilation. The person on the receiving end should meet the dog and get him out of the crate promptly. The dog should then be given some cool water and a light meal and allowed to rest. Most airlines and express companies take special care of animals.

WINTERIZING

During the winter months, when sickness and disease are especially prevalent, the dog's health should be under constant surveillance. His health is dependent on housing, diet, exercise, and general treatment.

By keeping the dog healthy his natural resistance to disease-producing germs is increased. Annual booster vaccination of D-H-L each fall is especially recommended. Probably two of the most neglected predisposing sources of infection are bad ventilation and unsatisfactory sanitation in the kennel or living quarters.

Housing

Indoor Dogs. In primitive days dogs had thick coats and rugged bodies. With heated houses, their coats don't have to be so thick and they need the protection of a coat or sweater when they go outside into cold temperatures. Even heavy-coated dogs should wear a blanket when left in a car for long periods of time in cold weather.

The toy breeds and small pets need the warmth and dryness of our houses because of their rearing and their dependence on us to provide them with warmth. Be sure to keep a dog's bed away from radiators, as the heat is drying to the coat.

Most of our pets sleep indoors, sometimes under sheets and blankets. Some pets even sleep on their backs with their feet in the air, mimicking their masters, complete with such sound effects as snoring.

Outdoor Dogs. For the indoor dog a good temperature to maintain is about 65 degrees. For the outdoor dog, if the temperature goes down into the 20's or even below zero, so long as he is protected from the wind and drafts and has good bedding, he will stay warm and snug. Few breeds of outdoor dogs need their living quarters heated.

The most important thing is dry, draftless sleeping quarters. In other words, if the dog sleeps outdoors he should have a dry, well-insulated house protected from wind. It should not face the cold north. In severe cold an empty burlap sack or curtain should be nailed over the opening of his house, and he will soon learn to walk under it. If there is more than one dog, usually they will sleep curled up together for warmth. Where the weather is severe, if the dog is old or a nursing bitch, infrared bulbs or regular electric bulbs are recommended for added heat.

There are many refined types of houses, but a simple box that is waterproof can be suitable living quarters for the out-

117

door dog. If possible, put the house against a protecting wall and certainly away from the north winds.

If possible, keep the dog's bed at least 4 inches off the floor. Use good bedding, at least 5 inches thick, for the dog to curl up in. Old blankets, old rugs, or cedar or pine shavings are best.

Diet

During the cold winter months there should be an increase in starches and carbohydrates to provide more heat and energy. Nourishing foods, warm foods, and extra vitamin supplements are advisable. I recommend increasing by one quarter the amount of food in the winter months. The dog should not be allowed to drink freezing water; it will chill his tummy and upset his bowels. Water should be at room temperature.

Exercise

In winter weather, no matter how cold or damp, there should be daily exercise. When a house pet is outside, so long as he is active let him stay, but he should not be allowed to sit around or lie on the cold ground or in the snow for any length of time, else he will get chilled. He will then be susceptible to tonsillitis, pneumonia, or other disease.

When there is snow, it is safer to walk a dog on a leash. Dogs have a natural tendency to walk in the ploughed areas and dart across the road heedless of cars. Most dogs love to wade in snowdrifts, and it is amusing to watch a puppy in his first snow. The minute he gets inside, dry him to keep him from chilling. Outdoor dogs love to be outside all the time, and the colder it gets the more they seem to enjoy it, but the indoor dog should not be allowed outdoors for long periods.

After he has been out in snow and ice, special attention should be paid to the dog's feet. Ice and snowballs develop in the webbing between the toes. If the dog has come in contact with sanded walks, the defrosting agents can be irritating to his sensitive pads. The chemicals should be washed from the feet immediately. If allowed to remain, they can cause severe irritation, and should the dog lick his pads the chemicals can irritate his tongue.

All dogs should be routinely checked twice a year: before cold weather and before hot weather—a 1,000 mile checkup! Also, all dogs should be given an annual booster shot of D-H-L in the fall of the year to fully protect them during the dangerous winter months.

Young animals and older ones should be given extra consideration. In the older ones, if they have arthritis or rheumatism, the cold weather increases the pain, and extended exposure to cold increases the suffering.

Bathing

Baths should be given less often during cold weather. An outdoor dog should not need bathing at all during the winter months except under emergency conditions. How often to bathe your dog is up to you, and if he sleeps with you or is in your lap most of the time, you probably will want to bathe him more often. But don't take him outdoors for at least 3 to 4 hours after bathing, when he is thoroughly dry.

Brushing, sponging, and dry shampooing at weekly intervals are usually sufficient for the average indoor dog, bathing him only when necessary. Corn meal or corn starch does a good job in short- or medium-haired breeds. For white dogs corn starch brushed in removes the dust and dirt and leaves the dog as white as a snowball.

Both young and old dogs are susceptible to chilling after a bath, and any dampness of the coat will render them prone to tonsillitis, bronchitis, and distemper.

TRAVELING BY CAR

As mentioned earlier, during the summer months always park the car in the shade with the windows open as far as possible, because the car can quickly become an oven.

When traveling with a dog during summer, a thermos jug of crushed ice and water should be readily available. I also advise wetting several towels with cold water and putting them on the floor for the dog to lie on.

Before going on a long trip, visit your veterinarian for a health certificate (in some states, and in Mexico and Canada, this is required) and get a rabies booster shot if he is due for one.

For a dog who is excitable, a wire cage is a good idea because then the windows can be lowered sufficiently to give him ample air circulation while you are parked or away from the car.

Don't leash a dog to the window, or tie him up inside the car, as he might easily hang himself.

Don't feed the dog much before you start on the trip. It is wise to carry a supply of water in a thermos. Stop every few hours to exercise the dog—the roadside parks are becoming popular for both humans and animals.

Most dogs curl up and sleep during a long car ride. However, there are some excitable animals who need sedation, and your veterinarian can prescribe tranquilizers that will keep your dog quiet and prevent drooling or vomiting. Sedatives or tranquilizers with anti-nausea qualities seem to give better results than dramamine or bonamine, which don't seem to work as well on dogs as on humans.

7 NURSING CARE; DRUGS; VETERINARY RESEARCH

Not only is the human population exploding; the canine population is exploding as well. There are about 25 million dogs in the United States. More than 4 million of these are registered purebreds. Throughout the world there are about 225 well-defined breeds of dogs, but only 115 of these are recognized by the American Kennel Club. In 1915 there was one pureblooded dog to every 300 people; in 1949, one to every 75; and in 1967, one to every 22. At the present time it is estimated that there is at least one pureblooded dog to every 5 to 6 households, and figuring in the mixed breeds and mongrels, I would estimate there is at least one dog to every 3 to 4 households. A recent survey has shown that 26 percent of all U.S. households have one dog, 10 percent have a dog and a cat, and 9 percent have a cat only. Over 8 percent of all U.S. householders have 2 or more dogs.

Canine longevity has been extended to an average of 10 to 12 years, and it is not uncommon to see a dog 18 to 20 years of age. This has been brought about by a decrease in puppy mortality, better home care, and better veterinary supervision. The public is demanding better food, more services, and completely up-to-date veterinary care.

The pet industry has progressed to where some of our dogs parade in the streets with mink coats, painted toenails, and bows in their hair. Our pets deserve the best, and it is obvious from the money being spent on them for food, clothing, and medical supervision that most dog owners are indeed taking excellent care of their animals.

NURSING CARE

The first thing one of my professors in veterinary school told me was that the doctor's job is to help nature along, not to impede it, and that if we interfere with nature, we are not doing our job as doctors.

Even with antibiotics, new drugs, the latest in laboratory equipment, and expanding medical knowledge, the value of nursing care cannot be overestimated. A dog can be given every known drug and yet not respond until tender loving care is instituted. Penicillin will not cure a lonely heart. There has to be a combination of veterinary supervision and tender nursing care to stimulate the dog's response to the drugs and to restore him to health.

At the Hospital

There are some conditions that definitely require hospital care, such as surgical cases, accident cases, cases which require oxygen and blood transfusions, and animals so critically ill that constant supervision is necessary to keep them alive.

Fortunately the average dog does well in a veterinary hospital. He is quick to respond to the gentle voices of the attendants and to the soothing treatment.

For animals who are highly emotional and need the human touch, most up-to-date veterinary hospitals have veterinary nurses in attendance who give individual attention and try to substitute the tender loving care pets miss from their owners.

Visiting Sick Animals. This is not generally advisable, because it gets the animals unduly excited, and they tend to be disappointed when left, but there are some cases when this should be allowed. Sometimes a critically ill dog will seem to give up—not care whether he lives or dies. Such a dog needs

121

an emotional lift, and at this point I usually call the owner to the hospital to bring some favorite tidbit of food. In rare cases I have allowed an owner to stay overnight in the hospital with the animal.

Some veterinary hospitals have special rooms where owners can visit critically ill dogs, away from the rest of the patients so that the hospital routine is not interrupted.

There is the occasional dog who will not respond to anyone but his owner, and for such a problem child I recommend home treatment, even if it involves daily or twice-daily trips to the veterinary hospital.

Whether to leave a sick dog in the hospital or nurse him at home is often a question. There are some dogs who emotionally don't do well in the hospital away from their loved ones, and yet some critically ill animals require hospitalization.

Common-Sense Home Nursing

Although love itself will not cure a sick animal, the close affection of a dog and his master will often overcome a dangerous disease with proper medication. In nursing a sick dog, persistence and patience are primary in maintaining life.

Most people try home remedies when their animals first show signs of illness and then seek veterinary help when the aspirin or the milk of magnesia doesn't seem to work. If the illness is such that the animal can be treated at home, the veterinarian will prescribe drugs that can be administered along with rest and quiet and tender loving care. Fortunately few animal diseases are contagious to humans; even canine hepatitis is not caused by the same virus as human hepatitis and is not contagious from one to the other.

Since sickness knows no time, nursing care is 24-hour duty, and most people will stay up day and night nursing a sick pet. But they must follow the veterinarian's advice. Some people, upon returning home with the animal, disregard the prescriptions. It is not fair either to the animal or to the veterinarian. If the animal doesn't recover, the veterinarian will likely get blamed even though the nursing care is what was lacking.

The Bed. The bed should be warm and free from drafts. The bedding should be kept clean so that when the dog soils it he doesn't have to lie in a wet or dirty box.

For a dog who cannot move about, bedsores become a problem. He should be turned from side to side every few hours and kept clean with a washcloth so that his urine doesn't burn his legs. He will need enemas or suppositories to aid in elimination. In all ill animals comfort is important for recovery.

Peace and Quiet. The sick dog should have peace and quiet with as little handling as necessary and with as few strangers to excite him as possible.

Exercise. Never allow the dog to go outdoors in extremely cold or wet weather if he has a cold or fever. And don't allow him to overexercise when he is recuperating. If the animal is so housebroken that he will not eliminate in the house, put a sweater or blanket on him and allow him a few moments for sniffing the grass and for his relief. Avoid overexposure to the elements and dry him thoroughly if he has gotten wet. Any convalescent dog is susceptible to secondary pneumonia.

Food. In the early stages of sickness a dog with an upset stomach or a fever will likely refuse food, and this is good because he will be prone to nausea, and a full stomach will aggravate his condition. However, if he persists in refusing food and liquid, he will dehydrate quickly. A puppy is critically prone to dehydration, and if he does not have intake of food or water for as little as 12 hours, he will dehydrate to the point of death. If food continues to nauseate the dog, he will then have to be fed by injections of saline and glucose, and other nutrients will have to be given intravenously.

If the dog refuses food, but it doesn't seem to nauseate him, don't hesitate to force-feed him. Bits of food every 15 to 20 minutes will often maintain an animal from dehydration and prevent him from going into coma and shock. To some people, if a sick dog refuses food, they take it away, thinking to starve him into eating. Others will sit by the hour feeding their dogs piece by piece minute amounts of food. Obviously the latter dog lovers are much more apt to save their animals.

Dehydration in the sick dog is a symptom which especially has to be watched for. Also called "drying out" or being "hide-bound," it is usually caused by diarrhea and vomiting, when more fluids are lost than are taken in. For survival the dehydration must be treated, and the vomiting and diarrhea must be stopped. Normally the loose skin on the back of the neck will quickly bounce back into place when pulled out, but with dehydration the skin remains pulled away from the neck and returns slowly. In the clinic the veterinarian combats dehydration with intravenous administration of saline and glucose and with injections to stop vomiting and diarrhea.

When a dog is sick, his diet must be changed. He generally will refuse his normal food; and the regular commercial foods are too harsh for a sick or convalescing dog. Don't hesitate to try many combinations of food until one is found that seems to stimulate his appetite. Some dogs will eat the strangest things when they are ill, and every bit of food that they ingest is that much in their favor, for they need the strength to fight off the germs and the aftereffects of the illness.

In feeding a sick dog, give small amounts of nutrients at frequent intervals. It is much worse to overload the stomach at one time than to underfeed. Liver is the best all-around food but should be given carefully; too much will cause diarrhea. It gives black stools due to the iron content. Good ground meat with broth is good, and so is lamb. The addition of minerals and vitamins is recommended.

One of the best foods in force-feeding a sick dog is eggs. Simply pouring raw eggs down a dog's throat may save his life. If possible remove the raw white. Boiled eggs are more satisfactory than raw.

Some dogs cannot tolerate milk or fats while ill, and so liquids in the form of broths—beef or chicken—or homogenized baby foods should be given. A pinch of salt can be added to help combat dehydration.

Try any kind of food you can think of. Some dogs who have always turned down fish will suddenly take to canned mackerel or salmon or tuna or sardines; the fish flavor seems to whet the appetite. Foods flavored with garlic, sugar, or syrup are often enticing to a sick dog. Other things that may entice him are candy, ice cream, filet mignon, caviar, or even plain old hamburger. Some dogs will even eat apple, orange, or grapefruit when ill.

A sick dog will be more inclined to "people" food, and so he may be more likely to eat if you make believe you are eating it. Hand feeding is certainly advocated for a sick dog— and don't worry about spoiling him, not with his life at stake. As you are feeding him talk with him; because he loves to be loved and pampered, especially when sick, affection will account for at least half the cure.

The Temperature. When nursing a sick dog, his temperature should be checked constantly. The normal temperature is 100-101 degrees. A fall below 100 is a serious sign that the body is weakening and radical treatment is necessary. The dog should be wrapped in warm blankets with a hot-water bottle or an electric heating pad until gotten to the veterinarian. A stimulant—brandy or any other alcoholic beverage—should be given. Don't worry about the dog's becoming an alcoholic; at least his life will have been saved. He can take the "cure" later.

Any temperature over 102 degrees should be regarded as fever. Some diseases, such as distemper, cause a fever of 103-104, while other infections can cause fevers as high as 105-106. Many times high fevers result in convulsions, as seen in such brain diseases as meningitis.

Aspirin is helpful in reducing fever and in alleviating pain and discomfort, but it will not cure an infectious disease. Any temperature above normal for 24 hours or more necessitates professional help.

Symptomatic Nursing. Even though I use all the drugs available to the veterinary profession, I am still old-fashioned enough to believe in symptomatic treatment. For example, the use of a vaporizer with a drop or two of tincture of benzoin or camphor in the water is beneficial in the treatment of pneumonia, distemper, or a chest infection. Vick's salve or something similar on the nose is helpful because the dog will lick it, and it is soothing to the throat and is a good expectorant, useful in bringing up phlegm from the chest.

In pneumonia, rubbing the chest with camphorated oil or some other liniment and using a sweater or chest protector will help the animal breathe easier.

For an irritated throat condition, pure honey is soothing and is a good food as well. However, if infection is present, antibiotics and other drugs should be administered simultaneously.

Symptomatic nursing involves what common sense tells one to do. If a dog's nose is running, it should be kept washed and protected with soothing ointments. Boric acid solution or warm salt water can be used to keep the nostrils clear, and baby oil or vaseline can be used to soothe them. If the dog has diarrhea, the condition should be treated with bismuth or Kaopectate. If constipation is present, a laxative (such as milk of magnesia), a suppository, or an enema should be given. Continual diarrhea can cause dehydration, and constipation can cause discomfort, gas, and a toxic condition.

Any sudden change in a sick dog, such as fast breathing, spasmodic coughing, bleeding from any body cavity, swelling of the head, welts on the body, sneezing, or rubbing of the eyes, should be reported at once to the veterinarian because it may be a drug reaction. An occasional animal shows susceptibility to a drug and can quickly go into "anaphylactic" shock.

Aspirin. Although aspirin is excellent for most dogs in the relief of fever and pain, there are some who apparently cannot digest aspirin. It seems to irritate the stomach, and causes vomiting. Some of these dogs can use buffered aspirin, which is less irritating. One aspirin for a 20-pound dog 3 times a day is beneficial in reducing discomfort.

It has recently been proved that in both animals and humans aspirin can cause ulceration of the stomach and intestines if taken in large quantities over a long time.

Misuse of Medicines. When using human medicines on the dog, the dosage should be regulated—a medium-sized dog of 40 to 50 pounds will take the same dosage as an average-sized human—but most human medications should be used only on the advice of a veterinarian. For example, some simple human laxatives contain strychnine, which can be fatal to some dogs if used incorrectly. Also, some drugs deteriorate with age and not only lose their effectiveness but concentrate in strength and can be harmful and toxic. Medicines should not be kept over 1 year.

Giving a Dog a Pill. Most patients will take a pill crushed or broken and inserted into the food dish or wrapped in a choice morsel. But with some dogs it is a battle between master and patient. For such dogs not so easily fooled, a certain amount of force is necessary, but never, never brute force, as it will frighten the animal and the pill may go down into his windpipe and choke him.

Stand on the dog's right side (if left-handed, use the opposite procedure), grasp the muzzle above his nose with the left hand and squeeze his lips against his teeth. This will open his mouth, and if he attempts to bite he will cut his lips because they are curled between his teeth. Push the pill straight back over the top and to the rear of his tongue, making sure it is in the center of his mouth, otherwise it will not go down. Quickly take your hand away and close the dog's mouth. His head should be held upward at a slight angle while his throat is stroked or tickled to make him swallow. Another way to make him swallow is to startle him by blowing into his face, which will cause him to gulp.

Giving Liquid Medicine. Don't fight the animal or frighten him; he should be relaxed before the procedure is attempted.

126

If not administered properly, the liquid can go down the windpipe and subsequently into the lungs, to cause a foreign-body pneumonia.

For dispensing liquid medicine, a long plastic squeeze bottle can be used, or a medicine dropper, or a syringe. The dog's head should be tilted at a 45-degree angle (but not any more, otherwise it will be difficult for him to swallow, and he can strangle on the solution). Stand on the dog's right (if left-handed, reverse the procedure) and grasp his muzzle with the left hand. Insert the tip of the device into the corner of the lips and pull the lips away from the teeth. Thus a funnel-like pouch is formed, and the jaws need not be opened. Pour the medicine into the pouch, and the liquid will seep between the dog's teeth, which will cause him to swallow without a fuss. Give small amounts at a time, and don't pour fast, as it will waste medicine and might choke the dog.

A problem dog can be backed into a corner to keep him from shying away. With a small or medium-sized dog it is best to give medicine on a table in order to have more control.

DRUGS

Antibiotics

Some kennel owners believe that a shot of penicillin will cure anything. By indiscriminate administration of antibiotics, they decrease resistance to certain drugs and also cause some dogs to have a drug sensitivity. Before any antibiotic is used, a veterinarian should be consulted.

Germs will develop immunity to certain antibiotics if these are given over a period of time, and the animal will be helpless when an antibiotic is really necessary.

Continual use of antibiotics will destroy the normal bacteria in the intestinal tract, and some dogs will develop diarrhea.

Dogs who are sensitive to certain drugs can quickly go into anaphylatic shock. These animals need immediate administration of cortisone, antihistamines, or adrenalin to save them from further drastic symptoms (see p. 212).

Caution is required in treating pregnant bitches with antibiotics, which go through the blood stream and affect the unborn puppies.

Some combinations of drugs hinder nature in fighting disease.

Antibiotics give some dogs a vitamin deficiency.

Tetracycline can cause puppy teeth to turn yellow, but fortunately the permanent teeth come in white and healthy in structure.

Should an amateur attempt to inject antibiotics, extreme care is necessary. Faulty administration can cause abscesses, or if the needle hits a nerve, partial or complete paralysis.

Hormones

I heartily approve of the use of male and female hormones, under the guidance of a veterinarian, for many conditions discussed in this book—spayed bitches, castrated males, prostatitis, certain ailments—but I deplore the use of hormones to interfere with nature.

The misuse of hormones to keep bitches out of heat has ruined much good breeding stock by making hysterectomies necessary to save the bitches' lives because of female infections.

There has also been misuse of hormones to bring females into heat. When they come into heat, they don't ovulate and don't conceive.

However, there is a valuable fertility drug which has been used in human medicine to help sterile women conceive and have multiple births. This drug is often used in dogs to help them ovulate, and otherwise barren bitches have been able to conceive and raise healthy litters.

There is a place in veterinary medicine for the *proper* use of hormones.

Tranquilizers

Tranquilizers have transformed many a bad dog into a manageable one, but like any other drugs, when used incorrectly they can adversely affect an animal's personality. The occasional dog reacts badly to tranquilizers and changes into a raving, man-hating beast.

Stimulants

Benzedrine—"goof balls"—and other stimulants are dangerous to a dog and can even cause death. They are too hard

128

on the heart and other vital organs. Some dogs go into convulsions, and others are permanently affected with lifelong epileptic seizures or similar muscular conditions. Giving stimulants to show dogs is frowned upon by the A.K.C. If a dog ever needs a stimulant, I advise nothing stronger than black coffee or brandy. Any artificial stimulation should be used only on the advice of a veterinarian unless emergency treatment is being administered.

Cortisone

Cortisone has an important role in veterinary medicine because of its value in the treatment of arthritis, skin diseases, traumatic injuries, shock, snake bites, and anaphylactic shock, but it should be used only on the advice of a veterinarian. Overdosage and prolonged use cause a toxic condition and is detrimental to the kidneys. The symptoms are excessive water drinking and urination, with bloating. There is an increase in appetite and an increase in weight, with retention of fluids.

VETERINARY RESEARCH

Through the combined efforts of researchers, veterinary practitioners, veterinary schools, and commercial dog-food companies, new surgical and physical techniques and new drugs for prolonging pets' lives are daily being discovered. Research is going on in every phase of animal health covering the scope of diseases, including contagious and inherited diseases, congenital defects, and the various ailments and disorders to which dogs are susceptible.

As canine medical research has always been the handmaiden of human medical research, the boundaries that are constantly being extended prove equally beneficial to man and dog. Incidentally, the experimental dogs suffer no pain, and they experience better treatment and more gentle and loving care than some of our pets.

Without dogs, heart, kidney, and other organ transplants would not be possible in humans. Most transplants are first tried on dogs. The kidney machine used in the treatment of human kidney diseases will soon be in common practice to help our dogs with their kidney problems.

All types of drugs and vaccines are being tested in the quest for a diagnosis and cure for cancer in both dogs and humans.

Because congenital heart diseases occur in puppies as well as in human infants, researchers throughout the world are conducting tests in evaluating heart and valve defects in dogs.

Brain and spinal disorders are being challenged by prominent veterinary researchers, and it is not uncommon for surgery to be performed on the brain or spinal cord to save a dog.

Research in canine geriatrics and in human geriatrics is proving equally beneficial to both species.

The research being done in animal breeding and sterility is opening new doors in human reproductive disorders. Embryos have been transplanted from an original mother to a host mother and sometimes back again. Some are conceived in one mother and born in another, while others are given to a host mother for a few days and then returned to the original mother. It has been found that the first few days of pregnancy are the most critical time in the life of the embryo and that environmental forces affect the development of the embryo in the first week. The stresses of overheating or excitement seem to be the prime factors in embryonic death the first few days after conception.

As with humans, no drug is allowed to be used on dogs until thoroughly tested and approved by the FDA.

The veterinary profession is ever aware of the many diseases and ailments that can plague a dog, and many researchers are working around the clock to find new cures and relief. Articles on new techniques, new drugs, and new ways of prolonging pets' lives are steadily appearing in all the veterinary journals and are a great aid to the local practitioner.

The Next 25 Years

There is no doubt that the next twenty-five years will see even more incredible advances in veterinary medicine and in the longevity of our pets.

I am convinced that research will find cures for such diseases as cancer, leukemia, hemophilia, and a new "bleeding disease" found in dogs in Vietnam and other Asian countries. Common ailments affecting the dog, such as skin diseases, will result in perfected skin-allergy tests and subsequent desensitization to the irritants.

Organ transplants in dogs will become commonplace once the researchers perfect their techniques. Even now, kidneys of dogs are being successfully transplanted.

Plastic surgery to correct harelip, cleft palate, elbow dysplasia, hip dysplasia, esophageal dilation, and other congenital defects will be possible in future years.

Acupuncture as an anesthetic works just as well on dogs as on humans, according to Chinese veterinary surgeons. Its practice in the United States already is widespread both as an anesthetic and as a treatment for a variety of ailments such as arthritis, spinal disc syndromes, hip dysplasis, and skin conditions, just to name a few. Ultra-high-frequency sound has similar applications.

Other modern developments which will probably gain in usage are: artificial hip joints, for otherwise incurable cases of high dysplasia, arthritis, and hip injury; and radiotherapy for treatment of malignant tumors.

Birth Control

There is very promising preliminary research with a vaccine to prohibit the reproductive function of male dogs. It is also being tried on females where it would permit them to skip a season. Although temporary, it would seem at this time to be very safe and could be a breakthrough for future birth control in dogs. The effect of the vaccine on the pituitary hormone prevents conception.

Ultimately, it may be possible to have sterilization vaccines for both male and female pets, and vaccines of both a permanent and temporary nature. A temporary vaccine would permit female show dogs to skip one or more seasons and be bred at a future time, if a litter is desired.

There is a new plastic device (similar to the IUD used by women) that can be inserted into the vaginal tract of a bitch in season to prevent conception. It is inserted by a veterinarian, ensuring proper blockage of the cervix. Its effectiveness has not been ascertained.

Fortunately there is an effective birth control pill for preventing heat periods. Further solutions to canine birth control will come from a variety of new methods being developed, including a vaccine, a mechanical vaginal device (IUD), a steroidal hormone implant (DES—Diethylstilbestrol), or a dietary additive. There is a test being undertaken at this time with a compound called Mibolerone, under the joint venture of a pet food company and a drug company, to produce a drug to prevent the bitch from coming into heat without harmful reactions.

Intensive Care Units for Animals

The first intensive care unit for dogs has been established at Cornell University Veterinary College. Its equipment is comparable to the best units in similar use for humans. This laboratory machinery will enable the staff to pinpoint the exact ailment within one minute. Included in the unit is a "blood-gas" machine, a cardiac defibrillator, an electrocardiograph, an instrument to measure arterial blood pressure, a respirator, and an oxygen tent. Quick diagnosis and help oftentimes save many patients' lives that otherwise would not have made it. Eventually, intensive care units will be set up for dogs in most good progressive veterinary hospitals.

Part Three

GOOD, BAD, OR INDIFFERENT BEHAVIOR

8 PERSONALITY AND INTELLIGENCE

PERSONALITY

Because of behavior patterns the origin of the domestic dog is still being debated. Most scientists believe that today's dog is a descendant of the true northern wolf, although some experts in the field, and especially Lorenz, foremost authority on animal behavior, believe that the Asiatic jackal is the ancestor of certain of our breeds.

Regardless of origin, the ancestor of the dog was a pack hunter and strictly monogamous. Even today there's great chivalry in male dogs toward bitches and puppies. It is rare indeed for a male dog to pick a fight with a female dog. He normally will let her get away with a lot of female temperament, including being attacked by her, although he will defend himself from destruction.

Just as with the human species, and even though you may find yourself swearing that they are identical, no two dogs are exactly alike, be it in features and traits, temperament, personality, or intelligence—and certainly in behavior. In a group of dogs we will often see almost every personality type and temperament: the leader, the follower, the brave one, the coward, the sly one, the dumb one, the friendly one, the timid one, and of course always the bully. And even though you may often have heard, from numerous "authorities" that mutts are smarter than pedigreed dogs, and other sweeping generalizations such as that poodles are exceptionally smart, retrievers are very friendly, and German shepherds are suspicious of people and not to be trusted, none of these statements is true. Every degree of intelligence and every personality type can be found in every breed and mixture.

As the dog's personality is the sum total of his physical, mental, emotional, and social characteristics, and of the organized pattern of his behavioral characteristics, experience and training in early puppyhood determine the animal's personality and temperament. Dogs are born with certain instincts, and the training of these instincts, and the surrounding environment, mold their temperaments and personalities. Proper training and a favorable environment produce a dog of even temperament with a pleasant personality.

INTELLIGENCE: ROTE OR REASON?

Dogs seem to be getting keener of mind, and in fact many are progressing faster than humans. They're more aware of us—know us better than we know them. Their lives are centered on us. We are their reason for being—to love us, comfort us, serve us, help us in any way. I firmly believe that dogs understand more than people give them credit for, that they understand what we're saying—not every word and detail, but they get the gist, the essential meaning, of our conversation.

There is growing controversy between psychologists and dog owners on whether remarkable performances of dogs are the result of training or indicate reasoning power and judgment. I am not a psychologist, and I am prejudiced. There is much evidence that convinces me that many dogs have a high degree of intelligence. Psychologists contend that as dog training mostly involves repetition, dogs learn only by conditioned reflexes. But anyone who has ever trained a dog has surely found that the time comes when he really has to exert himself mentally to stay one step ahead of his canine pupil; the dog shows reasoning power to either avoid the work at hand or, if he cares to, to become an obedience champion. I have seen many dogs show judgment in thoughtfully appraising certain situations and then carefully take the right action. And certainly the judgment exercised by some Seeing Eye dogs shows intelligence far beyond conditioned reflexes and irrespective of training. During their daily work they make many on-the-spot decisions to safeguard the safety of their blind masters.

Reasoning Power

An amusing example of reasoning power was told to me the other day by the mother of a new baby. She had trained her dog to fetch a clean diaper from a shelf in the closet every time the baby needed to be changed. On the day of this story the infant had an upset stomach and needed changing every half hour or so. Nine times the dog made the trip to the closet and returned with the requested diaper. On the

135

tenth trip, obviously fed up with diaper toting, he pulled all the diapers off the closet shelf and deposited them in a neat pile beside the baby's crib. He then stalked out of the room with his head high in the air.

Another example concerns a German shepherd who loved to kill rabbits. He would proudly bring home the mutilated rabbits to show them off to his master. The master was never pleased with his dog's "accomplishment" and told him so (but not very sternly) each time he arrived home with his prey. The master decided he would have to take more drastic measures to break the habit, and the next time the dog brought home a mutilated rabbit the master whipped the dog severely. The next time the dog killed a rabbit, he was found burying it, trying to hide it. Since he knew he would be punished if he came home with the dead rabbit, to me this was reasoning power, not instinct or training.

One of my patients is a very intelligent Kerry blue terrier who is always brought to my kennel for boarding when his family goes out of town. He loves the kennel and especially seems to enjoy being with all the other dogs. One time his family decided to let him stay at home with a babysitter friend while they went away for the weekend. The dog wasn't apprised of the arrangement and disappeared from the house when he saw his family drive off. While the babysitter was frantically looking for her charge, the dog was walking the three miles through town to my kennel, where he presented himself to be boarded. Another time this same dog appeared at my hospital, scratched at the door, and demandingly barked to be let in. He limped in holding up his front paw, which he had somehow cut. I examined, sutured and bandaged it, and he went on home.

INTELLIGENCE: ACUTE PERCEPTION

Telling Time of Day and Day of Week

It is an accepted fact that dogs are able to tell the time of day and also the day of the week. Just about every dog owner has at least one story to corroborate his dog's time sense.

I know a cocker spaniel who wakes his mistress every weekday at six o'clock but knows when it's Saturday and Sunday and lets her sleep later. Every evening at five he is at the bus stop to meet her, but on Friday nights she goes right

136

from work to the beauty parlor and he knows to meet her bus at seven.

Whatever the explanation, dogs certainly do have a much more acute sense of time than most humans.

Predicting Storms

This also is a faculty that dogs are accepted as having. Sometimes hours before an impending storm they become restless and start to whine and to act in a peculiar fashion. Vibrations, rhythms, and barometric pressures beyond the threshold of human perception are felt by dogs. As a result they often "know" when a thunderstorm is coming.

INTELLIGENCE:
EXTRASENSORY PERCEPTION (ESP)

Scientists believe that dogs are blessed with a sixth sense that gives them psychic powers. From time immemorial people have attributed to dogs all kinds of uncanny powers.

There have been many amazing stories of unexplainable behavior of dogs which suggest some power of premonition, some attunement with nature that is not possessed by man.

The homing instinct in dogs has been described in many newspaper stories of dogs' returning to their old homes after traveling hundreds and even thousands of miles. ESP scientists believe that some of this ability can be accounted for through the regular senses and remembered experiences, such as territorial instincts of a dog leaving his "calling card" at various posts throughout his territory. However, behavioral scientists are attempting to get to the root of animal navigation and at the present time cannot account for all of their migratory habits. Some researchers are now agreeing that dogs do possess some powers of logic and thought deductive processes.

Some scientists believe that a dog has a built-in compass and can allow for the time of day and seasonal changes in showing his homing instincts.

It has been shown that some dogs possess more potential ESP powers than others, similar to the differences in ESP in various people.

One of the earliest and most famous cases of ESP concerned a dog named Prince who crossed the English channel during World War I and traveled until he found his master in the trenches in France.

ESP scientists are investigating case stories of dogs who seek and find an owner who is newly located in a place that the animal has never been. This type of story rules out any of the regular senses, as well as memory. The ability is called "psi-trailing." Hundreds of cases have been reported.

One typical case of psi-trailing involves a dog whose family moved from New York to California. The dog was left behind in New York, and eleven months later he appeared at the new home in California. This astonishing story was thoroughly checked by the scientists and passed all the tests set by the parapsychologists to authenticate it.

Dr. Joseph Banks Rhine, world famous parapsychologist at Duke University, and I exchanged many dog stories, and we both believe that a dog can sense what his master is thinking, and what his mood is, from the slightest gesture, from a fleeting facial expression. A great dog lover himself, Dr. Rhine reported to me that he had seen dogs in close harmony with their masters receive mental messages and perform feats of command without a word, a gesture, an expression, or a blinking of the eye passing between them.

Telepathy and clairvoyance predominate in the stories from Dr. Rhine's files. One story concerns an airplane accident some distance from home. At the exact moment the owner of the dog was injured in the crash, the dog started to behave in a peculiar manner and ran under the house. The master remained unconscious for several days, and during this time various members of the family tried to coax the dog out from under the house and to get him to eat, but he paid no attention to them. By flashlight they observed that his eyes were glazed and that he appeared to be in a coma. Dr. Rhine's records show that the dog came out from under the house at the exact moment his master regained consciousness; and he then appeared normal in every way.

The second story is about a little mongrel who lived with a family in Richmond, Virginia. One night the dog was at home with the family, and two of the sons were away from home on an overnight camping trip. In the middle of the night the dog started to howl in a most peculiar way. This, of course, woke the family, and as the dog had never howled before the family decided she was trying to tell them something. There didn't seem to be anything amiss in the house or around it, and yet the dog continued to howl. They became apprehensive about the boys and decided to drive out to the campsite, about ten miles away. They found the woods on fire and rapidly burning toward the boy's tent. Quick evacuation saved the boys.

Another story concerns a little terrier named Penny, who found her way in a strange place and performed an uncanny act in a cemetery. A year and a half after the death of a mother in a family, one of the daughters came home and made a visit to the graveyard. Penny was left in the car while the woman went to a water spigot in another section of the cemetery to freshen up some flowers. When the woman returned, she saw that Penny had jumped out of the car and way lying on the mother's grave whining and moaning. No other member of the family had been to the cemetery for several months, and the dog had never been there. What explanation do we mortals have for this type of behavior? How did the dog find the gravesite among the thousands of other graves?

The last story—a psi-trail case—is one of the most incredible I've ever heard. It concerns a female dog adopted by a family who found her at their summer vacation home. By the end of the summer they had become very fond of her; and they were thrilled with her new litter of puppies. Not wanting to abandon her and not being able to take a mother dog and five puppies back to their city apartment, they found a good home for her near their summer cottage. A month later the dog appeared at their apartment in New York City—thirty miles from the summer vacation home! This dog had never been to the city before, and of course had never seen their apartment. She had a puppy in her mouth; she deposited it on the apartment floor and then asked to go out. She returned the next week with a second pup and continued her trips until she had her own family and her human family under the same roof. Hard as this story is to believe, it has been completely investigated and authenticated.

All these stories prove there is a strong bond between a dog and his beloved human being—a bond that testifies to the presence of a mysterious sense in dogs that is greater in scope than we humans can imagine.

9 NORMAL BEHAVIOR AND INSTINCTS

BEHAVIORAL INFLUENCES

Behavior is never wholly inherited or wholly acquired but is always developed under the combined influences of heredity and environment. The object of socialization of a dog is to produce a well-balanced and well-adjusted animal.

The ideal dog, according to trainers, is self-assured, outgoing, and friendly with people and other dogs, with a strong pride in his own intelligence. He'll greet guests with a wag of his tail, rather than jump on them. He will not bite nor will he fight unless for the protection of himself or the family he loves. He is not overfriendly, and he is not shy. He is a "well-adjusted" dog because he has no bad personality traits that have to be corrected before he is trained.

Each dog is very much an individual and should be regarded, treated, and handled as such. If you study your dog's individual traits and mental reactions, you can train and manage him more effectively. By knowing his personality and his normal behavior patterns you will be quick to notice the slightest deviations. The normal-behaving dog is usually the happy dog. The happy dog is the product of your association with him.

It is difficult at times to establish a line of demarcation between normal and abnormal behavior of either dogs or humans. A docile little pet might turn into a ferocious tiger when being groomed or having his nails clipped. It would not be considered abnormal behavior if he were to bite his owner. This is his normal reaction to the grooming, and although he is untrained he is acting quite normal by being hostile to the person trying to perform the grooming atrocity. Usually the pet wins the battle, and his hair doesn't get combed or his nails cut. Although this is considered normal behavior, it is disconcerting to the owner to have his dog tell him when grooming is to be allowed.

Usually the so-called master has brought this unnatural

and unpleasant state of affairs upon himself. The pet realizes that he has the upper hand and will often press his advantage. Don't underestimate these "dumb" animals. It is obvious that this dog needs some training, and most dogs actually want obedience and discipline; they respect you more if you teach and demand obedience and discipline; and they like to learn. Your dog is pleased when he masters a command and you praise him for it. It is satisfying to him to be taught to fetch things for you; he desperately wants to be needed.

His demands are so few—mainly affection and companionship. He needs to know that you like him. Treat him as an individual, praise him when he does right, punish him when he does wrong, and you are on the road to producing a normal dog. Words of praise are food to his ego, and he'll do more and more things for you for this praise. Play with him occasionally. Throw things for him to fetch, wrestle with him, and even groom him (even if he may dislike the actual grooming, he likes your spending time with him, caring for him, giving him companionship). Spend as much of your leisure time with him as possible. He lives for it, and it is a thrill for him just to be near you. This association with the greatest thing in his life—you—makes for a healthy, happy dog.

The dog is a social animal and doesn't like to be left alone. Dogs suffer from claustrophobia too. Loneliness breeds many problems. When he is not worked with, is neglected, mental deterioration sets in because of his boredom and lack of reason for being. He becomes a neurotic and unhealthy dog, much to the displeasure of everyone.

Prenatal Influences

Research has proved that environmental influences can prenatally affect the behavior of puppies. Gentle handling of the bitch during pregnancy results in the offspring's being more docile and less easily aroused by sudden disturbances in the environment. On the other hand, certain drugs given to the pregnant dog can alter the behavior of the offspring, and experimentally, electric shock to pregnant bitches results in the puppies' being more excitable.

The mother-puppy bond is established after normal delivery, and there is a relationship between the warmth, food, shelter-seeking behavior of the pup.

NORMAL HANDLING OF PUPPIES

In discussing normal behavior we must understand the normal handling of puppies. It is the early impressions from puppyhood that set the characteristics for future personality.

Nursing

A puppy should be handled as early as possible. During the first 3 weeks the mother usually provides all the food, warmth, and love that a puppy needs. The pattern of puppy behavior is sleeping, feeding, and playing. At the end of that time the puppy becomes receptive to the outside world, and he begins to learn. The human treatment that the puppy receives between 3 and 4 weeks of age is likely to influence its temperament as an adult. Emotional stresses such as long separations from his mother, being roughly handled or frightened by strangers, loud noises, or being left in a strange location are experiences that might have a detrimental effect on the puppy's personality.

From the 4th to the 8th week of his life the puppy begins to investigate the outside world. He learns to recognize by scent the human beings that he comes in daily contact with. He learns to recognize the voice of his caretaker, and other animals and objects that he meets every day. It is these new experiences and impressions that help to form the stability or instability of the yearling.

Most puppies raised under kennel conditions with little human contact will at five weeks show fear reactions. However, if the puppies are handled within the next 2 weeks, this fear will disappear. Puppies should be handled before 5 weeks of age; then there will be no fear reaction evident. Puppies who are not handled until after 12 weeks become increasingly timid and may be extremely difficult to catch. They can be trained but will always be more timid and less responsive than those who socialized with human beings at an earlier age.

Weaning

The period of investigation usually ends at weaning time, when the puppy is confronted with new problems. It is at this time that his intelligence develops quickly in favorable surroundings. By the time he is 3 months old a puppy can learn almost anything that is properly taught him. Even though his body may be too weak and immature to perform some of the activities he learns at this age, later in life he will show the results of his proper early education.

A properly reared puppy is happy and naturally sociable and eager to make friends. He desires patting and gentle handling and will respond favorably by growing up without fear. After weaning, a puppy should be handled by strangers and given a chance to learn that there are other gentle human beings. You should attempt to take him with you on short car trips to the market or shopping center so that he can get accustomed to the car and to city noises. He has to learn that these will not harm him. An animal learns by association and repetition. The more often he's exposed to tenderness and love, the more favorable will be his impression of human beings. A puppy must be encouraged at an early age to form his own impressions and must have confidence in human beings.

A puppy's basic instinct is to love and be loved. However, if he suffers an unhappy puppyhood, his love for the human race can turn to anxiety and distrust. We then have a problem dog.

The Orphan

Although dog psychologists say that a puppy should be put into a new home between the ages of 6 and 8 weeks and that any time after 12 weeks the dog is likely to be maladjusted, I am still old-fashioned enough to believe that dogs can adjust to a new family life at any age if they are basically of sound disposition. I know of countless cases where a close and mutual relationship has resulted from the adoption of dogs of all ages. Many strays have made wonderful family pets. Daily, people adopt dogs of all ages from animal shelters and dog pounds, and good master-pet associations are achieved. In raising an adult dog, as in raising a puppy, tender loving care goes a long way in establishing a firm relationship. But it must be emphasized that disposition is of primary importance in choosing a puppy or an adult dog.

DISTINCTIVE BEHAVIOR OF BREED

Certain breeds have distinct inherited physical and behavioral characteristics which are bred from generation to generation. The guard dogs (Doberman pinscher and German shepherd) have a strong body with a great desire for territorial defense, and so they make excellent watchdogs. It is interesting to watch these puppies as they begin to assume protective custody of both the house they live in and their human family. Although this is a natural instinct and cannot be taught, it can be developed as the dogs mature.

Hunting dogs, because of their keen eyesight and keen sense of smell, have been bred for years to various game. The Saluki hound and the whippet, because of their great speed, can catch their game. The larger breeds, such as Irish wolfhound and Scottish deerhound, see their game. The bird dogs, such as spaniels, setters, pointers, and retrievers, also hunt by eyesight but primarily employ the sense of smell. The hound breeds, such as bloodhound, English foxhound, and beagle, hunt mainly by scent, with their noses close to the ground. Small breeds, such as terriers, were originally trained to hunt rodents. They are aggressive and quick and go after their prey assertively. Dachshunds were bred for hunting badgers, and their body and leg formation makes them ideally suited for catching their particular quarry.

Breed selection has given rise to a large variety of dogs, and each dog, through generations, has been bred for distinct physical and behavioral characteristics. Some dogs have been highly trained in a specialized way for specific jobs—for example, the German shepherd as guide dog for the blind, in police work, and for the armed forces—each requiring specialized training and certain characteristics.

Through the years dogs have come to be adopted more and more for companionship, and for this purpose a small, easily controlled pet is the most practical type. Most people want an affectionate dog, easily trained, not too aggressive, and not vicious or destructive. For them the small or medium-sized dog is the most suitable.

TEMPERAMENTAL DIFFERENCES WITHIN BREED

There can be great differences in temperament in the same breed due to breeding. For instance, although the German shepherd is a watchdog and working dog by heritage, he may become unpredictable, aggressive, or shy because of indiscriminate inbreeding. Through inbreeding many breeds are becoming disoriented from their original purpose. Years ago cocker spaniels were hurt to some extent by indiscriminate breeding—by the lure of profit and of developing champion dogs. Another prime example is the poodle, currently enjoying great popularity. To make quick and easy money, much inbreeding and unselective breeding are going on, producing and reproducing undesirable traits and physical anomalies. To continue at the present pace may spell doom to the breed.

INSTINCTS

Your dog has many curiosities and strange instincts which are inheritances from thousands of years of life in the world. In reality you have a breath of the wild in your home, still retaining traces of the days when his ancestors roamed the woods, matching wits and courage with wild boars and tigers. One of his curiosities is his nose: it is split into a backward curve and trembles with sensitiveness. Keenness of scent was especially necessary to the primitive dog. Incidentally, he always slept with his nose pointed upward to catch the scent of enemies approaching, which involved walking in circles to catch the proper direction of the wind before bedding down. As you've no doubt noticed, the dog still walks in circles before lying down.

The Maternal Instinct

One of the basic instincts is the mother-pup relationship. The mother acts in an instinctive manner; thought processes are not involved. The mother cares for the young, and the father, in some cases, assists, depending on how much motherly instinct he has inherited. In the wild state the father helped rear the puppies, but the domestication process has eliminated him from this role.

The maternal instinct is a prominent factor in raising puppies. One of the earliest signs of this instinct is nest-making before the onset of whelping. The licking and eating of the placenta by the bitch seems to be a necessary preliminary to the cleaning of the young. It also seems to be the basis of the maternal attachment to the offspring; experience has shown that if the bitch is prevented from cleaning and eating the placenta, the usual close link between mother and puppy is not formed. Quite normally the bitch will push aside sick and dying puppies and will sometimes even bury them.

Normally the bitch tends the litter and stays close for about 3 weeks. Then gradually she leaves the box more and more. She will clean the puppies by licking them and by ingesting the urine and feces until they are about 4 weeks old; by then they have been taught to leave the box to take care of their elimination. At about 3 weeks she starts their training period; she punishes them, growls at them, knocks them over. At the onset of the weaning period, by way of introducing her puppies to solid food, she regurgitates her food for them. The bitch begins to lose her maternal affection when the puppies begin taking solid food, at around 4 to 5 weeks.

Puppies are blind until about 9 or 10 days old. Since they cannot see, they stay snuggled close to the mother's warm breast. In the wild, with sight, many of these puppies would have wandered off and quickly perished.

Litters usually have one particularly rough member, and there will often be a tendency to fight. These slight altercations can be considered normal.

An interesting phenomenon in dogs, which is also seen in humans, is that no matter how roughly a mother treats her young before weaning, the suckling retains its love and affection for her.

The Maternal Instinct Altered or Inhibited. The normal maternal instincts may be altered somewhat in a bitch who is overattached to her owner or has been reared as an indulged "perpetual puppy." She may be deficient in maternal behavior and refuse to nurse her offspring. Such a bitch should have her owner close by when she whelps and in the subsequent nursing procedures. There should be no strangers present during this period, as she may be thrown into hysterics and harm her puppies, or even kill and eat them.

The maternal instinct may be inhibited in some dogs when there is a Caesarean section. When they awake from the anesthetic, some of them are indifferent to their puppies and

146

will even harm them. This is not a general rule fortunately, but you should be all means stay with the bitch while her newborn puppies are given to her.

The maternal instinct can be affected by hormonal imbalance. Sometimes there will be no breast formation or milk for the puppies, although there may be a normal delivery.

Always, if the bitch is emotionally disturbed about her puppies, or indifferent, the puppies should be removed from her and raised by hand, both because of the harm that might befall them and because it is easy for them to assume some of her emotional unstableness. With hand-raising they can be normal puppies in all traits and not inherit the mother's tendency toward indifference to maternal responses.

The Care-Giving Instinct

This is an aspect of the maternal mother-pup relationship which involves instinctive action. The mother dog sometimes engages in an advanced type of social behavior—a grooming which is a toothful combing for fleas or foxtails either in her young, in another dog, or in her master. We often see a dog "groom" someone in her human family or a canine playmate. She will lick the ears and neck in an affectionate way which is her expression of extreme love. This is her desire to mother her human family.

The Suckling Instinct

This, of course, is a strong instinct. If puppies are not suckled by the mother, there should be some substitute. Even a pacifier will do. However, it is best to use a bottle with a small opening so that the puppy will have to work to get the milk out. If a puppy is not allowed to suck, a non-nutritional sucking habit will sometimes develop and persist in later life.

The Sexual Instinct

Domestication has so relaxed the dog's morals that today's concept of the dog is that he will breed with any female. Not unlike their human counterparts, male dogs play the gallant to every bitch in heat, even complete strangers.

When puppies are about 4 weeks old, some sexual activity will be noted—there will be some copulatory movement—but the phase lasts only about 2 weeks and then disappears until sexual maturity.

In the male dog the raising of the hind leg is usually hormonally controlled and is not learned by the pup from other male dogs. The male hormones affect the behavior of the male dog. There is also a strong link between the sexual urge of the male and the hormonal smell of the female urine. Male dogs are attracted to female dogs in heat by the odor of their urine and instinctively know when the bitch is ready for breeding.

Normal Sexual Behavior

Puppies are like children in early stimulation and sexual sensations. The mother licks her puppies, stimulating the genitals and other sensitive areas. Litter mates rub against one another and their mother for pleasurable sensations. During early growth long before sexual maturity, they have oral and bodily contact during which they exhibit sexual excitement. There is no differentiation between the sexes—males ride males and females are stimulated by females. This is normal behavior and is not considered homosexuality until sexual maturity. If the animal does not change after sexual maturity, it remains a homosexual the rest of its life.

Sex play or forepleasure is normal in dogs and important in breeding. The mating pair should be put in a room by themselves and allowed to undergo the pleasure of sex play. It is stimulating to both sexes, and often an aggressive romantic male can win over a latently frigid female.

During normal sex play dogs lick one another around the sensitive area: penis, vulva, clitoris, nipples, anus, lips, mouth, tongue, eyelids, ears. Often the female will roll over on her back like a puppy and allow the male to lick the smooth and tender (usually hairless) skin on her abdomen, thighs, and elbow regions. Sometimes the male will allow the female to ride him, and this may enable her to have an orgasm. The normal female doesn't usually have an orgasm at the time of copulation but may have one during the foreplay, while riding the male.

Frequently when a female in heat is kept from male dogs, she will become so sexually aroused during the middle of her estrus cycle that she will ride other females to try to satisfy her sexual needs. Likewise, males cooped up for long periods without female companionship will ride one another. After returning to normal conditions, most dogs will return to heterosexuality and enjoy the normal pleasures of sexual contact.

The Signature of the Dog. The habit dogs have of smelling one another under their tails is a normal instinct called the "signature" of the dog. It has to do with the odor that is eliminated from the anal glands. Under severe emotional stress, and fear, evacuation of these glands can occur, and the odor is quite putrid. These are the same anal sacs that are used as a defensive mechanism in the skunk.

There are some who believe that the anal-sac secretions may be a source of sexual attraction. The hypothesis is that the secretions of the anal sac contain the hormonal odors depicting the sexual period of the female.

The Herding-Roaming Instinct

The dog is born with an urge to roam and form packs. We should all try to prevent our pets from traveling with a pack, because this is when dogs revert to the call of the wild. They usually get into trouble by attacking other dogs and animals and even people. It is normal for a male during the mating season to join with a group of dogs and follow the trail of any female in heat.

Communication between Dogs

There are many normal communication patterns between dogs. When danger is threatening, there is a certain posture to a dog's body. He has a distinctive way of slinking when he is submitting to a new threat. When his tail is between his legs, he is submitting to a danger. Raising his paw is a sign of submission.

Urinary scent is one of the commonest ways dogs communicate with one another. The male dog uses this device for marking his territory, as does the female dog. It is normal behavior for territorial rights.

Vocalization is another means of communication, and it varies from breed to breed. Some breeds, like the hound, howl, while some small terrier types are yappy. Guard dogs bark to let both people and animals know that they are protecting their territory. Hunting dogs bay to express themselves.

Only tame or domesticated dogs bark. Wild dogs and

149

wolves don't bark; they howl. Barking is an imitation. As the master urged him with shouts to go after game the dog in his excitement imitated these sounds and in time developed the barking habit.

The scientific explanation of howling in the domestic dog is that it is merely the outcropping of instincts developed through the ages when wild dogs hunted in packs; the howl was their rallying call.

The dog still retains many of his primitive instincts, but these impulses can be guided through training and education, and we can mold our dog into the temperament and personality type we want. He wants to be taught and is eager to learn. It is up to us to teach him.

10   TRAINING FOR NORMAL BEHAVIOR

FIRST PRINCIPLES

It must be evident by now that it is next to impossible to have a normal, well-behaved, even-tempered dog without discipline and some training. Once a dog is trained he is a better pet and a greater source of pride, and he himself is happier for knowing that his master is pleased with him.

There are many books devoted to discipline and training which are well worth reading. There are also many fine obedience-training classes throughout the country, and I heartily recommend this form of training. Of course, you must be willing to accept the fact that if your dog fails the course and becomes a dropout it is entirely your fault, not the dog's. He is a willing subject; it is your responsibility to help him become an apt pupil.

Any sincerely interested dog owner can train his own dog, and it can be a most rewarding education for both master and pupil. Patience and plenty of self-control are the most important ingredients for successful training. At times you have to be firm, you have to be gentle, you have to scold, and you have to praise. You must temper punishment with praise. You and your dog must share mutual love and confidence, and your seriousness of purpose must be sincere.

Basically dog training is built on reward and punishment. A kind word or a caress makes any dog feel that he is pleasing his master. Other meaningful gestures of affection that a dog can understand are taking his muzzle playfully in both hands, rubbing him behind his ears, rubbing your hand gently over his flanks and back, or taking his nose in your hand affectionately. A pat on his head, running his ear through your hand, or just the words "Good dog" make for a happy, grateful dog.

Men and women alike can be trainers, but there is a tendency in women to be less strong and authoritative in their commands than men and less stern in their punishment. Just the same, some of the best obedience trainers in the country are women, because they have a way of giving commands that dogs seem to like and pay attention to. So I appeal to you women to be strict and to follow up your training with stern enough punishment when the dog doesn't obey.

My answer to the frequent question, What is the best age at which to start training a dog? is 3 months for minor commands and a minimum of 6 months for any intensive training. Don't start too early, for a puppy can easily be intimidated. Too severe training and discipline can destroy his confidence and attachment and have a permanent affect on his personality. Severe punishment, rough handling, loud and harsh words can turn the puppy into a distrustful pet full of antagonisms toward the human race. Start slowly and gently in training the puppy, and use incentive and praise.

Most puppies form a strong attachment to an individual human being which may persist or wane, and there is often a phase of adolescent independence when the dog will become disobedient and defiant—just like a teen-ager. Discipline is needed during this critical period, but it must be mixed with patience and must not be overbearing.

Although it can be too early to start training, it is never too late. I don't for one moment believe that you can't teach an old dog new tricks. He can be taught new tricks and all the basic commands whatever his age. It is bound to be a little more difficult to break old habits like barking, chasing cars, and sleeping on satin cushions, but here too, with perseverance, new tricks can replace old habits.

I don't intend to get into the fine points of discipline and training, but I will briefly discuss the rudiments of normal behavior.

Your dog must be relaxed before you begin a training

151

session. He can't learn while he is tense and timid and in a nervous state. If he is confused and defiant, he will subconsciously resist your teaching. Complete relaxation is essential to successful dog training.

GET TO KNOW YOUR DOG

To train your dog to the best advantage of both of you, you must get to know him. For example, there are sensitive dogs who squeal at the slightest slap with the disciplinary newspaper, the merest jerk of the training lead, or even the touch of a grooming comb. A word of ridicule, to hurt his feelings, should be enough to bring him into line.

Then there's the pesty dog. He's the aggressive type who is always pushing himself at you for your attention. He jumps on your guests, nuzzles them, brings a ball to be thrown. This dog needs special firmness and sternness to rid him of his overdemanding trait. He's basically good, but he has to be taught that he's not number one in the world. He's the type of dog that if allowed to will take over the entire family and run the whole show. He usually has to be taken down a peg or two before any good training habits can be evolved.

If your dog is shy, he must not be overpunished. I would give exaggerated praise and patting when he does something right and gentle but firm correction when he does something wrong. It is possible for the shy dog to learn, and learning will improve his personality by allowing him to gain confidence in himself.

Various breed require different kinds and degrees of punishment. For instance, in beagles mild punishment is usually enough to inhibit undesirable activities. However, in a larger dog, such as collie or German shepherd, your punishment most likely will have to be more severe physically because the determination to resist you will probably be stronger.

You have to know your dog's personality when you are training him because each dog has to be handled differently. Each animal has a threshold of sensitivity which you must determine in order to know how far you need to jerk the leash for response. Train him according to his temperament and anticipate his next move.

GETTING THE MESSAGE ACROSS

Anyone can train his dog so long as the animal is able to understand what he is being taught. It's strictly a matter of communication. That he loves you and wants to please you is a big plus factor on your side in learning how to train him. As with people—getting on the same level when you want to communicate with them—so it is with dogs. You have to get down on your haunches, crouch beside your dog, and win his confidence. Talk "man to man" with him, in quiet, soft tones.

I can't overemphasize that you should constantly talk to your dog while training him. But please don't raise your voice, or shout, or yell, or scream. And don't, for goodness' sake, lose your temper and kick at him or throw things at him. He'll not only be frightened and confused, but he's liable to lose some of his respect for you. If you feel a fit of temper coming on, dismiss the class forthwith!

Your dog can tell by the tone of your voice whether you mean the command. He has to know you mean it; he has to be convinced. Don't be wishy-washy; your dog will understand your tone of voice better than he will understand words. Try to develop voice tones that will convey the meaning of your commands. He will learn the significance of your voice tones and ultimately the meanings of some words.

In getting the message across, word commands have to be augmented by body contact so that the dog can associate the two. By repeating the body contacts with the same words, he will soon learn what you are trying to tell him. I advocate a choke collar; it is one of the few ways of communicating your message. (It is not a cruel instrument and can be used on the smallest and most fragile dog when handled properly and gently.) In time, when he understands your message, your voice commands will suffice. It is a matter of repetition until he understands what you want. The whole aim of training is to teach the animal to react to your voice commands and hand signals.

For disobedience and discipline, sometimes words such as "Bad dog" or "Phooey" are enough, but for some strong-minded individuals I am not against discipline with a rolled-up newspaper or a switch, or in some really tough dogs, a leather strap. Although it may be necessary to give stiff physical correction now and then, remember never to hold a grudge in training. Follow up an admonishment with a re-

153

ward or praise for some other deed. It will encourage your pet to do better next time.

Failure to respond to his master's wishes is usually due to confusion or to physical illness or incapability. Patience and understanding can correct all but physical inability.

One of the strongest methods of punishing a dog is to grab him by the scruff of the neck and shake him. This goes back to primitive days when dogs roamed in packs and the leader punished an errant follower by grabbing him by the neck and shaking him severely. This technique, although not practiced much nowadays, is still an effective way of making a dog feel bad. He knows that he is really being punished when you shake him by the scruff.

MAKE THE LESSONS ENJOYABLE

Dogs get bored with long training sessions. If you work with them over 20 minutes at a time, they will lose interest and stop listening to you. For a younger dog or a puppy, 5 to 10 minutes is long enough for any one training session. But do it frequently, and don't punish him if he does something wrong. When he does well, praise him, give him a reward. And make the rewards worthwhile—favorite tidbits. If he does badly, a verbal "Bad dog" is usually enough. Vary the lessons and intersperse the hard things with easy and known commands—and make them as much fun as possible.

BE CONSISTENT

Dogs are constantly observing their masters, trying to figure out what is wanted of them. Be consistent in your requests and responses, and be consistent in your aims and methods, so as not to confuse or deceive. Follow up the same learning procedures with the same praise, reward, or disapproval response. And don't let the dog get away with something one time and punish him another time—you'll just bewilder him.

TEACH RESPECT

A dog has to be taught to respect his master. He automatically will love you out of his respect for you. You have to be his master, not let him be yours. He wants to know what you, as his master and teacher, expect of him. As you communicate your wishes and he learns to understand you, he will forever be your loyal follower and try to please you. Once the dog knows his master is the leader, he will be a happy follower.

As well as the five fundamental training points, there are five basic commands which I believe all dogs should be taught. They are Heel, Sit, Down, Stay and Come.

BASIC COMMANDS

Heel. You teach your dog to walk on your left side without pulling in front of you; he is always to walk in back of you, at your left heel. When he tries to get in front of you, you jerk the choke collar while repeating, "Heel."

Sit. You will pull the leash straight up with your right hand while pressing on his hindquarters with your left hand, repeating the word "Sit."

Down. You grasp the leash under the dog's neck and push straight down on it while holding the other end of the leash in your right hand. The voice command should have a downward inflection. Sometimes in a stubborn animal it's necessary to pull the front legs forward to weaken his support and then pull down on the collar as you say, "Down."

Stay. You put your dog in a sitting position and push gently against his chest or nose if he tries to move forward. You command him to stay and move slowly from him. Keep repeating, "Stay" as you gradually increase the distance between you.

Come. Be sure to do this with a leash or a long rope. First put him on the "Stay" command. Use the word "Come" with an inviting tone and inflection and give the leash a little tug toward you. When he gets to you, praise him or reward him.

I can't in all conscience end this chapter without a word of sympathy for the weak owners—and I include myself—who sneak bits of food to their dogs under the table, reward them with a cookie for every little expression of affection or funny-ism, or let them get away with all kinds of "favored" idiosyncrasies. Hopefully we can manage to exert enough training and discipline to keep our permissiveness and our dogs' "advantages" within bounds.

11 ABNORMAL BEHAVIOR: THE NEUROTIC DOG

We are seeing an increasing number of nervous dogs in our midst. While some of these dogs owe their nervousness to inherited faults of temperament, most of them owe it to a variety of unfavorable environmental conditions. From their normal primitive ways we have changed dogs' normal behavior patterns so much in recent years that it is small wonder their neuroses are increasing apace. Also, because dogs imitate their masters closely, and unfortunately even the bad aspects, they seem to be acquiring many of the neuroses and mental ailments of the human race.

I feel obliged to interject that not all owners of misbehaving nuisance pets are maladjusted. Most of these owners are nice people who just happen to be victims of circumstance. They own a juvenile delinquent dog and can't bear the thought of parting with it. It is to these victimized dog owners that most of this chapter is dedicated. We will discuss ways and means of handling problem dogs.

At a renowned clinic for mentally ill dogs, in Copenhagen, last year alone more than 2,000 mentally disturbed dogs from all over Europe received treatment. Patients are usually fit to return to their owners in about a month—although it takes up to 3 months to cure canines addicted to tranquilizers. A high proportion of the disturbed dogs are sent to the clinic to be cured of biting people. "Dogs that bite children or handicapped people," theorizes Arne Soerensen, founder of the clinic, "are not necessarily mean, but frightened when pushed up to a small child or a stranger."

CAUSES OF ABNORMAL BEHAVIOR

Inherited Nervousness

Although most cases of nervousness are basically due to environmental factors, some dogs do inherit the tendency. If a nervous dog was bred from two non-nervous parents, then we can be fairly certain that the nervousness is environmental. Inherited nervousness should be eliminated from the strain by not allowing such dogs to breed; they should be castrated or spayed. Behavioral abnormalities that should be watched for before allowing an animal to breed are excessive timidity and fear of strangers; refusal to leave a familiar environment; sound, touch, and sight shyness; fear-biting; fear of sudden changes; and excessive activity. Any of these traits would be inherited in offspring and establish and compound many abnormal traits.

The vast majority of descendants of the shy, fear-biting bitch will shy at friendly animals even though the sires are normal and friendly creatures. Furthermore, in addition to the direct inheritance of shyness, the behavior of the mother is likely to teach the puppies to react violently, as she does, to strangers and other disturbing influences. Nor is this shyness modified by training.

Physical Disorders

When I examine a dog that is brought to me because of abnormal behavior, there are many factors that I consider. We must always investigate the possibility of a physical disorder as the cause of any abnormal behavior before we can incriminate a mental problem. Many times the animal doesn't feel well and acts in a peculiar manner because of an organic problem. I usually give the animal a complete physical checkup, looking for one of the following disorders which can affect behavior: worms, thyroid disease, a spinal-disc disorder, poisoning, constipation, diarrhea, urinary ailments, allergic reactions, milk fever in a nursing bitch, sex-organ malfunction, anal-gland infection. Many diseases, such as rabies, spinal meningitis, distemper, and epilepsy, can cause abnormal behavior. Brain tumors, abscesses, and such traumatic things as a blow to the head or an inner-ear infection can cause abnormal behavior and even affect a dog's temperament. I have seen dogs with head injuries undergo such abnormal behavior as loss of social and sexual drives, loss of hunting tendencies, and complete lethargy, and I've seen them regress to puppy habits and further—back to the point of primitive wild canine behavior. Sometimes a goodnatured animal will turn vicious and unreliable. After elimination of the organic problem, the abnormal behavior generally will clear up.

An overdose of tranquilizers or sedatives will change

157

behavior. Some drugs accumulate in the blood stream and gradually over a period of time will cause a derangement in mental abilities. If the dog becomes dopy or sleepy, or acts stupid under certain medication, have your veterinarian check it out to make sure there are no sedatives in it that are affecting the dog's ability.

A dog behaving abnormally can conceivably be under the influence of alcohol, especially around Christmas time, when always at least one pet is brought to us who has consumed too much eggnog. At a recent veterinary convention there was a discussion about the increase in the number of alcoholic dogs. You can tell when a dog is hung over; he's bleary-eyed and listless and looks like he's got a headache. However, he can't get the stuff himself; someone has to give it to him. The drinking generally starts as a gag at a party, when someone gets the dog to lap up some booze. He takes a liking to the stuff and becomes a sneaky party drinker.

Unsuitable Environment— Undesirable Youthful Experiences

If a puppy is reared in seclusion or in an unsuitable environment, he may be expected to grow up to be unhappy, nervous, and timid. When he's confronted with a new situation, he sometimes goes to pieces. He doesn't know how to cope with new problems. If he's under 3 months of age, he can easily be taught to deal with crises. The older he is, the more difficult it will be and the slower his response to treatment. The one thing that all dogs of any age respond to is tender loving care. It takes a lot of patience and consideration to deal with the problem dog. The pet has to first of all believe in you as an individual and trust you as the one person in his life. He's more apt to do what you want if he has this confidence.

There are certain conditions in the family life of an owner that can affect a dog's behavior: a tense and stressful family life, a shy owner, a fearful owner, an anxious owner, a tense owner, an excessively permissive owner, a bored owner, and a person who isolates himself, such as an introvert.

In order to suggest an atmosphere of family life, one progressive kennel owner pipes in radio soap operas to comfort homesick dogs. Experts have discovered that matronly voices and gruff but friendly voices of middle-aged men have a soothing effect on dogs.

158

So remember, if music fails to soothe your bored and lonesome dog, let him hear some radio soap operas.

The Aging Process

Senility affects the various organs of the body, so as the dog gets older there will be a slow, gradual change in some of his behavior patterns. His toilet training is one of the earliest things to go. Where he was once well housebroken, we get an animal who begins to dribble urine—much to his embarrassment. The muscles of the bladder gradually lose their control. Certain kidney diseases, such as nephritis, and also diabetes can cause the dog to wet through inability to hold urine. Sometimes it would seem that an animal is being spiteful and getting even with his owner by wetting the floor, and this does happen, but most of the time it's a physical problem. In older dogs have your veterinarian check the kidneys at periodic intervals. As the male dog gets older his prostate gland often enlarges and produces an inflammation which causes him to urinate often. It is painful and needs medical attention.

In an older dog you will usually notice a loss of hearing. At first it is very gradual, and you may not realize that he is having trouble hearing you. As he deafens you might use high-pitched sounds, such as whistles, rather than voice commands.

Cataracts form in older eyes, and your dog may have trouble recognizing you. There is a gradual graying and loss of vision, accompanied by changing behavior patterns.

In the older dog you may notice a change in his attitudes toward the members of his human family. Although he still loves them dearly, he wants his comfort and solitude more often. He wants to be left alone instead of romping and playing as he once did. This is not of his desire but because of his physical disabilities. It will be easier for him if you can adapt to his dilemma and be sympathetic and patient with him. As long as he is near you, he is happy. Of course, like older people, he may sometimes get a little irritable and not want to be handled. Accede to his demands. He has been and still is your loyal companion.

NEUROTIC MANIFESTATIONS

It is the consensus of the experts that the tensions of our modern-day civilization have a deteriorating effect on our pets.

The present-day neurotic dog is unfortunately a development of easy living, particularly in homes where he is coddled or, at the opposite extreme, where the people attempting to train him use such overbearing methods that they cow the puppy and make him mentally timid and frightened.

Oher causes of neuroticism among dogs are loneliness, lack of exercise, lack of proper training, and overfeeding.

In describing a neurotic dog I would say that most of the time he is restless. He whines and whimpers, and barks excessively. He is not dependable when strangers are in the vicinity; he doesn't like their presence, and if they come near him he is apt to snap at them without warning. The neurotic dog is usually a finicky eater; overfeeding and too frequent feeding have helped to make some neurotic dogs what they are. It's best to keep certain neurotic dogs slightly hungry so that they'll respond to commands with more obedience, in anticipation of a reward of food.

Psychosomatic Ailments

Psychosomatic ailments are a form of abnormal dog behavior. They're closely allied to emotional reactions and are resorted to as a means of gaining attention. These animals aren't faking a sickness—they are actually ill. Various emotions are responsible for psychosomatic illnesses, but the outstanding one seems to be jealously. Psychosomatic ailments are actual organic ailments of which emotional factors are a cause. They can range anywhere from sexual maladjustment to human beings to animal self-mutilation and suicide. Psychosomatic medicine is a fairly new field in veterinary medicine, and in certain cases of emotionally caused physical disabilities help can be instituted.

Discovering the cause of each emotional ailment is a special challenge to every veterinarian. An interesting case I had involved a dog brought to me with a seemingly incurable skin condition. The poor dog scratched constantly. The owners had used everything from burnt cylinder oil to highly refined cortisone preparations without effect. While I was questioning the master, it came to light that there had been no skin trouble or scratching until a cat had joined the household. We checked the dog for sensitization to cat hairs but found none. We then decided to work on the theory that the dog was jealous of the cat and scratched to gain attention. When a new home was found for the cat, the dog's skin condition promptly cleared up—and no medication was necessary.

In an effort to gain attention dogs have done some strange things, but the queerest case I ever have seen is a male dachshund who goes into psychosomatic labor pains when his mate is about to have puppies. The male resents his mate's being the center of attraction whenever motherhood is imminent. In order to get into the act he goes through labor pains with his mate. He climbs into the whelping box with her and grunts and groans and strains and carries on like the real thing. As each puppy is born he cleans and attends to it. At the completion of whelping the mother dog chases him out of the box and takes over her puppies. This pair has had several litters, and the male has behaved similarly each time.

Asthmatic Seizures

Asthma seems to be an ailment of emotional origin. I have seen dogs that were jealous of either a human or another dog go into loud asthmatic wheezing when things weren't going their way and they wanted to gain attention. Some excitable dogs will have a seizure when the doorbell rings and strangers come into the house.

With a seizure the animal works himself into a frenzy and begins to pant and to breathe with loud gasps. Sometimes his tongue turns blue; and some dogs faint from lack of oxygen. Medically the bronchial tubes become constricted, and the dogs can't get enough oxygen into their lungs.

The best treatment for a dog in this state is to pick him up, talk to him, soothe him, and relax him; soon the breathing will return to normal. Some animals have to be kept on respiratory sedatives or tranquilizers to prevent recurrence of these attacks. In preventing attacks, when you expect a lot of people in your house, or neighborhood children playing nearby, I advise giving the animal some sedation, for asthmatic bronchial attacks can prove fatal if the dog has a weak heart.

The short-nosed breeds, such as bulldog, Boston terrier, pug, and Pekingese, are the prime victims of this ailment.

Loss of Appetite

Loss of appetite can be a psychosomatic ailment, especially when the dog is obviously on a hunger strike. Almost any dog in new surroundings may refrain from eating the first day. However, if after 2 or 3 days the animal still is not eating, it is usually due to emotional trauma. For example, a dog's feelings can be hurt when you put him in a boarding kennel as you go off on a trip. He feels left out, unwanted, unloved. Most normal dogs will go right to food as soon as something is presented to them to their liking. The psychosomatic dog who will not eat usually shows other symptomatic signs, such as hiding in a corner, involuntary urination and defecation, resistance to handling or walking with the new sitters, and a fearful attitude, with the whites of his eyes showing.

Even in their own familiar home, there are some dogs who won't eat if everything isn't perfectly in place, or when there's company, even though their owners are near.

Loss of Bowel or Bladder Control

Severe emotional stress, anxiety, or shock can produce loss of bowel or urine control in almost any animal. This is expected and normal. However, there are mentally disturbed animals who lose bowel or urine control without any apparent cause. In such a disturbed dog anything that is not to his liking can produce these ailments.

Pseudopregnancy, or False Pregnancy

This is a fairly common psychosomatic ailment, and it is frustrating to both dog and owner. The dog is definitely affected physically; she becomes very uncomfortable, with large, swollen breasts full of lactating milk dripping from her nipples. Some animals drip milk whenever they lie down and continue lactation during the 4- to 6-week normal nursing period. Often they will stop eating and lose a lot of weight.

Some females at the time of delivery give all the signs of impending whelping. The vagina becomes enlarged, and there is a discharge. I've seen them go through false labor pains, tearing up newpapers and making a bed just as if they were preparing for puppies. During the period for nursing their puppies they usually stay in bed, or lie under chairs and other objects, and even refuse to eat. They have the maternal instinct of a nursing mother and will frequently carry objects (rubber toys, shoes, pillows) around in their mouths and snuggle them close to their breasts to simulate puppies. They are suspicious, protective, and disagreeable to anyone who goes near. At times they get upset and depressed, looking for their puppies.

Why the female does this, no one seems to know, but we do know how to treat it—to relieve the poor bitch of her feverish breasts, her anxiety over her "puppies," and her depressed state. She definitely needs treatment. Your veterinarian can treat her with hormones; and if there is fever, with antibiotics; and if she's emotionally upset, he will use tranquilizers to calm her down. I believe in applying camphorated oil to the breasts. Just apply it lightly to the nipples, and it will relieve the pain and dry up the milk; don't rub or massage it, as it will stimulate the milk flow. Some bitches self-nurse, and this is a disagreeable development which prolongs both the physical and mental anguish. When there's a profuse flow of milk, these bitches can be used as wet nurses to orphan puppies.

As well as medication, there should be a lot of tender loving care. Give the bitch as much love as she will allow. Don't punish her if she growls at you. Be patient and gentle.

There is disagreement between veterinarians and research scientists on whether false pregnancy is an emotional disorder or strictly a hormonal malfunction. I believe that there is an imbalance of hormones in the body, with a consequent emotional change in the animal. There's no supportive evidence that false pregnancy is hereditary. Usually if a bitch has one attack, she will be susceptible to further pseudopregnancies. Such animals may have to be spayed; they are undesirable as breeders. However, for those who had intended to breed a dog, I would advise trying to breed her at least once. Sometimes having a litter of puppies will straighten out the hormonal disorder. But if it's not successful, I would advise a hysterectomy. It will prolong the health and happiness of the animal, for she does suffer terrible physical and mental anguish during false pregnancy.

Occasionally during false pregnancy a bitch will work out her own solution. A dog I know, a devoted member of family, became jealous when her mistress had a baby—the first baby. While the mistress was nursing her baby, the dog developed a false pregnancy, filled up with milk, and tried to cuddle many objects around the house. However, her make-shift puppies were not satisfactory, so she went out looking for living objects to suckle. She came home one day with three baby rabbits, put them into her bed and began nursing them.

Fortunately jealousy of a new baby in a household works itself out in ways such as the above. Usually the dog will accept the baby as part of the family and lie by its crib and protect it. When the baby starts crawling, the dog will play with it. I have never heard of a dog harming a baby or willfully injuring a baby because of jealousy.

Sexual Disorders

There are many psychosomatic sexual disorders. Even with two normal dogs the mating process is a strained one for our home-grown pets—those who don't roam the streets breeding with any dog that comes along. In some of our planned breedings tension and excitement will occasionally prevent dogs from getting together. There are some emotionally disturbed pets, those who have been spoiled by overpermissive owners, who show little inclination to mate with their own species, and the females often make poor mothers even if they are bred. Many overdependent females are so attached to their human masters that they will be frigid to the point of being vicious to the male attempting to mate. A spoiled male may not show any desire to breed and even upon stimulation will show impotence. Sometimes a male dog who has been raised with an older female who has dominated him will show no inclination to normal mating.

It is well known that miscarriages can occur because of emotional trauma. In highly excitable dogs almost any disturbing event can cause premature whelping. In such dogs puppies sometimes arrive without the accompanying normal flow of milk. The bitch sometimes will refuse to care for the puppies and may even kill and eat them. The theory behind this is that she fears someone will hurt her puppies. In my opinion there's also the possibility that she feels disdain for the puppies and an unwillingness to share family affection with them.

Although car sickness is usually caused by an inner-ear disturbance, motion sickness can sometimes be classified as psychosomatic in origin because some carsick-prone dogs begin to drool and show nausea before they get into the car. It is controlled by emotional factors.

This ailment can be helped and controlled with anti-motion-sickness pills or tranquilizers to calm the anxiety of the dog before he gets into the car. If the dog has a tendency toward drooling or nausea, a drug such as dramamine or bonamine, with a tranquilizer, is advisable. In my opinion the tranquilizer is more important than the dramamine or bonamine because it's fear of the car that makes the animal drool.

Animals can be trained not to be fearful of a car. Of course, it's easier if done in early puppyhood—taking the puppy for short rides (preferably on an empty stomach). Some dogs are taken in the car only to the veterinarian or to the boarding kennel, and as these places are often distasteful to the dog, the association can be unfortunate and traumatic. It's good to take him on rides for pure enjoyment, with something he likes to do as part of the trip—a run in the woods, a food treat.

OTHER NEUROTICISMS

Claustrophobia

Just like humans, dogs are subject to claustrophobia. Some dogs during and after confinement show abnormal behavior patterns. One manifestation is tail chasing; the dog chases his tail continuously until he collapses from exhaustion. Another is spot attacking. The dog stares rigidly at a spot on the floor for about five minutes and then springs into the air to attack the spot. He will repeat this behavior continually while in confinement. Claustrophobia is offset by giving the dog some freedom and exercise.

Antisocial Tendencies

These tendencies can vary all the way from seeming disdain for association with other animals to active association with humans only.

Anxiety

Anxiety is a neuroticism dogs acquire from humans. The symptoms are restlessness and rapid or loud panting. The anxiety can become so intense that the animal loses control of his bowels and bladder.

Compulsive Behavior

Much of the dog's behavior is compulsive, and so long as his uncontrollable desires are not harmful or vicious, they usually don't present problems. Behavior is easily learned and tolerated in a dog; he enjoys the security of behavior patterns and established guidelines. This is one of the reasons dogs take to obedience training and like to learn tricks.

Coprophagy (Stool Eating)

Although coprophagy is distasteful in appearance, it is not harmful to the dog except for the control of intestinal parasites. The exact cause isn't known, but experts agree that it's a mental or dietary deficiency, or both.

I've noticed in many cases of parasitism that the dog gets a perverted appetite, eating feces, or possibly dirt, or he will chew on stones or other inedible objects. Another possible cause is a mineral or vitamin deficiency causing the dog to have a craving for something he's not getting in his normal diet.

In young puppies one of the commonest causes of stool eating is incomplete digestion of meat. Meat is passed in the feces in the same condition as before ingestion. This is likely due to intestinal worms, too much meat at one meal, or too large chunks. Sometimes cooking the meat for the puppy will cure this habit.

A new theory attributes coprophagy to an enzyme deficiency which can be corrected by the feeding of glandular organs (e.g., heart muscle) and by the use of enzymes in the daily diet.

Once a physical abnormality is ruled out, I would apply pressure on the dog regarding this habit. It is seen in young puppies more often than in adult dogs, and I approve of punishment for ridding the dog of the habit.

Many people have tried to discourage the habit by making

the stools distasteful to the dog by the addition of various preparations. For example, a commercial drug called Ectoral which is used to kill fleas and ticks seems to give the stools an offensive taste. Other substances, helpful in some cases, are monosodium glutamate (sold commercially as "Accent"), oil of anise, and papain (an enzyme used in meat tenderizers). Any of these added to the dog's food should make the stool undesirable.

Extroversion

This classifies the dog who makes friends with everybody and is in love with the whole world.

Hallucinations

Under stress some dogs will snap at and chase imaginary objects, such as flies which aren't there.

Hysteria

Hysteria is not uncommon in nervous dogs. A prime example is dogs who are afraid of storms. I've known some on a hysterical binge to practically take a house apart during a storm. Such a dog begins pacing and panting well in advance of the storm. When he gets uncontrollable, it's impossible to calm him; he snaps and bites at everything. The treatment is to slip him a "Mickey Finn" at the first sign of an impending storm—a tranquilizer or sedative.

For some nervous dogs just the threat of a bath, a pill to be taken, or toenails to be trimmed is enough to make them hysterical. Such high-strung dogs often chew at themselves, causing lesions on their bodies which we classify as neurodermatitis.

Mass hysteria can be precipitated in a group of dogs quite easily. All it takes is one dog to get overexcited and hysterical, and they all lose control of themselves. Unfortunately they often pick on one poor defenseless dog and mutilate him.

Introversion

This is the opposite of extroversion. These dogs stay close to home and will have nothing to do with strangers.

Phobias

A phobia is an abnormal fear of someone or something which is the result of a conditioned learning reflex. Dogs develop certain phobias for individuals and events which can start in a small way and build up to a hysterical condition. A good example is a phobia to the postman or to garbagemen.

Some dogs have an abnormal fear of the veterinary hospital—but not any more abnormal than some people's fear of a dental appointment.

Sexual Abnormalities

Sexual abnormalities are common in dogs of all ages and both sexes.

The female will mount other dogs, male or female, and even children, in the manner of the male and try to perform the sex act. If the bitch is in season, this is not abnormal, but some females show more or less constant signs of heat every 3 or 4 months instead of every 6 months. This is due to cystic ovaries which produce excessive female hormones. The condition might be counteracted by the injection of hormones, and if not, a hysterectomy is indicated, as these bitches are difficult to breed.

Male dogs will also perform this riding of legs and will even mount a child who is crawling on the floor. This is not uncommon during the normal breeding season, but some dogs who are confined and not allowed to roam develop the habit from sexual frustration. It can become intolerable, and dangerous to children. We use female hormones to try to counteract the condition, and if not successful, and it's impossible to breed the dog, castration is indicated.

Homosexual masturbation is common in the canine kingdom. Males ride males, and females ride females. The pleasure is derived from the clitoris or the penis rubbing against the body of the other animal. The female receives a clitoridean orgasm when she rides another female, and by her reactions it is obvious that she enjoys the sexual act. The male may even penetrate the anus of the other male dog.

The male dog also masturbates by having intercourse with such objects as towels, shoes, and stockings. He will also lick his penis until he has an erection and subsequent ejaculation.

168

This dog when confronted with a female in season may or may not show any interest.

Pseudohermaphrodites are dogs having both male and female sex organs, and with such abnormal sexual features and hormonal imbalances their behavior is distinctly abnormal.

In one female dog whose sexual organs appeared normal, I found signs of a penis inside the vagina. This male organ would enlarge upon stimulation. The dog would allow herself to be mounted or would mount a female and attempt to copulate, depending on her mood or the stage of her irregular estrus cycle. She attracted male dogs but would not let them penetrate her.

There are male dogs that attract other males because of secondary female characteristics. They show signs of large nipple formation and a pendulous, soft scrotum with abnormally soft testicles. The sheath of the penis is large and flabby. The testicles secrete a female hormone which affects the dogs both physically and mentally, and usually causes a chronic skin disorder.

For the physical and mental well-being of these dogs surgical intervention is recommended.

Temper Tantrums

Dogs display tantrums just like spoiled children and often are just as temperamental. They have emotional ups and downs much like their masters, whom they are trying to imitate. Sometimes it's difficult for the owner to recognize an outright case of temper tantrum, and he may attribute the abnormal behavior to other causes. When a mature dog chews furniture, rugs, and clothing, tears up curtains and draperies, and destroys other property in the house, he is having an unadulterated temper tantrum. Often the owner rationalizes the behavior by saying that the dog is difficult to train or isn't intelligent. This is seldom so; usually the dog is downright angry at being left alone.

By inadvertently leaving his television set on one time when he went out, a friend of mine found the answer to his dogs' destructive tendencies when left alone. The dog had obviously become so engrossed in a program that he hadn't gotten around to destroying anything by the time my friend got home. It turned out the dog was perfectly content to be left alone watching TV. For some dogs, leaving a radio on will help.

If the problem isn't this easily solved, the dog should be punished immediately after the act is performed. If necessary, go out and when he thinks he's alone sneak in the back door and catch him in the act. Impress his wrongdoing upon him very sternly.

If you have a dog who is rebellious and won't respond to punishment, confine him to areas of the house where there's nothing that can be destroyed.

NEUROTIC ROLES

The Vicious Dog

Dogs aren't born vicious unless they're mentally unbalanced. The vicious dog isn't necessarily a nervous or neurotic dog, usually his viciousness is a product of his early environment, just as bad dispositions are more often the result of early environment than heredity. Viciousness per se is rare; animal acts of violence are rare. It is not inborn for a dog to fight without provocation—to fight unless for his life, his mate, his young, his possessions, or his human family. Even German shepherds and Dobermans trained for guard duty or armed forces service have to be taught to attack, and some of them can't be induced to bite, regardless of training.

When dogs run in packs, they revert to the call of the wild and become vicious. Keep your dog from joining a pack. With security in numbers, dogs have much more bravado and will attack other animals and even people. They should be considered dangerous.

The Aggressive Dog

Some dogs are downright bullies. They bully other dogs in the neighborhood and at times will try to scare and push people around too. This comes from primitive times when their instinct would have been to become leader. There are usually several dog fights in the neighborhood before a leader is established. Sometimes the other fellow feels that he still should be leader, and the fighting goes on. For certain male dogs who fight constantly, I recommend castration; it takes away some of their aggressiveness.

The male is generally larger and stronger and usually more aggressive, owing in part to the stimulus of male hormones. Females given male hormones will begin fighting, and males who are castrated will become more peaceful and try to avoid fights. Male dogs seldom will attack female dogs, but there are exceptions; there are some quite ungentlemanly males. But the aggressive tendency in females is serious because spaying will not relieve it. Some females are vicious with other females. The only suggestion I have is confinement, or a muzzle when you let the female out. Muzzling somewhat slows up aggressiveness because of the obvious handicap in a fight.

Breaking Up a Dog Fight. When trying to part two fighting dogs, be extremely careful. Even though your dog loves you, in the heat of battle he may bite you severely. It is best to try to pull him off by his tail or by a rear leg; or if there's a broomstick or a pail of cold water handy, that may dampen the battlers' enthusiasm. Never, never put your hands near their heads or mouths.

The Tramp Dog

There are four main reasons why dogs run away from home: (1) The call of the wild—the search for a mate. (2) Boredom. There's not enough excitement or companionship at home. (3) Unhappiness. The dog doesn't feel wanted by his human family and will go elsewhere to find people who appreciate him more fully. Sometimes jealousy is an underlying factor. (4) Love for children. Dogs will seek out children because children usually will take more time to play with them than adults.

The tramp dog leaves home at the slightest provocation, and teams up with other dogs to become one of the pack, even for a few days. If his reason for wandering is sexual, or if he hears the call of the wild at certain times of the year, this can be quite normal. And the dog who leaves the house in the morning when everyone goes to work and school and then returns at the hour of their return is quite normally bored at being around the house by himself and goes out to seek adventure and playmates.

But there are neurotic dogs who are habitual wanderers. They will stay away from home for days at a stretch. Usually they leave home because they're lonely and are seeking the companionship of other dogs and humans.

In curing this habit you have to counteract the cause. If the dog is lonesome at home, you have to provide more companionship. You have to show him he's loved and wanted.

Just feeding him plenty of his favorite food won't keep him at home. In trying to correct a wandering dog, when he finally does return from a prolonged trip, don't punish him when he first comes to you; this will make him wander even more. He'll associate returning home with punishment, and his trips will be longer and longer. Treat him rather coolly. Then, after a few hours, he'll come to you. That is when you start giving him lots of affection, and some of his favorite food, to make him recognize the love he's missing when wandering.

Of course, during breeding season the sexual urge is strong. But there are some dogs who wander in search of females the year round. For these dogs I advise castration; it will incline them to stay home. Attitudes change, and without the sexual motive as their main concern in life, the dogs become wholly concerned with their human families.

The Chaser

Some dogs seem to have a compulsion to run after small children—barking at them but not biting or even intending to bite. Occasionally the child falls and hurts himself and is scared half to death. The more the child screams and the faster he runs, the more persistent the dog is in the chase.

The performance of your dog is your responsibility. You are legally subject to arrest and conviction for owning a dog who is a public nuisance. You must attempt to stop his habit at once.

Here, too, you must catch the dog at the beginning of the tendency. It's best for the young puppy to grow up with children so that they become fast friends. At the slightest suggestion of his chasing a child, even though the puppy is only 3 or 4 months old, he must be punished. Be strict with your dog. Keep close supervision over him. Don't allow him to run free. In training him not to run after children, take him out on a rope 30 to 50 feet long, and when he attempts to go after a child, jerk him back strongly so that it pulls him off his feet. You have to reprimand him sternly and punish him severely. Then you have to supervise the dog closely as children play with him, until he loses his desire to chase them.

Other Animals. The three commonest objects of a dog chase are poultry, sheep, and cats. This is a serious problem because once a dog is accustomed to killing other animals and gets the "taste of blood," it's difficult to rehabilitate him.

172

To him it's rare sport. He doesn't kill animals for food but rather for the thrill of the chase. He loves to see them run from him and to show his speed and dexterity with the subsequent kill.

Your dog is your personal property, and thus you are responsible for any damage that he may do, to either property or people.

If you intend to raise a puppy in the country where there are chickens or sheep, begin at an early age to get him used to walking among the poultry and animals. You should be with him at all times during his indoctrination period.

I've seen dogs chase horses and cows, and seen them receive a sharp hoof to the body or head while trying to nip at legs. I've seen large German shepherds kill young colts, and I've seen them kill calves. At this age it's difficult to rid them of the habit. I'd muzzle them or move them to the city.

There are many methods for curing the bloodthirsty habit. One method of curing a dog of chicken killing it to whip him over the head with the slain chicken and then tie the dead chicken around his neck until it practically rots off.

Another method is the use of a BB gun. When the animal walks among the chickens (or sheep) and gives the slightest growl or indication of viciousness, he receives a BB shot in his hide. Usually the owner is out of sight, and the animal doesn't know where the shot is from. However, he soon associates pain with his aggressive act.

Many dogs love to chase cats. If the cat would stand its ground, hiss and become ferocious, most dogs would stop short and think twice about attacking those sharp teeth and raking claws. In the main, tomcats and Siamese cats are a match for any dog and can handle themselves in any fight.

Your treatment should be about the same as with poultry and sheep. Severely punish your dog if he shows any tendency to chase cats. Of course, the best prevention is to have your puppy grow up with a kitten; they'll become the best of friends. Unfortunately, once a dog has the feeling for chasing and killing cats, the habit tends to persist.

Cars. Chasing cars is a sporting event for dogs, as it takes them back to primitive times when they chased game for their food. Nowadays chasing the big things on wheels is a substitute for the food-finding instinct. Also, it is possible that some of the dogs are trying to protect their neighborhoods from the monsters and that others, like the collie, are trying to herd them. Some breeds are worse offenders than others, and without a doubt the collie dog is the worst, but any breed is susceptible to the lure of the chase.

Most dogs are smart enough when chasing a car to stay right at the side of it, snapping and barking at the tires. However, occasionally there's a mishap and a good dog is killed. Numerous accidents have occurred because some motorists try to swerve or stop suddenly, with bad results to the human beings involved.

It's a habit that should be stopped if at all possible, but it's not an easy one to deal with. I've treated some dogs three and four times for being run over by an automobile. But the victims, as soon as the casts are off their legs, instead of being scared of cars, are off to the races again. Some dogs can be cured of the habit if the trainer is strict enough. There are several methods.

The most widely used method is to have a stranger in a strange car (dogs will not chase the cars in their family) drive by with a water pistol loaded with ammonia water (1 tsp. of household ammonia to a pint of water). The liquid is squirted into the dog's eyes and face as he approaches the car. This has to be repeated several times. The ammonia solution is strong enough to impress the dog with pain when he chases the car, but not strong enough to damage his eyes.

Another method is to get a friend who is a stranger to the dog drive by with a whip. As the dog approaches the car, he has to let him have it. Several sharp blows to the body should impress on him that there is pain associated with chasing cars.

A third method is to tie a piece of wood—a two-by-four—or an empty gallon tin can to the dog's neck so that when he attempts to run he trips over the wood or can. All these methods have to be repeated often until embedded in him mind.

The Biter

The biter is usually an animal who is aggressive. Some of these dogs are quite neurotic, and anything that moves in front of them—motorcycle, bicycle, running child—they will go after. It's almost like a game to them—like attacking an enemy. As the dog usually has his reasons for biting, we should attempt to get at the root of the problem and try to correct it. In most communities a dog is allowed three bites and after the third one is condemned to death.

The bad habit is sometimes brought about by excessive roughness when playing as a puppy. Some people do play too roughly with their puppies—teasing them with their hands and feet. As the dog gets older—his teeth larger and his jaws stronger—this play becomes more dangerous.

Biting should be corrected in the early stages before it's deeply ingrained in the dog's mind. Obedience training is helpful in that the dog will learn to follow your commands. The punishment for biting should be a sharp slap across the muzzle to show him that his mouth and the biting are what you are displeased with. Use either a newspaper or a leather strap, depending on the severity of the bite. Biting is a reprehensible habit and should be dealt with promptly and sternly.

Castration will slow down extremely aggressive male dogs. Although their motives for biting may not be entirely sexual, the operation takes away some of their male aggressiveness and they calm down to a walk. But castration will not help the neurotic dog who bites because he's panicky.

It is sometimes necessary to resort to a muzzle when turning the biting dog loose in the neighborhood. There are cities and towns where muzzling the at-large dog is required by law. I don't believe that muzzling is cruel to a dog. There are comfortable muzzles on the market; and sometimes a dog can be kept in the neighborhood who otherwise would have to be sent away or put to sleep.

Occasionally we get a dog who is incorrigible and can be classified as a canine criminal. No amount of training will correct his biting. If he's a large dog, such as a German shepherd or a Doberman, I advise military service if possible. Such dogs might also be used for guard duty in certain organizations. I certainly don't advise them as home pets; they're untrustworthy and the danger to children in the neighborhood is too great to take chances. These animals should either be given away to places in the country or, in some drastic cases, be put to sleep.

With the millions of dogs in the United States, there is the occasional criminal act of a dog attacking a human being. In my opinion this dog has flipped his lid—has become mentally unbalanced. If he were being defended in court, his attorney would plead that his act was committed during a fit of insanity. There is the age-old expression that the barking dog never bites. This is not so. If a dog is growling or barking at you, don't run from him. Stand your ground, and more often than

not he'll leave you. If you run from him, he'll likely take after you and attack.

The Barker

There are many neurotic dogs who love to bark; they're
enchanted with the sound of their own voices. The neurotic
apartment-type dog barks from loneliness and boredom. He
craves attention and wants everyone to know he's there. Every time he hears someone in the hall, or sees someone outside the window, he barks to let the world know that he's a
member of the family and also its protector. Every dog has
the protective instinct of the guard dog, even if he's not
trained for it.

The worst offender is the night barker. This dog usually
has slept all day and is coming alive when the master is ready
for bed. Sometimes a hard run before retiring will get the dog
too exhausted to bark. As for the other barkers, since dogs
bark because they're lonely and crave companionship, spend
as much time as possible with your pet when you're home.
Needless to say, the barking habit is best corrected in the
puppy before it becomes embedded. Here again sternness and
consistency are required. If your dog barks only when you're
away, sneak back to catch him at it and punish him so he'll
be able to associate his barking with disapproval. There are
comfortable muzzles which you can put on your dog to prevent him from barking. Muzzling is not a cure, but is an answer when it is imperative that he be quiet. Sometimes a dog
will associate the muzzle with punishment for his barking and
will be cured.

Female hormones given to adult male dogs eventually
reduce or even suppress excessive barking. The female hormones suppress the male hormones and reduce the aggressive
and territorial-defense barking. If the male is not desirable
for breeding purposes, I recommend castration as a permanent cure; it will quiet him down in many ways.

The Wetter or Dribbler

Most of these dogs are so neurotic and such a bundle of
nerves that they can't help wetting the floor. When you approach them, they wet the floor out of fear and apprehension.
Yelling at them makes matters worse, and they wet even
more.

In primitive days when an older dog pushed a younger dog around, the younger dog would usually wet as a sign of submission. He was plain scared of the larger and older animal.

It's not an easy neuroticism to correct. The dog has to first believe that you're not attempting to hurt him when you approach him. You have to fill this dog with kindness—be gentle and tender with him; bring him along slowly.

Of course, not all wetting is neurotic per se. There are some dogs who show such behavior out of pure orneriness or stubbornness; and some of it can be considered abnormal. They are completely housebroken dogs who wet curtains, floor, and furniture just to get even with their masters. Some male dogs wet the house and one another as part of the territorial instinct—to mark off their property.

Before you severely punish one of these dogs, you should have him examined for a kidney problem. With certain kidney diseases the dog can't control his urine. In older dogs prostatitis is common, and it gives the dog an uncontrollable urge to urinate often.

The House Nuisance

This is the neurotic dog who either has been neglected in training or has been allowed too much of his own way around the house. He's usually everywhere and in everyone's hair. He carries his food from room to room, sleeps where he pleases, takes over the best furniture and loves to lie in doorways. He jumps up on your guests with his dirty paws, and when they sit down he jumps into their laps and licks their faces. He is the dog who sits under the dining-room table at mealtime begging for food.

It is difficult to punish these sweet brats, but most of us have friends who find such behavior reprehensible. Should you have such a dog and decide to take things in hand, if he's out of puppyhood a lot of the dies have been cast, and stern and consistent discipline is the only cure.

A tip on jumping up on people: As the dog jumps up to you bring your knee up to meet his chest or chin. Several such clips with your knee should discourage the habit. Or step on his hind toes as he jumps. Usually light pressure will suffice.

In scolding him for jumping onto Aunt Phoebe's needle-point chair, I suggest you hit him lightly with a rolled-up newspaper or a bit of strap to make him associate the punishment with the crime. Then leave the disciplinary object in the chair; that will add emphasis and accessibility.

The Digger

In digging, dogs are reverting to primitive instincts; they're looking for a gopher or other hunted game, making themselves a place where they can lie down in the cool ground, burying a bone. Often they pick a spot near your favorite shrubbery.

It's a difficult habit to cure. Punishment at the scene of the crime may help in time. You have to wait until you catch the culprit in the act of digging. Then you can shout at him to stop and throw objects, such as tin cans, to scare him. If he leaves the scene of the crime, catch him by the collar and haul him back to the hole, reprimanding him by calling him "bad dog" and other well chosen words. At the same time give him a good shaking by the collar. Repeating this a time or two should cure him. Another method is to clip nails very close so digging hurts dog's paws.

The Timid-Shy Dog

A timid-shy dog is not necessarily a coward. He lacks confidence in himself because of a traumatic experience in puppyhood. The cowardly type will fight only in packs. If he's alone and sees another dog coming, he'll put his tail between his legs and go off. The cowardly dog is not necessarily a neurotic dog; the timid-shy dog usually is.

If the timid-shy dog isn't properly rehabilitated, he will be forever retiring and shy. You can't rush at him or approach him quickly, for in his fear he might bite you. In rehabilitating him, it takes patience and tender loving care to renew his confidence in you and the human race. In the female, if the shyness is not inherited, breeding her will sometimes help. Raising puppies may give her confidence.

Where the shyness is inherited it's doubtful whether you can train the dog to be an outgoing personality. You should teach him in a quiet voice with lots of praise and patting. Never make a sudden movement. Obedience training works well on these dogs if done gently.

The Runt of the Litter. Litter mates, sometimes with the

aid of their mother, will combine to persecute one individual in the litter. This usually occurs between the 9th and 10th weeks. Whenever the persecuted puppy tries to get back into the nest, the others continually harass it. This puppy will be timid-shy and undernourished, but can be rehabilitated.

The Overdependent Dog

The overdependent dog is the one who is reared as a perpetual puppy. There's a close emotional bond between this pet and its owner, and any disturbance in the daily routine will send the dog into a hysterical state.

The cause can be visitors, the absence of the owner from the house, or a visit to the veterinarian or boarding kennel. When they're severely disturbed, such dogs when left alone in a house over a long period may become destructive. Usually a babysitter is in order. If not a human babysitter, you might get another puppy or a kitten; even a TV set may help the dog's anxiety and depression. Such animals are good subjects for tranquilizers.

The Dope Fiend

There are some dogs who get hooked on certain narcotics or sedatives. They become dependent both on the drugs and on the attention they receive.

One of my patients became so used to getting phenobarbital for his twitching body (chorea, as a sequela to distemper) that every night at ten o'clock he sat up and begged for his pill. He wouldn't go to sleep without it. Finally, after months of barbiturates, we changed the pill to aspirin and he was completely satisfied—slept like a baby.

HOW TO HELP THE NEUROTIC DOG

Dogs respond to proper treatment, and it's up to each of us to find the proper way for his dog.

To fight excessive nervousness in a dog here are some good rules to follow:

—Don't give him many commands at once. Go slowly.

—Don't teach him more than he can comprehend in a 10- to 20-minute session.

—Be firm with him and make him understand that when you tell him to do something, he must do it or be punished.

—Give him plenty of companionship.

—Give him plenty of play and exercise.

—Allow him to be in the company of many strangers, preferably the children in the neighborhood. Most dogs are gentle with children.

TRANQUILIZERS

Tranquilizers play an important role in veterinary medicine and especially in handling and quieting nervous and neurotic dogs. But drugs are potent and should not be used without the advice of a professional.

Tranquilizers are useful in calming dogs fearful of storms, cars, firecrackers, and guns.

They are helpful with the bitch undergoing false pregnancy, to overcome her anxiety over the missing puppies; with the shy bitch, to overcome her fears of the male during mating; with the nervous bitch, when she is whelping and to overcome the possibility of refusal to nurse her puppies; and with the bitch who has been known to kill her puppies.

They are useful in the control of itching skin, in some coughs caused by irritation, in asthma, and in vomiting.

Tranquilizers are helpful when training animals, to overcome their neuroses. They calm the animal down to the point where he will listen to the owner or trainer.

They are also used by veterinarians for minor operations, such as surgery, eye treatment, teeth cleaning, and even grooming and clipping. And they are helpful to kennel owners when nervous pets are boarding at the kennel—barkers, finicky eaters, etcetera.

But tranquilizers are not a permanent cure for any neuroses. They are just in-between treatment until proper training and rehabilitation can be initiated. The causes of the neuroses should be delved for and dug out.

With the vicious dog, tranquilizers should be used with care and not be depended on entirely. Even in a moment, if the tranquilizer doesn't sedate the dog, or before it takes effect, he may perform a criminal act and hurt a child or a dog. Sometimes instead of helping him, the tranquilizer seems to mix him up even more and he becomes more unstable and more difficult to handle.

BRAIN SURGERY FOR THE VICIOUS DOG

Guard dogs retiring to home life and vicious dogs in need of rehabilitation can be helped by brain surgery. A prefrontal lobotomy, similar to that performed on human beings, has given consistently good results. The animal becomes timid and within a few weeks develops a desirable personality.

Part Four

THE AILING DOG

12 SYMPTOMS AND THEIR INTERPRETATION

Even though your dog will never learn to open the medicine cabinet to seek out an aspirin tablet or a laxative pill when he feels pain or constipation, and even though he cannot verbalize his wishes and fancies, he can communicate his needs, and especially when he's ailing. For the health and welfare and often the *life* of your pet, the slightest symptom out of the ordinary, the slightest deviation from any of his normal habits or any change in his appearance, should be carefully watched!

Early treatment of any ailment or disease is much easier and less traumatic for your dog. Early diagnosis is much easier and less traumatic for your dog. Early diagnosis by the veterinarian is helped considerably by your early recognition that your pet is not up to par.

Your dog's tail, the barometer of his feelings, is your principal guide to his well-being. No matter how badly he feels, he will *try* to wag it. And that trying can be worth a thousand words.

As you know your dog, his responses and his actions can tell you a great deal about the state of his health—a little less enthusiasm in his welcome, less nimbleness in his step, less anticipation for his dinner. . . .

This chapter discusses the various visual and other symptoms of illnesses, their interpretation, and their causes. Even though your dog can't say, "I have an awful earache," he shows you he has an earache by shaking his head persistently and by holding it to the side of the infected ear. By careful observation of the symptoms your dog displays you should be able to determine the next step for his welfare. It may be something simple that can easily be treated at home or can be watched at home for a few days. It may be something requiring early veterinary diagnosis and treatment. Or it may be an emergency requiring immediate professional care.

This chapter is meant not for diagnosis and treatment but to guide you in knowing when you should get your dog to your veterinarian. You should have as close a relationship with your veterinarian as with your family physician.

INDEX OF SYMPTOMS

185

Hair Loss (see Shedding)
Head Shaking
Head Swollen
Hives

Incoordination (see also Paralysis)

Jaundice (see Yellow)

Limping (see also Feet, Tender)
Lumps

Mouth, Frothing (see Frothing at the Mouth)
Mouth, Pale or Red (see Gums, Pale and Fiery Red)

Nose, Cold, Dry, Hot (see also Temperature Rise; Temperature Fall)
Nose, Running (see also Eyes, Running and Sneezing)

Odor (see also Bad Breath)
Overweight (see also Abdominal Enlargement; Bloat)

Panting (see also Breathing, Fast; Coughing)
Paraylsis (see also Incoordination)
Penis, Discharge from
Penis, Enlarged

Rectal Growths
Rubbing Rear along Ground
Rumbling or Noisy Intestines

Scratching
Shedding
Shivering and Trembling
Sneezing (see also Colds; Eyes, Running)
Snoring
Sores
Stiff-leggedness

Temperature Fall
Temperature Rise
Testicles, Enlarged
Thirst

Trembling (see Shivering and Trembling)
Twitching (see also Convulsions; Paralysis)

Underweight (see Weight Loss)
Urinary Abnormalities: Dribbling; Frequent Urination;
    Straining and Blood

Vaginal Discharge
Vomiting

Weight Loss
Wetting (see also Urinary Abnormalities)
Wheezing (see also Coughing)
Whining (see Crying and Whining)
Wobbling

Yellow (Jaundice)

INTERPRETATION

ABDOMEN TUCKED UP (*see also Back Hunched Up*)
This is a symptom in which the animal has a tucked-up belly and hunched-up back, and walks slowly and stiff-leggedly. It is due to abdominal pain which can be caused by constipation, foreign-body impaction, intestinal infection, or a severe case of worms.

ABDOMINAL ENLARGEMENT (*see also Bloat; Overweight*)
In the female, if the swelling is not pregnancy, it may be infection of the uterus (metritis), which causes the uterus to fill with pus, giving a bloated or pregnant look; or it may be dead puppies. Severe impactions from constipation—with a lot of gas forming from the putrefactive material—will bloat the dog. In gastric bloat there is severe and dangerous enlargement of the stomach. Tumors of the abdominal cavity can be another cause. In older dogs we sometimes see an enlargement of the abdomen due to a heart and kidney abnormality called dropsy; the abdominal cavity fills with fluid.

ABDOMINAL STRAINING
When your pet seems to be in distress, straining every few minutes while trying to have a bowel movement, the first thing to suspect is constipation. And the second cause may be diarrhea, making the animal strain because of the severe in-

187

testinal irritation. If the normal treatment for either of these symptoms doesn't give relief and the animal still strains, professional help is indicated, as the cause can be impaction with bones or some other foreign body or even possibly a tumor growing in the intestinal tract.

APPETITE, LACK OF

When an animal misses more than one meal, start looking for causes. It is a symptom which can have many causes, beginning with an emotional one—strangers, a visiting or new dog in the house, a new cat. It can also be caused by an infection, such as sore throat or tonsillitis. Worms will cause intermittent appetite. In the case of a bad tooth or a gum infection, the dog wants to eat but won't pick up food because of pain. In the acute stage of any disease appetite will be affected. As the temperature rises the dog begins to go off his normal routine. He will usually lack pep and sleep a lot. If he does go to his food, he will smell it and walk away. Occasionally a dog gets bored with one type of food. A variation in diet will often help; just a change in the brand of dog food, and the appetite may pick up.

APPETITE, PERVERTED

At times you may notice your pet eating rocks, dirt, feces, or other inedible materials. This perverted craving generally signifies a dietary deficiency of minerals or vitamins, usually caused by worms in the intestinal tract. Stool eating can be caused by an enzyme deficiency or may be only a bad habit. It is not unusual for an extremely nervous and high-strung dog to sometimes display a perverted appetite. Oftentimes boredom results in perversion, a resultant of confinement and insufficient exercise.

APPETITE, RAVENOUS

If your dog suddenly eats a lot more than normal, the cause may be internal parasites, such as worms. Some females during their heat period have an immense surge in appetite without pathological significance. A happy dog will eat more than an unhappy dog; hand-fed dogs tend to eat more than they need.

BACK HUNCHED UP

We usually see a dog in this position when he has abdominal pain. He walks laboriously, with his back hunched up and his abdomen tucked in. The condition is caused by kidney disease (nephritis), or in the female it can also be caused by metritis. It also manifests itself in any painful condition in the abdominal cavity, such as severe constipation, foreign-body impactions, diarrhea, and bladder infections.

In certain breeds that are more susceptible to spinal-disc lesions, such as the dachshund, any hunching of the back may indicate a spinal abnormality.

BAD BREATH (see also Odor)

The odor emanating from the dog's mouth can be putrid at times. It is caused most often by tartar on the teeth; it can also be caused by infected teeth and gums. There is also an infection of the lips (similar to trench mouth)—seen mostly in long-haired dogs—caused by fungus, which gives a bad odor. These conditions have to be treated because without proper care the animal will lose his teeth and be forced to eat chopped and homogenized food the rest of his life.

In severe kidney diseases the breath smells like urine; this signifies uremia. Various digestive disturbances can also cause a foul odor, from the stomach gases.

BEHAVIOR, CHANGE IN

Any deviation from a behavior pattern should be regarded with suspicion; there is always a cause. An animal's physical ill-being will usually affect his behavior. A significant early symptom of rabies is a change in behavior—the animal can either show an unusual overfriendliness or turn on you with extreme viciousness. Look for other symptoms and causes with any sudden personality change.

BLEEDING

This is a symptom that requires prompt action because any loss of blood can be critical. In all accident cases, to stop hemorrhaging is of primary importance.

The causative agents of bleeding from the rectum can be worms, foreign bodies, tumors, and poisoning.

Bleeding from the kidneys and the urinary tract signifies kidney or bladder stones, cystitis, or some other kidney infection.

Bleeding from the ear can mean either infection of the ear or brain concussion.

In bleeding from the mouth the blood can be coming from the stomach or the lungs. If it is from the stomach, it is usually mixed with stomach juices, and there will be vomiting. If the blood is frothy or bubbly, it can mean that there is hemorrhaging in the lungs and that drastic treatment is needed immediately.

Bleeding from the nostrils indicates a ruptured abscess in the sinus cavity, a tumor in the nasal passages, or an abscessed tooth.

In the female, bleeding from the vaginal tract means either her normal heat period or a female infection.

BLOAT (see also Abdominal Enlargement; Overweight)

Bloat is a serious ailment, and immediate professional care is necessary in order to save the animal. Luckily it is not common; and it occurs usually in the large breeds—Great Danes and St. Bernards most commonly. The earliest symptoms are extreme restlessness and swelling at the abdomen. The swelling is rapid and acute; the stomach will stretch to two or three times its normal size. It is an emergency condition, since the stomach may rupture. The cause of bloat is not known, although rapid gulping of large amounts of food and excessive exercise immediately after eating can be contributing factors.

BOWELS, LACK OF CONTROL OF (FECAL INCONTINENCE) (see also Diarrhea)

There are times when a dog can't control his bowel movements, much to his embarrassment. We see this condition in older animals because of a partial paralysis of the nerves controlling the rectal muscles. It also occurs following a cerebral hemorrhage; an automobile accident where the spine or the anal ring has been damaged; or a dog fight where the anal ring has been injured, bitten or badly torn. Tumors inside the rectum can also produce fecal incontinence.

BREATHING, FAST (see also Coughing; Panting)

The dog's normal respiratory rate is 12 to 30 per minute while at rest. Any time there is an increase in respiration at rest, some abnormality is indicated. Of course, after exercise or excitement a dog can breathe rapidly, 60 to 90 per minute, without pathological significance. Persistent fast breathing while at rest, when accompanied by rapid, weak pulse and dilated pupils, means the dog is in shock. Fast breathing is present in pneumonia and in a ruptured diaphragm, which is a hernia caused by an injury—usually an automobile accident or a severe blow to the midsection. It is present in the early stages of some poisonings.

BREATHING, SLOW
A lessening in the rate of respiration is found in narcotic poisoning, diseases of the brain, and in later stages of infectious diseases.

COLDS (*see also Eyes, Running*)
Although there is no conclusive evidence or scientific proof that there is a correlation between the human head cold and the canine cold, often the dog will come down with a running nose, red and running eyes, red throat, and fever. Just as the symptoms are similar to those in humans, so is the treatment.

CONSTIPATION
Normally a dog will have at least one bowel movement for each meal that he eats. The average adult dog will have 1 or 2 movements a day. Puppies who eat 3 or 4 times a day will usually have that many bowel movements. If a dog goes over 24 hours without a bowel movement, we classify this as constipation.

Simple causes of constipation are lack of exercise and unbalanced diet (too much meat and not enough vegetables or roughage). Too many bones can cause constipation; or they can become impacted, as can other foreign bodies, and cause serious constipation. Another cause is infected anal glands. In older male dogs enlargement of the prostate (prostatitis) tends to obstruct the rectum and cause constipation. In long-haired dogs there can be blockage at the anus due to matted hair.

CONVULSIONS (*see also Fits; Frothing at the Mouth*)
Convulsions are a condition of generalized, severe, spasmodic jerkings of the entire body. While having these seizures, the animal is usually semi-conscious or in severe cases completely unconscious. The convulsions usually last from 2 or 3 minutes to 10 minutes, with periods of quiescence in-between. Other symptoms include "chewing gum fits" (rapid chomping of the jaws), lying on one side with the mouth twitching rapidly, and the feet moving as if running. When the animal comes out of the convulsive attack, he usually staggers for 10 or 15 minutes and appears blind—walking into objects and snapping at anything that comes near him.

Convulsions have many causes. The foremost is distemper. Certain brain diseases cause convulsions—some types of brain tumors and epilepsy. Dogs with very high fevers can go into convulsions, and sunstroke can be included in this category. Poisons are another cause, the most notable being strychnine, which is very quick-acting and sends the victim into a severe and prolonged type of convulsion. The heartworm and the hookworm, in their migration through the blood stream, may end up in the cerebral vessels, produce pressure on the brain, and then convulsions. Eclampsia, in nursing bitches, can cause severe convulsions. Overexcitement or apoplexy, in some extreme cases, can cause convulsions.

COUGHING (*see also Wheezing*)

Coughing is a symptom of a respiratory affliction. It can be symptomatic of something as simple as a too-tight collar pressing on the windpipe or something as serious as a severe lung infection. Of the variety of causes of coughing, one of the mildest is laryngitis. Tonsillitis is also a common cause. The cough in these ailments—a dry, hacking one—is intensified by exercise and excitement. The lower down the infection is, the deeper the cough. Tracheo-bronchitis, an infection of the lower respiratory tract, is accompanied by a deep cough which is productive of a white frothy matter from the bronchial tubes. If not treated it can go into pneumonia or pleurisy, and the deep cough will be accompanied by labored breathing. Coughing can also be symptomatic of distemper, heartworms, and such other worms as hookworms, roundworms, and whipworms. Lung tumors will produce a cough, as will chronic sinus infection (sinusitis). Dogs can have, but not commonly, tuberculosis, with its typical hacking cough. If a dog swallows a foreign object, it can end up penetrating the esophagus wall and pressing on the windpipe. This causes a cough of emergency proportions.

CRYING AND WHINING

When a dog cries or whines, it means pain which shouldn't be ignored. In puppies it is usually colic. Any digestive disturbance will result in crying. But it can be caused by many painful abnormalities.

DEAFNESS

Deafness is often seen in older dogs as the nerve controlling hearing degenerates. Excessive wax in the ear canal will partially block hearing. Some puppies are born deaf; this occurs most often in the Dalmatian. Usually congenital deafness is seen in white dogs.

DIARRHEA

In this condition the bowel movements are loose, varying in color from light tan to dark brown to a black, tarry mass. The color of the stool often tells the cause of the dysfunction. In many diseases, such as distemper, hepatitis, and leptospirosis, diarrhea is but one of the symptoms. In chronic tonsillitis the swallowed discharge seems to infect the intestines and cause diarrhea. In simple diarrhea, although the movements are watery and loose, they have their normal color. This simple diarrhea can be caused by such things as overeating, a sudden change in diet, or an emotional disturbance. But a change in stool color is usually symptomatic of a more serious condition. A black, tarry mass most often means the presence of blood in the upper intestinal tract, while bright-colored blood in the feces means bleeding in the lower intestinal tract. There is also a bloody mucous stool which usually signifies extreme irritation in the upper or lower intestinal tract or both. These bloody stools can be caused by an infection, by certain poisons, by sharp foreign bodies, and by worms; hookworms and whipworms are the most common culprits, then roundworms and tapeworms. Coccidiosis, strongyles, and giardia—protozoan-type parasites—also cause bloody, mucous stools. Overeating of bones sometimes gives a white or light-colored stool. Black stools can be caused by iron in such foods as liver.

DROOLING

When we notice our pet salivating excessively, we should immediately look into his mouth for one of several causes. A foreign body such as a bone or a wood splinter may be causing irritation, or an infected tooth or gum infection may be involved. Nausea from an irritated stomach also can cause excessive salivation.

EAR-FLAP ENLARGEMENT

This can vary in size from a dime to a grapefruit. Called a hematoma (a cyst filled with blood), it is the result of a ruptured blood vessel in the ear flap. Usually it is due to an injury to the ear or is brought about by excessive head shaking or scratching. It can also be caused by ear-mite infestation, or a bee, insect, or snake bite, and will be aggravated by head shaking.

EYES, BLINKING
The eye is a sensitive organ, and excessive blinking usually means pain caused by a foreign body, an ulcer, a scratch on the cornea, an abscess or sty on the eyelid, or the simple irritation of dust in the eye.

EYES, COLOR CHANGE
When the normal color of the eye turns to a grayish or bluish white, this signifies an infection or inflammation of the outer covering of the eye (the cornea). It can also be diagnostic, along with other symptoms, of hepatitis.

EYES, RED
Sometimes identified as "pink eye," this condition, called conjunctivitis, is an inflammation and infection of the conjunctiva, or covering of the eyelid. It can be caused by dirt and dust or by a bacterial infection.

EYES, RUNNING (see also Colds; Sneezing)
There is normally a small amount of a clear-looking discharge in the eyes. When the discharge becomes a yellowish matter which gathers in the corners of the eyes, there is some abnormality which may be caused by a foreign body or some type of infection.

Any slight irritation of the eye caused by dust, dirt, extremely cold air, etcetera, will produce watering. This secretion will go down the tear duct into the nasal passages, producing a nasal discharge with subsequent sneezing. If the tear duct becomes clogged, the discharge from the eyes will spill over the side of the face and cause staining of the hair and skin.

FEET, TENDER (see also Limping)
When your pet holds up his paws or walks gingerly, look for trouble on the bottom of his pads. There may be a fungus infection, an embedded foreign body, a wound, or even too-long nails. Some dogs have thin pads, and even severe exercise can produce bleeding and irritation.

FITS (see also Convulsions; Frothing at the Mouth)
A fit is not quite so severe as a convulsion. In "running

fits" (hysteria), the dog appears very nervous; he looks every which way frantically and runs blindly—bumping into things, barking and yipping. He may be calmed down by talking to him quietly and soothingly; the symptoms will gradually subside. Running fits can be caused by a heavy infestation of worms producing cramps and pain in the intestinal tract or depriving the body of normal nutrients, especially minerals and calcium. Some white breads and biscuits will cause fits when self-rising flours trigger cramp-like pains in the stomach. Fits sometimes occur in puppies when they are cutting their teeth and the blood calcium level drops. The other type of fit is similar to apoplexy in the human, and can happen in excitable dogs. They appear to just crack up; they take off in circles for no apparent reason. They are best left alone to calm down by themselves, as they tend to bite. When such a dog is back to normal, it is wise to seek professional help to prevent recurrence.

FROTHING AT THE MOUTH (see also Drooling; Fits; Convulsions)

Unfortunately the first thing many people think of when they see a dog frothing at the mouth is that it has rabies and has gone mad. This is an age-old fallacy, and countless wonderful dogs have been wrongfully destroyed. A simple irritation of the mouth caused by eating something distasteful, or cuts, foreign bodies, and bruises, can cause frothing. A simple upset stomach can cause excessive salivation and frothing. Teething puppies, with their sore and tender gums, will often drool and froth at the mouth. Encephalitis and post-distemper fits can cause frothing. If the dog shows other signs of illness along with the frothing, professional help should be sought immediately.

GAS (FLATULENCE)

Excessive gas is usually caused by a digestive disturbance in the alimentary tract, generally from improper diet or from scavenging. A diet composed exclusively of meat, without enough roughage, can cause this condition, as well as certain types of food, such as hard-boiled eggs, cabbage, cauliflower, turnips, onions, and certain brands of dog foods. The breed most commonly afflicted with this embarrassing condition is the boxer. High-strung animals also have the problem. As dogs get older you can expect more digestive disorders and more interference with assimilation of certain foods, and they will pass more wind.

GUMS, FIERY RED
When the normal gum color becomes fiery red, it usually signifies a gum infection. The gums are swollen and bleed easily. The condition should be treated as soon as possible; neglect can result in the teeth's becoming loose, with premature loss.

GUMS, PALE
When the gums look pale—whitish or grayish—anemia is indicated. The foremost cause of anemia is worms; parasites such as hookworms feed on the blood. Other causes of pale gums are disease, malignant tumors, and blood loss in the intestinal cavity from foreign bodies or poisoning.

HEAD SHAKING
This symptom indicates ear distress. The dog also scratches at his ear and cries with pain when he hits a tender spot. In the beginning the head shaking is mild, but as the infection progresses the dog walks with his head tilted on the same side as the ear infection. Ear infection can be caused by ear mites, bacteria, or fungi, and all three can occur at the same time. Parasites such as fleas and ticks can work their way into the ear canal; also an assortment of foreign bodies stuck into dogs' ears by children. Because of the proximity of the brain, if the infection is allowed to progress to the middle ear or inner ear the consequences can be severe, with high fever and convulsions. Head shaking can also be caused by fly infection at the tip of a dog's ear, especially an upright ear.

HEAD, SWOLLEN
It is disturbing to see one's pet with part or all of his head swollen to an astonishing size. Sometimes the eyes are swollen shut. The condition can be caused by several things, the most common being an allergy similar to hives in humans and brought about by the dog's eating something that doesn't agree with him—generally from a garbage can, or table scraps given as a treat. Crab and lobster meat seem to be especially common culprits.

HIVES
These are bumps on the dog's body, most often on the

head. The bumps are accompanied by intense itching, and the cause is usually, as in humans, an allergic response to food or drink. Occasionally an anaphylactic reaction to an injected drug or vaccine is responsible.

INCOORDINATION (*see also Paralysis*)

This is any deviation from the normal gait of the animal. Sometimes he will hold his head to one side and walk in circles. It can be caused by a head injury, a brain injury, an inner ear infection, or a brain tumor.

LIMPING (*see also Feet, Tender*)

When a dog begins to limp, there are several possible causes. The most likely cause, and the first thing the dog should be examined for, is an injury to the pad of his foot involving a foreign body such as glass, metal, or wood splinters. Although the pad has a tough covering, it is not invulnerable.

Sometimes cockleburs and matted hair balls are found between the toes, causing lameness.

Dislocations, sprains, and fractures are common causes of limping. In a simple sprain the symptoms should abate in a day or two. With a fracture the symptoms will depend on the severity of the break—whether it is a simple hairline crack in the bone or a compound fracture with pieces of bone penetrating the skin.

Dislocations and fractures can occur even in the toes—fracture and phalangeal dislocation. In each toe there are three phalanges—three parts, three bones. Sometimes a running dog will take a wrong step, stumble, or step into a hole and one of these tiny bones will fracture or dislocate, causing a lameness.

Bursitis, arthritis, and rheumatism can also be responsible for limping. In bursitis and arthritis the joints usually get quite feverish. Rheumatism is often seen in middle-aged and older dogs, and on cold, damp days the signs are more pronounced.

Congenital hip dysplasia, which is a malformation of the bone socket in the hip, causes a painful lameness. However, dysplasia is not confined to the hip and can cause lameness in any joint of the body, including shoulder and elbow. Bone infections can cause lameness and are usually the result of injuries, bite wounds, or gunshot wounds. Rarely, limping can be caused by bone tumors. In the puppy rickets can cause limping. It is a bone disorder due to a nutritional deficiency of the vitamin D, calcium, and phosphorus necessary for the growth stage. In the fast-growing breeds, such as the Great Dane, a puppy can develop rickets in 3 to 5 days on a poor diet. When you see a puppy with bent legs or with his toes spread out loosely, it means that he doesn't have enough solid bone formation.

A good rule of thumb for limping is that if the symptom continues more than 24 hours, or if the limping steadily worsens, medical care is indicated.

LUMPS

Most growths are soft hairless "lumps" in the skin, and are usually seen in dogs over the age of 6. They vary in size from a pea to a walnut. Some people refer to them as "old-age tumors." They are generally benign but occasionally show signs of malignancy, as in mast-cell tumors. These are seen most often in boxers and Boston terriers.

Another type of lump can be a sebaceous cyst. In appearance and size is is similar to the tumor, but it contains a cheesy substance. At times the cysts rupture and then begin to fill up again. The breeds most commonly affected are Norwegian elkhound and Kerry blue terrier.

Any lump on the body should be attended to as soon as an increase in size is noted. Fast removal of tumors can save your pet's life.

NOSE, COLD, DRY, HOT (see also Temperature Fall; Temperature Rise)

Although the dog normally has a moist nose, a dry nose doesn't necessarily mean a sick dog. Nor does a hot nose necessarily mean a fever. I've seen dogs with cold noses and temperatures at 105 degrees. This is one of the commonest fallacies about dogs—that a cold nose is normal and a hot nose means fever. The condition of the nose can vary with the temperature and humidity inside the house and the climate outside.

NOSE, RUNNING (NASAL DISCHARGE) (See also Eyes, Running; Sneezing)

A clear watery discharge from the nostrils is not necessarily significant, and can be normal. If the discharge is excessive or turns to a thick mucous or yellow puslike secretion, there is infection present. A running nose, with purulent matter, is a symptom in distemper and pneumonia.

Any eye irritation or infection is accompanied by nasal discharge because the eye drains down the tear duct into the nostril.

Sinus infections can cause a running nose. Also, the sinuses can become clogged, infected (sinusitis), or abscessed (caused by an infected tooth).

Nasal tumors—cancers of the frontal sinuses—are fairly common. Also, a nasal worm occasionally gets into the frontal sinuses.

Foreign bodies are another cause of nasal discharge. I have removed all kinds of objects, including pieces of straw, wood, and even needles.

ODOR ("D.O.") (see also Bad Breath) . .

An unpleasant odor emanating from the dog's body can be due to several causes, and sometimes a tentative diagnosis can be made just from the odor. Among skin diseases, seborrhea has a typical rancid odor; sarcoptic mange has a typical musty odor. Some ear infections give a putrid odor. An anal-gland infection can give a discharge which has a distinctive odor synonymous with the anal glands' being called skunk glands.

OVERWEIGHT (see also Abdominal Enlargement; Bloat)

Lack of exercise is a major cause of obesity in dogs. In spayed and castrated animals the lack of hormones sometimes causes obesity. With a hypoactive—underactive—thyroid the dog is listless and rapidly gains excessive weight. If an older dog has an extreme gain in weight, it may be fluids collecting in the body, due to congestive heart failure or inadequate kidney function.

PANTING (see also Breathing, Fast; Coughing)

Normally a dog pants after exercise, and in hot weather, since this is one of the only two ways he has of perspiring (the other is through the pads of his feet). Some breeds—those with short heads, such as bulldog, Boston terrier, and Pekingese—normally pant more than others.

Excessive panting is usually a sign of an abnormality. In such pathological conditions as fever, lung disease, and heart disease there is excessive panting, and also a blueness or paleness to the tongue if not enough oxygen is reaching the lungs.

199

PARALYSIS (*see also Incoordination*)

Usually paralysis starts in the rear legs, and the animal drags himself, unable to walk. It is generally caused by disease or an injury to the brain or spinal cord. There is also paralysis with a slipped spinal disc and more seriously with a ruptured disc. The symptoms come on gradually, starting with slight incoordination in the rear legs, reluctance to move, an arched back, and pain when the back is touched.

Tetanus, or lockjaw, can cause paralysis or stiffening of the body. It is a rare disease in dogs and is usually caused by a puncture or wound infected with the tetanus germ.

An injury to the nerves of the front leg can cause a paralysis, and the dog will drag his toes. This, called radial paralysis, is usually seen after an automobile accident. Tick paralysis is a completely generalized paralysis caused by tick infestation. A single tick which attaches itself to the skin over the spinal cord can be responsible for the paralysis.

PENIS, DISCHARGE FROM

In adolescent males a slight yellowish discharge—a secretion from the prostate gland—is normal. When this discharge increases and thickens, with a foul odor, it usually signifies infection of the glands at the base of the penis.

Dripping blood from the penis requires close scrutiny to determine if the blood is coming from inside the penis—through the urethra—or is external. Inside, it generally means infection or stones in the bladder or kidney. Outside, it usually means an injury—a bite or a foreign body embedded in the sheath.

PENIS, ENLARGED

Occasionally a dog cannot retract his penis into the sheath because of its enlarged and inflamed condition, caused by sexual intercourse or other excitement. If the penis stays exposed for a long time without moisture, it becomes infected. This condition requires professional help. Also, when the dog gets excited, either emotionally or sexually, a large knot appears between the penis and the testicles. It is transitory and will usually subside when the animal quiets down.

RECTAL GROWTHS

Occasionally tumors are seen growing on the outside of the anus. Male dogs are more prone to this condition than females. As the tumors are usually malignant, they should be treated immediately.

There is a condition, called prolapse of the rectum, in which a large mass protrudes from the anus. It is usually caused by a severe case of diarrhea where there is continuous straining.

Rubbing Rear along Ground
When an animal drags his rear along the ground, it doesn't always mean worms, as many people think. Ninety percent of the time infected anal glands are the cause. Certain types of worms can be the cause, notably the tapeworm. Segments of the tapeworm will often crawl out of the anus, and the dog will scoot himself along the ground to relieve the irritation.

Rumbling or Noisy Intestines
When the dog's intestinal tract carries on a rumbling and growling, it is usually due to some intestinal upset. Infection can be the cause; or chronic colitis can bring on the noisy spells. If the dog apparently is not sick and the attacks are only intermittent, the cause can be worms.

Scratching
Discern which area the dog is concentrating his scratching on. External parasites—fleas and lice—are the commonest skin irritants. Skin diseases are also a common cause—eczemas, dry skin—and can be brought on by many things, including too much bathing with harsh soaps, inadequate diet, and allergies. Scratching is also associated with any skin lesion.

Shedding
Normally dogs shed twice a year, in the spring and in the fall, when they're changing their coats. Some dogs who live in warm houses shed profusely the year round because the heat dries out their skin and hair. Excessive bathing with strong soaps can cause abnormal shedding. So can worm infestation. In high fevers, during disease, the animal will begin losing his hair, and the shedding will continue after recovery. Dogs can shed after any severe traumatic or emotional experience.

Shivering and Trembling
Most often shivering and trembling mean that the dog has a fever. Almost any type of ailment that causes a fever brings

on shivering and trembling. Certain types of poisons, both external and internal, cause a nervous reaction and trembling. Insecticide powders, lawn sprays, and fertilizers cause toxic reactions. A nursing bitch can show signs of trembling and shaking in the early stages of eclampsia.

SNEEZING (*see also Colds; Eyes, Running*)
The dog will have spasmodic sneezing when trying to rid his nostrils and sinus passages of certain secretions. Allergies are a common cause of sneezing: in spring, plant pollens, and in the house, dust and wool rugs, are culprits. Drainage from an eye infection will cause the dog to sneeze. So will infections of the sinuses.

SNORING
Snoring is normal in dogs, as in humans. It is especially prevalent in the short-nosed breeds—bulldog, Boston terrier, Pekingese—because of the large size of the soft palate. If breathing is difficult, surgery may be necessary.

SORES
Sores can appear on any part of the body, and the word describes a multitude of infections. They can be caused by insect bites, bites from lice, fleas, ticks, eczemas, and other skin infections, such as ringworm.

Sometimes self-mutilation will greatly magnify a simple sore. The old saying that a dog's tongue can heal his wounds is not quite correct. Although a dog can keep a wound clean by licking it, he can also mutilate it badly by biting and scratching it.

STIFF-LEGGEDNESS
In male dogs stiff-leggedness is usually caused by an injured testicle or an enlarged prostate gland. We also see stiff-leggedness in arthritic or rheumatic older dogs.

TEMPERATURE FALL
Any temperature reading under 100 degrees should be considered abnormal. When the temperature begins to drop, the body is weakening, and emergency measures should be taken immediately. The exception is the whelping bitch, who gives fair notice of the blessed event when her temperature drops under 100 degrees twenty-four hours before delivery of her first puppy.

Temperature Rise

The normal body temperature of dogs is 100 to 101 degrees. In young dogs the temperature may go up to 102 degrees without cause for alarm. In the adult dog temperatures ranging from 101 to 102 degrees aren't necessarily disturbing, since there can be variation with room temperature, exercise, and excitement in the veterinarian's office. But anything over 102 degrees should be considered abnormal. Although the insides of the ears and thighs indicate if there is a fever, the best way of telling a dog's temperature is with a rectal thermometer. The temperature is a sensitive indicator of the normal or abnormal metabolism of the body. In any infection and in many diseases there is usually a temperature rise in the early stages.

Testicles, Enlarged

When a male dog jumps over fences or other objects and the scrotum or testicles are injured, there can be severe swelling with pain and stiff-leggedness. If the swelling continues, in either or both testicles, inflammation develops which requires professional treatment. An enlargement can also mean a tumorous growth of the testicle.

Thirst

Dogs normally drink more water in hot weather and after exercise. But at any time any dramatic increase in water consumption is a danger signal. Excessive thirst is a symptom of some kidney diseases, one type of diabetes, and fever. With any inflammation of the stomach, such as gastritis, the dog will try to drink water but will vomit it immediately. In all cases of extreme thirst your veterinarian should be consulted as quickly as possible.

Twitching (*see also Convulsions; Paralysis*)

This nervous disorder, called chorea, is a twitching of the muscles similar to St. Vitus's dance in humans. The commonest cause is a disease like distemper, and it manifests itself after the animal has seemingly recovered from the disease. The twitching starts off mildly, in almost any part of the body (but most likely leg, head, jaw), and gradually worsens, increasing in severity.

Urinary Abnormalities

Dribbling Urine. This is common in the spayed female as

she approaches middle or old age and is due to a female-hormone deficiency. In older dogs, male and female, there is a relaxing of the muscle tone in the bladder and the urethra, and consequent leaking, over which the animal has no control. Whenever a completely housebroken dog starts urinating in the house, there is a medical or psychological cause. Most of the time a urinary-tract infection is involved. Some animals do it out of spite or jealousy and develop a psychosomatic urinary-tract infection.

Frequent Urination. Several urinary disorders can be involved in this symptom. It can signify an inflammation of the bladder known as cystitis; because of a burning sensation the animal feels the need to urinate often; and sometimes there will be no urine. After a prolonged attack there is blood from the irritation to the lining of the bladder wall. The animal is in extreme pain and usually walks with a hunched-up back and cries when palpated (touched). It is seen more often in females and is sometimes caused by getting wet and chilled and lying in damp places.

Straining and Blood. This is the opposite of the dribbling syndrome. The animal does a lot of straining, and pain is evident. Only a few drops of urine appear, usually accompanied by blood. This is a symptom of bladder or kidney stones.

VAGINAL DISCHARGE

The normal vaginal discharge, which is bright red, occurs the first week or 10 days of the heat period (estrus). The discharge turns paler and finally colorless as the time for breeding is attained. After whelping, for several days there is a normal discharge from bright red to brown in color.

However, if after whelping the normal color turns to either a purulent or black or greenish color, this is always a danger symptom of infection, retained afterbirth, or a dead puppy. A red discharge when the bitch is not in heat can signify a false heat (cystic ovaries) or tumors in the uterus or the vaginal tract. If the reddish discharge is followed by a large mass protruding from the vagina, the animal has prolapse of the uterus. This is caused by a breakdown of the musculature of the vagina and uterus either from undue straining or from tumors.

If the bitch is not in heat but the males in the area seem to think she is, this usually indicates the presence of an infection in the uterus called metritis. It can occur at any age but is more prevalent in middle-aged and old dogs. In an acute attack the animal is obviously sick; she has a high temperature, and has a hunched-up back or will stay in a curled-up position and not want to move.

VOMITING

Vomiting commonly occurs in all dogs and is due to many varieties of ailments and diseases, from simple to serious. The dog vomits frequently because he can regurgitate at will. We often see our pet eating grass and then vomiting. This is his way of relieving his indigestion. We also see dogs regurgitating food immediately after eating it and then eating the vomited mass. It's not a pretty sight, but it's their way of predigesting their food. Often a mother will regurgitate her food so that her puppies can eat it—softened and homogenized. Occasionally a dog will vomit in the morning before he has eaten any food. It's a yellow, frothy mass, like beaten egg yolk. Generally this means simply that he is hungry and empty; the yellow mass is bile. If the vomiting is persistent, though, examination is needed for a more serious cause.

Breeds with short heads—bulldog, Boston terrier, Pekingese—are very susceptible to vomiting; the slightest excitement may provoke it. The ailments that cause vomiting include:

—Brain injuries.

—Car sickness.

—Constipation or impaction.

—Constricted stomach (pyloric stenosis). This occurs in puppies and is characterized my vomiting shortly after eating. After persistent vomiting the puppy gets weak and dehydrated.

—Diseases. Among them are distemper, hepatitis, leptospirosis, metritis, nephritis, and pancreatitis.

—Emotionalism (psychogenic vomiting). Highly nervous dogs often vomit when they get excited. Dogs have been known to vomit when they're jealous or want attention. They are usually dogs who are overindulged and undertrained. Tranquilizers work very well on this type of psychosomatic problem.

—Fatigue. Caused by strenuous play and exercise after eating.

—Foreign bodies.

—Gastritis. Caused by eating spoiled, greasy, fried foods or by overeating improper food or too many bones.

—Intestinal infections in enteritis.

—Obstruction or interception of the bowels. This is caused by a twisting of the intestines, and the symptoms are acute. The animal is in severe pain, and your veterinarian is needed immediately.

—Overheating.

—Poisons. The symptoms are severe—fast breathing, twitching, severe cramps, diarrhea sometimes with blood—and immediate emergency treatment is necessary.

—Prostatitis; tonsillitis; worms.

WEIGHT LOSS

Along with loss of weight, the animal usually becomes rough-coated, and begins to lose his hair. Loss of weight is serious, and the cause must be ascertained as soon as possible. As the dog loses weight he will likely develop anemia; he will be tired and listless. The first thing to be suspicious of is one of the following diseases: diabetes, distemper, hepatitis, leptospirosis, nephritis.

In diarrhea of any extent there is loss in weight; if this persists, the cause of the diarrhea must be discovered.

Other causes of weight loss:

—Chronic colitis. This is a persistent and intermittent diarrhea from a variety of causes. The animal is not assimilating his food properly, so that part of what he is eating is being wasted—passing through his body undigested.

—Chronic tonsillitis. This condition keeps the animal from eating properly.

—Dental problems. Because of an abnormality—abscessed tooth, loose tooth or teeth, gum infection, etc.—the dog can't eat properly.

—Emotional disturbances. Can cause "hunger strikes." Excitable animals often exert so much energy running and jumping that their weight stays at a minimum.

—External parasites. Animals become emaciated when heavily infested with ticks, fleas, lice, from the parasites' feeding on their blood.

—Inadequate diet; malignant tumors; intestinal worms.

WETTING (*see also Urinary Abnormalities*)

Many dogs, especially puppies, when they get excited will have an involuntary urination. For older dogs see Urinary Abnormalities: Dribbling Urine.

WHEEZING (*see also Coughing*)

This is almost like an asthmatic condition in humans. The wheeze is a sound made on inspiration, while the cough is made on expiration. Wheezing is caused by allergies or bronchial diseases. Short-nosed dogs such as Bostons, boxers, pugs and bulldogs are more susceptible to this condition.

WOBBLING

This is known as the "wobbler syndrome" because the dog walks in an uncoordinated, wobbling fashion. It is caused by narrowing of vertebrae in the spinal canal. It is painful, and results in eventual paralysis. It is seen in the large breeds, especially the Great Dane and Doberman Pinscher. Surgery—a dorsal laminectomy—relieves the pressure and the results are usually gratifying.

YELLOW (*Jaundice*)

When the animal appears yellow—skin, membranes of the eyes, mouth—it is a serious symptom. It signifies a dysfunction of the liver and can also mean an obstruction in the bile duct due to stones or growths. It is seen in hepatitis and leptospirosis. Certain poisons can affect the liver so that the animal shows up with jaundice. An overdose of worm medicine can affect the liver. For jaundice quick professional care is recommended.

13 FIRST AID IN EMERGENCIES

THE MEDICINE CHEST

A medicine chest is essential for every dog owner. There are many times when drugs are needed for minor ailments or until your veterinarian can be reached in an emergency. I advise discussing the matter with your veterinarian; he will be pleased to tell you what preparations to stock. The following can serve as a basic guide:

absorbent cotton
adhesive tape
cotton swabs
enema tubes: Fleet (disposable)
gauze bandage
nail clippers
rectal thermometer
scissors

alcohol
ammonia, aromatic spirits of
aspirin
boric acid
calamine lotion
  (for skin lesions)
camphorated oil
charcoal (activated) for
  poisoning
disinfectant (such as Lysol
  or Clorox)
Epsom salts (to soak minor
  infections)
hydrogen peroxide
iodine
Kaopectate
Metaphen or Mercurochrome
milk of magnesia
mineral oil
paregoric (for pain or
  diarrhea)
shock formula
soap (germicidal, such as
  tincture of green soap or
  Phisohex)
styptic powder (to stop bleeding)
talcum powder, medicated
vaseline

STEPS IN
FIRST AID TO AN INJURED ANIMAL

Hurt animals are usually frightened and confused. Even normally friendly ones may bite and scratch the person attempting to help; so keep your safety in mind. Here are a few points to be followed when aiding an injured animal:

1. Move slowly, speaking in a quiet voice.
2. Restrain the animal with a loose rope around his neck.
3. To prevent biting, muzzle the animal.
4. To control bleeding, use a pressure bandage.
5. Cover the animal with a blanket or coat to keep it warm.
6. Call a veterinarian for further instructions.

To Move an Injured Animal:

1. Spread a coat or blanket along and under the spine.
2. Gently put the animal on the blanket.
3. Holding the corners of the blanket, carry it as you would a stretcher.

THE AUTOMOBILE ACCIDENT

Since being hit by a moving vehicle is the most common of all emergency situations, I shall use it to illustrate the "steps in first aid to an injured animal."

The main concern following an automobile accident must be the presence of shock and internal injuries. Broken legs and external injuries are relatively unimportant in the beginning. Saving the life of the animal comes first. X rays and broken bones can be taken care of afterward.

When a dog is hit and you rush to him, be careful because in his pain he might bite you, even though he would never do so if completely conscious or normal. In his delirious thrashing about he can possibly hurt you.

Approach him cautiously, and before you put your hands on him, try to assess his injuries. It is best to put a muzzle over and under his mouth and behind his ears (handkerchief, necktie, or soft rope will do).

If a leg is broken, apply a temporary splint (stick or any straight object), wrapping it with a towel or cloth so that the leg is kept motionless. Excessive movement of broken limbs can cause tearing, further bleeding, and blood clots.

The next thing is to put a blanket or coat over the dog. Keeping the animal warm is imperative because shock almost always accompanies severe injuries. Usually the blood pressure drops, and if there's any loss of blood the body temperature goes down quickly.

If there is apparent bleeding, it is well to try to put a covering or pressure bandage over the injured area. If the wound is squirting blood, it means that blood vessels have been ruptured, and a tourniquet should be applied to the points of pressure where the blood vessels enter the area. The less blood lost, the greater are the chances of recovery.

If there are spinal or head injuries, or other internal injuries, it is advisable to put the dog on a stretcher (a large board, an old door or plank, and for a small dog even a cookie sheet) to keep the body as rigid as possible. If necessary, tie the dog down on the stretcher to keep him from moving about or getting up.

Don't attempt to feed or water him. This may aggravate internal injuries and begin a chain reaction of vomiting and further internal bleeding from severe vomiting spasms.

The next step is to rush the animal to a veterinary hospital. He will need injections, oxygen, and possibly blood transfusions to save his life.

ARTIFICIAL RESPIRATION

Artificial respiration is indicated in any condition where the animal's breathing has stopped and so long as there is a heartbeat. There are several traumatic experiences that can cause respiratory failure, such as drowning, electric shock, anaphylactic shock due to snake bite, bee stings, and vaccination reactions.

The dog needs immediate attention because his body cells desperately require oxygen, and if the brains cells don't have oxygen for 10 to 15 minutes or less, permanent brain damage results.

Artificial respiration should be given as follows:

The animal should be lying on his right side with his head and neck extended and his tongue out of his mouth as far as possible.

Place your two hands on his chest over his ribs and apply your weight down firmly to squeeze his chest together, emptying his lungs.

Repeat this procedure every 5 seconds in a rhythm timed to the normal breathing rate of the dog, which is 12 to 30 times per minute. Do it slowly but with strong pressure to the chest cavity. The firm pressure also massages the heart.

Don't give up quickly. You may have to work on the animal an hour or more. There's always hope of reviving an animal as long as there's a heartbeat.

As soon as the animal starts breathing by himself, let him sniff some spirits of ammonia, and then treat him as a shock victim with stimulants and warmth. Professional help should be sought to treat the cause of the respiratory failure.

Mouth-to-mouth resuscitation can also be administered if there are two of you. While one is applying artificial respiration, the other can be breathing directly into the dog's mouth, forcing air into the lungs. The hands should be cupped to form a cone over the dog's mouth and nostrils, and the

210

breathing should be hard and continued until the dog begins to breathe by himself.

HEMORRHAGING

Any signs of bleeding should be regarded as a critical emergency. The animal should be kept as still as possible and taken immediately to a veterinary clinic. For external bleeding in the interim, cold water, ice packs, pressure, and tourniquets are the basic first-aid principles.

External Bleeding

Arterial. The severing of an artery is serious. The blood is bright-red and spurts out in rhythm with the heartbeat.

Venous. When a vein has been severed, the blood is darker and seeps in a steady flow.

Capillary. This is an oozing of small surface blood vessels. It can be hazardous if the wound is extensive.

Bleeding can be stopped by direct pressure either to the blood vessels or to the hemorrhaging area itself, by means of fingers or bandages, by use of a tourniquet, or by direct pressure to the pressure points on the dog's body.

To apply a tourniquet. Any emergency article that can be tied will do (handkerchief, rope). Always tie the tourniquet above the wound—between the wound and the heart. Loosen the tourniquet every 5 to 8 minutes so that the area doesn't become deprived of the normal blood necessary to keep the tissues alive.

Pressure points. To stop bleeding you can apply direct pressure to one of the three main pressure points.

1. There is a pressure point near the jugular vein and carotid artery along the side of the neck. There is a groove running down the neck in which you can find these blood vessels. Press your fingers at this point, where the neck meets the shoulder, to control hemorrhaging on that side of the body.

2. There is a pressure point on the inside of the thigh where the femoral artery passes over the thigh bone. Pressure at this point controls bleeding in the hind legs.

3. The third pressure point is directly above the elbow on the front leg. The brachial artery crosses over this bone, and direct pressure will stop bleeding in the front leg.

Any internal bleeding should be regarded as serious. Professional injections to help coagulate the blood are needed to stop the bleeding. If there is an extreme loss of blood, as the blood pressure drops the animal will go into shock.

Hemorrhaging from the eye is the result of a blow on the head or on the eyeball.

Blood coming from the mouth can indicate a broken jaw, a broken tooth, or a cut gum. Foreign objects such as bones and sharp sticks can cause various injuries to the mouth and the soft tissues of the throat. When a dog retches blood and it is frothy, it is mixed with air and is coming from the lungs. If it is darker, it is mixed with the gastric juices and is coming from the stomach.

Bleeding from both nostrils signifies fractured bone in the sinuses and a foreign object in the nostrils. Bleeding from one nostril indicates an abscess or tumor in that one sinus.

If blood from the rectum is bright-red, it is from the lower intestinal tract. If it is darker brown or black, the blood is mingling with the digestive juices and is coming from the upper intestinal tract.

Bleeding from the urinary tract can indicate stones in the bladder of kidneys. In the female dog, if she is not in season, bleeding can signify tumors or cysts in the female passages or an infection in the uterus.

SHOCK

One way to tell if a dog is suffering from shock is to look at the gums. If they are pale and grayish, shock is indicated, as well as possible internal bleeding. Other symptoms are weak and rapid heartbeat and a cold body, producing the classical cold, bluish skin and pale mucous membranes (seen, for example, in the lips). The dog may be panting and showing hard breathing. He may go into a coma.

The management of shock should be understood, as it has wider application than mere fright. It covers most cases in which something unusual has happened. The body—its organs and nervous system—seems to be so stunned that death may result from the shock and not from the injury itself. For instance, in burns as well as in other injuries the shock condition may be the direct cause of death rather than the burn or other injury. Most often shock is a result of trauma, hemorrhage, intense pain, certain toxins, or severe fright.

In the treatment of shock *never give liquids to an unconscious or semi-conscious animal*. Inhalation of liquid can strangle the dog or produce a foreign-body pneumonia. If the conscious animal being administered a stimulant fights having the liquid poured into his mouth, refrain from continuing, as the excitement and distress are worse for his condition than any good to be derived from the stimulant.

If the dog is conscious, and until he reaches the veterinary clinic, stimulants such as warm coffee or whiskey or brandy spilled into the corner of the mouth often help to save his life. They are good heart and blood stimulants in small doses. Spirits of ammonia or smelling salts can also be used. Another effective first-aid measure for shock is a mixture of 1 teaspoonful of salt and ½ teaspoonful of baking soda in a quart of water, given by mouth. This can also be given in place of ordinary drinking water for the first few days following injury or burns. The intensive thirst attending burn injury will make the patient receptive to the solution despite its unappealing taste. The salt and soda are helpful in replenishing the body with the essential elements lost during the shock syndrome.

For treatment of shock, keep the pet calm and warm; use blankets and hot-water bottles. Administer stimulants if the animal is conscious and able to swallow. Examine for injuries and stop any bleeding; then rush the animal to a veterinarian. There is nothing more effective in shock than blood transfusions and oxygen.

Shock Formula

This is a very useful preparation to have on hand in your medicine chest as it might save an animal that otherwise would have died of shock. It is prepared by putting 4 tablespoons of rock candy in a small covered jar and adding 3 tablespoons of brandy or whiskey (depending on dog's taste). Allow the jar to stand for several days for candy to melt and form a thick heavy syrup. This syrup can be used in an emergency to prevent and treat shock. If you do not have this ready when an emergency strikes, a simple mixture of honey, or syrup, mixed with equal parts of brandy also will help pull animal through.

EMERGENCY CONDITIONS

Abscesses

An abscess is a large, painful, feverish swelling which gathers beneath the skin on almost any area of the body. It is an infection caused by a bruise or a puncture which closes up and doesn't drain. The animal is feverish, and reluctant to move because of the pain.

The infection in the beginning causes a swelling which is hard to the touch. At this stage hot Epsom salt or table salt packs should be applied to bring the abscess to a head so that the core can be removed. The abscess should be lanced by a professional to avoid the dire results of punctured blood vessels or arteries.

Sometimes the abscess ruptures itself and exudes a thick, foul-smelling, brownish-red mass. When this happens, the opening should be flushed out with hydrogen peroxide and then an antiseptic, such as boric acid solution or mild tincture of iodine, applied into the wound. Gradually the opening will close; but don't allow the outside skin to close completely until all the pus has stopped draining.

Bee Stings and Insect Bites

I've seen many dogs with terrible-looking lumps and bumps on their heads. And usually with a mild bite or two, relief can be gotten with warm compresses of bicarbonate of soda, and antihistamines to relieve the swelling. Some animals, however, react violently to a sting or bite. As some humans do, they get an anaphylactic reaction and require immediate medical attention if they are to survive. They have to be treated as an animal in shock (p. 213)—kept warm and given stimulants—until they reach the veterinary clinic.

Bees, wasps, hornets, and spiders produce violent reactions in those sensitized by previous stings. In the sensitive animal, after the sting, pain is felt at the site where the barb was inserted. This is followed by redness of skin, hives, and intense itching. Shortly thereafter the animal feels weakness and dizziness. Fainting, wheezing, shortness of breath, and choking may also be seen. These symptoms may all manifest themselves within a few minutes, or may be delayed up to 24 hours. Call your veterinarian immediately; an injection of epinephrine or cortisone may be necessary.

Burns

It's fairly common for dogs to be scalded with boiling water or other hot substances, or to be burned by electrical wires or chemicals, such as certain types of disinfectants.

In severe cases the animal has to be treated for shock before the burns are treated.

In superficial burns the animal can be washed with a bicarbonate of soda solution and then vaseline applied to the area to coat it and keep it clean. If possible the area should be covered to prevent secondary infection from setting in.

Where there are extensive burns, and deeper burns, all the necrotic (dead) skin and hair have to be removed. The areas are then covered with vaseline bandages, and your veterinarian gives antibiotic therapy. These burns are dangerous and require expert professional care to save the animal.

Burns caused by electrical wiring and chemicals are treated in the same way. In the treatment of chemical burns, however, if the burning chemical was an acid, you wash the wound with an alkali, such as bicarbonate of soda; if the burning agent was an alkali, such as lime or other garden products, you counter with an acid, such as vinegar. After the initial washing the wounds should be covered with vaseline and bandages.

Diarrhea

In simple diarrhea the bowel movement is loose, with a normal color. The disorder is usually caused by such things as overeating, a sudden change in diet, or an emotional upset.

Some dogs can't digest horse meat, and the slightest bit of it in their foods gives them diarrhea. Too much liver can give some dogs diarrhea. Organic foods cause diarrhea in others. Some animals can't take milk, and in diarrhea milk should be immediately removed from the diet, although buttermilk is good. Fried or greasy foods upset some dogs; also spoiled or decayed foods.

Very nervous dogs and emotionally disturbed dogs can have diarrhea almost at will. Any time something goes wrong in the household, they have diarrhea.

A bland diet should be given, which will include most starchy foods (rice, macaroni, noodles, grits) flavored with any type of lean meat. You can also give Kaopectate (1 tbsp.

for an average-sized dog, repeated 3 or 4 times a day), or milk of bismuth with paregoric. The diarrhea should be cured within 48 hours if it's a simple type. If it is not, professional consultation is needed.

Drowning

The first thing to do for a dog who has been under water too long is to hold him upside down and let the water run out of his mouth and nostrils. Then apply artificial respiration, and in extreme cases mouth-to-mouth resuscitation (p. 210). It may be necessary to continue for some time—half an hour or an hour, or as long as the heart continues beating.

After the dog starts to breathe by himself, you have to treat him for shock (p. 212) and keep him warm against pneumonia. The animal may show foreign-body pneumonia caused by water in the lungs. It is best to get the dog to your veterinarian after he is revived so he can be examined and complications prevented.

Electric Shock

When a dog is knocked unconscious by stepping on or chewing into a live wire, be sure the electric current is turned off before you do anything to help the dog. Then you must try to stimulate his respiration, which is the first thing to stop in electrical shock. As long as the heart is beating, you can possibly revive a dog who is not breathing. Give artificial respiration either by pressing on the rib cage in a rhythmic motion or by giving mouth-to-mouth resuscitation.

Fits and Convulsions

The best way to handle one of these animals is to stay out of the way until he quiets down to where you can throw a blanket over him and try to calm him. Don't try to give him medicine during an attack or you'll surely be bitten; he will not know friend from foe. After the attack is over, give him a sedative and get him to your veterinarian.

Foreign Object Swallowed

Animals often get foreign objects into their mouths and throats. Bones and pieces of wood become wedged in the mouth between the teeth and gums and get stuck in the throat. Needles, fishbones, and chicken bones easily become embedded in the tissues of the mouth and tongue. If the object will not come out with your fingers, the dog will likely have to be put under an anesthetic and forceps used. If the foreign body is down past the throat, your veterinarian has special instruments that go down into the esophagus and windpipe.

If your dog swallows a questionable object, use a solution of hydrogen peroxide or table salt to make him regurgitate the object.

Frostbite

In certain areas of the country animals occasionally are overexposed in cold weather. Usually it is their toes that are frostbitten. The affected parts should be thawed out slowly with a minimum of abrasion, since the frozen parts have little blood circulatory action and gangrene or necrosis can easily occur. After thawing, the affected parts should be covered with vaseline or grease to ward off possible injuries. Bandages should then be applied but not tightly, as the circulation must not be interfered with.

Heart Attack

As in humans, a heart attack can occur while a dog is strenuously exerting himself out in the yard or relaxing in front of the fire. The animal will gasp for air and go into an unconscious state. The tongue may turn blue, indicating he isn't getting enough oxygen.

In emergency treatment give artificial respiration (p. 210), and a stimulant, such as warm coffee or brandy, to get the heart and respiration going again.

Applying pressure to the chest cavity does two things: it empties the lungs, and it massages the heart (pressure on the chest cavity presses on the heart muscle and is almost like open-heart resuscitation). By pounding on the chest cavity firmly, but not roughly, the heart muscle can sometimes be stimulated into beating.

When the animal regains consciousness, he should be treated as a shock case (p. 212) and kept warm, as his body temperature will drop rapidly if he is left uncovered. A veterinarian should be contacted, as the animal's heart needs digitalization and other forms of stimulation of a more permanent nature.

Heatstroke

This is a drastic condition seen during hot weather. Particularly affected are highly excitable animals and the short-nosed breeds, such as Pekingese, English bull, Boston terrier, pug and boxer. The Pomeranian also seems susceptible.

A common mistake people make is to leave their dogs in parked automobiles while they go shopping for a "few moments." The causes of heatstroke in susceptible animals are high atmospheric temperatures, high humidity, and lack of ventilation.

The first signs of heatstroke are excessive panting, weakness, inability to stand, and dilated pupils giving a blank expression. In later stages the tongue turns various shades of blue; it is difficult for the dog to get air and he becomes cyanotic.

Quick action is needed to save the animal. Move him into fresh air or into a cool, ventilated area. His temperature usually goes up to 106 degrees or more, so he has to be cooled as fast as possible. If there's a bathtub available, get him into it, but don't have the water so cold initially as to shock him. It is preferable to soak the animal with wet towels to allow the heat to evaporate slowly. Apply ice packs to the head. Then rush the animal to your veterinarian for oxygen, intravenous saline and glucose injections, and general treatment for shock.

To prevent heatstroke when traveling in a car without air conditioning, keep the windows open and allow the animal to lie on towels which are kept soaked with cold water. At home be sure to provide the animal with adequate shade and protection from the sun. Avoid strenuous exercise in hot weather. The addition of salt to the diet during the summer months is advisable, as the dog's body loses salt rapidly in hot weather. A pinch in the dinner every night is all that is needed.

Injuries

Ear injuries usually entail cuts and bruises to the ear flap received in a dog fight (in which case there may be punctures and tears) or in blows to the head (in which case there may be a hematoma or hemorrhaging). When there is a hematoma, the ear flap swells, and a soft mass can be felt inside the ear. Because of its painfulness the dog shakes his head continually. The more he shakes it, the more it hemorrhages and the more it swells. The best emergency treatment until you reach your veterinarian is cold packs to the ear.

Eye injuries should be treated with great care. Any injury to the outside covering, the cornea, or the eyeball should be looked upon as an emergency. Keep the eye moist with cold-water packs and keep it covered (the dog will try desperately to scratch it) until you get to your veterinarian.

Eyeball protrusion (ruptured eyeball) is not uncommon in the breeds with large bulging eyes; but it can occur in any breed when there's a hard blow to the head which forces the eyeball out of the socket. Quick action is necessary if the eyeball and eyesight are to be saved. Cold-water packs will keep the eyeball moist and control the swelling. Rush the patient to a veterinarian, as each minute the eye is prolapsed reduces the possibility of getting it back into the socket.

Foot and leg injuries are common. To avoid having a lame dog the rest of his life, an injury should be properly attended to immediately. At the first sign of limping the leg should be carefully examined from the paw up.

Although the dog's pad has a tough covering, it is vulnerable to penetration by such foreign objects as glass, metal, and wood splinters. Any wound to the pad should be washed thoroughly with an antiseptic and then bandaged to prevent further dirt and debris from entering the wound and to keep it from opening further. Often wounds to the pad have to be sutured and are slow-healing because of the constant pressure of the dog's weight on the wound.

When dislocations, fractures, and sprains to the leg are not readily diagnosable, an X ray should be made. Heat should be applied and aspirin given to relieve the pain. If limping continues more than 24 hours or is more severe, the injury is more serious than a simple sprain. Even certain sprains where the ligaments are torn require surgery to repair the ligaments and splints for immobilization.

Often a dog will get his tail caught in a door or cut by a sharp object such as the edge of a metal wall or a fence. These injuries are painful and tend to be difficult to treat because of constant wagging (and hence bruising). Antiseptics should be applied, and the tail bandaged with a thick padding.

Paralysis

Paralysis is a disturbing sight. The poor dog is unable to move and sometimes is unable to swallow. It can be due to a variety of causes ,suc has cerebral hemorrhage (p. 200) or food poisoning (p. 229). Spinal-disc rupture can cause a complete paralysis of the rear parts. This is seen mainly in dachshunds. A severe infestation of ticks can cause a generalized paralysis.

For emergency treatment, move the dog carefully and get him immediately to your veterinarian.

Porcupine Quills

In certain parts of the country porcupine quills are a painful reality. The muzzle and head generally bear the brunt, as the dog is usually trying to attack the porcupine. Because the quills are so painful to remove, the dog has to be given a general anesthetic. Don't try to remove them yourself; you might be badly bitten.

Skunk Odor

After unpleasant contact with a skunk, the dog's feelings are badly hurt, as is the air around him. The best thing you can do is wash him with soap and water. You might also rub into his coat an old country remedy that works—tomato juice; it seems there's something in the juice that works as an antidote for the skunk odor. Then you can rinse the animal with a 5 percent solution of ammonia, being careful not to get any into the eyes. You may have to repeat the washings several times.

Snake Bite

During warm weather when a dog comes home with a large swollen mass around his face or neck or his front leg, it is wise to suspect snake bite and to get it treated immediately.

Immediate first aid is the same as for humans. Put a tourniquet between the bite and the heart. Cut open the area with a blade (razor or knife), and if possible carefully suck out the venom. Soap and water is the best detergent for the wound; and then rush the dog to your veterinarian. With antitoxins and cortisone, most snake-bitten animals can be saved.

Stroke

A stroke, sometimes called apoplexy, is a sudden-rupturing of a blood vessel in the brain. It may happen in a dog of any age but is usually seen in older dogs.

The blood vessels affected may be on one side of the brain, or there may be a complete generalized hemorrhaging with total collapse and paralysis of the entire body. When one side of the brain is affected, the animal will usually show partial to complete paralysis of the limbs on the opposite side of the body.

Emergency treatment with stimulants, such as spirits of ammonia, whiskey, or brandy, is imperative. The animal should be rushed to a veterinarian.

Suffocation

Some of our hunters put their dogs in the trunks of their cars and often when they arrive at their destinations find the dogs unconscious. Not only can a dog suffocate for want of oxygen, but there is danger of carbon monoxide fumes leaking into a trunk.

Immediate artificial respiration (p. 210) may save the animal.

Unconsciousness—Coma

There is always the terrible prospect of finding a pet in a coma or unconscious. Various conditions can cause such a frightening syndrome. A heart attack is a common cause of unconsciousness; owing to circulatory failure, the animal faints. There is usually shallow and fast breathing, pale gums, and a faint pulse. Shock can cause a comatose state and can be brought about by a variety of conditions (p. 212). Brain injuries, such as concussion, or a cerebral hemorrhage as seen in strokes, can cause a coma. Fits and convulsions can end in unconsciousness.

Emergency treatment should begin with stimulants—not by mouth but inhalants, such as spirits of ammonia or smelling salts. Artificial respiration and mouth-to-mouth resuscitation are indicated. As the animal revives you may pour whiskey or brandy into the side of his mouth. Your veterinarian should be consulted, since diagnosis is essential to prevent a repeat performance.

Vomiting

Until professional help is received and the causative agent found, symptomatic treatment should be commenced.

A dog who is vomiting is very thirsty, but the more water he drinks the more he vomits. Remove all water dishes and replace them with a few ice cubes in a dish.

For causes of vomiting, see p. 205.

Treatment during the recuperative period should involve a bland diet to help nature heal the lining of the stomach. Remove all commercial dog food from the diet. No horse meat and no milk should be given. And no bones! A basic diet can be cooked rice, grits, noodles, or macaroni, flavored with lean beef, chicken, or lamb. Broths, either chicken or beef, can be given, with noodles or rice added. Cooked cereals, such as oatmeal and farina, and Pablum and other baby cereals and baby foods, are excellent. Buttermilk, cottage cheese, and other cheeses are also acceptable.

Wounds

One of the commonest wounds is a dog bite. Dogs enjoy fighting with one another—to show superiority, or to gain the affection of a female in heat, or two females will fight each other to vent their female frustrations. The most dangerous bites are the deep puncture wounds that dogs give with their long canine teeth. Often a puncture will have hair and debris in the wound and be deep enough to hit the bone. This can cause an osteomyletis, which is an infection of the bone. In one chronic subterranean wound I worked on, none of the antibiotics had any effect and upon X ray we found the end of a dog's tooth embedded in the bone.

In first aid for a deep, penetrating bite wound I recommend first pouring hydrogen peroxide into the wound to prevent contamination. Next any suitable antiseptic, such as Mercurochrome, should be used. Then an antibiotic ointment should be inserted into the wound and the dog put on a generalized antibiotic to prevent serious infection.

Wounds such as occur when a dog tears his skin going through a barbed wire fence are frequent. To prevent infection hydrogen peroxide should be poured on the wound, and for cosmetic reasons the wound will subsequently have to be sutured.

Gunshot wounds are frequent hunting accidents. Also, sad to say, some hunters train their dogs with a light load of buckshot as punishment. Sometimes the buckshot is too much for the dog at close range, and he is more seriously injured than the hunter had anticipated in his fit of anger.

The first thing in emergency treatment is to stop the bleeding (p. 211). If the dog goes into shock, treat him for this immediately by wrapping him in a blanket and giving him stimulants (p. 212).

PLASTIC SURGERY FOR INJURED ANIMALS

Veterinarians are now considering the appearance of the animal following an accident and are employing many techniques commonly used on humans by plastic surgeons. Disfiguration may be avoided in many cases, and cosmetic surgery is a daily routine in most good veterinary hospitals. For instance, a dog with a broken jaw can have it repaired with wires so that instead of a monstrosity with a protruding row of teeth and a misshapen jaw the appearance will be normal.

Recently a toy poodle was presented to me that had been severely burned by chewing into a hot electric wire. Part of the tongue was burned off and also one side of the cheek and lips. Besides cosmetic surgery, the animal needed surgery to help control the muscular action of the tongue. After a series of plastic-surgery operations, the dog was restored to a normal-looking and normal-acting pup.

14 POISONS

Most dogs are exposed to poisons every day. Around the house are many common household items—sprays, paints, polishes, detergents—that can prove toxic to pets under certain conditions. Medications such as worm medicine and boric acid are potentially toxic. Nor is food poisoning uncommon. Outside the house there are pesticides that are dangerous to dogs. Even certain trees, shrubs, flowers, and weeds—for example, foliage of delphinium, foxglove, and rhododendron—are poisonous when eaten.

Many times a day we receive patients in our hospital who have been poisoned. Although most of the cases are accidental, there are sadistic fiends who poison dogs deliberately, and I have often gone to court to help convict such despicable humans.

Poisoning is one of the principal causes of pet deaths. In many localities it is second only to the automobile. Although deliberate poisonings are comparatively rare, it is well to be able to recognize the symptoms of the two most commonly used poisons—arsenic and strychnine. They are readily available for rats and are so quick-acting that immediate attention is necessary to save the animal.

GENERAL SYMPTOMS OF POISONING

—Intense pain in the abdomen
—Crying
—Vomiting (usually)
—Trembling and perhaps convulsions
—Hard breathing

PESTICIDES

Arsenic

Arsenic causes severe abdominal pains, and the usual symptoms are watery and sometimes bloody diarrhea, salivation, vomiting, staggering, trembling, and convulsions. In the final stages there is a coldness of the extremities and paralysis of the body.

Emergency Treatment: It is effective only in the early stages. As quickly as possible attempt to induce vomiting. Use hydrogen peroxide (3%), one tablespoon for every 10 pounds of body weight, mixed half and half with water. Also give the dog 2 to 3 tablespoons of milk of magnesia and half a cup of strong tea. Then get him quickly to your veterinarian.

Strychnine

The early symptoms are dilated pupils and twitching and stiffening of the neck muscles. In the later stages there are severe muscle spasms and usually convulsions. The limbs are extended and rigid; the neck is bent up and backward. At the slightest noise, such as the clapping of hands, the animal goes into severe convulsions. This hypersensitivity is diagnostic.

Emergency Treatment: In the early stages you have to give an emetic, such as hydrogen peroxide or soapy or salty water, to induce vomiting. Then give several tablespoons of strong tea to inactivate the strychnine. In later stages when the animal is showing convulsions, don't try to force anything into his mouth, as it would most likely go into his lungs and cause a fatal foreign-body pneumonia. The sooner you can get the dog to a veterinarian, the better are his chances; the veterinarian will intravenously inject a contra-active agent for the strychnine and then wash out the stomach and intestines.

Antu

This rat poison is used by many exterminators. It causes fluid leakage in the lungs, and the animal practically drowns in his own fluids. The early symptoms are mild stomach distress and increasing difficulty in breathing. As the stages progress there are bubbling sounds from the lungs. As the dog weakens he becomes prostrate and then goes into a coma.

Emergency Treatment: If an animal is seen eating a dead or obviously poisoned rat, induce vomiting immediately. Use one tablespoon of dry mustard in half a cup of water, or a solution of soap in water, and pour the liquid into the side of the mouth.

Warfarin

Although this rat poison is supposedly nontoxic to pets, it is one of the commonest sources of poisoning that we see today. The poisoning can be caused by repeated small doses over a period of time or by a single large dose. One of the first symptoms is vomiting. In mild cases the vomitus is gastric contents; in severe cases there is blood and also bloody mucous stools. In milder cases there is weakness, sometimes lameness, and generally a bloody diarrhea. If the case is severe, the animal exhibits the same symptoms as those of shock: the blood pressure drops, the body becomes cool, breathing becomes shallow and weak, the pulse fast. Usually there is hemorrhaging in the body cavities and under the skin in the regions of the joints.

Emergency Treatment: It will usually require immediate attention by your veterinarian for blood tranfusions to restore clotting power. Injections with vitamin K are a specific for this poison.

Thallium

Thallium is a chemical used in rat poison, and in recent years many cases of thallium poisoning have been reported. Thallium is an insidious type of poison, because although it is rapidly absorbed in the stomach, clinical signs don't always appear immediately; there may be a delay of several hours and even 1 to 2 days. Two types of symptoms may show themselves—acute or chronic.

When the condition is acute, severe intestinal distress is noted. The animal regurgitates, and there is diarrhea with blood.

One of the most characteristic signs of thallium poisoning is hair and skin changes. The superficial areas of the skin become reddened, the hair falls out, and the skin becomes necrotic, or deathlike in appearance. The skin spaces between the toes show these changes early. The skin about the muzzle becomes dry, cracked and bloody, and then encrusted.

A significant sign of chronic thallium poisoning is alopecia, or falling out of hair. The hair begins to fall 12 to 14 days after ingestion. As the disease progresses there are respiratory infections, which can turn into pneumonia, and neurological signs, such as muscular tremors, incoordinated walking, and convulsions.

Emergency Treatment: As soon as possible after ingestion a teaspoonful of table salt in water should be given. Then the dog should be taken immediately to a veterinarian.

INSECTICIDES

Insecticides are a growing danger to our pet population because of the increasing practice of spraying and dusting lawns and gardens. Although lawn sprays are not normally toxic to them, it is wise to keep dogs off treated lawns until the spray has dried. If your dog is exposed to a fresh spray, wash his feet with soap and water. Wipe the soles of your shoes after you have walked over contaminated ground so as not to take it into your house. Insecticides can be absorbed through the skin; if there's any question of an animal's exposure, get him into a tub and wash him off completely.

Pyrophosphates

These are compounds used in insecticides, such as Malathion, and are lethal. They are found in agricultural products as well as in flea and tick dips. The poison is absorbed through the skin, and overexposure can prove fatal. When preparing one of these dips, be sure to follow directions carefully. Many an animal has been killed because the dip was too strong. The symptoms are pinpoint pupils, salivation, violent abdominal cramps, respiratory spasms, watering of the eyes, vomiting, diarrhea, muscular twitching, and convulsions.

Emergency Treatment: It must be administered promptly. If the animal has been dipped in too strong a solution, wash him off immediately and rush him to a veterinarian for oxygen and antidotes.

Flea Powders, Sprays, Dips, Collars

When you apply flea powders, sprays, dips, and other insecticides to your dog's body, bear in mind that there is always the possibility of an individual susceptibility and a bad reaction.

Flea collars are an excellent addition to the canine world, but there are some dogs who are sensitive to the chemical in the collar. In some dogs there is a localized irritation around the area where the collar touches the dog's neck. In extreme cases a dog can become ill with an upset stomach, or worse still, with a generalized toxic condition due to absorption of insecticide from the flea collar.

Fortunately reactions are rare, although cases have been reported of severe reactions to flea collars in both dogs and humans. In dogs the reaction may range from light skin redness to purulent lesions. Falling out of hair has also been reported. When the animal is sensitive to the ingredients of the collar, he shows a toxic reaction in the form of nausea, and in extreme cases, dizziness.

The first time a dog wears a flea collar, check the skin, especially on the neck, for the first few days. Fastening the collar tightly may cause sensitivity to the flea-killing ingredients.

Occasionally a sensitive person develops a mild poisoning

227

type rash after close contact with a pet wearing a flea collar. In households with young children, make sure they don't chew on the collar.

TOADS

Most of the poisonous toads are found in southern Florida and in the desert regions of the Southwest. There are at least nine different species of toad capable of poisoning dogs. The toxin in the toad is carried in the wart-like lumps on the skin, and clinical signs show in the dog shortly after he has attacked the toad. The symptoms include evidence of pain, diarrhea, blindness, and convulsions.

Emergency Treatment: Irrigate the dog's mouth vigorously with water as soon as possible after his encounter with the toad. The dog should then be gotten to a veterinarian for sedatives and tranquilizers to control pain, and steroids to reduce inflammatory reaction.

WORM MEDICINE

Because worm medicine is strong enough to kill a worm, under certain conditions it is strong enough to kill a dog. There is no such thing as a 100 percent safe worm medicine. Any one of the medicines can be highly toxic if used incorrectly—either in overdosage or given to a sick dog.

Never, never give worm medicine to a dog with a fever. The fever likely signifies that the patient's body is not well enough to receive a jolt from strong worm medicine. Since there are four or five types of worms and a specific medicine for each type, good judgment and caution must be exercised.

Emergency Treatment: In any type of reaction to worm medicine, sugar in any form is an excellent antidote until you can get the patient to a doctor. After worming, if you see any wobbliness or incoordination, give Karo syrup or molasses (½ tsp. to 1 tbsp.).

BORIC ACID

Boric acid powder, which in solution is widely used by humans as an eye antiseptic, can be highly toxic to dogs when ingested.

Many dog owners use boric acid powder on white poodles

and Maltese terriers to counteract the brown discoloration caused by tear stain. However, when there is more than one dog in a house, and since animals tend to lick one another's faces, this can be dangerous. It can cause hemorrhaging in the stomach and the intestinal tract, usually fatal in the toy breeds.

Emergency Treatment: Contact your veterinarian immediately and give an emetic of powdered mustard (½ tsp.) in warm water until vomiting occurs.

CARBON MONOXIDE

Carbon monoxide is a deadly poison which is odorless, colorless and tasteless. In small doses, it will make humans only mildly ill with nausea, headaches and vomiting. However, three to four hours of inhaling this gas can prove fatal to a dog. When a dog becomes excessively sleepy while traveling in a car look for any leaks in the exhaust. Sometimes "car sickness" is really carbon monoxide poisoning. Many cases of carbon monoxide poisoning have been reported with dogs traveling in trunks or in station wagons with the air-conditioning turned on, windows closed and faulty exhaust systems.

FOOD

The dog's stomach is a strong organ which can digest many inedible objects. Most dogs can consume decayed or rotten food without suffering any ill consequences; usually the worse the food smells, the better the scavenger likes it. However, food or water can be contaminated with bacteria called *Salmonella*, or meat can be contaminated with bacteria called *Clostridium*, and both these bacteria cause food poisoning.

Salmonella poisoning gives severe intestinal symptoms. In young animals a severe case will be acute and sometimes end fatally. The onset and termination are quick; within hours a puppy with severe vomiting and diarrhea can expire.

There can also be a prolonged intestinal infection which manifests itself in fever, vomiting, diarrhea, and after a while, dehydration and weakness. There is an acute diarrhea in these cases, and the animal may pass some blood when the intestines are severely irritated.

The chronic form, which shows no symptoms, is known as the "carrier stage"; it usually follows recovery from one of the other forms. The animal is similar to Typhoid Mary, who carried lethal doses of typhoid germs to her relatives and friends while she herself appeared healthy.

Diagnosis depends on isolation of the bacteria by laboratory culture. Proper treatment would then be instigated by the veterinarian.

Sanitation is by far the best means of preventing and controlling this type of poisoning. Feeding dishes should never come in contact with any fecal material. Strong detergents and disinfectants should be used in cleaning the dog's quarters to prevent contamination.

Clostridium poisoning is characterized by partial to complete paralysis of the body. The bacteria give off a toxin which affects the nervous system.

The dog can remain paralyzed for a period of a few days to 2 to 3 weeks. He needs to be fed intravenously during this period, as he can't swallow food in severe cases. Constant nursing care is needed to save the animal. The urine and bowels need daily help in evacuation. The animal has to be turned from side to side at regular intervals to prevent lung congestion and bedsores.

Emergency Treatment: If there is any reason to suspect food poisoning, hydrogen peroxide to induce vomiting is the first step. This should be followed by a mild laxative, such as milk of magnesia or mineral oil, and in extreme cases by an enema. Evacuation of the bowel contents is imperative.

HOUSEHOLD POISONS

Puppies are like little children in that they will eat almost anything including household objects such as: nail polish, shoe polish, insect repellents, funiture polish, bleaches, soaps, dry cleaning fluids, mothballs and naphthalene, all of which can prove to be exceedingly toxic.

Alkalies, Acids

Alkalies such as lye and other drain cleaners are corrosive and will burn the dog's mouth and other membranes of the body that they come in contact with. Unfortunately dogs will drink these (a sip is enough) if exposed to them.

Acids, for example muriatic acid, present the same problem when left where a dog can get at them.

Emergency Treatment: Quick medical care is required to save the dog's life. In the meantime, for alkali poisoning pour vinegar or lemon juice (several tablespoons) into the side of the dog's mouth. For acid poisoning, bicarbonate of soda (one teaspoon) should be quickly gotten into the dog.

Lead

Lead poisoning is a common ailment of young dogs especially in the summer and fall. This usually comes about from licking or chewing on wet paint or drinking water out of paint cans or ingesting linoleum. Dogs also come into contact with some insect and rat sprays which have lead arsenate in them.

Another common cause of lead poisoning is feeding from ceramic (glazed pottery) dishes. Although lead components are widely used in ceramic glasses, they are normally harmless when properly applied and fired. If not fired long enough, acid in foods causes the lead to seep into the food causing a toxic condition. The FDA has recently banned importation of certain pottery from Italy and Mexico because it is a lead poisoning hazard.

In chronic cases, when there is a gradual exposure to lead, there is a bluish discoloration along the gum line. In large doses the acute symptoms are trembling, bloody diarrhea, fast breathing, convulsions and then coma.

Emergency Treatment: Give the animal an emetic immediately and some charcoal, which is a specific antidote, and then get him quickly to a veterinarian. If you have time, give him an enema and Epsom salts (1 tsp. in water).

Antifreeze

Dogs seem to like the taste of antifreeze, even though it's a deadly poison. Every spring and fall there are reports of dogs dying because they drank antifreeze drainage from cars or got into open containers of the stuff.

Emergency Treatment: Before rushing the dog off to a veterinarian, induce vomiting and give Kaopectate or Pepto-Bismol to coat the stomach and intestines.

Soap

Soap can be poisonous to dogs. Normally dogs will not eat soap but upon occasion a puppy or even a grown dog will be attracted by its odors and will eat some and become ill. In small amounts soap only causes vomiting, but when a large amount is eaten it can cause death. Don't be afraid to use soap in bathing a dog because even if he should eat some suds they won't bother him.

Talcum Powder

It has been shown recently that "baby powder" has been seriously affecting infants, oftentimes resulting in fatalities. It is an absolute poison to the baby's internal organs whether swallowed or inhaled into the lungs. This should caution the dog owners who indiscriminately use these powders to groom their dog for the shows. Pneumonia and lung congestion is not an uncommon result of powder used on the toy breeds of dogs.

Other Household Poisons

Dry-cleaning preparations and other chemicals used in cleaning clothing, and disinfectants with creosote, such as Lysol, can be toxic to the dog's intestinal system.

Golf balls can be fatal as the liquid center contains a substance that can be explosive as well as toxic.

Emergency Treatment: Follow the emergency instructions on the bottle or can and get the animal immediately to a veterinarian.

Plants

There are many household and garden plants that are poisonous to dogs and can cause serious birth defects if eaten by a pregnant dog. There is a wide range of birth defects that have been traced to eating certain toxic weeds in animals. Defects such as dwarfism, twisted bones, harelips, and cleft palates have resulted because of ingestion of these poisons in small amounts. Larger amounts bring death. The most common killer of poisonous plants in dogs is Larkspur, which is commonly found in most flower gardens. Other household or garden plants poisonous to dogs include:

—Ornamental plants: azalea, wisteria, laurel, rhododendron.

—Vegetables: rhubarb leaves (either raw or cooked) can cause convulsions and death in dogs.

—Houseplants: poinsettia leaves, castor bean, mistletoe, and lily-of-the-valley can be fatal.

—Field plants: hemlock, locoweed, jimson weed, and arrowgrass can also have a killing effect.

—Trees and shrubs: foliage of the cherry tree can give cyanide poisoning when eaten, as can peach tree leaves and elderberry leaves. The bark on all of these trees release these poisons when eaten.

GENERAL EMERGENCY TREATMENT FOR POISONING

Emetics

These are preparations which induce vomiting. At the first suspicion of poisoning you have to act quickly; seconds may save the animal's life. If you can get the dog to vomit up the suspected poison before it is absorbed into the bloodstream, this may be sufficient to save his life. The quicker the chemical is released from the stomach, the better the results and treatment.

Hydrogen peroxide (3%) is one of the best emetics. You can use it straight from the bottle or mix it with equal parts of water. Use one tablespoon for every 10 pounds of body weight. Common table salt: Use one teaspoon in a cup of warm water. Mustard powder: Use one tablespoon in a cup of warm water. Washing soda: use ½ teaspoon in a cup of warm water. Pour the liquid slowly into the side of the dog's mouth. Don't get panicky and spill it in quickly, as the animal might ingest it into his windpipe. Vomiting should occur in a few minutes. If it doesn't occur within 10 to 15 minutes, repeat.

Antidotes

Activated charcoal, which can be bought at most drugstores, is a useful antidote. It will absorb some of the poison in the stomach and intestines. Mix 2 to 3 tablespoons in a cup of warm water and spill it into the side of the dog's mouth.

On the can or bottle from which the poison came, most manufacturers give directions for antidotes on the label. Follow the directions carefully.

Consult your veterinarian immediately even if the animal appears normal after vomiting.

15 AILMENTS

ALLERGIES

Although allergies—in the form of asthma, hay fever, and eczema—have been accepted for many years as a major cause of human discomfort, it is only in recent years that the same allergy syndromes have been identified with canine discomfort. They show in the skin in welts and lesions; in the intestinal tract in diarrhea and vomiting; in the head and other parts of the body in hive-like swellings; and in the nasal passages in excessive sneezing and running eyes.

Allergic reactions in the dog can be caused by various foods; by certain insects; by vegetation and pollens; and by hundreds of different agents, such as house dust, floor polishes, woolen articles, nylon rugs, chicken feathers, cat hair, and tobacco.

A recent major breakthrough in veterinary medical research has produced tests for determining causes of allergic reactions and has developed protective antigens. When an allergy is suspected, skin areas are shaved, tests are made, and within 48 to 72 hours the veterinarian can read the results. When an allergy test is positive, it is correlated with the dog's history, surroundings, habits, care, and food; and usually by removing the cause, fast recovery is initiated. If the cause is ever-present, the dog can be vaccinated to desensitize him to the object(s) (there can be more than one irritant) he's allergic to. Dogs allergic to trees, grasses, pollens, etcetera, will have seasonal reactions.

Dietary

Just as with humans, not all dogs can assimilate all foods; they have their idiosyncrasies too. Some pets can digest only "people" food and in fact develop colitis, a chronic inflammation of the intestines, when given dog foods. With some dogs the simplest deviation from the normal diet will produce a chronic diarrhea, with or without vomiting, and a continuous growling of the intestines.

For determining dietary allergies a basic diet is used. The dog is taken completely off his regular diet and is put on a relatively allergy-free diet—mutton and rice. Foods are then added one at a time until an allergic response tells which food is the culprit. Protein sources should be tested first—chicken, beef, liver, egg, whole milk, cottage cheese—followed by cereal products—oats, wheat, corn, other grain cereals. By testing foods one at a time, a dog owner can determine which are the safe foods and which are not.

Flea

Hypersensitivity to flea bites is a fairly common allergic reaction. The bite of the flea produces intense itching. The animal scratches violently, often injuring the skin and predisposing it to secondary infection in "hot spots" and other dermatological conditions. For animals whose bodies reject the presence of even a single flea, injections with flea antigens are used. The injections rid the dog of his sensitivity to the presence of fleas; they don't destroy or banish the fleas.

Hives

Hives in the dog are characterized by a tremendous swelling of the head, usually around the eyes and mouth. The animal is uncomfortable and shows severe itching. The hives are usually caused by an allergy to a certain type of food not generally a part of the regular diet. Antihistamines are prescribed. Cold packs are used to relieve the itchiness, and in most cases the best treatment is a good laxative or enema to wash the intestinal tract of the causative agent. Hivelike swellings can also be caused by a bee sting. In snake bites the enlargement is much more dramatic.

Skin

White dogs and light-colored dogs seem to have a special susceptibility to skin allergies. (This is true in humans too; blond-headed, light-skinned people seem to have greater skin sensitivity.) French poodles, Maltese dogs, setters, wire-haired terriers, and Dalmatians seem to be the most prone. The initial symptom is itching skin with redness and inflammation. Scaliness follows, and the hair starts to fall out either from scratching or from dryness, leaving bare patches. Baby oil or lanolin rubbed on the irritated areas will soothe and relieve the skin, but to effect a cure the cause of the allergy has to be determined.

Allergic Symptoms

—Scratching
—Coughing
—Sneezing
—Eye rubbing
—Paw licking and biting
—Rubbing face against the floor
—Diarrhea
—Vomiting

Discussing any of the above symptoms with a veterinarian will save a pet from many hours of needless suffering.

Incidentally, there are two breeds, the Mexican chihuahua and the Mexican hairless, which apparently can be kept by persons considered allergic to dogs, and can actually help them. This statement might be repudiated by the medical profession, and I have no scientific facts to back me up—just observation that these two breeds, for some unknown reason, help people with allergies and asthma.

ANEMIA

Anemia is a condition of the blood in which there is a reduction in hemoglobin. It is characterized by loss of energy and pale gums. Usually the dog becomes listless, sleeps a lot and loses appetite. He loses weight and after a time becomes emaciated and dehydrated. Instead of healthy-looking red gums there is a paleness which goes from a light pink to a blanched white. The tongue also becomes pale-colored. The most common cause of anemia is infestation of hookworms.

A whiteness of the gums is indicative of an extreme loss of blood and is a serious condition. The blood loss can be the result of an accident or internal intestinal hemorrhage caused by hookworms or whipworms, certain types of poisons, or prolonged illness.

In the South there is an intestinal protozoan parasite—babesia—which attacks the blood cells and causes extreme anemia. This protozoan is spread from dog to dog by the brown dog tick, and to break the cycle and prevent reinfestation, the animal and his surroundings must be rid of ticks.

In the treatment of anemia the dog should be fed large quantities of liver and red meats, along with supplements of iron, malt, and vitamins, especially vitamin B_{12}. In severe cases the dog has to be given blood transfusions until his body can reproduce more blood cells.

BONE AND JOINT DISORDERS

Arthritis

This is inflammation of the bone in a joint. The end of the bone develops calcium deposits, and movement is painful. In all these ailments heat gives relief, and aspirn is helpful. A veterinarian may prescribe injections of cortisone, which can be rewarding.

Bone Tumors

Fortunately bone cancer is rare. The tumors spread to the lungs, and the condition is considered inoperable. Limbs affected by bone tumors can be amputated if detection is early enough—before spreading to other parts of the body.

Bursitis

Bursitis is an inflammation of the joint capsule in the leg. Any movement of the limb can cause extreme pain. Treatment involves heat, aspirin, and steroids.

Hip Dysplasia

This is an inherited abnormality in which the femur bone is displaced in varying degrees from the hip socket due to the improper formation of the ball and socket joints between the back legs. It can cause extreme pain and has been found in over 40 breeds of dogs. A full discussion of the condition can be found in Chapter 18.

Rheumatism

This is usually seen in middle-aged and older dogs. It is an inflammation of the joints and muscles similar to arthritis. On cold and damp days dogs tend to show more signs of the affliction; so warm, dry living quarters are prescribed for preventing repeated attacks. Heat and aspirin are also helpful.

CYSTS

Cysts are growths varying in size from a pimple to an orange. They can be found on almost any part of the body, but mainly there are four different types of cysts found in four different areas: on the ovaries, under the tongue, under the neck, and under the skin.

Ovarian

Cysts which grow on the ovaries of bitches cause frequent and prolonged heat periods. In some cases hormones, by injection, can be used successfully, but in severe cases surgical removal of the ovaries is the only relief. If the cysts appear on only one ovary, that ovary can be removed and the bitch can still be used for breeding.

Ranula

This is a cyst which grows under the tongue. It increases in size until it pushes the tongue upward and to the side. It is unmistakable in appearance. It causes the dog extreme distress, and surgery is the only correction.

Salivary

A salivary cyst can develop under the jaw along the neck. It begins as a mass, and when unattended can grow to large size. A salivary cyst is caused by a blockage to the salivary duct. The salivary gland secretion cannot be discharged into the mouth and forms a sac or cyst. Salivary cysts are difficult to treat, and the only complete cure is surgical removal, which is a complicated and delicate operation.

Sebaceous

These cysts are the commonest type and are found under the skin. They are discussed under Skin Disorders.

EAR DISORDERS

Next to smell, hearing is the dog's most acute sense—about 140 percent more acute than the auditory sense in humans. As in humans, the ear is divided into three sections: outer ear, middle ear, and inner ear.

Any time a dog is seen shaking his head persistently or scratching at his ear frantically, he's trying to say that his ear needs attention. Often there is an odor emanating from the ear which is diagnostic of trouble.

Also like humans, dogs have ear-wax problems, but since a certain amount of wax normally should be present, very frequent cleaning is not advised.

In certain breeds, especially French poodle and Kerry blue terrier, hair normally grows in the ear canal. When this hair is plucked, antiseptic powder or oil should be put into the ear to prevent infection.

Canker

This is the commonest ear infection to plague dogs, and is a serious condition of the middle ear. As the infection progresses it goes into the inner ear, which is close to the brain. When it infects the inner workings of the ear, the dog holds his head to one side and walks in circles, with a loss of equilibrium. This can prove fatal if the brain is damaged.

Ear canker is caused by either bacteria or ear mites. Ear mites are parasites which live in the dog's ear and lead to a chronic irritation of the ear canal. The irritation predisposes the ear to infection from bacteria or fungi. Puppies can be born with ear mites, and in fact a large percentage of puppies carry ear mites which they have acquired from their dams. In serious cases the mites penetrate into the inner ear, and the animal develops convulsions and an incoordinated gait. It is easy to diagnose ear mites even without a microscope; on looking into the ear one can see the diagnostic black, crusty, foul-smelling debris. Under the microscope the black debris shows tiny mites with tentacles that irritate and itch the ear canal.

The symptoms are head shaking, rubbing the ear against objects, and scratching at the ear with the back legs. The dog whines in pain when the ear is touched.

For treatment it is necessary to wash out the debris with an

239

insecticidal preparation that will kill the mites. Because the mites lay eggs in the ears, the treatment must be continued daily until all the eggs as well as the mites are killed, to prevent further infestation. As the mites don't always confine themselves to the inside of the ear but often take a stroll around the head when the host is resting, and because the head shaking disseminates the wax excrement and eggs, the treatment may have to be continued for some time. Also, the mites bury themselves under the skin in the inner side of the ear flap, and are difficult to treat and irritating to the skin of the ear membrane. That is why the dog continually shakes his head.

Inner ear infection must be prevented by properly administering to the ear at the first signs of head shaking or odor. In serious cases of middle- and inner-ear infection, external treatment alone is not always sufficent; internal antibiotics are needed as well. Sometimes the condition is so stubborn and resistant to chemical therapy that the veterinarian has to resort the surgery, removing part of the ear canal and in extreme cases removing the entire canal right down to the skull.

Ear canker is more prevalent in long-eared dogs, such as hounds and spaniels, because the pendulous ears close off the ear canal to air. Access to air is indicated in treating ear canker, and the hair should be kept cut away from inside the ear.

Ear Carriage

The way a dog's ears stand (carriage) is important in certain breeds. During the teething period, when the puppy is going from baby to permanent teeth (4 to 7 months), sometimes the ear will droop or completely flop because of the teething process. However, with the addition of certain vitamins and minerals, and with acquisition of the permanent teeth, the ears generally return to their original position. There seems to be a correlation between teething and the erection of the ear in certain breeds. If a dog's ears are not erect by the age of 9 to 10 months, it is certain that they will not stand by themselves. Upon the advice of a veterinarian corrective ear surgery is usually indicated.

Deafness

In checking hearing in humans, the person is asked if he hears sounds in different tones and intensities. Since these subjective tests can't be used for animals, their ability to hear must be judged by their actions, that is, how they use their ears in response to sounds. In general their hearing is discriminating as well as acute. Many dogs are able to distinguish the varied footsteps of members of their household and even the engine of the family automobile. There is one limitation, however, that seems to involve most dogs—they seldom can locate a sound from well above them; for example, if you call or whistle from an upstairs window, the dog will hear the sound but will not be able to locate it. Careful observation of the dog's reactions to different sounds is the only way his hearing can be checked, and one has to be wary that the dog is not compensating for a hearing loss with scent and sight.

Deafness can be caused by severe ear canker and inner-ear infection. Tumors growing deep in the ear canal can interfere with hearing. As a dog approaches 10 to 11 years of age there is a decrease in the acuteness of his hearing, since the nerve controlling the hearing degenerates. There is no cure. Gradually he is unable to hear voice commands. High-pitched whistles can then be used for commands. A deaf dog can also be directed by stamping on a floor; he feels the vibrations and responds to them.

Deafness seems to run in some breeds, and in white dogs (and cats) inherited deafness is prevalent. The breed most prone to inherited deafness is the Dalmatian. English setters and pointers also seem to have this tendency.

Hearing aids are being used more often for deaf dogs. They require special fittings, and the dog wears the aid for only a few hours at a time until he gets used to it. Eventually he can wear it most of the time.

Flies

Certain breeds are especially susceptible to fly infestation on the tips of their ears; German shepherds and chowchows are the commonest victims. In laying their eggs the flies bite the skin, which brings blood to the tips and edges of long, erect ears. This can cause a chronic skin infection at the ear tips.

For treatment most of the insecticidal fly sprays are helpful, but care should be taken that the spray is low in kerosene, which can irritate the dog's ears. Another remedy is a mixture of citronella, camphor, and olive oil applied to the ears. Tincture of benzoin is also good.

241

Hematoma

Constant head shaking can cause a blood cyst, known as a hematoma. It is caused by a broken blood vessel—the result of an injury, a blow on the ear, or continual head shaking and ear scratching. The blood vessel ruptures between the layers of the skin and starts filling up.

A hematoma needs intervention by a veterinarian. The only cure is surgical. If the dog continues to shake his head, as the bleeding continues with head shaking, a stocking or bandage should be put over his head while he is being taken to the veterinarian. Sticking a needle or knife into the soft painless swelling doesn't effect a cure; the ruptured blood vessel has to be gotten at. Also, the predisposing cause of the head shaking, such as ear mites or ear canker, has to be dealt with when the hematoma is treated so that the head shaking will stop.

Tumors

There are warts or tumors which grow in the ear canal, and these have to be removed surgically. They are irritating to the dog and can be serious. They can block up the ear canal, allowing infection to develop in the canal's inner recesses.

Cleaning the Ears

When swabbing the ear, don't probe deeply inside. Someone should hold the dog's head so he can't jerk or move suddenly, and then the swab should be inserted gently into the the ear, no further than an inch only until slight resistance is met.

I don't advise using water in the ear; a wet ear is always a major predisposing factor for ear infection. When bathing a dog, it is advisable to put cotton in the ears to keep out the soap and water.

For normal cleaning use a cotton swab saturated with ether, glycerine, or best of all, hydrogen peroxide. The ear should then be saturated with a drying powder, such as BFI.

The wax at the bottom of the canal is difficult to flush out, so sometimes a warm sweet oil may be used to loosen some of the hard crusty wax. Again, the ear should be left dry.

When the ear is infected and contains purulent matter, it should be syringed with a surgical soap solution, such as Phisohex, then left dry.

EYE DISORDERS

As the eye is such a sensitive and vital organ, treatment of an abnormal eye must be very careful. The normal eye has a slight clear-colored discharge, and normally the tear duct in the inside corner of the eye drains into the nostril and carries away the normal discharge. Whenever there is any trouble, there is a significant increase in the amount of discharge, and its color and thickness noticeably change. The excessive discharge is more than the tear duct can carry, and the mucopurulent matter spills over the outside of the eye and runs down the face of the animal.

If the excessive discharge is the result of a mild irritation to the eye caused by dust, dirt, smoke, or smog, a simple washing with warm water, or mild salt solution (a pinch of salt to a cup of water), or a boric acid solution, or a collyrium wash, should be sufficient to eliminate the irritation. However, if after 2 days the eye has not cleared up it should be looked at with an ophthalmoscope for something more serious, such as a scratch on the cornea, an ulcer, or a foreign body. Excessive discharge can also be caused by a deficiency of vitamin A. The deficiency can be due to inadequate diet or to a severe case of worms. Sometimes a simple worming of the dog will clear the eyes. In all cases of eye trouble, foods rich in vitamin A, such as eggs and carrots, should be added to the diet.

When a dog's eye is injured, it is painful, and sometimes he will try to paw at it and rub it. This can result in scratches on the eyeball and cornea, so it is highly advisable to tape the dew claws on the front legs to prevent further injury.

Cataracts

Cataracts are a partial or total opacity of the lens of the eye. They are most often seen in middle-aged to older dogs, but there are also juvenile cataracts which appear in dogs under 5 years. Most common in poodles, cockers and Boston terriers, juvenile cataracts are believed to be hereditary. Animals with this condition should not be used for breeding.

There is no medical treatment for cataracts except removal

of the lens so that the animal may perceive light. Veterinary medicine has perfected the technique of cataract removal so that many dogs blind with cataracts are given additional years of sight. The eyesight is not perfect—the dog cannot focus—but at least he can discern shadows and objects in his path.

Collie Ectasia Syndrome

This congenital condition can be recognized as early as 6 weeks after birth by the puppy's dilated and gleaming pupils. It is a recessive characteristic, and a carrier must be tested in order to identify it. A dog carrying this syndrome should never be bred. See Chapter 18.

Conjunctivitis

This is an inflammation of the tissue surrounding the eye and of the tissues of the inner circle of the eyelid. The inflammatory condition can be caused by foreign bodies, dust, dirt, smog, different types of pollen, or bacterial infection. Along with an excessive discharge, the dog does a lot of blinking.

A treatment for simple conjunctivitis is a drop or two of cod-liver oil in the eye daily; this relieves the irritation and helps to heal the eye. If a foreign body is in the eye, a boric acid solution may wash it out, but if it is embedded in the tissue, then professional help should be sought to remove the object. Amateur probing in the eye can do irreparable damage.

There is a follicular conjunctivitis caused when the follicles on the inside of the third membrane enlarge and become irritated. A substance is secreted that continuously drains out of the eye. The veterinarian will usually have to put the animal under anesthetic and scrape the follicles or possibly remove the third eyelid.

Ectropion

This condition of everted eyelids is seen in large breeds, such as St. Bernard, Great Dane, and even basset hound. It leaves a large area of exposed eyelid for the collection of dust and other eye irritants. These eyes continually appear red and eventually become infected. There is a surgical procedure to tighten the eyelids, and it also gives excellent cosmetic results.

Entropion

This, the opposite of ectropion, is an abnormality in which there is an inverted eyelid. It usually occurs in small breeds, such as Mexican chihuahua and terriers. The eyelashes continually scrape the cornea or the eyeball, causing severe irritation. Over an extended period the usual result is ulceration of the eye and permanent defects. The only correction is surgical: the eyelids are pulled outward, with good results cosmetically. Until the surgery is performed, keep a lubricating ointment or oil in the eye to protect the cornea from the constant irritation.

Glaucoma

This is an enlargement of the eyeball due to an increase of fluid inside it. Because of the abnormality the fluid can't escape, and pressure builds up inside the eyeball. Often it starts in one eye and sympathetically spreads to the other eye. The condition can be helped by drops in the eye, but there is no permanent cure. Some dogs respond to the eyedrops, and the pressure reduces. For others there are diuretic tablets which draw the fluid from the eye. There is also a surgical technique which provides continual drainage for the pressure, and it can be used with good results. It is a delicate operation but has helped prolong the eyesight of many a dog.

Harderian Gland Infection

The Harderian gland is under the haw, or third eyelid, a membrane on the inside of the eye at the nasal corner (in certain breeds the third eyelid is more noticeable and is sometimes a pink or black pigmentation). When there is an infection of the Harderian gland, there is a noticeable enlargement of the third eyelid and it extends out over the corner of the eye. Sometimes antibiotics and soothing ointments will reduce the swelling in the gland, but if not, the Harderian gland has to be removed surgically.

Often called "gray eye" or "blue eye," this is an inflammation of the cornea, or outside covering of the eyeball. It usually starts with an inflammatory condition of the cornea, and then if there is excessive irritation, there will be a graying or a blueing of the eye. In a serious case it turns completely opaque, a sort of whitish-gray color. The animal is unable to get any light and is temporarily blinded in the affected eye. Keratitis is usually caused by a foreign body, but whitening of the eye, along with other normal symptoms, is diagnostic in hepatitis. Keratitis should be treated by a professional.

Poodles: Tear Staining

This is a common condition and is caused by a constant tearing over the face. It can be seen in other breeds, such as Maltese, toy terriers, Mexican chihuahuas, and cocker spaniels, but is most common in the white poodle. It usually begins at the age of 2 to 3 months. The brown-stained face and the pink-colored third eyelid are prominent.

Direct causes of eye stain are chronic conjunctivitis; infection of the Harderian gland and third eyelid; blockage of the tear ducts; an allergy; and growth of hair on the inner corner of the eye. There are also some indirect predisposing factors for eye stain: poor physical condition of the animal; inadequate diet; inverted eyelids (entropion); matting of hair on the eyeball; a low-grade infection, such as chronic tonsillitis; lack of sunshine and fresh air; and lack of proper exercise.

Many home remedies (such as Vitamin A and Brewer's yeast) have been tried on these running eyes but if infection is present only cleansing the eye with eye washes and antibiotics such as tetracycline will improve the condition. Oftentimes, surgery is the only method giving any relief from this insidious and unsightly ailment.

To get rid of the brown stain once the condition is cleared up:

—Keep the hair clipped close to the face.

—Carefully wash the skin and hair with a hydrogen peroxide solution, being careful none gets in the eye. The bleaching of facial stain with chlorine bleaches or similar agents is not recommended, as they can cause discomfort or pain to the eyes and the fumes are irritating to the eye.

—After the hair is dry, some people put boric acid in the corner of the eye; but since it is so toxic when ingested, Desitin ointment or zinc oxide ointment is safer. Some people use white lipstick below the eye corners, and others use white clown makeup, both of which are good.

Progressive Retinal Atrophy (PRA)

This is a congenital degenerative eye disease for which there is no effective treatment and which inevitably causes total blindness. Mainly inherited by the miniature and toy poodle, it is also seen in Gordon setter, Irish setter, Norwegian elkhound, collie, Labrador retriever, greyhound, Kerry blue terrier, miniature long-hair dachshund, and spaniels.

Generally the first sign of PRA is a hesitancy in the dog to leave the house in the evenings while acting perfectly normal during the daylight hours. In poorly lighted rooms he may be fearful of walking around or of going down stairs. There is also a personality change. As the condition progresses he begins to bump into things. Gradually the pupils become widened, and one can see the back of the eye. The eye takes on a green-orange or bright-color appearance. The dog develops a high-stepping gait, feeling his way as he walks, and he carries his head in an exaggerated position. A conclusive diagnosis can be made by the veterinarian; with an opthalmoscope he can view the retina and see the degenerative changes.

In the poodle sometimes the blindness is complicated by cataracts. Surgery for the cataracts is then useless. A recently completed study indicates that 76 percent of poodles with PRA develop cataracts, and 30 percent of poodles with cataracts have PRA as well. There is a special test which allows the veterinarian to distinguish between PRA and cataracts.

PRA in poodles is generally considered to be hereditary; it is transmitted as a recessive factor. PRA is becoming more common because it does not show up until later in life, after the age of 4 or 5. A dog can have sired or whelped several litters before it is discovered. The only way this disease can be eliminated is by selective breeding. The male or bitch diagnosed as ever having PRA in the family background should not be used as breeding stock.

Retinal degeneration may follow canine distemper, but the hereditary form is the most common. Fortunately, a PRA diagnosis can be made by a veterinarian by the time the puppy is 10 weeks old. Early diagnosis will eliminate breeding PRA carriers.

Prolapse of the Eyeball (See Chapter 13.)

Ulcers

Ulcers of the eye are common, as dogs will rub into foreign objects or get into fights with cats and dogs. An ulcer is dangerous. The dog can lose his eyeball if it is not treated quickly; even a slight pinprick on the eyeball can enlarge and penetrate into the inner part of the eye, in which case the eyeball has to be removed surgically. It is painful, and the dog will try to scratch at it. Often the animal has to be put under sedation. The eye ointment used should contain local anesthetic to help relieve the suffering.

Other Conditions

The breeds with bulging eyes, such as Pekingese, Boston bull, and pug, are especially susceptible to eye trouble. In the Pekingese there are many eye ulcers, because the hair on the wrinkles beneath the eyes becomes too long and scratches the eyeball. The hair should be kept clipped.

White-colored dogs and dogs without pigmentation around the eye seem to have more eye trouble than pigmented dogs.

Some dogs develop tumors on their eyelids. There are also pimples or pustules, such as sties in humans. These all require professional treatment.

When dogs go blind, they adjust more quickly to their environment and with fewer emotional problems than do humans. It takes them only a day or two to learn the location of doors and furniture. In a two-dog family I know, when one of the dogs went blind, it continued to walk and run about as before—but always close beside the other dog, who had assumed the role of seeing-eye dog.

FEMALE DISORDERS

Metritis

This is an infection of the uterus seen in middle-aged and older bitches. It can be either acute or chronic. The veterinarian can determine the severity of the infection by the white blood count. When the count goes to a certain point, surgery is essential to save the bitch.

Often mild attacks of metritis occur after heat periods; anywhere from 2 weeks to 2 months after the bitch goes out of heat this uterine infection will appear. Antibiotics and douching can be helpful and can often avoid surgery.

If the bitch has many attacks, the veterinarian likely will advise a hysterectomy. This is recommended while the animal is still is good physical shape; if emergency surgery has to be performed in an acute attack, the chances of survival are less good.

Visible symptoms of metritis are fever, lassitude, enlargement of vagina, painful abdomen, and an irregular discharge ranging from red in color to a dark, foul-smelling pus.

Prolapse of the Uterus

This is a breakdown of the musculature of the vagina and uterus which allows the uterus to protrude from the vagina. It can be caused by undue straining during whelping or by tumors. Upon palpation of the vaginal tract the veterinarian can determine the cause.

In some cases the uterus can be pushed back into the pelvic area, with the possibility that it will come out again in a few hours. In other cases a partial hysterectomy can be done to remove the mass. In severe and repeated attacks I advise a complete hysterectomy for the bitch's furture health and well-being.

Prolapse of the Vagina

This occurs in the bitch during season and occasionally during pregnancy. The condition is seen in the boxer and Boston bull most often and is considered to be a hereditary weakness. It is recommended that such bitches should not be mated and should be spayed. However, surgical treatment can restore the prolapse. If you do breed these dogs, artificial insemination is the method of choice. However these dogs usually require Caesarean section as the prolapse recurs during the whelping process.

Ovarian Cysts

This condition is discussed under Cysts.

249

THE HEART

Heart disorders are generally seen in older dogs (discussed in Chapter 3). However, dogs of any age can have heart problems, including puppies born with a condition like that in the human blue baby. Such conditions sometimes can be diagnosed by X rays and can be surgically corrected.

A main symptom of heart trouble is shortness of breath—gasping for breath with any exertion—and extreme exercise will produce pronounced symptoms, with the gums turning cyanotic (bluish), because the animal can't get enough oxygen to his lungs. In certain types of congestive heart failure there is usually a coughing due to the presence of fluid in the lungs caused by inefficient heart valves. Sometimes there is a vibration in the chest which can be felt by putting a hand on the rib cage over the heart.

In extreme cases there is collapse or fainting; the dog is unconscious for a few moments. Such a case needs emergency treatment. The heart should be massaged by pounding on the ribs and artificial respiration given. Mouth-to-mouth resuscitation is helpful. These dogs need professional care to digitalize the heart. Digitalization is a strengthening of the muscles for more efficient heart function. With proper care these animals can have long and happy lives.

Heartworms

Heartworms are parasites living in the heart chambers, blood vessels, and lungs. They are acquired from the bite of an infected mosquito. There is a full discussion in Chapter 17.

INTESTINAL DISORDERS

Colitis

Colitis usually appears in a chronic form and is an inflammation of the large intestines. The exact cause is unknown, but we know that emotional tension and excitability are contributing factors. We also suspect allergic reactions to certain types of food. Certain traits, such as shyness, insecurity and anxiety, can bring on various psychosomatic illnesses, including an attack of colitis. Some dogs get this condition when their owners start packing valises to leave town. We see a lot of it in pets who are very emotionally interrelated with their owners.

The symptoms are diarrhea with mucus and vomiting. When there is blood in the stools, it usually signifies an ulcerated colitis. Ulcers form on the inside lining of the large intestines and occasionally bleed.

Colitis tends to recur, so we must try to eliminate the predisposing factors. In other words, don't let your dog worry; and anything that seems to disturb him should not be allowed in the house. The diet should be bland—cooked cereals, lean meat, cooked eggs, other soft foods. Animals with colitis usually cannot digest commercial dog foods; these are rough and harsh to a sensitive intestinal tract. If the colitis seems to be caused by a certain type of food, it is advisable to experiment with a bland diet, adding foods one at a time (see Allergies in this chapter). Above all, the animal should be kept quiet.

Periodic bloody diarrhea is also seen in eosinophilic gastroenteritis. Cockers and German shepherds are the main victims but any breed can be affected. It is diagnosed by a blood count.

Constipation

There are many causes of constipation. The main ones are improper diet, overfeeding, and lack of exercise. Too many bones will tend to cause an impaction in the intestinal tract, and so can too many hard dog biscuits. Overfeeding older dogs or dogs who live in apartments and get little exercise can result in a chronic constipation. Any sudden change of diet can upset the intestinal contents. Impacted anal glands (see Rectal Disorders in this chapter) can cause constipation because of the pain involved when the animal tries to relieve himself.

For treatment, sometimes compensatory foods that loosen the bowels, such as milk and liver, give relief. Mineral oil and milk of magnesia are the best laxatives for dogs. In severe constipation an enema is recommended. Use either warm, soapy water in a regular enema tube or a Fleet disposable enema tube, which when inserted into the rectum usually produces immediate bowel evacuation.

In the condition known as false constipation there is interference with the stools passing from the rectum. It is usually seen in long-haired dogs where the hair and feces mat up over the rectum and seal the exit. It can cause a painful condition resulting in severe impaction. The hair should be clipped away and infection around the anus treated. Vaseline or baby oil gives soothing relief to the rectum.

Diarrhea (see also Chaps. 12 and 13)

Diarrhea can occur in dogs from such simple causes as change in diet or excitement or from more severe causes, such as distemper or poisoning. In prolonged cases diarrhea is debilitating and can cause death if unattended. In a puppy one loose movement should be attended to immediately; diarrhea weakens and dehydrates puppies so quickly that there isn't a moment to lose.

If it is not a simple diarrhea, that is, if it doesn't respond to treatment and persists over 48 hours, professional help should be sought. There may be a severe infestation of worms, or infection, or disease.

Enteritis

Enteritis is an inflammation of the bowels with many causes. The infection of the intestinal tract can be due to a foreign body; to distemper, hepatitis, or leptospirosis; to severe worm infestation, and especially coccidiosis; to any type of poisoning, either food or chemical; or to twisting of the bowels.

Intestinal spasms and cramps are symptomatic of enteritis and show a painful abdomen which is extremely sensitive to touch. Vomiting usually accompanies diarrhea but it is not a constant symptom. The diarrhea is with or without mucus, and in severe cases there is blood. In young puppies I have seen fits develop from the intense pain of the abdominal cramps.

The first step in the treatment of enteritis is to find the cause and eliminate it. Antibiotics are used, and soothing drugs and a bland diet to heal the irritated intestinal-tract lining. Although the dog's stomach and intestines are strong, there are infections of these organs that are sometimes difficult to treat. Complete dietary and drug harmony is needed.

Gastritis

This is an inflammation of the stomach characterized by nausea and vomiting. Sometimes overeating or eating wrong types of food will cause gastritis. It can also be caused by certain diseases, such as distemper, leptospirosis, uremia, nephritis, and metritis.

When a dog is bothered with indigestion or nausea, he eats grass (long-stemmed blades) to empty his stomach or to serve as a laxative. If he does this repeatedly, he should be examined to find out the cause.

In gastritis, along with grass eating, the dog is very thirsty and demands water to soothe his inflamed stomach. However, the more water he drinks the more he vomits, so the water should be restricted. Substituting a few ice cubes in his water dish is a good idea. Kaopectate and Pepto-Bismol are both soothing to an inflamed stomach; in a simple case only 3 to 4 doses are needed. Use a bland diet with soft foods until the inflammation subsides.

Pancreatitis

This is an acute or chronic infection of the pancreas, a very important gland that helps to furnish digestive ferments that aid in the digestion of food. In the acute stage, there is a high fever, abdominal pains and persistent vomiting. In the chronic form, an intermittent vomiting usually presents itself. Dietary control is an important part of the treatment. Dogs cannot digest any fats so that the diet should be void of any fried or greasy foods. A simple bland diet is essential.

MALE DISORDERS

Orchitis

This is a condition in which there is an abnormal enlargement of one or both testicles. It requires professional treatment because the testicle may even need to be removed. The use of antibiotics is imperative.

An enlargement of the testicles can also mean a tumorous growth.

Prostatitis

This condition is commonly seen in middle-aged and older dogs. It is characterized by a hunched-up back and painful walking, as the prostate gland is situated between the hind legs in the pelvic cavity.

Age can be a contributing factor, or an inadequate love affair, or it can be seen in a male dog who has been on the town for a few days.

The syndrome usually requires professional treatment, as the enlarged prostate can cause subsequent infections in kidney and bladder. Its proximity to the rectum can cause constipation due to pressure on the rectal wall.

THE MOUTH

The Gums

Many dogs suffer from gum infections. The gums bleed easily, swell, become ulcerated and ooze pus. The accompanying putrid odor is caused by either tartar formation or infection working under the gums.

This pyorrhea type of infection causes loosening of the teeth, and the dog becomes toothless at an early age.

For treatment the gums should be massaged with a good antiseptic, such as salt and soda, and painted with tincture of iodine. Hydrogen peroxide, Bactine, and other mouth washes are also good. This treatment should be repeated at least once a week for badly infected gums.

Halitosis

This important problem usually comes from the same source as in humans—an unclean mouth and the resulting decaying particles among the tooth crevices. Tartar and infected gums are the prime causes of bad odor.

The fact that dogs gulp their food rather than chew causes some odor from the mouth. Overfed dogs usually produce an offensive stomach odor. To combat this the diet could be changed to food that requires some chewing. More outdoor exercise also helps.

Prophylactic treatment of the mouth and gums is beneficial. Chlorophyll tablets can be used as well as commercial powders and sprays.

Lip Infection

We sometimes see a lip infection in cocker spaniels and springer spaniels which gives a diagnostic rotten odor. Bacteria and fungi in the crevices of the moist lips and eventually produce a necrotic infected area which needs cleansing and chemotherapy to destroy the putrefactive odor.

Oral Warts

These are small to large growths found in the mouth and on the lips of young dogs, and can vary in number from one to several hundred. They are caused by a virus and are contagious from one dog to another. They also occur in cattle, horses, and rabbits, but these types are not contagious to dogs.

The warts appear suddenly and multiply insidiously and very rapidly. Some of them grow to about the size of a pea. They appear on the tongue and spread to the soft palate.

In extreme cases the warts interfere with eating and cause excessive drooling. Surgery is then recommended. Electric cauterization gives nice results. A vaccine is available that both helps eliminate the warts and prevents recurrence.

Teeth

The normal dog is blessed with a much stronger set of teeth than is the normal human. The tooth structure is stronger, the enamel is thicker, and the teeth have much more resistance to cavities. Dental caries is not a serious problem in dogs who receive a proper diet.

Normally the adult dog has 42 teeth, except for the short-nosed breeds (pug, bulldog, etc.), which normally have only 38 to 40 because of the lack of space in the jaw. Puppies normally begin cutting their deciduous, or baby, teeth at about 3 weeks of age and finish at about 6 weeks. All the baby teeth are shed and replaced by the permanent teeth at between 4 and 7 months of age.

Abscessed Teeth. An abscessed tooth gives the dog many moments of pain and fever. He will be reluctant to eat and will exhibit all the symptoms of a person in extreme difficulty with an infected tooth. His jaw may swell over the area of the tooth, and there is usually swelling under the eye. When this swelling appears, the tooth has to be removed. Once the tooth is pulled, the abscess drains into the mouth, and the swelling subsides. Occasionally an abscess erupts through the skin of the cheekbone under the eye, and we have a chronic fistula that continually exudes pus. Once the tooth is removed this disappears and clears up.

Broken and Worn Teeth. This is fairly common in dogs because of their bad habit of chewing and carrying stones or pieces of wood in their mouths. Many a tooth has been broken during the hunt by dogs tearing away at all manner of objects to get at the quarry. All these factors wear the teeth down, and when the enamel is worn off, cavities are possible where the surface of the tooth is gone. Chipped, broken, or loosened teeth can sometimes be corrected by capping or filling.

Although normally it is possible to tell the approximate age of a dog by the amount of wear and tear on his teeth, with animals who like to chew on bones, stones, and other indigestible objects, the teeth usually show signs of wearing down at an early age. I have been asked many times if it's possible to tell the age of a dog by its teeth, and my answer is that it's not so reliable as in the horse. Up to about a year of age in dogs it is not difficult to approximate the age.

Inherited Defects. The practice of dentistry on canines has progressed far in the past decade. There are even dogs in the show ring with caps on their teeth, and this is allowed if it can be proven that the dog's tooth was broken, that the defect occurred after birth and was not congenital. The correction of any congenital defect is frowned on by the AKC.

There are inherited tendencies of the mouth and teeth that must be watched carefully in breeding. These are undershot jaw, overshot jaw, and missing, loose, or misaligned teeth. There is a good possibility that if an animal with any of these defects is bred, the offspring will show the same defects.

The hereditary defect that breeders are primarily concerned with is that of missing teeth. Some breeds are born with missing tooth buds. This can hurt the dog's chances in the show ring, but it has no health significance.

Misalignment of teeth is becoming more and more of a problem among purebred dogs. There is a tendency for these imperfections to be inherited. Orthodontia—realignment of teeth—is being tried, but it must be done when the animal is still under 1 year of age. Also, it is difficult to get the animal to cooperate with the type of metallic braces that children wear.

Pitted Enamel. This is erosion in which there are openings and holes in the enamel. It is usually caused by diseases, aging, bacterial action, or chewing rocks or other hard objects. They are called "distemper teeth" because distemper, along with a high temperature, is one of the principal causes.

Even though the teeth don't look good, they are healthy and can be serviceable to the dog for many years. It is not possible to remove the dark spots.

Tartar. The commonest cause of dental problems in the dog is tartar formation. The tartar attaches below the gum line and causes oozing of serum from the gums. The tartar progressively builds up over a period of several months, and as it worsens it causes bad breath, sore gums, pus formation, loose teeth, abscessing of the roots, and general ill health. As the tartar works under the gums the teeth are loosened, and many a dog becomes partly toothless at an early age. A paucity of teeth shortens a dog's life.

In small dogs and in the toy breeds we see tartar formation and loosening of the teeth at an early age more frequently. Many of them eat specially prepared and home-cooked foods, and most of those are soft and require no chewing. Usually the front teeth are the first to go. They loosen at the roots and begin falling out when the animal is only 2 or 3 years old. When the teeth are loose in the sockets, they give a lot of pain to the dog and may cause him to refrain from eating. I have had to remove 8 to 10 teeth at a time in some smaller dogs, leaving them almost toothless and doomed to a life of soft-mashed foods to be consumed in a semi-liquid state. A periodic checkup with a veterinarian at least every 6 months can prevent a lot of these problems, as he will check the mouth and scrape off any tartar.

As the tartar forms, one of the first things the owner will notice is bad breath. On closer inspection he will find that the teeth that were once white and pretty are turning to a brownish color. If it is far advanced, the only way to rid the teeth of the tartar is for a veterinarian to use a tartar scraper. He can scrape off the tartar painlessly and quickly. In severe cases the dog may have to be given a tranquilizer or a general anesthetic because there can be a gum infection, or loose or abscessed teeth. If the tartar is extremely bad, some of the teeth may have to be extracted.

In its early stages tartar may be removed by a solution of salt and soda (a teaspoon of salt and a teaspoon of soda in a cup of water). This is an excellent solution that can be rubbed on the teeth and gums (with a piece of cotton) at frequent intervals. In some dogs once a month may be sufficient, but in others once a week may be necessary. Some people use toothbrushes, but most dogs resist them in their mouth. Some people use regular toothpaste or tooth powder, but dogs who don't like the taste will salivate profusely. If a dog will tolerate a toothbrush and a mild-tasting toothpaste, the gums may bleed when the teeth are brushed, but this will be helpful to the gums.

Also for the prevention of tartar formation, the feeding of hard or semi-hard foods, which require chewing, is recommended. There are excellent kibbles and biscuits on the market. A large shank bone or knuckle bone once a week will give a dog many hours of enjoyment and will help his teeth and gums.

Teething. The owner must keep close watch on the puppy's mouth to make sure that the baby teeth fall out when the permanent teeth appear. Should the baby teeth interfere with the normal position and alignment of the permanent teeth, unless they are removed by the age of 7 to 8 months, they can affect the mouth structure of the dog for the rest of his life. In toy breeds the double row of milk teeth that often are not shed at the proper time are a problem. When the permanent teeth don't loosen the baby teeth and make them drop out, the baby teeth grow longer roots that go straight down into the jawbone. The longer the milk teeth stay in the mouth, the deeper the roots and the more difficult they are to remove.

By the time a puppy is 8 to 9 months old, if he still retains any of his baby teeth, they should be pulled by a veterinarian. This should not be attempted by a layman; the baby teeth are often hard to remove, as they have long spurs at their base and require dental instruments to remove them properly. If they are taken out improperly, a root can break at the base and give problems for many years.

During the teething process there will probably be periods of fever, swollen throat glands, mouth hemorrhages with or without loss of appetite, and even diarrhea. If the symptoms persist for more than 12 to 24 hours at a time, a veterinarian should be consulted.

Yellow Teeth. Occasionally we see yellow teeth in puppies, and we are finding out that this can be due to the antibiotic tetracycline, given to the brood bitch while the puppies are in the womb or to a puppy during an illness while in the teething stage. There is nothing that can be done for this yellow discoloration, but fortunately the permanent teeth usually come in white.

NERVOUS DISORDERS

Nervous disorders lead to many distressing symptoms, such as fits, convulsions, shaking, twitching, paralysis, and various frightening exhibitions of hyperexcitability. The causes are many and varied, ranging from a highly emotional animal's getting upset over strangers to diseases of the brain, such as distemper, spinal meningitis, and rabies. With the rapid advances in neurological research in dogs the practicing clinician will soon know more both about the effects of disease on the brain and spinal core and about emotional factors concerning the dog's brain.

There is usually a cause for any nervousness in a dog whether it be a mild fever, a sore throat, a tummyache, or a severe case of worms. Any deviation from normal should be thoroughly checked and the condition corrected. When an animal doesn't feel well, he changes from his normal routine and normal personality. We all must admit that sometimes when we have a headache or indigestion, we feel like biting people too. So we should not be insensitive or impatient with our dogs when they don't feel well. Instead we should find out what the trouble is and have it corrected.

Chorea

As an aftereffect of distemper we see chorea, a spasmodic twitching of the muscles, gradually spreading over the body to eventually cause disability or death. If the progress of the disease is stopped and localized in one area, the animal can live a normal life even though subject to occasional twitching. Fatigue or overexcitement increases the severity of the twitching.

Convulsions and Fits

Convulsions and fits can be caused by worms, high fever, overexcitement, poisons, head injuries, internal parasites, and congenital types of epilepsy. The distemper virus in some cases attacks the brain and causes an encephalitis which results in fits and then generalized convulsions over the body. In disease of the brain, in the beginning there is usually a clamping of the mouth ("chewing gum fit"), and in the latter stages partial or complete loss of vision accompanied by a high fever. There is also a complete change in personality from a docile dog to a vicious animal that bites everything in sight.

Epilepsy

We are seeing more and more epilepsy in dogs. The cause is unknown. Much of it is in poodles but all breeds are susceptible. For no apparent reason the animal goes into severe convulsions, frightening both owner and dog. After regaining consciousness, the dog may wobble for 5 to 10 minutes and then be normal in every respect. Epileptic fits in dogs are controlled by the same drugs that are used for human epilepsy, and many dogs with the condition live out their years in health and happiness.

Incoordination

This is a nervous disorder symptomatized by staggering. It is usually due to an inner-ear infection. Sometimes long-standing chronic ear infections go into the inner ear and affect the brain. The dog holds his head on one side and walks in circles. It is a serious condition, and when there is brain damage, it usually leaves the dog with a permanent disability. However, there are excellent drugs at the disposal of the veterinarian for combating the infection. Sometimes radical surgery is necessary. Ablation, or removal, of the entire ear canal is performed and the diseased part of the inner ear removed. It gives dramatic results in some critically ill patients.

Poisons

There are some types of poisons that affect the nervous system, causing extreme nervousness or convulsions. Strychnine is a prime example. It causes a severe convulsive type of syndrome similar to the epileptic fit. However, in strychnine poisoning the animal does not recover in 5 to 10 minutes as in epilepsy but continues to worsen as long as the poison is in the blood stream.

When sensitive dogs are overdosed with some of the insecticide poisons, there will be trembling which increases in severity to a shaking and then convulsions. Unless these animals are given antidotes, they soon succumb (see Chap. 14).

Rabies

Rabies is a disease that causes extreme nervousness and is usually what people think of when an animal has a fit or convulsions or acts unusually vicious. By studying the various symptoms of the disease, usually you can be assured that an animal does not have rabies just because he snaps at someone (see Chap. 16).

Spinal Meningitis

This is an infection caused by either a virus or bacteria and affecting the covering of the brain or the spinal cord. It is an extremely painful and critical condition, sometimes resulting in convulsions and death. Quick treatment is needed if it is going to be at all possible to save the animal.

NOSE

The dog's nose is a marvel of nature. Its anatomic design is perfect for maximum functioning in surveying the surrounding world. All living things, be they animal or vegetable, give off an unmistakable odor to the dog, and he is able by instinct to recognize each. Weather conditions affect his scent greatly. Dry, hot weather cuts down on the intensity of odors. Damp earth with not much breeze and a moderate sun are favorable for aiding the dog's scent. Freshly fallen snow is ideal for holding scent; it helps the hound find the rabbit.

The world of the dog is composed of smells, sights, and sound. Because of his relatively poor eyesight, he relies more on his sense of smell and on his hearing. His keen sense of smell is used not only for hunting but in the more vital areas of defense, search, and rescue.

Even though the dog sees only contrasting shades of gray, his sensitive nose supplements his knowledge of the surrounding environment very vividly.

The sense of smell varies greatly in individual dogs and breeds, but in general it can be estimated that the dog's scent discrimination is about a million times keener than man's.

In obedience training the sense of smell is important in retrieving and in tracking where the dog is required to follow the trail of a given individual. In bloodhounds the tracking instinct is a highly developed art, to the dismay of criminals and escapees.

Since no two people smell alike to the dog, apparently the odor of a human is as individual as a fingerprint.

There are many recorded experiments to bear out the theory that the dog has the ability to smell emotional and physical conditions, such as illness, fear, and joy. When the dog smells fear, he often will take advantage of the adversary—a tangible reason why a person should try to appear calm and not run from a dog.

RECTAL DISORDERS

Anal-Gland Impactions

These are two sac-like glands on either side of the anus which discharge their contents into the rectum. They are sometimes called skunk glands, because they are the same glands which produce such wicked results in the skunk when used as a defense mechanism. However, in the dog they are just a vestigial organ and not really needed.

The anal sacs normally secrete a viscous, malodorous liquid ranging in color from light gray to brown and in consistency from watery to paste-like. Occasionally blood or pus is seen; this indicates infection, and a veterinarian should be consulted.

Several theories have been advanced about the purpose of anal glands in dogs. One theory has it that the secretion lubricates the anus as an aid in defecation. This is disputed by some experts. Another theory is that the anal sacs give off a characteristic scent for each individual which may account for anal sniffing in dogs. Some dog researchers think that the anal secretions give off a sex-hormone odor which increases in intensity when the bitch is in season. There is some evidence for the theory that the anal glands can be linked with the strong territorial instinct in dogs. The dog can voluntarily release the anal-sac fluid and does so to demarcate his territorial boundaries. When frightened, the dog will empty his anal sacs, to the dismay of his enemies or the examining veterinarian, as the case may be.

Regardless of their function, the anal sacs are totally unnecessary to today's domestic dog, and surgical removal is acceptable when indicated in chronic rectal and skin infections.

Normally the fluid of the sacs is expelled into the rectum. However, sometimes the ducts become occluded so that the sacs enlarge with the retained fluid. Irritation of the gland ensues, and extreme discomfort in the dog's rectum. The dog tries to expel the enlarged anal sacs and rubs his rectum along the ground. (Rubbing the tail along the ground is not always a sign of worms!) The commonest symptom of anal-sac trouble is licking or biting at the anus.

If there is no infection present, the veterinarian can treat blocked or distended sacs by exerting gentle pressure so that the secretion is expressed. In dogs who have constant trouble, periodic expression of the sacs is necessary every 2 to 6 months. I advise you to ask your veterinarian to show you how to empty these glands. Foods that act as roughage, such as bran cereals, are good for keeping the glands open. If the glands become chronically infected, I advise surgical removal.

Left unattended, injury to the anus with subsequent infection to the surrounding skin is possible. Occasionally segments of tapeworm migrate into the ducts of the gland, causing a blockage. Anal-sac infection can progress to such an extent that an abscess of the anal gland results; this requires surgery to relieve the pressure. At times we see a generalized infection manifested by an itchy dry skin, and at other times I have incriminated the licking of the discharge from infected anal glands as the cause of throat infections and chronic intestinal infections. Because of their close proximity to the infected anal glands when an animal is licking or biting, eye and ear infections can also occur.

Some people refer to anal-gland impactions as hemorrhoids, but actually dogs don't suffer from hemorrhoids as they are known in humans.

Anal Infection

Sometimes bacterial and fungal infections occur in the anal ring and cause severe irritation. In mild cases of anal infection, vaseline or baby oil can correct the irritation, but the condition should really be corrected under medical supervision.

Foreign Objects

Sometimes foreign bodies pass through the alimentary tract and become hung in the rectum. The subsequent infection is usually painful. Generally a veterinarian can manually remove these foreign objects.

This is a condition where a large mass protrudes from the anus. The predisposing cause is usually a severe case of diarrhea which breaks down the tissue holding the rectum in place.

In cases where the rectum has protruded for a long time and there is quite a bit of injury to the tissue, gangrene often sets in. Sometimes we have to amputate part of the rectum and insert it back into the pelvic canal. The cause of the diarrhea has to be corrected before a permanent cure can be effected.

Rectal Tumors

These tumors usually are not malignant and can be removed surgically. However, if they are allowed to remain and grow, they can obstruct the passageway and cause severe impactions and chronic constipation, and eventually can become malignant.

Sometimes X-ray treatment is advisable. In male dogs periodic injections of female hormones will often keep the tumors from growing.

RESPIRATORY DISORDERS

Kennel Cough (Tracheo-Bronchitis)

This is an inflammation of the upper respiratory tract, specifically the windpipe and the bronchial tubes. It is an infectious condition and contagious from one dog to another. It can spread rapidly.

It is seen more commonly in caged animals than in outdoor pets, hence its name.

There is a persistent dry hacking cough which becomes more severe with excitement or exercise. The animal may seem normal in other respects, with a normal temperature and a healthy appetite.

Recently, the para-influenza virus has been found the major contributing cause. Fortunately, a vaccine has been developed and is very effective.

Treatment is both aggravating and prolonged. The disease runs a course of 2 weeks to 2 months. I've seen kennels affected by this "bug" for as long as 2 years. Treatment consists of antibiotics and cough medicine for symptomatic relief. Complete isolation of infected animals and strict sanitary procedures are essential to control this ailment.

Pneumonia

This is an infection of the lungs or the lining around the lungs, and it can be as serious in a dog as in a human. The poor patient has a difficult time breathing and will hold his head in an extended position trying to get oxygen into his lungs.

Well-equipped veterinary hospitals have oxygen cages which help the animal to breathe, along with medicinals which are projected through the air into the cage. The oxygen and medicinals help him symptomatically while the antibiotics which he receives destroy the infection.

Pulmonary Emphysema

This is an abnormal collection of air within the lungs which is characterized by coughing and difficult breathing. It is similar to the emphysema suffered by humans. Any respiratory disease or disorder can result in emphysema. There is no medicinal cure. Cough medicines are useless and sometimes contra-indicated.

The best way to help a pet with this condition is to keep him quiet. Rest, proper diet, and avoidance of excitement and strenuous exercise are necessary.

Sinusitis

This is a nasal disorder which can be distressing to dogs. The symptoms include sneezing, nasal discharge, and if there's an infection present, loss of appetite.

Sinusitis can be caused by:

—An allergy to a type of pollen or other vegetation—similar to human hay fever.

—Infected teeth can result in an abscess in the sinus cavity. The diseased teeth have to be removed and drainage from the sinus has to be established.

—Head injuries can result in broken bones in the sinuses. Infection usually follows.

—Foreign objects can sometimes work their way into the

sinuses; either debris accidentally embedded, such as twigs and grass, or such things as peanuts and bits of plastic toys stuck into dogs' noses by children.

—There is a mite that is occasionally found in the frontal sinuses.

The first step in the treatment of sinusitis is ridding the animal of the causative agent. Antibiotics, antihistamines, and steroids are used at the discretion of the veterinarian. Unfortunately most dogs don't tolerate nasal sprays and nose drops!

Tonsillitis

The tonsils are two small glands in the back recesses of the throat which are troublemakers in some dogs. In small dogs and toy breeds particularly, these little glands seem to be the cause of a lot of woe. Tonsillitis can occur in any breed from Mexican chihuahua to Irish wolfhound.

The causes of tonsillitis are many and varied—from a chill in a drafty room to getting wet either by rain or by a bath given at the wrong time of day. Some dogs cannot stand a sudden change in temperature or moisture.

Whenever a dog gags quite a bit, vomits occasionally, or coughs intermittently, tonsillitis should be suspected. Running eyes are sometimes caused by tonsillitis. Tonsillitis can cause chronic conditions of the sinuses in which the dog sneezes and wheezes continually. Intestinal disorders can be caused by badly infected tonsils; also ear infection. I've seen chronic skin problems completely clear up after a tonsillectomy.

Sometimes infected tonsils are not serious enough to give a high fever. They give a low-grade infection which keeps the animal just a little under par with a finicky appetite, occasional coughing spells, or a vomiting spasm once in a while. By the time the dog is obviously ill, the tonsillitis is in the acute stage, with high temperature and loss of appetite. When one looks into the mouth, the tonsils are seen to be large and inflamed, sometimes with yellow spots on them.

The usual treatment is antibiotics, throat sprays, and painting of the throat. In most cases I don't advise tonsillectomy. The average dog may have only one or two attacks in his lifetime, and with injections of antibiotics the disorder can be dealt with. For chronic cases I recommend tonsillectomy, but since so many factors must enter into this decision, it should be left entirely up to your professional adviser.

Another method to relieve the dog's irritated throat sug-

266

gests the application of a dab of unsalted butter or pure honey to the dog's nose. As he licks his nose, his throat is coated and soothed.

Tonsil cancer in dogs is blamed on pollution. It has been shown that city dogs suffer more tonsil cancer than do country dogs.

SKIN DISORDERS

Skin ailments are common among our canine population, and the causes are multitudinous. When one sees a scratching dog, the first thing one usually thinks of is fleas or some other external parasite. Actually the scratching can be due to any of countless allergies, or a diet deficiency, or fungus infection; and there are hundreds of causes of internal disarrangement.

Just the same, the commonest cause of skin infection is the flea. Once the dog starts scratching and digging his claws into his skin to rid himself of the flea, he gets a secondary infection, and then he licks and bites, causing more irritation, and this sets off a chain reaction. By using the excellent flea collars on the market, and the flea soaps, sprays, and powders, and by grooming regularly during the flea season, we can rid our dogs of this cause of skin disorders.

Collie Nose

This is an inflammation of the skin on the nose which is caused by photosensitization (sunlight irritation of the dog's skin). When the sensitive area above the nose is irritated by the sun, the dog rubs and scratches it, and it forms a pustular infection. It is seen particularly in light-colored dogs, and we try to keep these sensitive dogs out of the sunlight. Sometimes we use soothing suntan lotions on the nose. We have tattooed the skin above the nostrils, making it a dark color, to protect it from sunlight. Hair dye can be put on the skin to darken the hair so that it will absorb the light of the sun. Cortisone ointments over the area are helpful in relieving itching and inflammation.

Eczema

Eczema is a condition of the skin which covers many varieties of nonspecific dermatitis, has hundreds of different

267

causes, and includes all types of skin infections. It is classified into moist and dry.

In moist eczema—commonly called "hot spots" and sometimes "weeping mange"—we see a red and angry pustular-looking area which can arise in hours. It itches terribly, and the dog licks it if he can reach it, or scratches it, and he spreads it quickly and furiously all over his body. To relieve this condition we give the dog tranquilizers or sedatives, and we use cortisone preparations and soothing healing ointments on the eczema. A good drying powder, such as BFI, is also soothing and helpful. If possible it is wise to bandage the affected area; keeping the animal's tongue and paws away from the infection is half the battle. (See the end of this chapter for suggestions on bandaging.)

In dry eczema the skin is dry and scaly in appearance. As in moist eczema, it is usually itchy, and the same treatment is prescribed, including bandaging to allay any chances of secondary infection. Something oily like lanolin or baby oil rubbed on the skin will relieve the itchiness, but the origin must be found.

One of the major causes of dry eczema is dietary imbalance—not receiving enough of the proper foods, or too much of one kind and not enough of another. Some diets don't have enough fats or oils, for example those limited to some types of commercial dry dog food, which cause the hair of some dogs to become dry and dull-looking and then start to shed. The simple addition of fats or oils to the diet will often correct the dry-eczema condition.

Another cause of dry eczema is hormonal imbalance. In spayed females we sometimes get this type of eczema with itching and shedding. The addition of female hormones clears the skin. We also see eczema in older dogs, both male and female. Usually with the addition of hormones we can help those animals and relieve their itchy skin.

Dry eczema is also seen when there are certain organic imbalances, such as underactive thyroid glands, kidney disorders, or digestive disturbances. Certain toxins are released into the blood stream. In nephritis we often see a severe eczema which usually clears up along with the kidney dysfunction.

Another cause is psychosomatic in origin. Dry eczema often occurs when a dog is envious of another dog or pet in the family. He will take to scratching to gain attention and liter-

268

ally scratch himself into a bad skin condition. (See Chap. 11, under Psychosomatic Ailments.)

Summer eczema is a condition some dogs develop every spring as soon as the weather starts getting warmer, and they scratch and itch until the frosts of early winter. The prime cause of summer eczema is fleas, along with other external parasites; ear mites and ear infection also cause a dog to scratch, with subsequent eczema or skin infection developing around the ears. The second most persistent cause is fungus infection. In some areas of the country there are certain types of fungus which live in grass, weeds, trees and other vegetation and which infect certain dogs (some dogs are allergic to the vegetation itself). A dog may have to be kept indoors to effect a cure, since the heat of the summer, and the sun, make the skin more susceptible to the fungus. During the early-morning dew and late at night when the grasses are wet, a dog with this condition should be walked by leash on the sidewalk or pavement.

Treatment of summer eczema requires medicated shampoos at regular intervals, antihistamines, and cortisones. But we must find out the cause, and then try to eliminate it. The promiscuous use of cortisone is dangerous to a dog's health. Cortisone can cause serious kidney disorders; it should be used only under the supervision of a veterinarian.

Elbow Callus

This unsightly condition can vary from a bare patch on the elbow to a thickening of the skin to a crusty elephant-like skin. Sometimes the enlargement grows until surgery is necessary to remove it. Occasionally the elbow joint fills with fluid because of a bursitis, and this also is treated by surgery. Elbow callus is usually seen in larger breeds and is caused by lying on hard, rough ground or on hard floors.

In simple cases vaseline, lanolin, or oil rubbed on the elbow joint will relieve the dryness and stimulate hair growth. In more serious cases we get a secondary infection in which pus exudes from the skin, and this requires cleaning with hydrogen peroxide and the application of antibiotic ointments.

Giving the dog a mattress or soft bedding will often eliminate the callus. Some people put stockinettes on the elbows to protect them from the bare floors. The condition can turn into a serious one if mismanaged.

Impetigo

Impetigo is little pustules seen on the abdomen. In young dogs these are also called distemper sores. They are seen any time a dog, especially a young dog, has a fever, and the condition is therefore associated with distemper because of the high fever involved. It is similar to impetigo in children, but it is not contagious to children.

Mange

Mange is of two types: demodectic (or follicular) and sarcoptic. Both are difficult to treat, but with present-day drugs the skin can be cleared up effectively. Occasionally there are secondary infections to deal with. The parasites of both types of mange can be examined under the microscope, and this is the only sure way of diagnosis.

Demodectic mange, "red mange," is the more difficult to treat because the parasite lives in the hair follicles. The mite burrows into the skin and finds its way into the follicles. Years ago this type of mange was almost incurable, but today, with the internal and external medications available, cures are commonplace.

Young animals are more easily infected with this mite, and volumes of research have been done.

Signs of mange usually are evident in puppies between 3 and 9 months of age. Predisposing factors to be considered in this infection are: diet, debilitating diseases, intestinal parasite infestation, any stress conditions (such as rapid growth, dentition) and certain breed susceptibility such as in Boston terriers.

Some veterinarians suspect that puppies may become infected before birth; others feel it is more likely that the mites are transmitted to newborn puppies from the dam. Good health in the puppy is important in combating the affliction. Some cases are uncontrollable in weak and sickly puppies.

The symptoms, usually lesions of bareness, start around the head, or around the eyes and mouth, but may appear on any part of the body. The lesions cause loss of hair and reddening of the skin, and the skin becomes thick and wrinkled. The skin changes are sometimes a hypersensitive reaction to the mite itself rather than the infection, and this is why some cases of mange are stubborn and resist all treatment.

We treat externally with such preparations as benzene hexachloride, benzyl benzoate, and rotenone, and we have injections and tablets to help kill the parasites in the blood stream at the hair follicles. Some veterinarians think that a high-protein diet is essential in treatment. Unfortunately some resistant cases don't respond to any treatment.

Dedicated treatment is an absolute necessity to rid an animal of the mite and prevent reinfestation. At times secondary infection with the staphylococcus germ appears, and the animal develops purulent sores all over his body. Constant use of the most potent antibiotics is necessary to save the animal.

In sarcoptic mange clinical symptoms are much easier to recognize. The sarcoptic mite causes an itchy skin which is not present in the demodectic type.

Scabs are formed on the skin, and hence the condition is called scabies by some people. The dog sheds its hair and in severe cases becomes almost totally bald. Sarcoptic mange spreads much more rapidly than demodectic mange, and it has an unmistakable diagnostic musty odor.

Sulphur preparations and insecticides kill this type of mange.

In general treatment for mange the bedding must be changed regularly to prevent the animal from becoming reinfected. Besides baths, ointments, and medications, it is necessary to observe strict sanitary procedures with the patient.

Incidentally—although it's not likely—these types of mange can be communicated to humans. Careful disinfecting one's hands after treating an animal with mange is recommended.

Old-Age Warts

In older dogs we often see small growths on the skin which we call old-age warts. They are not troublesome to the dog unless they increase in size. The animal rubs at them and breaks them off occasionally, with consequent irritation and bleeding. The warts can be removed if they give trouble; and if they start growing in the slightest, I advise having them removed. If they remain the same size and are not in an area vital to body functions, I would leave them alone.

Pustules

Pustules, or pimples, are often found around the mouth or chin, and because of saliva and continual moisture they are difficult to treat. Sometimes the eruptions show up in the eyelid. With the use of antibiotics and soothing lotions we can handle the affliction quite well. The pustules are usually caused by a staphylococcus infection. In severe cases the condition is called furunculosis. The mouth or eyes swell to tremendous size and usually cause the animal to lose his appetite. It is uncomfortable and can be fatal if not handled correctly, as these infections can spread to the internal organs, such as the lungs and kidneys. We institute antibiotic therapy, and open the abscesses to let the pus out.

Ringworm

Ringworm is a skin disorder caused by a fungus infection which involves the hair and hair follicles. It is contagious to other dogs, cats, and human beings.

Its appearance is indicated by ring-shaped, usually red-colored patches covered with scales. In some cases the red patches form honeycomb-like crusts over the hair roots and give off a distinctly moldy odor. When it affects the feet, it is called athlete's foot.

It is due to either one or two parasitic fungi. It can be gotten from the ground, from droppings of other dogs, and from manure fertilizer.

Because the fungus doesn't affect the hair above the skin surface, the treatment of ringworm is aimed at the fungus at the base of the hair underneath the surface of the skin. Clipping the hair from the affected areas is essential. Special antifungal shampoos and dips may be used on the affected skin along with iodine and other specific fungicidal solutions. Salicylic acid can also be prescribed. Ordinary sulphur ointments are not very effective.

The most efficient treatment for ringworm is the internal method in which griseofulvin is given by mouth over a month or more. This destroys the fungus at the base of the hair.

Sebaceous Cysts

These are growths which are found under the skin. They can be small, or at times they can get as large as a walnut. Occasionally a cyst erupts—a thick white cheesy-like mass—and after this is expelled, the cyst closes up and is small again for a while. Invariably it gets large again. Cysts are usually caused by a secretion from the sebaceous glands under the skin. The only correction is surgical removal. They resemble tumors on palpation, but generally one can feel the soft inner part, which shows that it is a sebaceous cyst rather than a tumor.

Seborrhea

This is an inflammation of the skin caused by an infection of the sebaceous glands. The infection causes an excessive secretion which forms a crusty foul-smelling condition. It is easily diagnosed by the cheesy-like scabs on the body and the unmistakable odor. It is seen mostly in cocker spaniels and dachshunds. The animal itches, bites, and scratches. The thick crusty condition is relieved by medicated shampoos, cortisone, and certain types of antibiotics.

Tumors

Skin tumors appear in malignant and benign forms. Any time there is a chronic ulcerated area of the skin that will not heal, a skin tumor should be suspected. The tumors are difficult to treat because they itch badly and the animal can't leave them alone. A chronic skin ulcer that doesn't respond to medication should be removed surgically, and a biopsy made for detection of malignancy. Skin tumors are seen especially on the legs, and as the dog will keep chewing and licking the infected area, it can quickly grow from pinpoint size. Great Danes are especially susceptible. Sometimes X-ray treatment is used. The area must be covered to keep the dog's mouth and claws away from it.

General Information on Skin Disorders

Skin ailments can occur as often in short-haired dogs as in long-haired ones. In the treatment of long-coated dogs it is generally imperative to clip and cut the hair so that the skin can be treated more efficiently.

All dogs suffering from skin conditions should be kept out of direct sunlight, which irritates the skin. Sometimes a

273

simple cure for eczema is to keep a dog in an air-conditioned house during the hot summer days.

In a bad skin condition use only mild medicated shampoos. Disinfect, and use insecticides in the living quarters of the animal to keep all ticks, fleas, and lice away. Droppings should be picked up promptly, and the beddings should be aired and sunned at least weekly.

Bandaging: Protecting Against Licking and Scratching

If the dog is scratching an area of skin with his hind legs, we make little booties out of gauze, bandage, and tape. Because the toenails are conducive to skin infection, with the nails covered the wound may clear up by itself.

If the lesion is on the body around the chest or rib cage, a sweater or a towel wrapped around the body and pinned securely will protect it from scratching and licking.

If an area cannot be bandaged, an "Elizabethan" collar can be made to prevent the dog from turning around to lick a certain area. Simply take a piece of plastic or cardboard and attach it to his collar around his neck.

The Coat

It is commonly believed that the more often one cuts a dog's hair, the richer will be the texture and color with each new growth. This is not true. You can cut your own hair every day for the next ten years and neither the texture nor the color will be affected.

The hair of the dog is hollow, and therefore the general health of the animal has much to do with his skin and coat. As the hair contains air and blood and as the hair root gets its nutrition and sustenance directly from the blood stream, disorders of the skin and coat have to be treated internally even more than externally.

Alopecia (loss of hair). This is usually caused by an internal condition—a dietary or hormonal imbalance. In many cases involving Pomeranians and dachshunds I've found a hypothyroid condition (underactive thyroid gland). By the addition of thyroid extract or thyroid-stimulating drugs we usually can cure the baldness. It is also seen in some spayed females and castrated males. These conditions have to be cured internally.

Dandruff. Flakiness of the dog's skin usually is of internal origin, such as insufficient oils or fats in the diet, and we usually advise adding these to the food, along with wheat-germ oil.

Dandruff is common in house dogs who stay inside most of the time. They don't get enough fresh air, and the skin dries out.

One of the main causes of "summer snow" is too frequent bathing, especially with strong soaps. The bathing robs the dog of the natural oils which keep his skin healthy.

In puppies a common cause of dandruff is worms. Worms seem to deprive the dog of needed sustenance. After worming, the dandruff usually disappears.

In the treatment of dandruff we should first find the cause and then try to prevent it. In symptomatic treatment we sponge the animal with alcohol, which gets rid of some of the flakiness, and then we apply a bland oil or a hair tonic containing lanolin. We give the dog an oil rubdown once a week, massaging the oil right into the skin. In dandruff it is not the hair but the skin that needs treatment.

Shedding. Many dog owners are constantly perplexed and irritated by their dogs' leaving hair all over the house. Normally dogs shed about twice a year—in the spring and sometimes in the fall—getting ready for seasonal changes. Also, there is a normal shedding when the puppy changes into an adult. He loses his puppy hair, and we can see a new type of hair, his adult hair, coming in. Depending on the size of the dog, and the breed, this occurs at 6 to 18 months of age.

Many of our pets who live in apartments and warm houses and love to snuggle up to hot-air or other heating units shed the year round. The heat dries out the hair and skin and causes excessive shedding.

Frequent shampooing with harsh soaps also causes excessive shedding. The dog has a normal oily secretion to keep his skin and coat healthy, so moderation is essential.

To prevent excessive shedding, you must see to proper grooming. The dead hair must be eliminated. The more you brush the hair and skin, the healthier they will be. Not all shedding is pathological. Bathe your dog occasionally with a bland soap. At times rub him down with oil on your fingertips to keep his hair and skin well oiled. Lanolin is probably one of the best ingredients for rubbing into the skin (there are also lanolin sprays to help the texture of the skin and hair). In diet the normal dry commercial dog foods generally don't have enough fats and oils for the dog with the dry skin, so I advise the addition of such things as bacon fat, beef trimmings, and wheat-germ oil. Vitamin E, which is in wheat germ, is an excellent skin conditioner, and a lot of show dogs are kept on this to keep their hair beautiful.

In warm weather I advise clipping, which removes a lot of dead hair and eliminates shedded hair all over a house. But don't have the dog's hair shaved down to the skin. Always have a minimum of a quarter of an inch of hair on the body to give the skin some insulation against the hot weather and sunlight.

SPINAL DISORDERS

The spine is a sensitive part of the body. The symptoms of a disorder at first may be ambiguous—the animal may refuse to jump onto his usual couch or chair or will not walk up or down stairs. A spinal disorder may go unnoticed until the animal refuses to move or moves gingerly. As the condition progresses he will cry out in pain when he tries to move into a certain position. He may hold his head either straight outward or to one side if the injury is in the region of the neck.

Accidents

In automotile accidents we sometimes get fractured bones in the spinal cord. These can be repaired surgically if the spinal cord has not been severed. If there is a complete severance of the spinal cord, there is no hope for recovery, as the cord will not regenerate itself.

Sometimes there is temporary paralysis of the spine caused by bleeding inside the spinal cord due to an automobile accident.

There is also a syndrome called "shock paralysis" in which the animal lies paralyzed for several days owing to the shock of the automobile accident or some other trauma. This often shows signs of recovery in 2 or 3 days and complete recovery sometimes within 2 to 3 weeks.

One of the commonest injuries to the spine is injury to one of the spinal discs, which are paddings between the vertebrae. Sometimes when there is strenuous movement or an injury to the back, the disc slips out of place or is completely ruptured ("slipped" disc; "ruptured" disc). The condition is seen most commonly in dachshunds—due to the elongated body—and Pekingese, poodles, and cockers are also susceptible.

In any painful condition of the body where the animal refuses to move in his usual fashion and will not jump and romp, an injury to the spine should be considered. There is incoordination in the rear legs, and gradually the animal goes down on his rear legs and begins dragging. There is severe pain when the back is touched.

Definite diagnosis has to be made with X rays. There are several methods of treatment, and sometimes surgery is the only recourse. Symptomatic treatment with hot baths, heat, ultrasonic waves, and drugs such as cortisone and butazolidine are all benefical in recovery from a slipped disc. Bed rest is essential, and confinement to an area of the house where the animal cannot jump into his favorite chair or sofa. Jumping is probably the most predisposing cause of a slipped disc is a dog.

In severe cases *complete* nursing care is as important as any medication or rest. Urine and bowel evacuation daily is essential. We often see a kidney stagnation due to the paralysis in the spine and a subsequent kidney infection. These often result in a uremic condition and death. Laxatives or enemas are needed to control bowel movements until the dog can evacuate by himself. Physiotherapy of the hind legs is essential—massaging and rotation of the legs to counteract atrophy of the muscles. Bedsores usually develop from the animal's lying in one position and from urine. Daily baths are necessary, and vaseline or vitamin A or vitamin D ointment can be rubbed on the sores to prevent secondary infection. A paralyzed animal should be rotated from side to side frequently in order to prevent congestion in the lungs, which also can cause death. The animal should be propped up so that his head is in an upright position as much as possible. Lying on his side sometimes incapacitates the animal even further.

These conditions sometimes recur in animals, and they

have to be careful about jumping and other strenuous exercise. These points are often difficult to get across to the patient. He simply will not lie in traction for 6 weeks as will the human patient. Recovery is usually slow, varying from 2 to 6 weeks. There are some dogs who never recover completely; we have all seen pictures of these animals with their wheelcarts. They are strapped into these contraptions and run around to their hearts' delight, using their front legs to pull themselves along.

Spinal Arthritis (Spondylitis)

This arthritis of the spine causes extreme pain. It can be confirmed only by X ray, in which one can see little calcium deposits (spurs) developing on the vertebral column. Any excessive motion in any direction will cause pain and in severe cases can cause paralysis. Aspirin, butazolidine, and cortisone give some symptomatic relief.

TUMORS

Tumors can appear on any organ of the body, and each presents a different challenge. There are two types of growths or tumors: one is a benign, or harmless, tumor and the other is a malignant, or a cancerous, growth. It takes professional skill and medical facilities to distinguish between the two, and I certainly advise seeking the help of your veterinarian if you discover an enlargement. In my opinion early removal of all tumors is of utmost necessity, as it usually will forestall further complications in other parts of the body. Dogs also have a leukemia similar to humans, as well as tumors of the lymph glands which are always malignant, rapid in spread, and usually fatal. Hopefully the fruits of the extensive medical research in progress will soon be available to help both humans and animals. In the meantime surgery is the only complete answer for any type of tumor.

The Head

Dogs can be affected with tumors of the brain (see Nervous Disorders in this chapter).
Tumors of the ear occlude the ear canal. They are distressful and cause the dog to shake his head continually (see Ear Disorders in this chapter).

278

There are also tumors in the mouth, and unfortunately some of these tumors, either in the hard palate or in the soft palate, are malignant. Sometimes they attack the bone of the mouth and continue to spread if not detected in the early stages. Tumors also appear on the gums, usually in old boxers. These benign masses can be effectively removed with electrical cauterization (see The Mouth in this chapter).

Tumors appear in the nostrils and the sinus passages, either on one or on both sides. They are usually malignant and give a poor prognosis. If there is a discharge of blood from one or both nostrils, be suspicious of a tumorous mass in the sinus cavities (see Respiratory Disorders in this chapter).

Mammary Tumors

Mammary tumors usually are seen in older, unspayed females, and because they increase in size after the heat period they are believed to be correlated with excessive female hormones.

In some cases we treat breast tumors with male-hormone injections at periodic intervals, which seems to control their size.

Eliminating the heat period in the older bitch is the most desired approach to treatment. I therefore advise spaying older bitches; this helps to keep down the spread of mammary tumors and also eliminates metritis, and infection of the uterus.

One fact seems to be established: if a bitch is spayed when she is under one year of age, it is most unlikely she will develop mammary tumors. Surgery after the age of one can mean that the tumors can occur with about equal frequency in spayed and unspayed bitches. If the bitch is to be kept only as a pet, I advise spaying between 6 and 7 months of age.

When one breast is affected, often the adjoining breasts begin to have masses around them too. In such cases when we have to resort to surgery, we remove two or three breasts in a row. Usually the lymph nodes are removed to make sure the tumors are not spread through the lymphatic system to other parts of the body.

Mammary tumors can be either benign or cancerous. If they are malignant, they can spread to other organs. If an X ray reveals that the tumors have spread to the lungs or any place else, removing the breast growths will not help the patient.

Other Tumors

Tumors in the lungs usually give a poor prognosis. In a dog suffering from bone cancer, often the tumors spread into the lungs, giving chest abnormalities. In tumors of the bone, if there is any enlargement of the bone an X ray should be make immediately.

Tumors of the organs, such as the liver and spleen, are common, especially the spleen. The intestinal organ also can be affected.

Tumors of the kidneys sometimes appear, and if only one kidney is damaged, it can be removed with good results.

In the male dog we see tumors of the testicles which necessitate removal of one or both testicles to prevent further spread.

In the male dog, for rectal tumors, we inject female hormones which in some cases seem to help control the size of the tumors.

URINARY DISORDERS

Affliction of the urinary tract in middle-aged and older dogs is becoming the most prevalent type of abnormality that we see in our veterinary clinics today. With improved over-all treatment and longer life there is a preponderance of urinary disorders. It is a problem that the dog owner and the veterinarian must face together in order to prolong the life of the patient. It is not a simply problem that can be cured with a shot of penicillin. It is degeneration of the tissues of the kidney so desperately needed to support life. The animal can live with only one quarter of the normal kidney tissue functioning. When more than three-quarters of the tissue is destroyed, signs of kidney disease are quite evident. Although there is not yet a complete cure, with adequate diet and care the animal can enjoy life for many years to come. Veterinary medicine in the future will have artificial kidney machines that can be used on dogs in kidney failure. I'm sure that we will see the transplantation of healthy kidneys to dogs with kidney failure, which is becoming so successful in human kidney disease.

The principal symptom of bladder and kidney stones is straining to urinate, with the appearance of only a few drops of urine combined with blood. X ray and urinalysis should be done immediately.

The causes of urinary calculi are not understood in either canine or human medicine. However, three predisposing factors are noticed in cases of bladder- and kidney-stone formation: (1) infection, (2) high concentration of minerals in the diet, and (3) reduced water intake. These conditions start a concentration of crystals in the urine with subsequent stone formation.

Although stones can occur in all breeds, Dalmatians are notorious for their urinary problems. It is believed that they inherit their susceptibility to the formation of uric acid calculi.

Urinary stones are composed of either phosphates or uric acid, and which type is present is determined by chemical analysis. We must find out which type of stone is involved so that prophylactic diet to prevent recurrence can be instituted. If the stones are of the phosphate type, milk, cheese, and other dairy products have to be eliminated from the diet. For uric acid crystals, meat and poultry products should be avoided, and the diet made up of vegetables, cereal, eggs, and other dairy products.

In prophylaxis, water consumption must be kept at a high level even if it means adding salt to the diet. Other methods are chicken broth and beef broth flavored to the dog's taste; and if they are not the phosphate type of stones, ice cream and other dairy products containing water should be added to the diet. Diet must be controlled to produce either an acid or an alkaline urine as the case requires.

Any urinary infection should be treated and controlled as soon as possible.

Preventive measures are by far the best means of prolonging the life of a dog with bladder or kidney stones.

Cystitis

Cystitis is an inflammation of the bladder whose principal symptom is frequent urination. The burning sensation in the bladder causes the animal to feel the need to urinate frequently even when the bladder is empty. In chronic cystitis there is often blood in the urine due to irritation of the lining of the bladder wall. The animal is in extreme pain, he walks with a hunched-up back, and he cries when palpated.

It is seen more often in females than in males, and it is derived from getting wet or chilled and lying in damp places.

The veterinarian will use urinary antiseptics to soothe the irritated bladder lining and urinary antibiotics to combat the infection.

Nephritis

The origin of nephritis, which is an inflammation of the kidneys, is complex and under constant discussion by practicing veterinarians and researchers. The exact cause or causes still must be found. It is known that some infectious diseases, such as leptospirosis, can cause an acute infection of the kidneys, and in some cases after the disease has run its course it leaves the kidney tissue damaged, so that the animal will suffer from nephritis in the chronic form (chronic interstitial nephritis) later in life. Other diseases also leave the kidney tissue damaged—for example, distemper, hepatitis, pneumonia—and susceptible to nephritis. Since the kidneys are the excretory organs of the body, any infection anywhere is absorbed by the kidneys, ends up in the kidney tissues, and interferes with normal kidney functioning.

One of the first symptoms we notice in nephritis is extreme thirst. The dog consumes a great deal more water, and then of course urinates more. Although many other diseases can manifest this symptom, any dog that is abnormally thirsty should be checked with a urinalysis for kidney malfunction.

There are two types of nephritis—the acute stage, which comes on quickly, and the chronic form. When the condition is acute, the dog is in obvious pain, hunched up and sensitive to palpation on the back. He is reluctant to move around and has a high fever. Treatment is usually more successful than with the chonic form since the kidney tissue has not been destroyed or damaged.

If the attack is mild and the dog gets over it, he goes into chronic nephritis. Many middle-aged and older dogs are showing this deterioration of the kidney tissues, due to a very high protein diet. When there is a decrease in kidney function, the waste products in the body which are normally excreted in the urine begin to accumulate in the body, and we see depression, loss of appetite, and vomiting. As the disease progresses the dog shows signs of uremia, which is extremely toxic and critical. A dog with a kidney condition should be under the supervision of a veterinarian so that any complication can be treated promptly. Vomiting is one of the first signs of trouble; it means that the kidney function is not keeping up with the accumulated waste products.

In treatment, aside from the antibiotics now in use for nephritis—there are several good ones that are used in both human and canine urology—dietary practices are of utmost importance.

A low-quantity but high-quality protein diet is essential. There are some prescription diets on the market which have been maintaining many nephritic dogs for years with good results. Salt-free diets are important (salt is bad in kidney diseases), and so is free access to water to flush out the kidneys of any impurities and waste products that have accumulated in the body.

One of the problems with the prescription diets is making the food palatable. I advise using cottage cheese and cooked egg as a source of protein. It is best to eliminate as much meat as possible, since some types of protein are detrimental to the kidneys. A small amount of liver in the diet is good to provide certain iron and vitamins. Some chicken may be used both to flavor the food and provide small amounts of protein. Cooked oatmeal or rice with a little sugar or syrup will provide taste and carbohydrates. All salty foods, such as ham, bacon, sausages, hot dogs, and wieners, should be avoided, as well as other highly spiced meats and foods.

The dog should be given plenty of liquids, in small amounts but frequently, through the day. It is not good for a dog to gorge himself on a quart or two of water at one time; small pans filled every few hours are much more satisfactory. Milk and other fluid dairy products, broth, and fruit juices may be used if the dog will drink them.

In prevention a careful diet, well balanced and not extremely high in protein, should be maintained. When the dog reaches middle age (5 to 6 years), a urinalysis should be done every 6 months. Some of the commercial dog foods are extremely high in protein, and although most dogs love a high-protein diet, it seems to have a deteriorating effect on the kidney tissues. I suggest adding table scraps to these commercial foods.

In feeding a nephritic patient, high-quality proteins are

very important. With high-quality proteins less proteins are required and therefore there are fewer waste products resulting in less strain on the kidneys. There is also less strain on the liver in its function of coverting protein and fat into glucose.

High-quality proteins are contained in beef, horsemeat, chicken, and lamb. Corn, wheat, barley, egg, milk, corn oil, and soy beans are good examples of other foods containing high-quality protein.

16 DISEASES

RABIES

Although rabies, or hydrophobia, is a disease that has been known to man since the days of Aristotle, there is more confusion about it than about almost any disease, human or animal. The virus of rabies infects all warm-blooded animals, including man. Infection with the virus is 100 percent fatal in all species with the possible exception of the bat. It produces an infection of the central nervous system which leads to a most horrible death.

The word hydrophobia, which is of Greek derivation and means "fear of water," may have started all the confusion. The rabid dog doesn't actually fear water. He has an extreme thirst and wants water desperately. When the disease has progressed to the stage where the dog's lower jaw is paralyzed and he cannot drink water, the frustration causes his actions to become frenzied and mad.

Rabies is not a hot-weather disease, as is commonly thought. Although it is more in evidence during the spring and summer months, when animals are outside more and roaming about, it is a year-round disease.

It is not solely a dog disease. All warm-blooded animals can transmit it, and all warm-blooded animals are susceptible to the virus. It can be contracted only from an animal with the disease, and for the disease to develop, the saliva of the rabid animal must get into the blood stream of the victim through a lesion in the skin, a bite, a cut, or an opening.

Rabies in the initial stage is preventable. If a person is bitten by an animal, or an animal is bitten by an animal, professional help should be sought immediately, as the necessary steps for the prevention of rabies should be instituted as soon as possible. For a bite on the face or head, emergency measures should be taken at once because the closer the bite is to the brain, the more rapidly the symptoms will develop.

The incubation period, which is the time between exposure and the development of symptoms, is extremely variable—from a few days to a year, depending on many factors, including the virulence of the virus, the nature of the bite, and the location of the bite. It has been established that rabies virus can be present in the saliva of an animal, in the incubative stages, as long as 9 days prior to the development of the first symptoms, and that the dog can transmit the virus 3 to 4 days before any symptoms are seen in the dog. Therefore both confinement and observation for 10 to 14 days are essential. At the present time there are no tests that can be made on a living animal to determine if it is in the early stages of the disease. If no symptoms develop in the dog for 10 days after he has bitten a human or another animal, it is almost certain that he has no rabies virus in his saliva.

If, however, the dog does show symptoms of rabies within the 10-day incubation period, *there is still time enough for the human to receive treatment*—prophylactic injections of rabies, the Pasteur treatment, which is 14 injections given at daily intervals. When an animal has bitten a person, the animal should be under the observation of a veterinarian so that the earliest symptoms can be noted and the person's physician notified so that treatment can be started at once. Contrary to common fallacy, these vaccinations are not painful and don't have dire consequences. If one is bitten by a rabid animal, there's no choice in the matter: the treatment has to be taken for survival. The same procedures apply for a pet bitten by a rabid animal, and there is a similar treatment.

The commonest symptom of rabies, in the early stages, may be simply a change in the behavior of the animal. A quiet, friendly dog suddenly becomes irritable and starts biting at people and objects. Where he was affectionate, he becomes shy, hides under furniture and stays in corners by himself. In a word, he's a completely changed dog. As there are two forms of rabies—the "dumb" form and the "furious" form—as the disease progresses, the dog is affected according to the form the virus takes in him.

In the dumb form, or paralytic form, there is usually paralysis of the lower jaw. The dog is extremely thirsty but has

285

difficulty in swallowing and the jaw hangs open uselessly. People have been known to put their hands down into the dog's throat because they thought a bone or a foreign object was stuck in the jaw and causing the paralysis. To put one's hand in a rabid dog's mouth is insidious exposure to the disease, since any cuts or abrasions on the hands will allow the virus to enter the blood stream. Such cases are required to take the Pasteur treatment.

Also, in the dumb form, the animal is lethargic and tends to stay in one area. For this reason it is not so dangerous as the furious type, but it gives a false sense of security. As the disease progresses the dog undergoes further paralysis, and as the muscles of the voice box become paralyzed there is a change in the animal's voice. It is an eerie sound that is unmistakable and quite diagnostic once one has heard the sound of a rabid dog. In the later stages the dog is unable to eat or drink, paralysis completely overtakes his body, and death follows in a week to 10 days from the time of the biting stage.

In the furious stage there is a tendency for the dog to roam, biting at all moving objects he encounters. As the disease progresses his eyesight seems to diminish, and he snaps at everything around him. He shows a perverted appetite for all kinds of foreign matter, including sticks and stones. He may roam for miles and miles, which is one of the ways the disease spreads. As it progresses the animal becomes more and more uncontrollably frenzied.

Contrary to popular opinion, frothing at the mouth is not a diagnostic symptom of rabies. It may or may not occur. Frothing can be caused by simple indigestion or nausea, and unfortunately many innocent dogs have been killed because of this erroneous belief.

A suspected animal should under no circumstances be destroyed until the disease has been permitted to run its full course. The veterinarian has proper facilities for confinement of these animals, and public-health laboratories throughout the country have an accurate diagnosis for rabies, which consists in making slides of the brain cells. If the animal is killed too soon, the lesions in the brain cells may not be developed and may give a false negative.

Even if a vaccinated dog bites a person, he is legally required to be quarantined for 10 to 14 days to make sure the vaccine took. Rabies vaccine is as close to perfect as any vaccine can be, but there is always a chance of error.

Fortunately the use of rabies vaccine throughout the country has cut immeasurably the number of cases of rabies each year. Since most people realize the danger involved to them personally, they remember to have their dogs vaccinated. But once is not enough—or twice. *Annual vaccination of all pets is an absolute necessity*—or every 3 years when using a chick-embryo type of vaccine.

DISTEMPER

Distemper is probably the oldest known disease affecting dogs. It is sometimes referred to as the "canine plague" because of its characteristics and virulence. It may be compared to influenza in humans, as it is an acute infectious disease caused by a virus. The disease is spread by air-borne particles and by direct contact with an infected animal or a contaminated object, for example a food pan. It is not contagious to man but is easily spread among animals. Many species of animals can spread distemper to the dog; it appears in natural hosts, such as wolves, raccoons, foxes, ferrets, and minks. It is not confined to any area of the world and is not confined to any age. Although it is most common in the first year of life, it can be seen in older dogs, and even in dogs who have received "lifetime" immunity. Distemper is difficult to treat because it is usually complicated by secondary bacterial invaders. Because it is much more easily prevented than cured, it is extremely important that a dog be vaccinated as early as possible, before he can come into contact with the disease.

The incubation period from time of exposure to the virus to when symptoms begin to develop is 3 to 8 days. The virus which causes distemper has an affinity for the respiratory, digestive, urinary, and nervous systems. It can cause serious nasal and eye discharges, intestinal upsets with diarrhea and vomiting, and fever, which occurs 5 days after exposure. In the final stages it produces a neurological disturbance which results in chorea (muscle twitching) and convulsions. The next stages are blindness and death.

Specific symptoms usually begin to appear about 5 days after exposure:

—The temperature, taken rectally, rises to 103-104 degrees on about the 5th day.

—There is continuous squinting and batting of the eyes, which become very sensitive to light; and a clear watery discharge will be observed. This discharge thickens, becomes more profuse and then turns whitish or yellowish as the disease progresses.

—The dog develops a running nose with a mucoid, purulent discharge. As the disease progresses the discharge increases and turns to a bloody mass which cakes up continually around the dog's nostrils.

—The dog loses his appetite and becomes listless.

—Vomiting and diarrhea are followed by extreme thirst; and dehydration sets in. When the dog drinks, he often vomits the water immediately. The bowel movements get more and more watery and many change to blood as the disease goes on.

—As the dog dehydrates he loses weight rapidly.

—He may also develop a cough unproductive of any matter.

—As the fever and disease continue the animal becomes depressed.

—Sometimes there are "distemper sores," which are little pustules—fever sores seen on the skin of abdomen.

—When swelling is noted in the lymph nodes of the throat, death can follow in a few days.

Treatment for distemper is complicated and should be supervised by a veterinarian. At present there are no drugs that will kill the virus, so the treatment is aimed at stopping the secondary bacterial infections. Globulin, which is the immunizing serum, is important in treatment. The veterinarian has adequate antibiotics with which to combat the pneumonia and diarrhea usually present. Aspirin is helpful in keeping the fever down and making the dog more comfortable. The patient must be kept as strong as possible with vitamins, nutritious food, and constant nursing care.

Nursing care is second only to the serum and the antibiotics. Nursing chores include keeping the eyes washed with boric acid solution and keeping the nostrils clear to allow the animal to breathe more easily. The purulent matter which tends to form in the nostrils should be washed with saline or boric acid solution and the nostrils greased with a medicated salve, such as Vick's. A vaporizer in the room with the dog is recommended to help his breathing. If the animal refuses food, he should be force-fed. A nourishing preparation is eggnog consisting of milk, egg yolk, and syrup. Sometimes a sick animal will eat things he would not normally touch, so a large assortment of foods should be offered to tempt him—

even such things as ice cream or candy. If he won't eat, food will have to be spooned into the side of his mouth, because every drop of nourishment he receives is that much in his favor in fighting the disease. In extreme cases the dog will have to be fed intravenously with saline, glucose, and amino acids. The patient's room should be warm and free from drafts and dampness, and he should be kept covered so that he will not be chilled and take further secondary infection. As the disease progresses each symptom has to be combated as it develops. Pneumonia can develop, and may be complicated by a bronchial pneumonia of bacterial origin.

In the most severe complications neurological symptoms begin to develop. The animal may seem to be completely recovered from the disease, and then a couple of weeks later the muscles in one of his legs may begin to twitch. This, called chorea, is an affliction of the nerves which resembles the twitching of St. Vitus's dance in humans. With treatment, sometimes the twitching will stop. Or it will spread to the other legs and over the entire body until the animal is in complete spasms. The twitching can affect the head muscles and the jaws, and when it does the dog's teeth will click continually. Without a doubt it is much more humane to put these animals to sleep. However if only a small part of the body is affected, the dog may recover, retaining some of the twitching but leading a healthy and happy life.

The neurological symptoms can go into the brain and produce convulsions. They usually start with "chewing gum fits," which is a clamping of the mouth, and then go into a more complicated form with generalized spasms and convulsions. At this stage the disease is invariably fatal. The few who do recover from the disease are almost invariably left with blindness or paralysis and are unfit companions to their masters. One out of 100 patients may possibly recover without any aftereffects.

Vaccination and immunity. Normally a mother dog with some immunity imparts a certain degree of immunity to the puppies in her womb before birth. The antibodies can help the puppies for the first week or 10 days even if they don't suckle their mother. If the bitch had distemper or received distemper vaccine within a year of pregnancy, it is possible that the colostrum immunity received by the puppies will last up to 12 weeks. If, however, the bitch is not immune to distemper, the puppies will receive no immunity from her, and then they must receive globulin or measles vaccine as soon as possible, which can be the 2nd week after birth. If globulin is given, it should be administered at 10- to 14-day intervals because after 9 days the immunity in the globulin begins to wane.

If there is danger of a non-immune puppy being exposed to distemper, or for some other reason a newborn puppy should be immunized, there is an excellent measles vaccine, prepared from human measles virus, which is a temporary protection against distemper and can be given to puppies 2 to 3 days old when necessary. Distemper resistance is established within hours. However, usually this vaccine is given to puppies between 3 and 6 weeks of age. Immunity is maintained until the puppy is 14 to 16 weeks of age, when the more active or permanent type of vaccine should be given.

When a bitch has high immunity to distemper, her puppies are protected while they are nursing for the first few weeks. I would therefore recommend a booster vaccination for a bitch about midway in her pregnancy. This will boost the immunity and indirectly help her puppies.

There is a test which can be done on the blood of pregnant bitches which given an accurate antibody titer count. This makes it possible to tell the exact week the puppies will lose their colostrum immunity and therefore the earliest time the puppies can be successfully vaccinated. I advise giving globulin or measles vaccine to all puppies at 4 weeks of age. There are modified live-virus vaccines which are given at about 10 to 12 weeks of age. These vaccines combine distemper, hepatitis, and leptospirosis and give excellent immunity. I usually advise two modified live-virus vaccines at 12 and 14 weeks of age, to be followed at 9 months of age by a booster vaccine.

A dog should not receive a vaccination if he has received globulin or serum within a period of 2 weeks; antibodies will still be present in his bloodstream which will interfere with immunity production.

There can be failures in vaccination when animals are not in good condition. If a dog is heavily infested with parasites or has a fever, he will not receive the proper immunity and may come down with the disease at the time of the vaccination. If the animal is not in good condition, canine globulin should be given, which will confer a temporary immunity while he is being treated for the parasite or the infection causing the fever. Later, when he is well, he should receive active immunization against distemper.

Booster vaccinations must be given annually. Most veterinarians agree that no product is available which will produce permanent immunity. "Lifetime" immunity is merely an expression, and not a reality; even recovery from the disease may not give life-time immunity, as had been previously thought. Many pets have been lost to this misunderstanding.

As a dog gets older his immunity wanes. A booster vaccination of D-H-L should be given every 12 months. Since distemper is most prevalent in winter and spring, owners should be persuaded to have annual boosters given their dogs no later than early fall.

Other recommendations include a booster for a sheltered or closely confined dog when he is going to be mingling with other dogs or when distemper becomes widespread in a community. When a dog is going to be in a dog show and exposed to many animals, he should be given a booster at least 2 weeks before the show; when a dog is going on a trip he should have a booster several weeks before leaving home.

There are some commercial vaccines on the market which give a false sense of security. They are not handled or stored properly, and they are produced by certain drug companies which sell them at cut-rate prices because their procedures for producing them are cut-rate and inadequate. Be wary of vaccines available at "bargain" prices.

Final warning. Don't buy, accept as a gift, sell, or give away any puppy unless it appears healthy and until it has been vaccinated for at least one week.

HEPATITIS

"Canine infectious hepatitis" is not the same disease as the human form of hepatitis and is not transmissible to humans. It is caused by a virus which is spread from animal to animal by direct contact with infected urine, feces, or saliva. It is not indigenous to dogs; many wild animals can spread the disease. Foxes, coyotes, and raccoons are among its common carriers. Although young animals are more prone to the disease, dogs of any age can be affected.

There is a form of hepatitis, the paracute form, that shows no symptoms. It is so deadly and quick-acting that the first sign of anything amiss is a dead dog.

Years ago hepatitis was mistakenly diagnosed as distemper because in its early stages the symptoms of hepatitis are difficult to distinguish from those of distemper.

The most characteristic symptoms are loss of weight, inflammation of the eyes and throat, and severe tonsillitis. Other symptoms usually are loss of appetitie, extreme thirst, vomiting, diarrhea, and a fever generally higher than with distemper—104-105. There is humping of the animal's back because of the tenderness in his adbomen caused by enlargement and inflammation of the liver. The poor dog may take to rubbing his belly along the floor to get relief from the severe pain he's suffering internally.

The virus of canine hepatitis is eliminated in the saliva, urine, and other excretions of dogs in the acute stages of illness. Recovered, immune dogs eliminate the virus in their urine for a long time and thus spread the disease to other victims. As in distemper, having the disease does not give lifetime immunity.

The duration of immunity that puppies receive through the colostrum, or first milk, of the mother follows closely the pattern for distemper so that the use of triple vaccine (distemper-hepatitis-leptospirosis) is recommended when the bitch is given her booster halfway during her pregnancy.

There are excellent hepatitis vaccines available to the veterinarian, and they have also been combined with attenuated live-virus distemper vaccine, as well as in leptospirosis vaccine, so that all three devastating diseases are protected against with one vaccination. As with distemper and leptospirosis, annual vaccination is essential for highest-level safety.

Don't use any of the cut-rate commercial vaccines; they are of cut-rate quality too. They can sometimes give the disease in either mild or severe form.

In treatment, use tender loving care. Antibiotics combat the invasion of the infection and prevent complications. Because of the inflammation of the throat and tonsils the dog will likely have to be tempted to eat or force-fed. Give highly concentrated and easily swallowed foods, such as eggnog and baby foods. The symptoms should be treated as they develop, such as bathing the running eyes and the caked nostrils. And the dog should always be in a warm room, free from drafts and dampness.

LEPTOSPIROSIS

Leptospirosis is an infectious disease of man, dogs, cattle, pigs, horses, rodents, and certain other animals. It is caused by bacteria, known as spirochetes, which localize in the kidneys of animals. The urine is infectious, and the disease can even be contracted while swimming or wading in water contaminated with infectious urine. The bacteria seem able to penetrate unbroken skin and mucosae (the lining of the mouth, nose, and digestive tract), and that is how they gain entrance to the body of the susceptible animal.

There are three types of leptospirosis. The type most prevalent in dogs is spread primarily in the urine of infected dogs to other dogs, and occasionally to man, cattle, cats, and silver foxes. The bacteria are prevalent in rodents, especially rats. The urine spreads the disease to other rodents and sometimes to man, dogs, and other animals. Rodents in all parts of the world are found to be infected and yet give no visible evidence of the disease.

The symptoms in some instances are similar to those of distemper and hepatitis, but the veterinarian has become efficient in separating the three diseases and noting their specific characteristics. In leptospirosis one of the typical symptoms is the color of the urine. It darkens sometimes to a deep yellow or orange and has a strong odor. The principal symptom during the initial stages is fever, usually with chills. The fever generally lasts 4 to 7 days, and about the 5th day there will likely be vomiting attended by pain in the abdominal regions caused by the spirochetes invading the kidneys and liver. The membranes and skin turn yellow. This jaundice sign is serious. The bacteria settle in the kidneys and muscles. The eyes become bloodshot. The dog sometimes has painful muscular spasms and walks with difficulty and stiffness. As the disease progresses his stools become mixed with blood, the vomitus contains blood, and often there is a bloody discharge from the gums. The disease can attack the brain, causing minor convulsions, and symptoms similar to those found in sleeping sickness.

It is especially important to catch leptospirosis in its early stages, before degeneration of the kidneys and liver from the ravages of the spirochetes. Penicillin and streptomycin are the drugs usually administered by the veterinarian.

The best prevention, of course, is immunization with annual vaccination. All good vaccines protect the animal from all the types of leptospirosis. One attack of the disease does not give permanent immunity; a dog can contract the disease several times, and the several types, during his lifetime. After an attack immunity last only 8 to 16 months. Recovered animals can become carriers and pass the bacteria in their urine for long periods. Another preventive is to keep premises and alleys free from rats.

HARD-PAD DISEASE

This disease is under constant discussion among veterinarians: is it a variation of the distemper or hepatitis virus or a separate disease caused by a specific virus? It has many of the symptoms of distemper, such as running eyes and nose, and carries a high fever, usually 104 degrees or higher, while distemper carries 103-104. It is generally more protracted than distemper and with other complications.

The reason for its name is that gradually there is a thickening of the pigmentation of the nose and feet. The dog begins to walk as if he has sore feet. The pads begin to crack and large crusty formations appear. These phenomena are caused by the virus attacking the epithelial cells of the body and by the high fever over a long period of time.

Hard-pad disease is difficult to treat unless caught in the early stages because of the high fever which can go on for several weeks and usually ends in the brain or other parts of the nervous system. When the disease goes on for 2 or 3 weeks, the animal wastes away; he becomes emaciated and an easy target for other diseases, such as pneumonia and encephalitis.

In treatment, antibiotics, constant nursing care, and forced feeding are essential. For softening the pads of the feet and the nostrils, lanolin and oils are used.

The prognosis is not good. It is hoped that in the near future there will be more knowledge of the disease and a specific means of prevention. So far as is known at the present time, the best prevention of hard-pad disease is prevention of the "big three"—distemper, hepatitis, and leptospirosis.

ENCEPHALITIS

Like hard-pad disease, encephalitis is considered by many veterinarians to be a part of the distemper syndrome, but others consider it a distinct disease with its own specific virus.

It attacks the brain and is one of the more serious complications in distemper, hepatitis, and leptospirosis.

Here again the best prevention is annual immunity with D-H-L vaccine.

DIABETES

In diabetes mellitus there is a wasting away of the animal. There is extreme loss of weight; the dog is very hungry and thirsty but continues to lose weight. The disease affects the pancreas and is usually found more in females than in males and generally in middle-aged and older dogs.

Diagnosis can be made from examination of the urine and blood, where there is an excess of sugar. The treatment is the same as in humans. With insulin (tablets or injections) and a strict diet, these animals can continue to enjoy life.

Diabetes insipidus is caused by a tumor of the pituitary gland. It is characterized by enlargement of the abdomen, lethargy and a gradual wasting away, excessive thirst, continuous urination (pale-colored urine), and loose bowel movements. There is no cure yet for this type of diabetes.

PSEUDOMONAS DISEASE

Pseudomonades are bacteria which cause a serious problem in dogs because they are resistant to most antibiotics. Treatment is difficult. The bacteria are found in soil, water, and putrefying material.

The infection causes a chronic kidney problem which can take years of treatment with special drugs to clear up. It also causes a chronic infection of the ear and eye which is resistant to medication.

Pseudomonas disease usually develops after prolonged treatment for some other disease involving constant use of antibiotics and steroids. This is why indiscriminate use of drugs is ill-advised.

CANINE BRUCELLOSIS

Brucellosis is on the increase not only among dogs but among pet owners as well. The best control method in a breeding kennel is to eliminate infected animals by isolating new dogs until tested. There is a simple test that your veterinarian can do in his office.

Clinical signs in infected male dogs are painful testes, fever, and loss of appetite; in females the signs are abortion, fever, and loss of appetite. A dog can remain infected and remain a carrier of the nonfatal bacteria for over a year. This is the way it is spread, very much in the manner of a venereal disease in the human species. The disease can also be spread to humans or from one dog to another by contamination from urine or feces, most often through the mucous membranes or open sores.

17 PARASITES

EXTERNAL PARASITES

Fleas

External parasites are annoying little bugs which are the bane of many a dog's existence. Some dogs scratch themselves almost as often as they wag their tails, and although the cause may be fleas, ticks, lice, or a skin disorder, most times the culprit is the flea.

Some dog owners tolerate fleas as a necessary evil; others put up with fleas as entertaining little critters who have remarkable athletic abilities. But levity aside, once a dog begins to react to fleas there is scratching, biting, and irritation which produces eczematous lesions, and the dog leads a miserable life until his master and his veterinarian intercede with flea control and treatment of his skin. With so many excellent insecticides on the market, flea control should be given especially high priority by dog owners.

To be better able to completely eradicate the flea, a knowledge of the life cycle of this hardy pest is helpful. A female flea produces as many as 500 eggs in a lifetime. The eggs are smooth, white, and rounded, and they live in crevices (e.g., the dog's bed and bedding, his hair) where there is sufficient organic matter to satisfy the food requirements of the larval stages. The eggs hatch into larvae and go through a cycle into cocoons. The adult flea may emerge from the cocoon in a few weeks, or it may lie dormant for as long as a year if conditions are not favorable. Fleas have piercing mouth parts, and their food is blood. While the adult flea will not survive away from the dog for more than 10 days, the cocoon or freshly emerged flea can live without food for many months, up to a year. (This accounts for the "flea swarms" which are sometimes encountered in deserted barns or empty dwellings when dog owners go on vacation leaving the house dogless.) In long-haired dogs the entire life cycle can take place on the dog. Contrary to popular opinion, fleas don't fly and don't jump far. They generally confine their leaps to hopping from place to place on the dog.

The adult flea can withstand a certain amount of cold, but the onset of winter motivates it to seek warmth indoors. Also, in the winter there is a decline in flea production due to lowered egg production, late hatching, and a high mortality rate for larvae.

There is considerable variation in the number of fleas carried by each dog before it becomes sensitized. Collies and spaniels can withstand more than 500 fleas, sometimes up to about 1,200. The short-haired and coarse-haired breeds react long before they have 500 fleas, usually about 250. Puppies tend to support more fleas than adult dogs, but older animals may develop a tolerance that will permit a moderate flea infestation without discomfort.

Once a dog becomes sensitized to his flea burden—some dogs react violently to just two or three fleas—there is discomfort, and the dog must be treated. The veterinarian has at his disposal diagnostic tests to determine if a dog's skin lesions are the result of sensitivity to flea bites; and if so, there is a flea antigen that he can inject. The flea antigen is helpful; but it rids the animal not of fleas but merely of the effects of the flea bites, and rigid control still must be practiced to keep fleas from the animal's body.

Flea control depends on the destruction of eggs, larvae, and adults. Fleas must be eradicated from the dog and his environment. It is not difficult to remove fleas from the dog; there are excellent insecticides on the market. An insecticide is usually applied as a wash, a powder, an aerosol, or a dip. A good flea bath usually brings the fleas and insecticide into immediate contact and gives rapid-fire relief.

A powder carries insecticide into the coat, and the fleas move into contact with the toxic particles of the dust. Powders are slower in action during cold weather, when fleas are relatively inactive. The advantage of powders over washes is that the dust particles will drop into the bed where the animal sleeps, helping to achieve control over the flea cycle.

Aerosol sprays are a simple way to apply insecticide to the dog's body. Unfortunately some dogs are afraid of the whizzing sound of the spray. Don't get any spray into the dog's eyes.

In applying powders or sprays, start at the head and work to the rear. Fleas are clever, and if spraying is started at the rear, they escape to the head into areas where they can't be reached.

There are some excellent insecticidal dips—suspensions—which can be mixed with water and applied once a week or every 10 days to outdoor dogs. Their strong odor is not easily tolerated in the home, but they give effective control of all external parasites, ticks included, for hunting and outdoor dogs.

There are excellent flea pills that your veterinarian can provide you with. These destroy the adult flea and prevent reinfestation. This is mainly accomplished by maintaining a high blood level of the insecticide. For the average dog there are no toxic effects, but the pills should be used only under the direction of your veterinarian; some older dogs with liver or kidney conditions should not have them.

The flea collar has revolutionized flea control, and it works on the simple principle that because the flea has to go to the head of the dog daily for food it must pass under the plastic collar, which contains insecticidal poison. Some dogs are susceptible to this insecticide and either show local sensitivity in a skin rash or, in some cases, become ill. However, flea collars help many, many more dogs than they hurt, and I endorse them unless there is an untoward reaction in the dog.

Flea medallions which are attached to the collar of the dog have been introduced recently. They do not come in contact with the dog's skin and prevent reactions. Their effectiveness in killing fleas is still being compared to flea collars as some dog owners claim they are not as effective.

Once fleas have been eradicated from the dog, for complete flea control parts of the house frequented by the dog have to be treated. While it is easy to remove fleas from the dog's body, it is difficult to prevent them from returning. The house should be sprayed with an insecticidal compound, probably several times, every few weeks, until complete control of the flea cycle is achieved. The eggs and cocoons are difficult to destroy, and the larvae are destroyed only if the insecticide reaches them in the places where they are prone to hide, such as the dog's bedding, cracks and crevices in the floor, walls and ceiling, overstuffed furniture, and floor covering.

In homes, fleas can be eliminated by aerosol mist sprays used in each room separately and generously, leaving doors and windows shut 15-20 minutes. Then vacuum clean rooms carefully and burn the sweeper bag contents, spray cracks in flooring, along baseboards, cold-air ducts, rug edges and between cushions of upholstered furniture.

When you leave your house in the summer and it is to be left without a pet, be sure to spray the areas frequented by the dog; otherwise, when you return you will be attacked by multitudes and hordes of fleas looking for canine or human flesh. They prefer the canine body, but at that point they will be starving for any kind of blood.

Generally dog fleas are not troublesome to man and will not live on man. However, there are some people who are extremely sensitive to the bite of a flea. Just being near a dog with a flea causes them to develop a rash.

Unfortunately most insecticides can be poisonous to man or animal if there is overexposure. When using insecticides, follow directions carefully. Never use them except at recommended intervals. If there is any skin irritation, or open wound, apply the insecticide carefully. Often a thin coating of vaseline over the wound can help it to heal and make it less attractive to the flea.

Certainly flea bites are the number one cause of skin problems in dogs, and so strict flea control is essential. Good grooming practices are helpful protection.

Ticks

Of all the parasites that dogs are afflicted with, the tick is the most difficult and persistent to deal with. The American brown dog tick is the most formidable because of its tenacity, resistance to insecticides, rate of propagation, and debilitating effect on the host. Ridding a dog of ticks is a task that calls for thoroughness, patience, and vigilance. Every year as warm weather approaches many dog owners are given to warranted apprehension about tick control on their dogs and in their homes. These hardy canine parasites can indeed invade the privacy of the home, living in the warmth and safety of crevices in the woodwork.

Originally rabbits, squirrels, and field mice were the wild hosts of the brown dog tick, but in the temperate areas of the world the tick has become domesticated and has learned to live exclusively with dogs. It requires warmth, so it holes up

299

during the cold weather in convenient crevices and emerges when the weather moderates. In heated kennels and homes ticks breed all year round.

The life cycle of the brown dog tick runs about 10 to 23 weeks, depending on climatic conditions and the availability of a host. The tick will die unless it has a dog to feed on. The tick gorges on the blood of dogs in three separate stages of development. In the larval stage it engorges itself and drops from the dog, finding a crevice in which to live. The blood it has engorged sustains it until it goes into the nymph stage. Again it finds a dog, and feeds, and drops off. It then emerges as an adult, finds a host, gorges itself, and mates.

For easy reference here is a résumé of the life cycle of the brown dog tick:

1. The egg hatches 19 to 60 days after being laid, bringing forth a 6-legged larva.

2. The larva seeks a dog, becomes engorged with blood, drops from the host and hides.

3. Six to 23 days later the larva molts and becomes an 8-legged nymph. The nymph obtains a blood meal from a dog, drops off and goes into hiding.

4. Twelve to 29 days later the nymph molts and becomes an adult. As an adult it once more seeks the dog, engorges blood and mates.

Each adult tick can lay between 4,000 and 5,000 eggs, mostly in cracks and on vertical surfaces in kennels and homes.

The tick's leaving the dog between its blood banquets can give a false sense of security in tick control. Just one tick on a dog or a wall calls for emergency measures. An insecticidal spray should be jetted into all the crevices and cracks of the vertical surfaces in the house: the fumes have to come into direct contact with the various stages of the tick's life cycle. There are pest-control companies that will fog a house; this involves toxic gas seeping into all the crevices in the walls, the door and window frames, and the animal's sleeping quarters.

Insecticides are potentially dangerous and should be used with caution. Especially should all young children be out of a room when it is being sprayed.

After the tick or ticks are removed from the dog—by hand, dip, or spray—the dog and premises must be watched vigilantly for reinfestation.

In pulling ticks off the dog's body, reach to the base of the skin to get the head of the tick, which is usually buried in the superficial layer of the skin. A tweezer or forceps is much better than fingers. An aerosol spray can also be applied to the tick until it falls off. Ticks live inside the ears and attach themselves to the dog's eyelids, requiring delicate handling in removal. After a tick has been removed, an antiseptic should be applied to the spot on the dog's skin.

When a tick is knocked off or pulled off but the head is left under the skin, the embedded head can cause infection if not removed. If squeezing the skin doesn't make the head pop out, a razor blade or sharp knife may have to be used to slit a small opening in the skin. Hydrogen peroxide or other antiseptic should be applied daily until the sore is healed.

An infestation of ticks on a dog can cause tick paralysis— complete paralysis of the body—and unless the animal is rid of the tick, it can cause death. It can also cause a dog to be anemic from extreme loss of blood, which will show up in lack of vitality.

The wood tick, which infects man with Rocky Mountain spotted fever and for which the dog is one of several intermediate hosts, is not confined to the Rocky Mountain region as was once thought. The infection may be acquired over a considerable portion of the United States, east as well as west, and in Canada.

The disease is spread to man by the bite of the wood tick. The seriousness of the disease makes tick control by dog owners even more essential—in the dog and in homes and kennels or wherever ticks will live.

Lice

Lice are not particularly hardy parasites and cannot live away from the host. Some people recoil in horror when they learn that their dogs have lice. Fortunately dog lice will not live on the human body.

There are two kinds of dog lice: biting and sucking. Biting lice are light brown and move frequently. They eat the skin scales and cause a dog to scratch abnormally. The dog's skin thickens and gets scaly. Sucking lice are blue in color and don't move. They burrow their heads in the skin of the dog and suck his blood. This causes itching and anemia and in puppies can be quite serious. I've seen puppies die of severe lice infestation.

Lice have a 8-day cycle. The eggs are silvery and firmly attached to the hair. They are difficult to dislodge, and adhere for some time. They can be found by spreading the hair apart on the neck and the ears and around the face. Fortunately they can be killed with proper insecticides.

After use of one of the various effective insecticides on the market (powder, sprays, dips, pills, etc.), the animal should be treated about once a week, for several weeks, to keep newly hatched lice from forming on his body. Fine-combing the dog after each application of the insecticide will help to remove dead lice and lice that may have been merely stunned.

INTERNAL PARASITES

Just because a dog is under the weather doesn't mean he's afflicted with worms. Unfortunately many dog owners have a tendency to blame worms for almost every canine illness known. Dogs have many different types of worms, and many wrong diagnoses by many dog owners have inflicted many doses of vile-tasting worm medicines on many defenseless pets. Dog should be wormed only if worms are present, and then only with meticulous care because worm medicines can prove harmful and even fatal unless properly supervised. Many fatalities have been caused by overdosage, by worming sick dogs with fever, and by improper diagnoses.

Intestinal worms are common, and especially in young animals. Although they are a worldwide problem and should be constantly guarded against, they are more prevalent in some parts of the world than in others. In the southern states, for instance, the warmer weather makes the soil conducive to the growth of the worm from egg to adult.

Because of the varieties of worms and the dangers involved with worm medicines, a dog suspected of having worms is best taken to a veterinarian. A routine fecal examination will determine if the dog has worms and what type. All veterinary hospitals provide microscopic examination for parasites.

Puppies derive worms directly from their mothers or from contact with infected bowel movements. They can also become infested with worms in the mother's womb. A young dog is much more susceptible to the effects of worms than an older dog. As a dog gets older his body becomes more resistant to the effects of worms. However, he is still vulnerable to parasites and should be checked at least every 6 months. Young dogs should be checked at more frequent intervals, and puppies under 6 months of age should be checked at least every month.

There are four common dog worms: roundworms, hookworms, whipworms, and tapeworms. A dog can harbor more than one type at a time. These parasites have complicated life cycles and are resistant to many chemicals. Their control is best left to a veterinarian.

Every so often I am asked if dogs have pinworms and if humans can get pinworms from dogs. The answer is, "No!" The pinworm that lives in the human does not occur in dogs, nor in any animal other than man. A physician who advises an animal owner to dispose of his dog or cat because the children have pinworms is ignorant of parasitology. Dog worms will not live in the human body.

A medicated food has been developed which reportedly prevents heartworms, hookworms, and roundworms. Your veterinarian can give you advice and directions. A liquid medication—styrid-caracide—added to the daily food has similar effect.

Roundworms

Roundworms are the commonest of the worm parasites and are most often found in puppies. They can grow up to 5 inches in length in the dog's stomach and intestines and are similar in appearance to the earthworm.

The eggs of this parasite are hardy and can remain alive in the soil for years. The adult roundworm lays her eggs in the stomach and intestines of the dog. The eggs may hatch and the life cycle be run inside the dog, or the eggs may be passed in the dog's bowel movements, or may be vomited and develop outside the dog. About 10 days later the eggs are infectious to any dog who digs in the soil and eats food or other material on which the eggs are deposited.

It has recently been discovered that large black water bugs transmit roundworm eggs. They deposit the eggs in the dog's dishes.

In the nursing mother, roundworm eggs can adhere to the skin and be ingested by the puppies as they nurse. The eggs hatch inside the body. The larvae enter the blood stream and travel to the lungs, where they burrow into air sacs. They are usually coughed up by the dog and then swallowed. Back in the stomach, the worms mate, and once again the cycle begins.

The eggs are laid in 2- to 3-week periods, so treatment for roundworms should be at 2-week intervals. According to the life cycle, one worming will not completely rid a dog of roundworms.

Roundworms can cause diarrhea, anemia, dull coat, and potbelly. There can be serious injury to the lungs, and the puppy can develop pneumonia as the worms migrate from the blood vessels to the air sacs of the lungs.

The best prevention for roundworms is proper diet so that the dog will not be hungry and likely to pick up scraps from the ground. Keep the dog yard sanitary to prevent reinfestation. The kennel should be kept clean and dry, and thus conducive to hatching eggs.

Hookworms

Hookworms are leech-like creatures that suck blood from the intestines. They are tiny worms, about half an inch long, of reddish or grayish hue. A dog can become infected with hookworms in three ways: (1) direct ingestion of the larvae from digging and eating around infected stools; (2) prenatal infection while in the womb; and (3) larval penetration of the skin.

The hookworm lays its eggs in the stomach and intestines. The eggs are passed out in the stool and hatch outside the dog in 7 to 10 days. The larvae are infectious and either are swallowed by the dog or penetrate the skin and subsequently get to the stomach by traveling, via the blood stream, to the lungs, where they burrow into the air sacs, are coughed up and then swallowed. Once in the stomach the cycle starts again; the worms mate and lay eggs.

Adult hookworms are insidious bloodsuckers, and a heavily infested puppy can bleed to death. The worms puncture the lining of the intestines and eject a substance which prevents coagulation of the blood. With loss of blood there is anemia and loss of iron. There is also a bloody mucus diarrhea; and sometimes a black tarry stool, signifying blood high up in the intestines. Other symptoms are restlessness, apathy, and stunted growth. With severe infestation a critical amount of blood may be lost.

Diagnosis is based on the presence of hookworm eggs in the feces. Fortunately there are excellent medicines, both oral and injected, for hookworms. The injection called D.N.P. is especially good, as it can even be given to puppies as young

304

as 2 to 3 weeks to save them from infestation. A pregnant bitch should be checked for worms and should be in good health before she delivers her puppies.

In addition to relieving the hookworm infestation, the veterinarian will likely prescribe supportive treatment to help the dog recover from anemia. Blood transfusions and liver injections or iron supplements are used to help the animal gain strength in fighting off the effects of the parasites.

As in all worm treatment, one treatment is not sufficient.

Many veterinarians have long considered hookworms a debilitating and killing intestinal ailment—one of the most stubborn and frustrating problems they face. They can kill the worms that attach themselves to the small intestines of the animal but have trouble preventing continued infestation. Proper diet and careful sanitary measures are essential in hookworm control. Hookworm infestation constitutes an especially acute problem in crowded kennels with earth and shaded runways where young puppies are constantly mingling with dogs seeding the area with eggs and larvae. However, even well-kept lawns around the finest homes can be heavily infested.

The ability of hookworm larvae to live in the soil is dependent on temperature, composition of the soil, and amount of rainfall and drainage. They develop best in moist, coarse, sandy soil. There are three things that will kill hookworm larvae in the soil: (1) A saturated salt solution (table salt) spilled on the ground at 3- to 4-week intervals, to break up the life cycle, is effective. (2) A concentrated borax solution, used in the same manner as the salt solution, will kill the larvae. (3) A spray has recently been developed—VIP hookworm spray concentrate—which is proving to be highly effective in killing newly hatched larvae. A second application in 14 days is advised.

It is thought by some that hookworm larvae produce a degree of immunity in dogs. Researchers are working on vaccines to produce immunity. Possibly in the near future this will be a reality.

The species of hookworm which affects dogs is different from the species which is a major problem with humans in the southern and eastern states. Canine hookworms can't be blamed for infecting man. However, the hookworm larvae can cause a skin irritation in humans, a sort of "creeping eruption" which affects children who play in infested yards or sandboxes where infected pets have deposited their hookworm-laden feces. But remember: the canine hookworm will not live inside the human body.

Whipworms

Whipworms are slender parasites—not much thicker than coarse sewing thread—which resemble small whips. They have no immediate host. The eggs are laid in the dog and passed out in the feces. They develop in about 3 weeks and are then infectious. Dogs eat the larvae or eggs, and these mature in the dog, living in the caecum (appendix).

Whipworms form toxins which cause anemia. They also cause chronic digestive disturbances, such as persistent or intermittent diarrhea. A diagnostic syndrome would be a normal bowel movement until almost completion, when mucus or blood appears. The whipworm is insidious and causes a dullness in the hair coat, excessive shedding, and in some cases a cough.

Diagnosis is made by the presence of eggs in the feces. Years ago surgery for the removal of the appendix was the only cure. Today the veterinarian has at his disposal excellent drugs for the elimination of whipworms.

For the prevention of whipworms, since the eggs need a wet environment, the dog's kennel should be kept dry, with plenty of sunshine.

Tapeworms

Three types of tapeworm are seen in the dog:

1. The broadfish tapeworm, acquired when a dog eats raw parasitized fish.

2. A tapeworm common to farm dogs and acquired by eating raw meat and viscera from such things as rabbits, hogs, sheep, and beef.

3. The flea tapeworm, acquired by a dog eating a flea or a louse; fleas and biting lice serve as immediate hosts. Commonly called the cucumber worm because of its shape, it is the most widely distributed of the tapeworms. It is also the most difficult to remove because the slender neck breaks easily, leaving the small head embedded in the wall of the intestines so that a new worm is generated in about a month.

In appearance the tapeworm resembles a long, narrow band of tape made up of many segments. It can vary in length from several inches to many feet, being a collection of worms joined together. As the worm grows, segments are added to the rear.

The life cycle of the tapeworm is more complicated than that of the other worms. The segments bearing the eggs drop off and find their way out of the dog through the feces, or crawl out of the rectum and into the surrounding hair. The segments dry up into little particles that look like tiny grains of wheat or rice. These are eaten by fleas or lice, which in turn are eaten by the dog. Therefore, to completely rid a dog or a kennel of tapeworms, lice and fleas must be eliminated.

Tapeworms are a common intestinal parasite in dogs. When present in large numbers, they may cause a digestive upset. They can cause a dull coat and often dry, itchy skin. Usually in large numbers they cause a general unthriftiness, loss of weight, and lassitude. The tapeworm is not so harmful as the other worms, but it can cause infection in the intestinal tract and chronic colitis. The dog's appetite is huge, but he doesn't gain weight.

In diagnosis, the feces and the hair around the dog's anus should be examined for segments.

In treatment, the essential thing is the release of the head of the tapeworm from the intestinal tract. Fortunately the same drugs are effective in treating all three types of tapeworms. See your veterinarian. As for home treatment, I warn you that there are some extremely toxic drugs on the market specified for tapeworming. Some of them can make a dog much more violently ill than any group of tapeworms could ever do.

In the prevention of tapeworms diet and sanitation are important, but ridding the dog of fleas and lice is even more so. A dog cannot become infested with tapeworms directly from another dog, nor will canine tapeworms live in the human body.

Heartworms

Heartworms are becoming more prevalent not only in hunting dogs but in pets dogs as well. Once confined to the tropics and semi-tropics, heartworms are now being frequently seen in temperate zones. In the United States they are most common along the Atlantic and Gulf coasts, but with today's easy transportation, and many travelers to the southern states during the winter months, heartworms are being reported all over the country.

Although mosquitoes are the main carriers of heartworms, there is some suspicion that other bloodsucking insects, such as fleas, ticks, and flies, may be involved.

To understand the heartworm problem, we must have a knowledge of the worm's life cycle. The larvae are ingested by the mosquito as it sucks blood from a dog with heartworms. Larvae are then injected into other dogs' blood streams when the mosquito bites these dogs. When the larvae enter the blood stream of a dog, they travel to the heart, lungs, and large vessels, where they mature and eventually produce other larvae. It is not until 6 to 7 months after being bitten by an infected mosquito that larvae may be found in a dog's blood. For this reason heartworms are rarely encountered in dogs who are under 1 year of age.

It is the adult worms living in the heart, lungs, and large vessels that cause most of the clinical and pathological symptoms. The adult worms interfere with blood circulation, especially in the lungs. The heart and lungs have to work much harder to bypass the worms that are present. With such a handicap the dog soon tires, coughs, and shows other symptoms typical of the heartworm syndrome. There is a great variation in symptoms. Some dogs appear healthy with no noticeable symptoms, while others are anemic, cough, itch, and are dropsical. Any dog showing one or more of the following symptoms should be tested for heartworms: easy fatigue, chronic cough, eczema, anemia with a heavy infestation of fleas, and fainting spells from overexercise or strenuous play.

A dog infested with a small number of heartworms may show no clinical signs. He may be active and have good stamina. However, as the heartworms multiply, symptoms usually appear. Along with the above symptoms there may be labored breathing. The dog soon loses weight and becomes anemic. As the condition progresses fluid accumulates in the lungs and the dog is in a critical state.

The adult heartworm can be 4 to 9 inches in length and lives as long as 5 to 7 years in the heart chambers or the large vessels of the heart and lungs. Diagnosis is made by examining a sample of blood under a microscope. Positive cases will show wriggling heartworm larvae.

With techniques worked out by the veterinary profession the mortality rate in treatment has been reduced to 5 percent or less. Surgery is indicated when there are large masses of heartworms present in the vessels, causing heart and lung failure. The surgery is complicated and serious, but fortunately there are veterinarians specializing in this.

There are tablets and injections which have been found to be somewhat effective in attacking the larvae and the adult heartworms in the bloodstream. The treatment is usually given in two parts—to kill the adult worms, and then after a period of several weeks another drug is given to combat the larvae circulating in the blood stream. Supportive treatment for the dog at the time of heartworm treatment is important. It may be necessary for the veterinarian to use digitalis to strengthen the heart, antibiotics to combat secondary infection, cortisone to reduce inflammation caused by the worms, and vitamins and minerals to build up the body deficiencies. After the dog has been treated, as it takes several weeks for the heartworms to die, it is imperative that the patient be kept completely quiet, without any exercise, for 30 days. The reason is that as the large masses of worms die they pass into the blood stream and sometimes form an embolism or a clot in one of the vital organs.

The best way to prevent heartworms is mosquito control. Mosquitoes are rarely out on bright sunny days and do most of their damage at night. Dogs should be housed in screened areas if possible. In kennels, residual insecticides should be used to control mosquitoes.

The most promising means of control at this time is daily doses of a drug, diethylcarbamazine. The drug, either in pill or liquid form, is given daily to dogs during the mosquito season. In some states, such as Florida, year round dosing is necessary. Your veterinarian can advise you on necessity and dosage.

Although the drug has been found safe to give to pregnant or nursing bitches, there are some unanswered questions about its effect on reproductivity in breeding dogs. There is, as yet, no scientific evidence that it has a bad effect.

However, the drug can be given only to dogs who are free of heartworms; unless a blood test is made before administration, fatalities can occur.

Kidneyworms

The giant kidneyworm is the largest of all the roundworms. Some females grow to 40 inches in length. Dogs become infested by eating catfish, one of the intermediate hosts. The worm is found in the kidneys or in the peritoneal cavity. Diagnosis involves examining the urine for eggs. It is a rare parasite.

Lungworms

There is no such thing as a lungworm per se, but there are two parasites that affect the lungs: strongylidae and filariae. Fortunately both parasites are rare.

The larvae of the strongylidae attack the lung tissues and cause a chronic cough. They are found in the feces, and upon microscopic examination the larval forms move around at a lively pace. Diagnosis is difficult, but once determined there are effective drugs to attack these worms.

The filariae are found in the trachea, bronchia, and lungs. In young animals they may cause an infection which is identified by a hacking cough after exercise. Heavy infestation may result in severer symptoms, such as respiratory problems, diarrhea, loss of appetite, and stunted growth. Pneumonia is a constant danger. Diagnosis is made by examining sputum from the lungs; it will contain eggs.

Coccidiosis

The incidence of coccidiosis is increasing throughout the country. It is an insidious type of infectious disease caused by coccidia, protozoan parasites microscopic in size which are often associated with filth. It attacks parts of the small intestines, causing a bloody mucoid diarrhea. Young puppies are especially susceptible, though adult dogs are not immune. In young puppies it weakens resistance to many other diseases. Distemper or any stress factor reduces the puppy's resistance, allowing the coccidia to increase and bring the puppy down with clinical symptoms.

Puppies can acquire the infection from contaminated premises or an infected dam. The coccidia are passed in the feces. When sanitation is poor, the animal is constantly reinfected by his own feces, and infection can spread quickly throughout a kennel. Dogs exposed to chicken manure are exposed to coccidia. Although chicken coccidia are not infectious to dogs, they can give a diarrhea. All animals can harbor coccidiosis in the intestinal tract, but each species usually carries its own infections by its own type of coccidia, called "species specific."

Coccidiosis should be suspected in all cases of continuing unexplained diarrhea and anemia. Puppies are more severely affected. The first signs can be a mild diarrhea which progresses until the feces become mucoid and blood-tinged. The puppy becomes weak and debilitated. If the dog is untreated, a cough develops, along with running eyes and nose, much as in distemper. The infection progresses until convulsions occur and the puppy usually dies.

When puppies recover, they may be carriers, passing the coccidia on to other dogs. Dogs in good health can be carriers. Known carriers should be isolated and strict sanitation observed. The carriers should be treated, and their quarters and runs cleaned with an antiseptic.

For effective treatment sulfa drugs are of great value. However, there is always the problem of treating secondary infection, such as distemper or pneumonia.

Giardia and Trichomonad

These are two protozoan parasites found in dogs, but not often. They cause a chronic insidious type of diarrhea that does not respond to any of the normal treatments. They can both be found and diagnosed from cultures of the feces.

Coccidioidomycosis

This is a rare disease caused by a fungus. It is generally found in the southwestern desert region. It affects man as well as dog and usually attacks the respiratory system. It is diagnosed by X rays and skin tests.

Generalized Symptoms of Worms: Warning Signals

A fecal examination for worms is advisable if a dog has any of the following symptoms:
—Intermittent or persistent diarrhea with or without blood or mucus
—Intermittent vomiting
—Persistent eating of grass
—Lack of pep or energy—general lassitude
—Rubbing tail along the ground
—Bloated stomach
—Generalized symptoms of anemia, such as pale gums
—Dry, dull hair coat with dandruffy skin

311

—Persistent watery, running eyes
—Gradual loss of weight
—Unexplained nervousness and irritability

Since any of the above symptoms can also be indicative of other diseases or ailments that may be serious, a dog showing any one of them should be taken to a veterinarian for diagnosis.

Ground Rules for Worming

—A dog in good condition is less susceptible to worms than a weak dog. Good diet and proper sanitation help in preventing worms. The same applies to control of internal parasites. Also, the dog should have clean, dry bedding at all times.

—If worm medicine is strong enough to kill worms, it is also strong enough to do some damage to the dog's body if used incorrectly. Many dog owners accidentally poison their pets with improper medication. Certain worm medicines can act as deadly poisons when used in overdose, used too frequently, used when not needed, or used for the wrong type of worm.

—Never, never give worm medicine to a dog with an elevated temperature. Find out immediately why there is a fever. Distemper, hepatitis, leptospirosis, and various bacterial infections are sometimes erroneously diagnosed as worms. Many a dog in the early stages of distemper or infectious hepatitis has died as a result of receiving worm medicine rather than the specific therapy for the condition causing the illness.

—Never worm a weak, sickly dog.

—Never give worm medicine to a constipated dog, because he will retain the worm medicine in his system too long. If a dog does not have a bowel movement within 3 hours after being wormed, he must have an enema to empty his intestinal tract.

—There are rules that should be followed in properly preparing a dog for worm medicine. For a couple of days before worming he should be on a bland diet, such as rice, noodles, and soup. Twelve hours before worming, his stomach should be empty. After worming, the bland diet should be continued for a day or two or as long as is necessary to control the intestinal irritation that the worms have produced.

Part Five
BREEDING

18 PREBREEDING: SELECTIVE BREEDING

The breeding of dogs is a fascinating challenge, and an art and a gamble as well. The challenge to the breeder is to see if he can predict the resultant product of the breeding. What is hoped for is a perfectly balanced dog which meets all the breed requirements, with a good temperament and personality with all the style, spirit, and grace desirable in the particular breed. There is a further challenge that no hidden defects in the ancestry should crop up in a subsequent litter of puppies. It is incumbent on the professional dog breeder to have a complete understanding of dominant, recessive, and mixed characteristics. The same applies to the novice who seriously wishes to breed good dogs. If the novice intends to develop champions in either conformation or obedience, I heartily recommend the study of some good books on genetics.

Before any dog owner embarks on a breeding program, there are many principles of breeding that he should understand and anticipate, for the future of the individual puppy and of the breed depends on using the knowledge that is available. Many a fine family strain has been ruined by indiscriminate breeding.

Unfortunately, when a breed becomes popular, there is an influx of novices who are ignorant of the perfect specimen of the breed and haphazardly breed any two dogs so long as they have pedigree papers and possibly a few champions in their backgrounds. This is inviting disaster for the breed. Beginners must find out what a good specimen in their breed is and have a willingness to learn and study the breed and breeding per se. The learner should get to know the standards of perfection of the breed—attend many dog shows and talk with knowledgeable breeders before starting a breeding program.

A good breeder has a complete knowledge of the virtues and faults of all the ancestors of his dogs through at least 3 generations. He knows the desired and the undesired structural, temperamental, and intelligence factors of the various strains he is breeding. Good dogs are not produced by hit-

and-miss breedings. They are carefully scrutinized and the faults eliminated.

A bitch and a stud don't always give to their puppies the qualities which they themselves show. They may carry many recessive characteristics which will show up in later generations.

Before setting up a breeding program, each person should have his purposes clarified in his mind. To me, there are three main things to be bred for: (1) temperament, (2) mentality, and (3) conformation—listed in my own order of priority. Certainly obedience enthusiasts are not particularly concerned with structural perfection. They are more concerned with mentality and give prime consideration to intelligence and trainability in building a particular strain. The dog-show breeder is looking for the perfect body. He is seeking to produce animals who are genetically pure for all the dominant qualities demanded by the standards of perfection of his breed. The nearer he approaches that ideal, the more similar in type will be the dogs he produces.

It is rewarding to develop puppies which are good both physically and mentally. A dog show is primarily a beauty contest in which the entrants are judged solely on their appearance and ring behavior. Obedience trials are a test of the dog owner's ability to bring out the inherent mental capabilities and intelligence of the dog. However, in my opinion temperament should not be sacrificed to intelligence or beauty.

Since I do not have the time to be a dog show exhibitor or an obedience trainer, I am more partial to a dog's temperament than to its mentality or conformation. However, I assure my readers that I am in full accord with each breed's standards of perfection and heartily endorse breeding programs headed in the direction of breeding the ideal dog and one with a high degree of intelligence.

Although this chapter is mainly devoted to the purebred dog, I am cognizant that many dogs of mixed ancestry produce highly desirable puppies, and I endorse the further breeding of any good mongrel dog if it has the personality, intelligence and body conformation that a particular owner likes. Being of mixed ancestry myself, I am entirely sympathetic to breeding dogs of mixed parentage.

TEMPERAMENT

A shy and dangerous dog, even though he may have a magnificent body, cannot live in my household.

Good temperament should be the first goal of breeders; and it should be noted in passing that although temperament is basically controlled by genetic factors, not all temperamental failings are inherited. Environment must also be considered, since experiences a dog encounters after leaving the womb affect his personality. It is often difficult to decide which traits are inherited and which are acquired. Environment versus heredity has long been disputed by psychologists and geneticists without any definite conclusions.

Non-hereditary influences on temperament include such factors as a puppy's being reared in isolation without individual care or affection, or a puppy's being the victim of bullying by larger and stronger litter mates. These conditions can affect the personality of the dog in later life and his reactions to humans—neutral, friendly, or hostile role. A nervous or shy mother can influence a puppy in later life. The mother's attitude toward humans can affect each puppy's temperament.

Every breeder should be on the lookout for timidity, fear of strangers, refusal to leave a familiar environment, sound shyness, fear of sudden changes, sight shyness, and excessive activity. Any of these signs can be inherited in the offspring and would establish abnormal traits.

Traits such as shyness or bad temper can be due to either environment or heredity. Nervous and shy dogs seem to respond to an obedience-training course; giving them pride and a sense of usefulness helps.

Seeking to control temperament in a breeding program is a complex task. Good temperament is usually present in the ancestral genes. Good temperament is dominant and will pass on to the puppies. Two dogs of good temperament may have a puppy which is not of good temperament, but if a puppy is of good temperament it will not have been bred from parents of bad temperament.

TYPES OF BREEDING

Because breeding is so complex and requires so much study, I will discuss only a few of the basic principles of the

316

three main types (1) inbreeding, (2) line breeding, and (3) outcrossing.

There is a fallacy among the uninformed that inbreeding and line breeding cause mental deterioration, loss of vigor, weakened constitution, structural malformation, impotency, sterility, and other weaknesses and abnormalities to appear in a breeder strain when there is too-close inbreeding. This is positively not so. Inbreeding and line breeding cannot create either good or bad qualities, mental or physical. They just bring out the qualities that are already in the stock.

There is also a fallacy that puppies that are bred from father and daughter or mother and son or brother and sister are not eligible for registration. All purebred puppies are eligible for registration whether inbred, line-bred, or crossbred.

In the proper hands inbreeding and line breeding are excellent ways of helping a breed. In the wrong hands they make for deterioration of a breed. The purpose of both is to bring about breed improvement and to upgrade the stock. They make for the elimination of recessive faults and bring about purification of a strain if properly done.

Inbreeding

Inbreeding is first-generation breeding—that is, breeding father to daughter, mother to son, brother to sister, half-brother to half-sister, etcetera. It is frowned upon by many who do not understand the principles of genetics and by those who may find the moral implications shocking. The truth of the matter is that the best specimens of animals, the most beautiful, the truest in type, are gained through inbreeding.

When the breeder wants to retain as much of the blood of the sire as possible, he will often breed a daughter back to her sire. On the other hand, if it is the blood of the dam that is desired, a son is bred back to his mother. This also applies to a granddaughters and grandsons.

Inbreeding is dangerous unless handled by an expert. It doubles up and intensifies all characteristics whether they be good or bad, and so the resulting puppies can have either very desirable traits or some very bad tendencies. When inbreeding, the animals must be carefully selected, as no other method of breeding equals inbreeding for intensifying the bloodline—making the best of exceptional animals—and in building a strain within a breed.

Only fault-free dogs should be mated. If there is ever any suspicion about its temperament, a dog should not be used in a breeding program. Carefully scrutinize pedigrees for at least 3 generations. Don't inbreed unless both specimens are uniform in type, size, and general appearance, are good specimens in themselves and don't have a single common outstanding major fault.

I don't advise the amateur to practice inbreeding until he is fully aware of all the principles involved.

Line Breeding

This is the mating of animals who are closely related to the same ancestors—that is, parent dogs who are closely related to a common ancestor but are not, if at all, related to each other.

The danger in line breeding occurs when selection of parents is made by pedigree alone, without considering the physical or mental traits of the mating pair. Dogs with notable faults often result. Line breeding (and inbreeding) will ensure this failure more quickly and more certainly.

Outcrossing

The bitch is bred to a male not related in any way to the many generations represented by the bitch. In other words, new bloodlines are brought into combination. Care must be taken that along with good qualities, bad ones are not introduced into the new litter. Several different types of puppies can be expected by this method, and on occasion there will be an outstanding specimen of the breed.

SELECTION OF PARENTS

This entire chapter boils down to one thing: *careful selection of parents*. In the selection of a prospective mate—bitch or stud—we must ascertain that each is as free as possible from inherited or inborn faults. The breeder must have a complete knowledge of the virtues and faults of all the ancestors for at least 3 generations so that he will know what to expect in both desired and undesired characteristics. He should fully recognize the dangers and pitfalls—and the need for using only stock which is sound in constitution, organs, and structure, and which possesses outstanding points of

318

merit with no single fault common to the two orginal parents. He should be able to recognize all the shortcomings of his own dogs as well as their merits and be fully informed about their ancestors. And he should never, never mate two dogs with similar faults: the faults can be magnified many, many times in the puppies.

Unfortunately some breeders breed only to sell to the highest bidder, with little interest in breed improvement; and other breeders, hungry for stud fees, breed indiscriminately to any female presented to their studs. These practices rapidly bring about breed deterioration. The Boston bull, cocker, Airedale, boxer, German shepherd, and recently the Weimaraner, to name a few, have been injured by promiscuous and indiscriminate breeding. Fortunately these breeds have recouped under the guidance and tireless efforts of conscientious breeders.

In picking out a bitch and a sire it must be borne in mind that like produces like but that characteristics don't always blend to give the desired result. For instance, a female with a long head bred to a male with a short head may not always produce puppies with medium heads but possibly puppies with heads too long or too short.

The Brood Bitch

There is an old saying that no kennel is better than its bitches, and that is why such care must be taken in selecting the bitch in the beginning of a breeding program. One must look for a bitch of superior ancestry. The over-all quality type of the bitch is also important.

A brood bitch should be free from any inherited shyness or savageness, both of which would produce undesirable puppies. Careful selection of mates with proper temperament through several generations is the only way to eliminate these faults.

It is necessary to know how to detect a structural defect in the animal's makeup. For example, if a bitch is too long of body, she should not be bred to a male also too long of body. She should be bred with a short-bodied stud to help breed out the defect.

Size. It is thought by many that the size of the bitch determines the birth size of the puppies, but this has not been conclusively proved. Hereditary factors controlling size may be passed on by either the sire or the dam, and so people breeding a small dam to a standard size or large male can run into trouble during the whelping process. Before you mate a very small bitch, understand that the size of the puppies at birth will be governed not so much by the size of the parents as by the genetic characteristics of the puppies' ancestors.

There is a common fallacy that a small bitch mated to a large dog will produce a litter in which the female puppies will be fairly small but the males will likely be as big as, if not bigger than, their sire. Sometimes an unusually small puppy born to comparatively large parents will owe its smallness to unfavorable fetal conditions, such as poor nutritional state of the bitch or disease.

There is another belief which goes against all the principles of genetics. Some people think they can produce small puppies by withholding adequate supplies of food from the diet of a pregnant bitch. Undernourishment of the bitch to reduce the size of puppies is not the answer in a sound breeding program. Malnutrition may stunt growth, but it will also produce unhealthy puppies.

It is believed by some that if a bitch has three or four litters sired by the same stud, each successive litter will look more like the sire and less like the dam. This belief has no scientific basis.

Telegony. Years ago it was generally believed that if a pedigreed bitch was mated with a dog of another breed or with a mongrel, she would thereafter be useless for breeding pure stock—all her subsequent litters would be mongrel or otherwise impure. Although this has been disproved, there are still people who believe it.

The Stud

In selecting a suitable stud the breeder must know the pedigree for at least 3 generations. He should also personally examine the stud and scrutinize the virtues and faults.

Get the best male available regardless of related bloodlines, and use a stud strong in characteristics in which the background of the bitch needs improvement.

Sometimes a breeder, in attempting to obtain a wanted characteristic not present in his strain, or to correct a fault he has not been able to eliminate, will use a stud possessing the desired trait but also possessing some fault. This brings undesirable characteristics out and is more likely to destroy the good traits already possessed than to add traits that are missing or desired.

It is the stud that determines the sex of the puppies as he carries the sex-determining chromosomes. Contrary to the old-age fallacy, the female, by nature of the number of ova fertilized, determines the size of the litter.

COLOR

In color inheritance there is no definite rule in genetics. The inheritance varies in each breed, with some colors dominant and others recessive. However, some colors appear to be dominant in all breeds in which they occur. These colors are brindle and black.

For example, two brindle boxers may produce a fawn puppy, whereas two fawns can never produce a brindle. Fawn to brindle breeding can produce only fawns and brindles, or all fawns, or all brindles. Brindle to brindle can produce fawns or brindles. The fact that fawn can be bred from two brindles shows that fawn is the recessive color.

Black is dominant in most breeds. Yet in other breeds, for example dachshund and basenji, red is dominant to black and tan, white in the Gordon setter, black and tan are dominant to red.

In color determination bear in mind that there is no blending of colors. For instance, a pair of black and white poodles will usually produce spotted colors and never a litter of blues.

MARKING

For an example of selective breeding for a specific marking we can discuss a collie in which a full white collar is wanted. The simplest way is to select a breeding animal in which a full white collar is well developed. This animal is mated, and the best-marked in each generation selected. In the ensuing offspring the desired collar should soon be achieved.

EYE COLOR

In certain breeds—harlequin spotted, blue merle, Great Dane, collie, Sheltie, and old English sheepdog—one eye of one color and the other of another is permissible in the show ring. The color difference does not affect sight, and it is usually hereditary. Actually, however, such a dog is at a slight disadvantage in the show ring against equally good dogs with both eyes the same color.

SKIN AND COAT

Although normal and healthy in all other respects, some bitches seem to remain in a state of slight molt or shedding the year round. Scabby skin and brittle or falling-out hair may be attributed to either congenital conditions that are handed down from generation to generation or possibly to a thyroid deficiency.

If a bitch has a poor hair coat, try to mate her to a stud who has a particularly good coat and is known to have ancestors who were similarly endowed.

OTHER CHARACTERISTICS

Among characteristics which don't blend is the undershot or overshot jaw. It is a mistake to breed a bitch with an overshot jaw to a male with an undershot jaw and expect the puppies to have good mouths. The result will be puppies with overshot jaws and undershot jaws.

INBORN TRAITS AND ACQUIRED TRAITS

Inborn traits are the result of heredity. Acquired traits are not inherited by the offspring. Animals have to learn all over again the things their ancestors learned—their acquired traits—because such characteristics do not impress the brain cells of the offspring.

For example, in bird dogs, new puppies have to learn the art of hunting. Some are better hunters because they have a better sense of smell or are more intelligent and not because, as an old fallacy goes, they were whelped while the bitch was hunting. Also, puppies born to an old hunting dog are not better hunters than those born to a younger bitch; both sets of puppies contain equal hereditary traits.

As other obvious examples of non-acquired characteristics, housebroken bitches don't produce puppies that are housebroken when born; cutting the tails of puppies doesn't make succeeding generations shorter of tail; and trimming the ears of puppies doesn't lead to successive litters with smaller ears.

An ailment or disease acquired by a dog after birth is not

transmitted to any offspring; for example, rickets, an ailment of the bones, is acquired and not transmitted.

HEREDITARY DISEASES: INHERITED ABNORMALITIES

Breeding programs that have developed show dogs have also contributed to abnormalities in dogs. The veterinary profession has been becoming increasingly concerned with some of the abnormalities that dogs have been developing through generations of breeding. At a recent veterinary world congress in Paris, a resolution was unanimously adopted regarding inherited diseases. The resolution concerned the health and welfare of dogs whose breed standards hinder physiological functions of organs and parts of the body. There is an increasing list of inherited diseases which threaten health and breed improvements. Large skulls, protruding eyes, and shortened heads are among the examples cited as often being responsible for increasing incidence of eye injury, difficult whelping, and dysfunction of the musculo-skeletal, nervous, respiratory, and cardiovascular system.

Some abnormalities are difficult to recognize as being inherited—ulcerative colitis, hemophilia, deafness, eye disease.

It has been proved that the incidence of hereditary disease is significantly reduced when puppies are bred from parents who show no evidence of defects. Control of hereditary diseases should be possible, therefore, by constant careful selection of breeding stock. Defective animals should be automatically disqualified from breeding, as should any animal having any association with a litter of defective animals. These animals should not be bred. They should be castrated or spayed, and can still make excellent pets. It is up to the breeder, the veterinarian, and the researcher to try to control hereditary diseases.

There are two types of hereditary abnormalities: (1) selectional abnormalities, and (2) chance abnormalities. Selectional abnormalities include all abnormalities of structure and function which are favored by the selection policy of breeders. For example, bulldog breeders deliberately select for extreme reduction of the muzzle. This leads to many problems, such as a prolonged soft palate, which causes snoring, and a short head, which causes the nasal passages to be partly or almost completely blocked.

A prime example of a physical abnormality resulting from

323

selective breeding is the collie. The skull shape has changed, from large and rectangular to a narrow, triangular-shaped head, to provide for the long pointed nose desired. This has changed both the shape of the skull cap cavity and, in my opinion, has lowered the brain capacity of some of these dogs. Several eye defects that are commonly transmitted may have resulted from the breed's narrow eyes. The old fashioned collie with his long head was much more stable and more easily trained.

Two other breeds facing possible physical ruination are the dachshund and the Welsh corgi. Only the largest and longest bodies are being bred as the long body is desirable in the show ring. Many disc problems have appeared in these breeds.

Selective breeding of thick wooly coat in poodles, kerry blues, and Bedlington terriers has produced many dogs with chronic ear problems. The hair, growing in the auditory canal and ear canal, is an excellent place for mites, bacteria and fungus to live.

Other selectional abnormalities include skinfold dermatitis as seen in English bulldog, Boston bull, pug, and Pekingese. Because of the excessive amount of wrinkling desired by breeders there is often skin irritation and infection. Entropion (inverted eyelids), ectropion (everted eyelids), and trichiasis (eyelash irritation) are other inherited abnormalities bred for.

Chance abnormalities present a different type of problem since their elimination doesn't depend on standards of breed selection. The chance abnormalities are hip dysplasia, elbow dysplasia, deafness, abnormal temperament, uterine inertia, hemophilia, cleft palate, nasal cleft, epilepsy, monorchidism and cryptorchidism, lens luxation, and retinal atrophy.

Chance Abnormalities

Hip dysplasia. This is a condition causing great concern among dog breeders. Nearly all large breeds are affected with hip dysplasia, and generally the larger the dog, the greater the chance of it. The larger breeds which mature most rapidly and grow quickly between birth and the first 3 to 4 months—usually dogs 30 pounds or over—have the highest incidence of hip dysplasia. The notable exception is the greyhound; as yet hip dysplasia has not been found in the breed.

Hip dysplasia is hereditary, but it is not congenital, since the hip joints are normal at birth. Dogs confined to kennels and permitted only moderate exercise have less hip dysplasia than litter mates who are heavy and exercise a great deal. However, confinement is not the answer to prevention, as it would retard the development of intelligence and personality. It has been found that reduction of the pelvic muscle mass predisposes the puppy to hip dysplasia. This is why greyhounds have no signs of the disease; their muscles consistently have greater pelvic muscle mass than those of any other breed, and the greyhound puppy matures and takes on weight rather slowly for the first few months of life.

Owing to improved skills in radiology, many cases of hip dysplasia heretofore unnoticed are now being found. Diagnosis can be done only by X ray, but not at birth. Changes in the hip are rarely present before the 8th to 20th week. A final decision about hip dysplasia cannot be made until the puppy is at least 6 to 12 months of age. I advise more than one X ray for final diagnosis.

The early symptoms of hip dysplasia are weakness and awkwardness in the hindquarters. Any persistent painful condition of the hind legs, or slowness in getting up from a reclining position, should make one suspicious of hip dysplasia and an X ray should be taken. Once a dog has hip dysplasia, the abnormality will always be present.

There is no satisfactory treatment, no medication that will cure, since the bone changes are irreversible. But there are drugs which help relieve some of the pain—aspirin, butazolidine, cortisone, and selenium compounds—and a new surgical procedure that alleviates suffering, pectineus muscle operation.

The question that faces many dog owners, breeders, and veterinarians is whether to destroy the dog that shows up with hip dysplasia. Not necessarily. Most dogs with hip dysplasia lead happy pain-free lives as pets, or at least a comfortable existence. If the animal has only a slight bone abnormality, obedience training and hunting may be allowed so long as there is no evidence of pain. Strenuous and fatiguing exercise should be avoided.

While the pet dog can lead a normal life with hip dysplasia, the breeder is the key to prevention and control of the disease. No one should ever breed a dog with hip dysplasia, even though he may feel justified in breeding the affected animal in order to preserve certain bloodlines to maintain quality, intelligence, disposition, conformation, or behavior.

As part of a control program for hip dysplasia, the Orthopedic Foundation for Animals has been formed. The owner of an animal who wishes to have a dog certified as free from hip disease writes to the OFA at P.O. Box 8251, Philadelphia, for application forms and instructions for submitting pelvic photographs. The X rays are scrutinized by a team of experts who classify the animal in one of three categories, normal, near-normal, or dysplastic. Any breeder wishing to embark on a sound breeding program should submit X rays to his veterinarian or to the OFA for consultation. There is no place for hip dysplasia in selective breeding.

Elbow dysplasia. This is a deformity of the elbow joint. It is similar to hip dysplasia and causes a lameness. Such an animal should not be bred.

Patella dysplasia. Many small breeds have a recurring dislocation of the knee. It is seen most often in chihuahuas, poodles, and Pomeranians. It can be treated surgically, but the offspring will be subject to this inconvenience.

Harelip and cleft palate. With modern advances in medicine and surgery, these conditions can be corrected surgically. Although it has been a universal custom to dispose of young puppies born with these abnormalities, with careful nursing most of them can be saved. But they should not be bred, because of the possibility of the defect being transmitted to their offspring. The abnormalities are most common in the Boston terrier, cocker, beagle, and Norwegian elkhound.

Monorchidism and *cryptorchidism.* These are hereditary defects in which one or both testes don't descend to the normal position in the scrotum. When both testicles are involved, the dog is usually sterile. Although a dog with one testicle can be a successful sire, because of the hereditary nature of the defect breeding is not recommended. The dog may have an unreliable disposition; also, the testicles are prone to tumors. The AKC disqualifies any animal with monorchidism or cryptorchidism; and the only way the defects can be controlled is by elimination of such dogs from any breeding program, and of any dogs in whose pedigrees it has appeared.

The defects are most often found in the toy breeds. They appear to be recessive—that is, normal males can sire both normal and affected males out of bitches born of normal sires and normal grandsires. The idea that the defects are sex-linked (like hemophilia) is popular but has not been proved or disproved.

In treatment some veterinarians administer hormones to

help the testes descend to their normal position. The value of this therapy is questionable.

Hemophilia. This is another hereditary disease, and there are two types in dogs. The disease results in a subcutaneous bleeding after minor injury and excessive hemorrhaging after wounds. It is similar to hemophilia in humans in that the blood doesn't contain all the necessary elements for clotting. In dogs as in humans, it is the female who carries the disease and the male who becomes the bleeder (especially in Irish Setters and basenjis).

Cystinura. This inherited abnormality is seen mainly in Dalmatians. It is a tendency to form urinary stones. The exact nature of the biochemical defect is unknown, but we know that there is a tendency for it to be transmitted from generation to generation.

Achondroplasia (the "swimmer"). The puppies cannot stand, but move around like turtles with all four legs extended outward. It is a condition in which the bones don't harden properly. It occurs most often in such breeds as Pekingese, bulldog, Scottish terrier, and Sealyham-breeds with short, thick legs and heavy muscles.

Diagnosis can be confirmed by X ray.

There is no cure, and it is best to destroy all affected puppies. However, with proper mineral and vitamin supplements, sometimes a puppy will develop sufficiently to get on his feet, although weeks later than his litter mates, and sometimes will even catch up in size. The gait has a telltale stiffness.

Some experienced breeders have been successful in having these animals recover by the age of 6 to 7 weeks by giving them a rough bed of blanket or sacking and an old piece of carpet on the floor of the pen, with nothing smooth or slippery under them.

But even if a puppy does survive and grow stronger as he get older, it is a genetic defect, and he would be detrimental to a breeding program.

Congenital Abnormalities

Cranioschisis (soft spots on the head). This is a condition in which the bones are not closed at birth. It is common in the toy breeds, especially the chihuahua. Normally the spaces close by the time the animal is 3 to 4 months old, but occasionally an animal will go through life with a small unclosed area. There is no pathological significance to the soft spots;

the animal may lead a healthy life with the unformed bones in his head.

Hydrocephalus. This is "water on the brain." The entire head is enlarged. It is not considered a hereditary defect, although it occurs more commonly in certain breeds.

In puppies and young dogs there are two congenital abnormalities which cause persistent vomiting. Diagnosis is made with barium X rays:

Esophageal obstruction or *dilation.* This results from a congenital malformation within the chest. It obstructs food from passing down into the stomach. It is difficult to treat, and surgery is the only solution.

Pyloric stenosis. This arises from a congenital stricture of the pyloris (outlet of the stomach). Solid food collects in the stomach and is unable to pass through the narrow outlet valve. This mass is eventually vomited, depriving the puppy of the nutrients necessary for survival. A careful dietary program of soft semi-liquid cereals is an absolute necessity. In severe cases surgery is the only solution.

Familial renal disease. A rare, inherited kidney disease in young Norwegian elkhounds. It causes uremia.

THE CANINE EYE AND SELECTIVE BREEDING

Breed Traditions

Some breed traditions in the canine eye are from antiquity. The St. Bernard has the weeping eye. The cocker spaniel has the soulful, watery eye. The Pekingese has the eye of mystery. The Boston has the large eye of play. The bulldog has the round fearful eye. The setter has the soft, mild eye. The fox terrier has the shoe-button eye of mischief. The bull terrier has the devil-may-care eye. And the chowchow—the Chinese dog—has the almond-shaped eye.

Hereditary Diseases

Just as there are breed traditions, there are indicated breed tendencies in eye diseases. Eye diseases have been found in 60 breeds. Ectropion (everted eyelids) has been reported in 25 breeds: with the bloodhound and St. Bernard most commonly affected (see p. 244). Entropion (inverted eyelids) is associated with chihuahuas (see p. 245). Trichiasis (abnormal growth and irritation of the eyelashes) is found most often in cocker spaniels and bulldogs (see p. 324). Lens luxation (dislocation of the lens) is seen mainly in wire-haired terriers and Sealyhams (see p. 324).

One of the most rapidly increasing and devastating eye diseases is progressive retinal atrophy (PRA). In the past it was seen most frequently in the Gordon setter, Irish setter, and Norwegian elkhound, but in the past few years the poodle has become the leader (sometimes in the poodle we find a complication because of a cataract which usually accompanies PRA). The other breeds most often affected are the rough collie, Labrador retriever, cocker and springer spaniels, Cairn terrier, and miniature long-haired dachshund. It is a degenerative disease for which there is no effective treatment and which inevitably causes total blindness (see p. 247).

One of the reasons for the spread of PRA is that it occurs well after a dog has reached maturity and may have been bred and produced many litters before it is diagnosed. The averge age of onset in poodles is 4½ years; the range is usually between 4 and 6 years. Selective breeding is the only answer. No dog diagnosed as having PRA should ever be used for breeding stock, and no matron or sire who has ever produced a puppy with PRA should ever be used for breeding.

RD (rod dysplasia) is another hereditary eye disease and its symptoms are similar to PRA. However, RD is found primarily in Norwegian elkhounds; and clinical tests show it as a separate disease entity. There is a test—the electroretinogram (ERG)—which detects RD at an early age, before the animals are used for breeding. It is a specialized test available only at certain veterinary institutions.

Another prominent hereditary disease is the collie ectasia syndrome, which can generally be recognized in a 6-week old puppy. Since it is a congenital abnormality, it is dangerous to breed collies with even a minimal lesion, since this can spread to the puppies. It usually results in total blindness (see p. 244).

Other hereditary conditions of the eye are the wall eye in collies and Great Danes, and prolapse of the third eyelid seen in bulldogs, bull terriers, and spaniels.

Diagnosis of congenital eye diseases can be made in puppies between six and ten weeks of age. Diseases such as PRA, RD, collie eye syndrome, and day blindness (hemerolopia) can be detected before these animals are allowed to reproduce.

19 BREEDING

The commonest mistake that the novice breeder makes is to put a bitch and a stud together in a room and leave them alone to let nature take its course. This is assumed to ensure a litter of puppies. In the main it is a faulty premise, and breeding would be strictly a gamble following this procedure. Although normal healthy animals would be expected to be able to mate with alacrity under the circumstances, our "civilized" dogs are prone to problems, and there are many factors to be considered before conception can take place and a successful program begun.

SEXUAL MATURITY OF THE STUD

The male dog reaches sexual maturity anywhere from 6 months of age in the small breeds to 1 up to 1½ years in the large breeds. The larger the breed, the slower the maturity. An unscientific way of deciding when a male dog is ready for breeding is setting it at the moment he lifts a leg to urinate and has "become a man."

It is not a good idea to use a young stud on a regular basis until he has reached his full maturity. I don't advise using a stud, except under unusual circumstances, under 1 year of age, and in the large breeds, for example Great Dane and St. Bernard, I would say they are 1½ years old before they reach full maturity.

A stud should have a physical examination before he is bred. Particularly the semen should be examined to be sure that he can sire a litter. He should be examined for intestinal parasites, because he should be in good health. Also, for the older male dog a day or two before he is scheduled to mate, male-hormone injections will increase his libido.

SEXUAL MATURITY OF THE BITCH

Heat, or estrus, is nature's signal that the bitch is ready to mate. It is commonly described as being "in season." The bitch will begin licking her vulva preceding her heat cycle, and this is a good indication that the season is not far off.

The first period of heat usually occurs anywhere after 6 months of age, up to 12 months, depending on the breed. In the smaller breeds, such as the toys, the heat period can come any time after 6 months—usually 7 to 9 months. In the larger breeds—German shepherd, boxer, etcetera—it usually comes at 10 to 12 months. However, it varies with the individual and with the season of the year. It seems that spring and fall are most conducive to the sex life of animals. There have been some unusual cases of dogs coming into their first heat at 5 months of age and others not until 18 months of age.

As a rule the first heat is agreed upon as not the best time to breed a bitch. Usually she is not quite mature, and most breeders and veterinarians advise waiting for the second period at least.

A physical examination must be done on the brood bitch before attempting to breed her. It is not uncommon to find an extremely small vagina in a maiden bitch. The vagina does not enlarge properly in the heat cycle for natural breeding to be culminated. The veterinarian can dilate it, with or without anesthetic, depending on the size. The physical examination should include testing for parasites because bitches who are anemic or just recovering from a debilitating disease may not be good brood bitches.

HEAT CYCLE OF THE BITCH

The commonest cause of unsatisfactory or incomplete mating is attempting to breed at the wrong time of the estrus cycle. Consequently a complete understanding of the cycle is primary in establishing a breeding program.

The beginning of the estrus cycle, called the proestrus, is signified by a discharge from the vulva. Actually at first there is a slight white or yellowish discharge, and then the heat period, or proestrus, begins, with the appearance of a bloody discharge and swelling of the vagina. The proestrus blood usually continues from 7 to 9 days, in a normal dog, but it can vary anywhere from 2 to 27 days in some irregular cycles. During this period the bitch generally has a hostile attitude toward males. At the end of the proestrus period her attitude changes, and she becomes interested in the other sex, attempting to attract them and often mounting them in a teasing fashion.

The average duration of proestrus is about 9 days, but in an abnormal cycle it may last from 8 to 24 days.

The heat period usually comes every 6 months, but no bitch can be counted on to be exactly 6 months to the day. Several factors such as time of year and emotional state have a bearing on the heat cycle.

The optimum time to breed is about 24 to 48 hours after ovulation, and ovulation will usually commence 9 to 12 days after the first sign of blood, in a normal female. Usually a bitch will accept the male only during the middle part of her estrus. Most breeders consider the 13th day the best breeding day, but some bitches will accept the male after 8 days and some will wait until 14 or 15 days. It has been recorded that some bitches have bred on the 5th day after the first sign of blood and others have gone as long as the 25th day.

A good barometer of the correct time to breed is a change in blood color to pale red or pale yellow. At this point the congestion around the vulva has decreased, redness had begun to leave, and although the vulva is still swollen, it has become soft and pliable. The best indication of the readiness and willingness of the bitch is when she puts her tail aside and extends her vulva.

Many amateur breeders fail to ascertain the correct time and breed either too early or too late. The veterinarian has a vaginal-smear test for determining ovulation in the bitch. Knowledge of the approximate time of ovulation is essential in a productive breeding program, especially with bitches who have abnormal cycles and don't accept the male at the normal time. Although no test can fix the exact time for breeding, vaginal smears can be used to closely estimate the time of ovulation. When the shipping time for a female is critical, when a female has shown abnormal heat periods, or to avoid overworking a valuable stud, a vaginal smear should be done at regular intervals, at least every 48 hours.

There is another ovulation test, which determines the glucose contents of the cervical mucus. Strips of paper are introduced into the vagina, and by a change in color they indicate that glucose is present. This is a sign that ovulation is taking place. These indicator strips are the same as those used in the routine examination for urine and are easily obtainable from any laboratory-supply company.

There are people who use estrogens and other hormones to

bring their dogs into heat. They also use hormone preparations to produce large litters of puppies. I am against hormones for these purposes, as their misuse may damage a good bitch for life. Many times hormones are given to bring the female into heat in her off season, and this is unsuccessful most of the time because ovulation does not take place without further stimulation by hormones.

Irregular Heat Periods

If a bitch remains a maiden for a long time after full maturity, she may have irregular seasons. However, after she is mated and has proved fertile, she may have normal intervals between her heat periods.

As the bitch gets older her heat cycles become less regular, and this is one of the first signs of old age. Some old dogs come into heat only every year or two, much to the delight of their owners. As the dog gets older she may show signs of heat but may not be capable of conceiving, because she doesn't ovulate. This is also true in "false heat" periods, during which a bitch goes through the full symptoms of estrus, such as bleeding, enlarged vulva, and attraction of males, but are not ovulating and conception is impossible. I have seen bitches 15 to 18 years old with false heat periods attracting males as if they were young and pretty maidens.

Prolonged Heat Periods

Some bitches stay in heat longer than the normal 3-week period. This is usually abnormal, although some maiden bitches, in heat for the first time, will stay in estrus 4 to 5 weeks without any abnormal body changes. A prolonged heat period is usually caused by some abnormal factor.

Infection of the uterus can give all the external signs of a heat period, including attracting all the males in the neighborhood. A bladder infection which causes irritation and bleeding of the vaginal tract can also sometimes be misinterpreted as a heat period.

When there is a prolonged heat period, the bitch should be examined by a veterinarian to find out what is causing the condition.

I advise against attempting to breed any female with an abnormal or prolonged heat period; and the life of a bitch should not be endangered by forcing her to breed with a male while she is suffering from some female irregularity.

Silent Heat Periods

This is an abnormal type of period in which the bitch does not show any of the signs of estrus. Although she is willing to accept a male, she will be in and out of season before she can be bred.

This is a bitch who requires professional help. I personally advise vaginal smears at monthly intervals to determine the health of her female organs, when she is in estrus, and when ovulation will occur. The condition is usually caused by a hormonal imbalance and is difficult to treat.

I would be cautious of using such an animal in a breeding program because there is a probability that the condition is hereditary.

Other Abnormalities

Some bitches will breed from practically the first day in season until the last. A stud cannot tell when she is ovulating, and there will be males around her during her entire heat cycle. These are abnormal females with abnormal tendencies, and they should not be bred.

THE SPERM: EJACULATION

In a normal mating the male ejaculates many thousands of sperm cells, and although only one is needed to fertilize each egg of the female, it is assumed that the more sperm present, the more likelihood there is of the egg cells being fertilized. The quantity of sperm cells and their health and vitality, together with the number of ova shed by the female during her heat cycle, determine the size of the litter.

The ejaculated fluid consists of three fractions. The first fraction, which contains no sperm, takes about half a minute to be voided. It is a clear fluid from the glands of the urethra. The second fraction is the sperm and takes only 1 to 2 minutes to be ejaculated. The third fraction, which contains no sperm, takes from 5 to 30 minutes to be voided. It is fluid from the prostate gland and is usually what the male ejaculates while he is tied to the female. While the third fraction is not necessary for conception, it serves as bulk to be washed forward into the uterus. When the first two fractions have been deposited in the vagina, there is a good chance of conception even though mating may have lasted only 1½ minutes, or long enough for the second fraction to have occurred.

THE TIE

The purpose of the tie in dogs is not fully understood, although a number of theories and explanations have been put forward. It doesn't seem to have any special significance in the present-day domestic dog.

Unlike what happens in other mammals, the dog's ejaculation doesn't occur until after penetration into the vagina and the greatly enlarged glands of the penis is held firmly in place by the contractor muscles of the vagina.

Normally the tie lasts from 5 to 30 minutes, and the time has no particular significance or influence on conception or on the number of puppies that result. Any time over 30 minutes is abnormal; if it is more than 45 minutes, a veterinarian should be consulted.

It is best to leave the dogs in a quiet, relaxed position while they are tied together. The male may turn around so that he is headed in the opposite direction of the bitch, so that the two animals are rear to rear. By all means never try to pull them apart, as you might injure either or both of them. And *never, never* pour cold water over them or try to beat them apart. It is heartless and cruel to try to separate them before their bodies are ready to release them from their love union. Trying to separate them just terrifies them and often injures them. The quieter they are left, the sooner they will separate.

There are many fallacies concerning the tie, and I know one breeder who times the tie, claiming that for every 3 minutes the animals are tied together there is another puppy conceived. This is absolutely false, since ejaculation of the sperm takes only from 1 to 1½ minutes.

SEXUAL BEHAVIOR PATTERNS

According to the ancestry of the dog, certain breeds were pack hunters and strictly monogamous. They stayed with one female completely and bred only with her. Dogs who claim the wolf as their procreator seem to be in this group. The rest of dogdom, which goes back to the jackal, has different behavior patterns.

Samoyeds, chowchows, Eskimo dogs, huskies, and Russian laikas are definitely linked to the northern wolf. The males of the wolf breeds will extend courtesies only to females in the same pack while they will fight off female dogs of other breeds and other packs.

Most other breeds are descendants of the jackal. These males are courteous and gentlemanly to every female they encounter.

Through the generations domestication has relaxed the morals, and most males will breed with any females that allow them to. Most stud dogs today are of the "cave-man" type and will force their attention on any bitches presented to them.

Most bitches resent forced attention and have to be restrained or given tranquilizers. Many a bitch will fight off one male but readily accept the mating advances of another. Some bitches enjoy playing hard to get. It is common for a highly pedigreed bitch to fight off an equally highly pedigreed stud—absolutely refuse to be serviced by him—and readily accept a mongrel in the neighborhood whom she has fallen for.

NATURAL BREEDING AND PROBLEMS

A common mistake made by novice breeders is to throw two dogs together who have never met before and then expect a successful breeding. Certainly dogs can breed by themselves, and especially can any dog that roams the streets accomplish this natural act without any outside interference. However, because of the confinement that most pet dogs have nowadays, and their close relationships with their owners, they have been inhibited from some of their natural instincts, such as the procedure of breeding—and many of them need help. I've seen male dogs mount bitches' heads in pure ignorance of how to perform the act. Likewise, many females require tranquilizers to calm them down; they are terrified by male dogs attempting to make love to them.

The two most necessary requisites for a successful union are a stud who is keen and persistent and able to make a successful union, and a bitch at the correct stage of her estrus and willing. If the breeder attempts mating too early in the heat cycle, the bitch will usually be overaggressive toward the male and will growl and bite him. This will decrease his desire, and a young inexperienced male might be ruined for life as a stud.

We must have appropriate surroundings for the mating, that the bitch and male are accustomed to, or at least not frightened by. They should not be thrown into the room and expected to breed immediately. Their introduction should be correct and proper, and they should be allowed to have some sexual foreplay so that they may become accustomed to each other and increase their sexual excitement.

Although they should be allowed to be alone so that they can play and tease each other in an uninhibited way, I recommend that they be watched from the outside so that there can be assurance that the union has taken place and so that when problems are encountered someone will be available to help the dogs. Most breeders and veterinarians connected with dog breeding are aware of the many difficulties that can be encountered in mating. Many dogs will not mate if there is someone in the room with them. Some males will allow help in mounting and penetration; other males will stop as soon as outside help is attempted. Each case has to be handled separately.

Shy and timid females may be helped by tranquilizers. Massaging the prostate, and hormone shots, are of some help in the male who is timid or does not show desire.

If the male is too aggressive and frightens the bitch, someone should immediately step in and help.

For aggressive bitches help is needed by two or more people. I usually have the owner hold the bitch's head, sometimes using a muzzle to prevent her from biting when the male penetrates. I also have someone hold the bitch's legs up so she will not sit down when the male attempts to mount her. The same procedure applies for a stubborn bitch.

In large breeds—St. Bernards or Great Danes—I have used four or five soft-drink crates under their middles to prevent them from sitting down.

In breeding large bitches to small studs, or vice versa, we use large books for the animals to stand on so that their sizes will coincide. It is also necessary to have something non-slippery, such as rubber matting, for the animals to stand on.

Many a willing female turns frigid when the male penetrates her vagina for the first time because of excruciating pain due to her very narrow female organs. Thereafter when he attempts to mount her, she will not tolerate it and sits on

337

the floor. I can't emphasize too strongly that all virgin bitches should have a vaginal examination before breeding, with dilation if needed.

NUMBER OF MATINGS PER LITTER

In the mating of dogs most breeders agree that 2 or 3 matings are desired, although one is all that is necessary. It is good to breed 2 or 3 times for several reasons: to ensure the bitch's being served during the period of ovulation, which sometimes is difficult to ascertain; it gives the bitch the best opportunity to produce the largest number of puppies; and it gives the stud a chance to produce some good sperm if he has not been used for some time. It has been proved that if a stud is not used for a long period, the semen may lose much of its potency.

I don't advise breeding more than 4 or 5 days apart because of the possibility of conception at both breedings, and there will then be a premature puppy or two in a litter of normal healthy puppies.

More than one male can breed with a female, and she can have puppies by each of the studs. For this reason some litters are composed of many different colors, sizes, and shapes of puppies. The bitch, after a night on the town, can give birth to many different types of puppies.

AFTER MATING

It is the opinion of many experts that for at least 10 days after the bitch has been mated, she should not be moved into a new kennel or alongside a male other than the one who serviced her. It is believed that disturbing environmental conditions can possibly be the cause of abortion in some bitches, especially highly excitable and nervous ones.

MISMATING OF A BITCH

Accidents indeed do happen. Occasionally a bitch escapes from her confinement and is bred by a neighborhood Casanova. To avoid the whelping of undesirable puppies, the mismating can be aborted.

If the misalliance is immediately apprehended—within an hour—douching the bitch with cold water and vinegar (half and half) is an effective method of avoiding pregnancy. It must be done within an hour after breeding, before the sperm has had a chance to fertilize any eggs high in the uterus.

There is a method that is almost 100 percent successful if done within a week of breeding. It must be done by a professional. It is a female-hormone injection, and the earlier it is given, the more effective it is. The only disadvantage is that it prolongs the heat cycle a week to 10 days. Most people don't mind under the circumstances.

Another procedure, but which is rather risky and should also be done by a professional, is an intravaginal injection of ether. This must be performed within 24 to 48 hours following mating.

There is a drug called Malucidin which is used in advanced cases of pregnancy. It is injected prior to the 44th day of pregnancy and will dissolve fetuses within 48 to 60 hours. However, it entails danger to the bitch, and I personally would not use it unless the pregnancy was detrimental to the life of the bitch.

ARTIFICIAL INSEMINATION

Artificial insemination in dogs has been used for about twenty years. The AKC requires a veterinarian's certificate of confirmation regarding the breeding. Actually the procedure *should* be performed by a veterinarian, as many laymen have produced uterine infection in their bitches.

Where natural breeding cannot be accomplished, artificial insemination should be attempted. I would recommend artificial breeding to any breeder who is not successful with a problem bitch, but certainly natural copulation should be attempted first. Also, it is possible through artificial insemination for a stud in one part of the country to breed with a bitch in another part of the country. Frozen semen is now available for that purpose.

The technique involves depositing the semen, with a syringe, into and through the cervix. Conditions must be absolutely perfect; correct temperature of the syringe and the absence of any sperm-killing chemicals are among the primary requisites for successful results.

FERTILITY AND STERILITY IN THE BITCH

Any breeding program suffers a serious setback when no puppies are produced. The breeder is completely reliant on

339

the quantity and quality of puppies produced from the union of male and female. In the production of puppies, without a doubt the commonest cause of sterility in the female is failure of the owner to present her for service at the right time of the estrus cycle There are many factors which affect the fertility of the bitch, and her sterility can often be traced to the owner's ignorance of her dietary needs, her emotional problems, and her physical well-being.

A well-balanced diet is essential for the proper functioning of the bitch's body. Often an adjustment in diet will allow a sterile dog to produce puppies.

Sterility is often due to emotional or psychological factors. Often the bitch shows aversion or hesitation when a male approaches her. Bitches have their likes and dislikes, and one male may be refused but another perfectly acceptable. Sympathy and understanding are needed in treatment.

Environmental conditions can affect the bitch's fertility. Sometimes moving the bitch to a strange place and climate will affect her physiological and emotional balances. Often bitches shipped to faraway places will not breed, but in the confines of their own neighborhood will breed with the first male that makes them an offer. Before breeding, a dog should be allowed time to adjust to a new environment and climate.

Physical causes of barrenness in bitches include such things as poor hormonal production, blockage of the Fallopian tubes, a thick and tough hymen, and a juvenile vagina which is small and constricted.

Poor hormonal production often responds to hormone therapy with good results. Conditions such as failure to come into normal heat, frigidity, and abnormally long heat periods can often be corrected by hormone treatment. However, the careless use of hormones can do more harm than good, and the method should be left to the discretion of a veterinarian. The most effective hormones are those which are similarly used in humans to help ovulation—fertility drugs. Such other drugs as cortisones and thyroids should be used only on the advice of a veterinarian.

Bacterial infections, tumor formations, or any serious illness usually will result in temporary or permanent sterility. Infections which may result in sterility are metritis, vaginitis, and ovarian cysts. Tumors found in the vaginal passageway can be corrected by surgery, and the bitch will then conceive.

Cystic ovaries cause nymphomania by keeping the bitch in constant heat. Most of the time she is nervous, high-strung, ill-tempered, and inclined to fight both males and other bitches. This condition usually requires surgery on one or both ovaries. If only one ovary is affected, removal would still allow normal heat cycles and the bitch would be able to conceive and produce normal litters. If both ovaries are affected, complete hysterectomy is the only answer.

There is a bacterial infection which causes sterility in bitches. A bitch may appear in excellent health and may even have a normal heat period (or a short period or none at all). There may be a normal mating, but it will result in either failure to conceive, abortion, or puppies that die shortly after birth. The veterinarian can detect the infection with a vaginal smear, and treatment is with antibiotics. If complete recovery is effective, it may be possible to breed the animal in the future.

After a serious disease, such as distemper, a young bitch may become temporarily sterile for up to 2 years. However, if the animal recovers completely, the tissues of her female organs will usually revert to healthy functioning tissue and she will have normal reproductive cycles.

There is sometimes a temporary barrier in breeding due to an acid secretion in the bitch which neutralizes the male sperm. This secretion has not been fully comprehended and can be due to a disease of the uterus or a "lethal factor" in the vaginal lubricant of some bitches. It can exert its influence on the sperm within 16 seconds after the sperm is exposed to the vaginal contents. This acidic condition can be tested for by inserting blue litmus test paper into the vagina. For a bitch with this condition (paper turns red) I advise a douche with bicarbonate of soda solution one hour prior to breeding.

Poor health due to heavy worm infestation can hinder pregnancy.

A very fat bitch will often fail to conceive, and if she does she will be subject to uterine inertia or a difficult whelping. It is obvious that proper diet and exercise will possibly correct this type of infertility. It is bad policy to breed a fat bitch.

The Age of the Bitch

Because the number of eggs shed by the ovaries during the heat period affects the efficiency of the bitch's reproductive organs, as she gets older and her ability to produce eggs decreases she declines to complete sterility. Usually the first sign of approaching sterility in older age is the commencement of irregular heat cycles. Also, as she gets older the bitch is more prone to female disorders due to hormonal dysfunction.

There is a common fallacy that if a bitch is bred at least once in her young life, she will be immune from such female disorders as infections and tumors in her old age. This is not true; it has been proved that dogs that are not bred are usually less likely to develop growths, cysts, and tumors than the brood bitch.

There are several diseases that aging bitches may endure which cause sterility. One of these is pyometra, which is pus formation in the uterine tract.

Another is metritis—a dangerous condition. It is usually seen in middle-aged and older dogs following a heat period. This is a time for the owner to be especially aware of any fever or general lethargy in a female dog; and immediate professional help is needed to save her. In severe cases the only cure is surgery to remove the infected uterus before general blood poisoning occurs.

My personal feeling is that after a brood bitch has completed her productive years, she should have a complete hysterectomy so that she will not suffer in her later years from female disorders. I especially recommend this to owners who have bitches that are also valued pets or companions. It prevents trouble later in life, when surgery would be more dangerous.

Breeding Span in Bitches

The breeding span varies in female dogs according to many factors. A bitch may have a short breeding span due to ill health, bad rearing, or environmental changes. Sexual puberty is delayed in some females because of ill health, bad rearing, emotional changes in environment, arrested growth, or poor nutrition. Also, in the old dog the extent of the span varies. When the bitch stops coming into heat can be affected by climate, environmental conditions, housing, feeding, hormonal disturbances, and even temperament.

FERTILITY AND STERILITY IN THE STUD

Sterility in the male can be due to a variety of causes. Some can be helped by veterinary intervention, while others are impossible to cure. Degrees of infertility may be inherited; the potency of the stud dog seems to run in certain families. There are some studs who for generations have been known to throw large and healthy litters. This is a good reason for knowing the ancestry in a breeding program.

Some males' sperm is weak, immobile, or even absent. A microscopic examination by a veterinarian can easily tell the exact status of the sperm, and whether the dog is likely to be a good stud.

There is a condition, called phimosis, in male dogs in which they cannot extend the penis from the sheath. It is due to a tight ligament. Surgery gives good results, and dogs can be bred soon after.

Monorchids and cryptorchids are often sterile. Although it is not a good idea to breed such dogs, because the condition can be inherited, if there is one testicle it can be functioning normally. If both testicles are hidden inside the abdomen, the dog is usually lacking in viable sperm.

Canine brucellosis is a newly recognized disease which causes infection and sterility in males. It can be considered a canine venereal disease because it is contracted during sexual intercourse. It originates as an acidic condition in the bitch which kills the sperm. The male can be contaminated by such a bitch and can pass the infection on to other bitches whom he services. It causes an enlargement and then shrinking of the testicles, and skin infection on the scrotum. A purulent discharge from the penis may or may not be present. If the infection is found in time, it can be treated with antibiotics and will not have a sterilizing effect on the male.

Another cause of sterility can be a serious illness. Any serious illness in the male can affect sperm production. This is usually only temporary. After a long period of convalescence, with proper care, the male is usually restored to his full fertility.

Too-frequent breeding, underfeeding, lack of exercise, and confinement are all causes of sterility. Any stud used frequently should be kept on a high-animal-protein diet, with plenty of outdoor exercise and freedom. Close confinement and environmental conditions affect the nervous temperament of the dog. An extremely nervous stud may not father many good litters. Faulty nutrition usually deprives the stud of the vitamins important in sperm production. The male may have millions of sperm in his ejaculation, but if they are weak and anatomically deformed, they cannot reach the ova in the uterus and usually conception cannot take place. It has been found by researchers that the male is usually to blame in about half the failures in production of puppies.

Many dog breeders like to breed their studs not later than in the latter part of the adolescent period mainly because they want the dog to have experience in the act of breeding. It is astonishing how many of our house pets are ignorant of the mechanics of mating and often have to be shown. Once they are shown the proper way, there's no stopping them, and they do quite well by themselves. There are some male house pets who show absolutely no interest in female dogs although they get terribly interested in pillows and other objects around the house. These dogs may be in good health and produce good sperm, but they have no interest in the opposite sex. Their abnormal behavior follows psychological factors, which usually are a combination of hereditary indifference and rearing in an artificial environment. These shy breeders are usually pets who have had little contact with other dogs because they have not been allowed to roam around. They usually prefer the company of humans. Occasionally I've resorted to male-hormone injections to help the sexual drive.

Frequency of Use

Frequency of use varies with the health of the stud and the quality and quantity of his sperm. Most normal virile males can be used at least twice a week without any harm to health or decline in fertility. In dogs with a lower fertility rate, once in 2 weeks may deplete the body of active sperm.

It is recommended that a stud be used often, at regular intervals, rather than trying to conserve his potency by breeding him only rarely.

The Age of the Stud

As the stud gets older his fertility usually diminishes because of interference and reduction in sperm production. The quantity and quality of sperm cells affect the conception rate because the sperm have a long way to go through the vaginal passage into the uterus to reach the ova.

Most males if kept in good health are fertile until 7 to 8 years of age. After that time sperm production begins to wane, and although a dog may sire litters, he may need help with extra amounts of food and hormone therapy.

A male in poor health, even because of a severe infestation

of worms, can be reduced in potency and his value as a stud threatened.

Although the number of puppies in a litter sired by an old dog may be smaller, it is a fallacy that the quality will be poorer. Once the sperm makes contact with the ova, no matter how old the stud, the puppies will be of the same quality and have the same good points (and bad) as if the sire were only one year of age. The factors transmitted by him to his offspring are genetic and are not affected by his age.

Another fallacy is that unless a stud is used when he is young, he will be impotent in later years. Many males not bred before 3 or 4 years of age have sired full litters. If a male is in good condition, his potency is available for many years without his ever having been used as a stud.

BIRTH CONTROL PILLS

There is now a birth control pill for dogs—OVABAN. If given in time before the start of the heat cycle it eliminates the entire period; if given after the onset of the cycle it shortens the heat period. No untoward results have been noted to date. The pills are also effective in the treatment of false pregnancy.

I would not recommend giving these pills during all of the dog's life to prevent heat periods. Surgical spaying is the permanent answer.

Incidentally, human birth control pills will not prevent conception in dogs.

SEX AND SIZE OF LITTERS

There are two erroneous beliefs which some breeders stubbornly stick to. Some believe that the sexes in a litter depend to a large extent on the stage in the heat period during which the dam was mated. For instance, they believe that if a mating is made at a later time in the estrus cycle, more males will be delivered, and that if more females are wanted, service should be arranged early in the heat period. The other belief is that the age of the parents has a determining influence on the sex of the offspring. It is believed that with older parents male puppies are more likely to be born, and the younger the bitch or stud the more females will be born. Actually the sex of the puppies is fixed the moment a sperm unites with the egg during conception.

I have had breeders tell me that they can predict the sex of puppies according to the direction in which the animals were facing during conception. Facing to the east means more females, and in any other direction there will be more male dogs.

According to my knowledge, raising puppies with sex control in mind is not possible at the present time. But with the research in progress it would not surprise me if in the near future we can control sex in puppies.

It has been proved that litter size seems to run in certain family strains, and so it is advisable to breed dogs whose ancestry shows large litters if such are desired. However, too large a litter can affect the size and health of the puppies and often affect the health of the mother, who in some cases may require outside help in feeding and rearing the puppies.

SUMMARY: THE BITCH

1. Don't breed a bitch under a year of age; it is much better to wait until she is 18 months of age so that she is physically developed and mature.

2. Don't breed a bitch with physical defects or one who is shy or has a bad disposition.

3. Don't breed a bitch who has serious faults according to the standards of the breed.

4. Don't breed a bitch who is in poor condition, either recuperating from a serious illness or from a heavy infestation of worms, or who is nutritionally deficient.

5. See that the bitch has a complete physical checkup before breeding her to make sure she is free from worms and other parasites, is free from disorders of the body, such as female infections, and is anatomically able to accept a male.

6. Don't breed a bitch unless you are ready and willing to lose a few nights' sleep and to take care of puppies until they are ready for their new owners.

SUMMARY: THE STUD

1. Don't breed a stud on a regular basis until he has reached full sexual maturity.

2. Don't breed a stud who has obvious congenital defects. I suggest that all studs have an X ray of the pelvis to determine the absence of hip dysplasia.

3. A stud should be used only if in excellent health and a

good example of the standards of perfection of the breed. Although no dog is perfect, we should strive for perfection.

4. I would not breed any male showing emotional instability, such as timidity, aggressiveness, or viciousness.

5. Too frequent breeding, or not enough breeding, interferes with effectiveness of fertility.

6. If the male is not a proven stud, a sperm count is valuable in determining his fertility.

7. Studs that are used frequently for breeding should be on high-protein diets, such as plenty of steaks and dozens of oysters.

BREEDING CHART

1. *Premating*
   a. physical examination by veterinarian.
   b. laboratory examination of stools, blood, and urine.
   c. booster vaccination for distemper, hepatitis, and leptospirosis.
   d. general mating information, e.g., signs of ovulation and other pertinent information; vaginal smear (if indicated).
   e. vaginal palpation for obstructions or tumors. The veterinarian looks for anything that would interfere with penetration; if a narrow or constricted vagina, he dilates it.

2. *3-4 Weeks Postmating*
   a. physical examination.
   b. dietary information and supplements.
   c. pregnancy palpatation.

3. *2 Weeks Prewhelping*
   a. physical examination.
   b. whelping information.
   c. clipping hair on certain breeds.

4. *Postwhelping Examination within 24 Hours after Whelping*
   a. bitch: palpation for retained puppies.
   b. discharge examination and douching if indicated.
   c. injections if needed to expel afterbirth.
   d. puppies: examination for congenital defects and pediatric information to owner.

20 PRENATAL CARE

After the mating process has been accomplished, the chief concern of the breeder should be the brood bitch and the need to maintain her at optimum nutritional and muscular level. Under such conditions she can be expected to produce healthy offspring. In the bitch, successful production of healthy puppies depends on (1) fertility, (2) fecundity, (3) the ability to carry her young the full term, (4) a successful whelping, and (5) normal development of the nursing instinct and sufficient milk to nurse her puppies.

SIGNS OF PREGNANCY

1. Increase in body weight. Usually an increase in abdominal fat occurs after the 5th week of pregnancy.

2. Abdominal enlargement. Usually this is observed about the 5th week as a slight filling out of the flanks, but if the bitch is carrying a small litter, the enlargement may go unobserved. Abdominal enlargement can also be due to an infection of the uterus, or to tumors in the uterus or elsewhere in the abdominal cavity.

3. Changes in the mammary glands. Usually about the 35th day of the pregnancy the teats begin to enlarge and pinken. They continue to enlarge and become softer in texture until about the 50th day. The breasts begin to fill with milk and get larger each day. A few days before whelping the breasts secrete a watery solution. The milk usually does not come down until whelping, although some brood bitches express milk several days before parturition.

A non-pregnant maiden bitch will have an enlargement of the mammary tissue after her first heat period. This is normal, and there is no need to become upset and believe that the virgin has cheated and become pregnant in an illicit romance.

4. Abdominal movement. During the last week of pregnancy, when the bitch is in a relaxed position the unborn puppies can usually be seen moving in the uterus, changing positions.

348

5. Temperamental deviation. During pregnancy a bitch may change in her behavior habits. Usually she becomes quieter and more affectionate, although a very nervous bitch may become aggressive.

6. There is generally an increase in appetite. But within a few days of whelping the bitch goes off her feed. When the bitch altogether refuses food, whelping is imminent. When she stops eating, and then does not deliver within 24 hours, it is a signal for a veterinarian to take over and find out what is causing the abnormality.

If none of the above signs of pregnancy are observed, there are methods that can be used by the veterinarian to determine if the bitch is pregnant. A reliable diagnosis is abdominal palpation—feeling the puppies in the uterus. Between the 24th and 30th day it is possible to feel the fetuses in the womb. With a fat bitch or a nervous one, palpation is more difficult. If only one fetus is present and is carried high in the uterus, it is difficult to make a definite diagnosis, as the puppy is under the rib cage and cannot be felt. In extremely difficult diagnosis, X ray is usually resorted to, but an X ray will not show a puppy until after the 49th day. It is not possible to use biological tests with rabbits or mice as in humans.

FALSE PREGNANCY

This is a common problem in dogs. To all intents and purposes the animal believes that she is pregnant and shows many of the symptoms of pregnancy, such as enlarged mammary glands with the production of milk, swelling of the abdomen, and appetite change. At whelping time she shows extreme hyperexcitability, such as panting and trembling. Many of these bitches go through labor pains at about the time they normally would be delivering. Often the bitch makes a nest and proceeds to protect her "puppies," which may be toys, bones, or other objects which she carries around in her mouth. She usually curls up with her "puppies" tightly snuggled to her breasts. Bitches in false pregnancy have been known to adopt entire litters of real puppies and to produce enough milk to raise them during their entire 6 weeks of suckling.

Varying symptoms are restlessness, looking for puppies, whining and crying, and scratching at rugs, trying to make a bed for her "litter." These are extreme symptoms. The dog generally doesn't go through all these antics but instead may become quiet, go off her feed, and curl up in a corner, wanting to be alone.

Certainly the behavior is abnormal for a non-pregnant dog, and while a bitch is undergoing this condition her temperament may be adversely affected. Mannerisms and normal behavior patterns are changed. Fortunately, with cessation of the false pregnancy, the bitch returns to her normal self.

Some dogs show a strong maternal impulse. In some bitches false pregnancy makes them more affectionate with their human companions, and sometimes they will mother a young puppy, or a young animal of any species. Their maternal frustrations can drive them to many things, and there are cases of bitches' stealing puppies from other bitches. Some bitches produce so much milk that it drips, stimulated by the highly emotional state. I don't advise milking such a bitch, as it will just stimulate further milk production. However, if her breasts are extremely swollen and feverish, some milk should be expressed to give relief. I would then apply camphorated oil gently to the breasts to help relieve the inflammation and dry up the milk.

The signs of false pregnancy usually last from about the 5th week following the termination of the heat period until the normal delivery date, had she been bred. Milk production sometimes lasts 4 to 6 weeks after the onset of the false whelping.

False pregnancy has been widely discussed. It is caused by retention of a growth on the ovary. The retention affects the bitch both physically and emotionally, and the abnormal behavior seems to be controlled by the ovaries that have gone astray.

Researchers have reported that an injection of certain hormones at the end of the normal heat period can prevent this condition in the ovaries and consequently false pregnancy. In treatment of false pregnancy the veterinarian usually resorts to a variety of hormones to counteract retention of the growth on the ovary.

Many times during false pregnancy the animal becomes feverish either because of enlarged breasts full of milk or because of conditions in her uterus (there are definite uterine changes during this period). A veterinarian will usually prescribe tranquilizers, and if fever is present, put the animal on antibiotics. The animal is definitely in distress both physically and mentally and needs help in both respects.

If the condition is chronic, I would advise hysterectomy to

keep the animal from undue suffering. Most bitches with histories of irregular heat cycles and false pregnancies usually will not conceive when bred. However, I advise attempting to breed such a bitch, because sometimes this will cure the occurrence of false pregnancy. It has been proved that bitches who have false pregnancies are not diseased and actually when bred make excellent brood bitches.

In the maiden bitch the symptoms are usually less severe and less prolonged than in an older dog. I personally advise breeding the bitch on the next heat period, as this is one way of satisfying her maternal instincts and returning her body to that of a normally functioning brood bitch. If the owner doesn't want to raise puppies, the bitch should be spayed. Bitches who have repeated false pregnancies are prone to female infections, such as metritis and mammary tumors due to excessive lactation development.

If hysterectomy is resorted to, it is not wise to spay these dogs while they are undergoing false pregnancy, as all their female organs are swollen and hemorrhagic and the operation is difficult for them. Also, while they are lactating, an operation might prolong the production of milk from several weeks to several months. It is much wiser to wait until the bitch has completely recovered from her false pregnancy.

In the treatment of false pregnancy it is best to reduce the diet and especially the fluid intake. The more fluid the bitch drinks, the more milk she will produce. Try to feed her food as dry as possible and give her plenty of exercise to keep her bowels moving so as to excrete all the excess fluid produced by her body.

I advise keeping the bitch away from other dogs, and especially nursing bitches and young puppies. It is difficult to tell how she will react; she might jump on a nursing mother and attempt to kill her so that she can have her puppies.

False pregnancy is not to be considered a neurotic tendency, but should be considered normal behavior due to an abnormality of the ovaries. It is also incorrect to consider a bitch sexually abnormal if she undergoes a false pregnancy. Actually her maternal instincts are great, and she should make a good brood bitch.

If a bitch has a false pregnancy and then is bred and produces puppies, it does not mean that this will prevent her from having false pregnancies again. She can have further false pregnancies, although it is the experience of most breeders that if this happens, they are usually less severe and don't last as long as in unmated bitches.

PHANTOM PREGNANCY

Many a fetus dies within a day or two after mating so that there is no indication of conception, or fetuses may die and disappear several weeks after conception. Often the bitch will show all the signs of being in whelp up to the end of 6 weeks and then gradually become slimmer until she passes her whelping date without any indication of puppies.

Phantom pregnancy is entirely different from false pregnancy. It is seen in a bitch who has been mated and appears to have become pregnant with all the symptoms. Failure to whelp is usually due to the death of the fetuses in the uterus and absorption of the fetuses during some part of the gestation period. There is no secretion or discharge from the vagina to signify a miscarriage—all residue is absorbed by the body of the bitch. Sometimes a bitch will lose part of her litter, some of the fetuses will die, and she will have fewer puppies than were conceived.

Fetal death and absorption is due to some lethal factor not completely understood at this time. It is thought to be either a hormonal inbalance or a deficiency of vitamin E or a lack of certain ingredients in the maternal blood.

Having a phantom pregnancy does not mean that the bitch is sterile and unable to bear future litters.

BRUCELLOSIS ABORTION

There is a condition called canine brucellosis which is on the increase throughout the world. It causes abortions in affected bitches, without any warning signals, in the 40th to 50th day of gestation; the 50th day is the most common. Some of the aborted puppies don't have developed hair, and others show a swelling around the umbilical area.

Bitches who have aborted should be isolated and the contaminated area thoroughly disinfected. The affected dogs are treated with antibiotics but should not be used for further breeding until completely negative for the bacteria. Exposed males should be examined and isolated if infected, and also treated with antibiotics.

It is most commonly found in beagles and occurs in a few other breeds. After the female has aborted, there is a prolonged vaginal discharge. Diagnosis is made by a blood test or by a smear from the vaginal tract. Laboratory confirmation is the only way of knowing if the disease has affected the bitch. Any apparently healthy bitch who aborts about 20 days before her term, or who fails to conceive after 2 or 3 matings, should be suspected of having this disease (see also Phantom Pregnancy).

GESTATION

We should know at the earliest possible time that a bitch is pregnant so that suitable arrangements can be made for her prenatal care.

The gestation period in normal bitches varies between 58 and 66 days; the average is 63. It varies in different breeds, and also fluctuates with the size of the litter, the time of mating, the breeding season, and enviromental conditions. The smaller breeds whelp slightly earlier than the larger ones. Gestation periods have been reported from 53 to 71 days, although these should be considered unusual. Puppies born under 58 days are considered premature.

In determining the whelping date, always count from the first mating period even if there were subsequent matings. The supposition is that the bitch conceived at the first mating.

NUTRITION

Prenatal nutrition should be complete and balanced because obviously nutrition of the bitch influences the nutrition obtained by the developing puppies. If certain elements of nutrition are not supplied by the mother, the embryos will not develop normally. The bitch must have optimum nutrition for production of superior puppies.

A balanced diet should contain high-protein foods rather than dry, bulky and mushy types. Instead of giving only dry commercial food mixed with water and milk, I would supplement it with a good amount of meat, either raw or as a canned dogfood meat. High-protein foods, such as eggs, liver, milk and cheese, are also good.

When she is first bred, the bitch should not be fed too much (rationalizing that the new puppies immediately need food), or she will get fat and lazy. And during the first 4 weeks of pregnancy her food intake should not be increased. Quality food, not quantity, is what she needs.

After 4 weeks of pregnancy she should have about a 20 percent increase in food intake, while at the same time not giving her all she asks for. The increase should be in proteins rather than in starch or carbohydrates. A bitch should be in good muscular condition with no excess fat added during her gestation period.

I advise dividing the daily ration into 2 or 3 feedings, because if the bitch eats too much at one meal, it will cause discomfort from the pressure on her already overcrowded abdominal contents.

Mineral Requirements

Bone formation of puppies is largely dependent on the mineral consumption in the pregnant bitch's diet. The absorption of minerals from the diet depends on the vitamin A and vitamin D content of the diet. If the diet is deficient in these vitamins, the bitch's body will be the first to suffer from lack of minerals even though the puppies may seem normal.

If the diet is deficient in calcium and phosphorus, the bone structure of the puppies at birth may be soft, brittle, or malformed, and there will be defective teeth later in life. Rickets is a common result of mineral deficiency.

Birth defects often appear when the diet is deficient in copper, niacine, iodine, pantothenic acid, and riboflavin. Such defects include cleft palate, eye defects, and skeletal malformation.

If there is a deficiency of vitamin B_2 (riboflavin) in the bitch's diet, the puppies may be born with umbilical hernia, cleft palate, or congenital heart defects.

The last 2 weeks of gestation the puppies put on flesh, and there is little bone growth. They don't need many extra nutrients. Keep the bitch down in weight the last 2 weeks. Rearrange her diet so that she gets more animal protein and less starch and carbohydrates. And keep up the vitamins and minerals.

There is a belief that feeding the bitch supplementary vitamins and minerals while she is in whelp will produce abnormally large puppies at birth. This is a fallacy. Although inadequate nutrition in the bitch will produce weak and small puppies, the size of puppies in the prenatal stage is controlled by genetic factors and by growth hormones of the bitch.

THE FAT BROOD BITCH

Fatness in the brood bitch reduces the chances of conception and also reduces the chances of trouble-free whelping. Fat bitches often produce malformed puppies, attributable to the crowded conditions in the uterus. The brood bitch who is overweight usually has a prolonged labor process, and the puppy mortality is high.

NUMBER OF PUPPIES

Gain in body weight during pregnancy does not reflect the number of puppies in the litter.

Some people are so anxious to know how many puppies will be born that they cause the bitch undue anxiety by poking at her tummy, trying to feel the puppies. Patience is indicated.

It is possible, after the 6th week of gestation, for the veterinarian to determine the number of puppies to be born. This is done by X ray, but it is not advisable unless, for the health of the bitch, there is a need to know.

Some people think they can tell the number of puppies by counting the nipples, and the breasts that are filled with milk, believing that there will be one nipple for each puppy. This has no scientific basis.

VACCINATION

All pregnant bitches must have immunity against distemper, hepatitis, and leptospirosis. Although it is a requisite of breeding to give a bitch a booster before she is bred, it is possible for the bitch to have a booster vaccination of a modified live-virus vaccine after breeding without danger to the unborn puppies.

The importance of the booster vaccine cannot be emphasized too strongly. The mother's colostrum (first milk) gives immunity against the various diseases puppies are prone to and should be as full of immunity as possible. Unvaccinated bitches with extremely low immunity can seriously affect the chances of puppies' surviving should they be exposed.

PARASITES

The same factors as above apply to worming. If possible, it should be done before the bitch is bred or very early in pregnancy. *A bitch should not be wormed during the last 6 weeks of pregnancy.* Worming is dangerous and can prove extremely toxic to the developing puppies. If it is necessary, be sure to see a veterinarian: he has some types of worm medicine which can be used safely on pregnant bitches. Commercial worm medicines can cause abortion or interfere with development of the embryos.

PREPARING THE BITCH FOR WHELPING

A few days before whelping it is advisable to give a bitch a good bath to be sure she is rid of external parasites, such as fleas, lice, and ticks. She should also be free of any skin diseases, such as mange, ringworm, or fungus infections, which might be transmitted to the puppies.

In the week before whelping it is advisable to clean the bitch's teeth and gums every other day. This procedure reduces the chance of navel infection in the newborn puppies. I advise using on the teeth and gums either hydrogen peroxide or salt and soda (1 tsp. of each in a cup of water).

Clip the hair around the bitch's breasts and vagina fairly short so the puppies won't become entangled during whelping and so the excess hair around the nipples will not get in the way of the hungry puppies. The inner thighs on each side of the vagina should also be clipped.

After clipping, the bitch's udder should be washed with a mild soap to cleanse it thoroughly and to wash away all parasite eggs that might be around the nipples. The nipples should be softened with baby oil and any encrustment removed. If there is dirt present on the breasts, roundworm eggs that infest so many puppies may be present. They are usually obtained by puppies in this way.

ADDITIONAL ADVICE

Bear in mind that a pregnant bitch needs special consideration in time, affection, and tender loving care. She wants to be spoiled a little bit, and I for one would be the first to give in to her demands except for extra amounts of food and in-between snacks that might cause a hazardous overweight problem. She wants to be close to you as the whelping date approaches, and she looks to you to give her the physical and emotional comfort that she will need during this especially trying time—especially the maiden bitch with her first litter.

During the last week of gestation the bitch must be watched carefully so that she doesn't injure herself and overdo herself trying to keep up with her daily chores and play periods with the neighborhood dogs. I would not allow her to roam free, as she might not be able to resist a leap or two. I would not allow her to jump over large objects; this can cause a misplacement or wrong positioning of the puppies. Or a hard fall might injure the unborn puppies. If she must be picked up, she should not be picked up in the middle but by placing one hand between her front legs and one under her hindquarters. Never, never pick up a dog by the scruff of the neck when she is heavy with pups—and I'm not in favor of picking her up in this manner even when she is not pregnant.

Normal exercise is desirable to maintain the tone of the muscles and to keep the bowels functioning normally. But the bitch should not be taken for many car rides, as hitting bumps may cause premature labor pains.

During pregnancy the bitch should be given a dose of milk of magnesia once a week to ensure regular bowel movements. I also advise a teaspoonful of bicarbonate of soda in her drinking water every day during the last half of her gestation period; this will help keep excessive acidity out of her system.

PREPARING THE WHELPING PEN

Get the whelping quarters ready for the bitch during the last week or 10 days before she is due to whelp so that she will know where you desire her to have her puppies and so she can become accustomed to it. Of course, some bitches will have their minds made up and will have a favorite bed or closet chosen where they know they will feel relaxed and be free from outside interference. However, the bitch should be somewhere near you when she starts going into labor.

The whelping box should be in a quiet corner, free from noises, from strangers, from excitement, and from cats and other dogs in the household. If disturbed, the bitch is apt to jump up to protect her puppies and possibly hurt one of them.

The box should be about double the size of the bitch so that she can stretch out with her brood and not be in cramped quarters and liable to roll over on a puppy or step on it. For large breeds have a shelf around the bottom of the box so the puppies can crawl under the shelf and be protected from a large brood bitch.

The box should be free of any debris and in a sanitary condition. It should be scrubbed with a good disinfectant, such as Clorox or Lysol.

For the litter in the whelping box there is no substitute for shredded newspapers. Many puppies have died of strangulation from becoming entangled in blankets or towels. Cushions can also be dangerous because the bitch usually will tear them to shreds and the puppies are liable to ingest some of the stuffing. Wood shavings and straw are strictly taboo in a whelping box; the puppies may ingest or inhale particles, which would be fatal. Newspapers are easy to clean and readily available, and the price is right. The newspaper is highly absorbent, provides a good footing for young puppies and allows the bitch an opportunity to dig and scratch preceding labor. The digging and scratching reverts to ancestral days when the bitch would dig a hole in the ground for her whelping nest. Domestication has provided newspapers for the same primitive satisfactions.

The new indoor-outdoor carpeting makes ideal lining for whelping boxes. The carpeting gives the puppies good traction and is easily sponged clean. Several layers of newspapers folded under the carpet will absorb all the puddles, leaving the carpet dry.

A heating pad is a useful object to have around in case of cold puppies. It has been estimated that 50 percent of early puppy losses are due to chilling. Therefore the whelping box should be indoors, in the home, at regular room temperature, 70-72 degrees; or if it is out in the kennel, it should be provided with adequate heat and be free from drafts.

THINGS TO HAVE ON HAND FOR WHELPING

There should be a good supply of clean newspapers; delivery tends to get a little messy.

You will need towels for drying the puppies and also for grasping them in helping the bitch to deliver.

By all means don't start boiling water at the first sign of labor. Even though this is always done in the movies and on television programs, the bitch doesn't need boiling water at any time. Hot soapy water is sufficient for sanitary purposes.

You will also need a sharp pair of scissors and sewing thread or dental floss for cutting and tying off umbilical cords. Boric acid powder, BFI, or alum powder should be used on the cord when it is tied off.

You should also have a medicine dropper in case it is necessary to suck out fluid from the nostrils and mouth of a puppy.

You might have a bottle of brandy close by for the bitch, possibly for the puppies, and especially for yourself should you feel a fainting spell coming on.

21   WHELPING

No two bitches whelp in the same manner. Each bitch has her own idiosyncrasies which have to be dealt with individually. Close association between dog owner and bitch is of great help in interpreting the bitch's emotional and physical feelings as she prepares herself for the whelping process. Although it takes constant watchfulness and understanding, I should say that overindulgence is sometimes much worse than neglect. It is upsetting to the bitch to be under constant inquisition—with a thermometer in her rectum every half hour or so and pokes and jabs at her tummy. All she wants is peace and the comfort of your presence.

Each bitch varies in emotions according to her psychological outlook, and each bitch usually goes through the same patterns each time she whelps. There are some bitches who would have their puppies in Times Square without any help in their whelping, and there are many bitches who are much more relaxed when left alone in the security and consolation of familiar surroundings. The timid, high-strung, or nervous dog should be kept under constant surveillance to be sure that she will go through all the normal instincts, including the care of her puppies when they are born. Some bitches will allow the owner to do almost all the whelping chores, such as cleaning the puppies and tying the cord; others will shy away and have nothing to do with the puppies if the owner interferes. You must know how the bitch will react to help or interference. The only way to know is to understand the bitch. (The central theme of this book is getting to know *your* dog.)

Although whelping is a critical time in a bitch's life, there is no immediate emergency during the whelping process that the owner should get panicky over. There will always be time to consult a veterinarian and get the bitch to the hospital if it should be required. Panic in the owner will produce panic in the dog, with possible loss of puppies and even of the bitch herself. Nature will take care of most of the situations that arise, and nature should not be interfered with but just helped along. Most bitches are capable of handling ninety-nine out of a hundred situations with their natural and maternal instincts, and the owner should not interfere with these God-given talents. The purpose of this chapter is to prepare the uninitiated to cope with the normal processes of birth and to alert them to abnormal situations so that they will know when to consult their veterinarians.

GESTATION

Although the "normal" gestation period is 63 days, there is no definite day for whelping. Puppies can be born as early as 58 days from the time of conception and survive, although they are usually a little more difficult to raise for a week or so while they catch up with their older litter mates. If they are born prior to 58 days, they usually will not survive; they are too premature, without all their body functions normal. There are reported cases of puppies born at 53 days and surviving, but such puppies require a great deal of artificial care, and probably would be lacking in normal functions.

There is no cause for anxiety or alarm unless the bitch is 4 to 5 days late. The bitch can go 65 to 68 days with normal puppies being born. However, at the 65th day the bitch should be examined by a veterinarian. If she is eating normally, seems lively, and has no off-color vaginal discharge, such as black, brown, or green, there is likely nothing to worry about.

Any normal delay in whelping, as long as 24 hours, is not endangering the puppies, because they are still enclosed in their sacs, which nourish and maintain them.

WHELPING SIGNS

One of the most reliable signs is a drop in the dam's temperature a few days before she is due. Her normal temperature is 100-102 degrees, but within 24 hours of her delivery time her temperature will begin to drop. When it reaches 99, the puppies will be born within 24 hours.

As another sign that whelping is close, the bitch lies on her side for about 12 hours. Her uterus during this period is contracting, getting the puppies into position for birth.

At this time there is usually a clear-colored discharge from the vagina. A clear discharge signifies a normal delivery. If the discharge is black, green, or brown, a veterinarian should be called immediately; something is going wrong with the delivery.

Usually about 12 hours before the puppies are born, the bitch will begin to refuse food. This is not a positive sign, because some bitches will eat right up to labor.

At about the same time she will start tearing newspapers or other objects into shreds, rugs, pillows, making a nest. And at this point she will probably go into her whelping box.

Within a few hours of delivery time the bitch will begin panting excessively, in a steady rhythm which increases as birth becomes imminent. She should be watched closely; this is a critical time. Her body will contract for a minute or so and then relax with less time between contractions as she reaches whelping. The contractions push the puppy along the uterus toward the outside world. In actual labor the uterus contracts and dilates as the puppies get into position for each stage of delivery.

NORMAL WHELPING

The first object to appear from the vagina is the water bag—the sac around the puppy which acts as a cushion to protect it from shock or injury while it is in the uterus. It also serves to dilate the vaginal passageway as the puppy moves down and out into the world.

Usually the head is the first part of the puppy to emerge, although in a normal delivery the tail or hind legs emerge first almost as often as the head. If the head comes through first, the body usually follows easily and quickly, and generally little or no assistance is required of the owner. Difficult delivery positions of puppies and how to assist are discussed in a following section.

Generally the sac surrounding the puppy bursts, or it is ruptured by the bitch as the puppy is born. Normally the bitch will instinctively tear it away with her teeth, but if she has no inclination to do so within 30 seconds after delivery, I would then interfere—as described in the next section—since the puppy cannot breathe until the membranes are torn away.

After the bitch removes the sac, she will bite through the umbilical cord and proceed to lick the puppy, rolling it around to dry it and to stimulate its respiration.

A bitch will clean her puppies roughly at times, washing their faces and rear ends and cleaning the umbilical cord. She should not be stopped unless she mauls the puppies. Most of the times her maternal instinct will motivate some degree of roughness as she is trying to stimulate breathing. The licking produces a stimulation to the blood circulation, and one can often watch pale white membranes pinken as a puppy starts breathing and his heart starts pumping blood through his body.

The afterbirth, which normally follows each puppy, is voided by the bitch within 15 minutes after the puppy is born. Most bitches then eat the afterbirth—long a subject of much controversy. Some breeders believe that the bitch needs the afterbirth because the hormones that it contains will give her a more personal feeling toward her puppies. Others think that the afterbirth is needed for certain nutritional hormones for her general well-being and to help stimulate milk production. Most experts agree that it does no harm to allow the bitch to eat the afterbirth, even though her health and well-being will not suffer should she not eat it. It is up to each owner whether to allow nature to take its course or to keep the afterbirths away from her.

Remember that there is one afterbirth for each puppy, and they should be counted to be sure they have all passed. Retention of the afterbirth results in uterine infection in the postnatal period which seriously affects both bitch and puppies.

After the first puppy has been delivered, the rest of the puppies should be delivered within 10-minute to 2-hour intervals. This varies among types of bitches. The fat bitch will take her time. The old bitch, past middle age, will usually be tired between puppies and will wait a long time. In general, a normal bitch should deliver her whole litter within an hour or two. However, it is not uncommon for it to take as long as 12 hours in a large litter, and in some extreme cases it make take 24 hours, depending on the age and condition of the bitch. Sometimes two puppies will be born within minutes of each other and then there will be a 2- to 3-hour interval. Over 3 hours between puppies is a sign of trouble.

When the second puppy is about to appear, remove the first puppy to another box to allow the bitch to concentrate on the next birth. The puppies might distract her, and in labor she might roll on one. Also, only leave one puppy at a time with her until all the puppies are born. During this process, when the puppies are away from her, they should be in a box which has an electric heating pad or a hot-water bottle. The temperature change is radical from inside the mother's womb to the outside world, and to ensure against chilling—the greatest cause of death among newborn puppies—the puppies must be kept warm.

After a few hours of whelping the bitch may get thirsty and want some warm milk or water. I would not give her any solid food; it might nauseate her. The milk or water should be presented to her in her whelping box. Don't make her get out of the box, as she most likely will not want to.

After the bitch has delivered her last puppy, wash her rear parts and her breasts to ensure that the puppies are not exposed to any soiled material that could upset their digestion. Then put the puppies on her breasts so that they can begin nursing.

Newborn puppies can go without feeding up to 12 hours after birth—in an emergency—but I would put them on the bitch as soon as she is cleaned up. The puppies should be carefully watched to be sure that each one is strong enough to grasp a nipple so that it can indulge itself in some of the colostrum which is such a vital part of its first few hours.

Once the contents of the uterus are expelled—both the puppies and the afterbirths—the uterus begins shrinking to its normal size within 24 hours after delivery. There is a normal bloody discharge for several days to a week after delivery. If the blood continues for more than a week, a complication is indicated and professional help should be sought.

Within 24 hours after birth, the bitch and puppies should be taken to a veterinarian for examination. He will expel any afterbirths that may be present and douche the bitch if purulent discharge is present. She may need pituitary to expel some of the contents, and it will help in "letting down" her

363

milk. Most important of all, the veterinarian will ascertain if there are any unborn puppies left in the bitch. It is not uncommon for a bitch to tire out near the end of her labor and leave one or two puppies inside. She appears to go out of labor and goes about the business of nursing her puppies as if nothing were wrong. However, within 2 to 3 days, if not attended to, she develops an infection. The veterinarian will examine the vaginal tract for any tears in the cervix that might have been caused by a large puppy passing through or a difficult whelping. Such abrasions can result in infection and can also affect the bitch's future breeding status if not handled professionally.

HELPING IN LABOR

The Sac

Occasionally the sac will rupture inside the vaginal tract, causing a "dry birth," which makes whelping slightly more difficult. In a dry birth, to expedite delivery of the puppy, mineral oil can be injected into the vaginal canal to lubricate it, or a greased finger covered with vaseline can be inserted as far as possible.

Once the puppy is expelled, the sac must be removed almost immediately to initiate the puppy's breathing. If the bitch doesn't attempt to remove the sac within 30 seconds, the owner must step in and take over. The sac should be torn quickly from the puppy, taking it away from the mouth first and then off the head, enabling the newborn animal to breathe. It should be done with the puppy's head downward so that any fluid will run out of the nose and mouth.

Sometimes a puppy is born covered with a slimy dark-green sac instead of the normal healthy transparent one. This is a sign of some abnormal condition in the uterus and means either that the puppy has been in the uterus too long before delivery or that an infection has taken place in the uterus. Usually such a puppy is weaker, and I would consult with a veterinarian, as he might want to put that puppy on an antibiotic to counteract any possible infection. The green material should be washed off completely, including the mouth and nostrils. The puppy may have a greenish color for several days but soon will appear normal.

The Umbilical Cord

The puppy is attached from its navel inside the womb by the umbilical cord, which varies from 6 to 15 inches in length. The bitch must lick the puppy immediately and chew the cord within a few minutes if the puppy is to survive.

If the bitch doesn't chew the cord immediately, then the owner must take over and cut it with scissors, leaving 1 to 1½ inches of cord next to the puppy. The cord should be tied with thread or dental floss (dipped in alcohol first), and the tie should be a knot near the base of the cord to prevent bleeding. Boric acid powder, BFI, or alum powder should then be applied to the tip of the cord.

Some bitches with short mouths, such as the English bull or Boston terrier, sometimes have trouble severing the cord, and the owner should step in and do the job.

There is a hint that I would like to give owners in helping puppies—giving them a little extra blood. If the afterbirth is still attached to the umbilical cord, you can squeeze the afterbirth with your hand, forcing some blood down the umbilical cord into the puppy's body, before you sever the cord. This little extra blood can mean a life-death difference in a weak puppy.

Be careful not to pull on the cord, because this can cause an umbilical hernia and can injure the puppy fatally if there is a rupture of the blood vessels where the cord meets at the navel. Sometimes a bitch will be too rough with a puppy. She will pick it up, holding the umbilical cord in her mouth, and this is one of the predisposing causes of umbilical hernias. If you see this happening, take the puppy from the bitch, cut and tie the cord, and then give the puppy back to her if she is gentler with it.

Once the puppy is detached from the umbilical cord, he has to breathe and circulate his blood on his own. If the bitch doesn't immediately start to lick the puppy and stimulate its breathing, the owner must step in quickly and take over. Once the puppy is crying, a sigh of relief can be breathed; the instant between life and death has been successfully traversed.

Drying a Puppy

Dry a puppy by rubbing briskly with flannel or a soft bath towel. This substitute for the mother's tongue is a good stimulant for respiration and circulation. Once a puppy starts breathing normally, place him on a warm heating pad for 15 to 20 minutes. When his body temperature seems normal, he should be put with his mother to get some of her milk into him.

Difficult Delivery Positions

Although a breech presentation—when the hind feet come first—is considered normal, sometimes the bitch doesn't have enough power to pass the puppy through her pelvis. If the feet appear and the puppy is not expelled within 15 minutes, the owner should attempt to help.

Grasp the two feet (you may have to use a towel to grasp the slippery feet) and pull gently, as the bitch labors, in a downward rotating motion. If only one foot is present, find the other inside the vaginal tract before pulling on the puppy. Be very gentle, and don't use a jerking motion, as you might damage the puppy.

There are other positions which cause whelping difficulties. The puppy's head may be turned backwards—may be twisted—coming on the side. Sometimes puppies are born in an L-shape—coming at right angles. There is an upside-down position in which the puppy comes out on its back instead of its chest. All these difficult positions require professional help, and an immediate decision has to be made whether to attempt to pull the puppy or to save the bitch and the puppy intact with a Caesarean section.

Dry Birth

Occasionally a bitch that has had a difficult and long delivery will lose all the lubricating fluid in her vaginal tract. This will prevent the pup from slipping out during her uterine contractions. A solution for this problem would be to insert some lubricating substance such as mineral oil, vaseline, or olive oil inside the vagina. This lubrication will help release the puppy from the vaginal tract.

Another whelping problem is an extremely large puppy stuck in the pelvic canal. To save the puppy, it should not stay longer than an hour. Sometimes the owner can insert a finger (thoroughly scrubbed) into the vaginal tract and pull out the puppy. Gentle movements, from side to side, while pulling the puppy downward out of the vaginal tract will help some bitches during a difficult labor. Be gentle with the puppy, not only for the puppy's sake but also to keep from tearing the bitch's vaginal tract. If the owner cannot help the puppy to be delivered, then the bitch should be gotten immediately to a veterinarian. His expert fingers will deliver the puppy, or he will do a Caesarean section.

Another difficulty is two puppies entering the pelvic canal at the same time. This difficult delivery requires professional help.

If no puppy appears within 2 hours after the preceding one, I would seek help. By no means insert any instrument into the bitch's vaginal tract. Besides mutilating the puppy, instruments can tear and puncture the mother's soft internal tissues and cause a fatal infection. A thoroughly washed and scrubbed finger, with or without rubber gloves, is the only thing that should enter the bitch's vagina.

Get any puppy out within an hour, dead or alive, because the rest of the litter has to be considered. If the bitch labors too hard and too long, she will become exhausted, and the longer the puppies remain in the uterus the smaller will be their chances for survival. Once labor begins, it is best to get the puppies out with the least procrastination.

Stillborn Puppies

Some puppies are born squirming, while others appear dead and lie still and cold. Don't give up on the still puppy. Rip off the sac and grab the puppy up (with a dry towel) with its head down and with a tight grasp on its body. Rub it vigorously. Swing it in a downward motion to propel any fluid from lungs, mouth, and nostrils. Do this several times. A medicine dropper or syringe is also useful in drawing fluid from the nostrils and mouth if necessary. If the puppy breathes with a gurgling sound, there is fluid in his nasal or respiratory passageway, and this should be cleaned out and dried so far as possible.

If the puppy is cold, immerse it in warm water for a minute or two to help stimulate circulation. Immerse it in water up to the neck while rubbing the chest cavity, giving a heart massage. Sometimes a stimulant, such as brandy, on the tongue works well.

Sometimes after a hard and long delivery a litter of puppies are depressed and need help in reviving. If tongues and gums are blue, it means that the puppies need oxygen badly; and some breeders keep a small tank of oxygen close by. The head cone is left in the box until all the puppies are pink and active. If the puppies have mucus or fluid in the lungs, oxygen can save them.

If no oxygen is available, mouth-to-mouth resuscitation with artificial respiration should be administered. Blow hard enough to expand the lungs of the puppy—one breath every 2 seconds. It usually will be several breaths before a puppy will give any indication of respiratory commencement, and then he will likely begin gasping about every minute or half minute. Keep up the artificial respiration and mouth-to-mouth resuscitation until he begins breathing at a steady rhythm. If fluid develops in his mouth, keep swabbing it out or syringing it. I've worked as long as 30 minutes on a "dead" puppy, so don't give up easily. When the puppy seems to be breathing normally and is squirming about in a vigorous manner, give it to the mother and let her lick it and dry it with her tongue.

A stillborn puppy is usually due to lack of oxygen and too much fluid in the lungs caused by staying in the pelvic canal too long. It also occurs in a dry birth when the afterbirth has been severed.

CAESAREAN SECTION

The Caesarean operation has saved many a bitch and many offspring. When done in time, it is a fairly safe procedure in the hands of a skilled veterinary surgeon.

It is best not to have a Caesarean as a last resort—when the bitch is exhausted and just about dead. Blood poisoning is a dangerous thing and has shortened the life of many a bitch through neglect and delay in doing the Caesarean. Many breeders, knowing their bitches are going to need a Caesarean, will have the operation performed as soon as the cervix dilates and she is ready to deliver. Some breeds, because of their anatomical structure, for example English bulldog, Boston terrier, Pekingese, toy poodle, and Chihuahua, are prone to whelping difficulties, and the Caesarean section has been a boon to them.

As a rule of thumb, if there is a delay of more than 24 hours after labor has begun, a Caesarean section should be the procedure of choice. The sooner the puppies are gotten out of the bitch, the better chance she has for survival and the better will be the chances for raising live puppies.

There is no need for an owner to fear a Caesarean. Bitches are fully awake and able to nurse their puppies within 2 hours after surgery. They suffer no traumatic difficulties from their inability to deliver their puppies normally. There is a common misconception that once a dog has a Caesarean, she cannot be used again for breeding. I have performed four or five Caesareans on the same bitch, and she has maintained good health throughout.

Having a Caesarean operation does not necessarily mean that the next time the bitch whelps she will require another Caesarean. Some bitches have been known to undergo 4 or 5 Caesareans, and then have a normal whelping.

Factors determining the need for a Caesarian section:

—A bitch that has gone to the 65th day and does not go into active labor, yet still shows no signs of toxicity and does not respond to pituitary or tranquilizers.

—A bitch that exhibits obvious signs of difficult whelping (such as rupture of the placental membranes and loss of placental fluids, inability to deliver the fetus, or exhaustion after a protracted period of third-stage labor and no delivery of pups).

—A bitch with a prolapsed uterine horn still in labor.

—An older bitch with severe heart disease.

—Bitches with deformities of the pelvic canal that would impair delivery of the fetus.

In conclusion, let it be remembered that your veterinarian will be the one to make the decision whether to do surgery or not.

CAUSES OF PUPPY DEATHS

Uterine Inertia

The commonest cause of death in puppies—and in bitches—is uterine inertia, which is lack of contraction of the uterus and inability of the bitch to expel her puppies.

The contractions, or labor pains, are reflex in action, and the reflex actions are thought to be controlled by hormones present in the bitch's body. However, the uterine activity which starts the labor process doesn't start the actual uterine contractions.

Uterine inertia is thought to be hereditary in origin, as it seems to run in some breeds. It may occur in bitches of any age, but the shy and nervous bitch is more susceptible. The nervous or excited animal liberates adrenalin into her blood stream, and adrenalin is a known inhibitor of uterine contractions. Such a bitch should have her owner present to help her feel more relaxed and to keep her from panicking. She should be in her normal housing environment and not in a new kennel or hospital. Anything alien to her can affect her labor pains.

Another cause of uterine inertia is hypocalcium—a lowered calcium level in the blood. A fat or lazy dog has a greater tendency toward uterine inertia. An emaciated or debilitated dog with hormonal deficiencies can also be affected by this condition. Although the causes are not exactly known the condition is thought to be due to a deficiency of necessary hormones at the termination of pregnancy.

The best way to prevent uterine inertia is to keep the bitch's weight down and to keep her active with plenty of exercise.

Dogs with uterine inertia seem normal in every respect and show all the preliminary signs of whelping, such as nest making, restless, and a slight discharge. But instead of their going into labor, the signs disappear and nothing happens.

If the puppies are not expelled after 24 hours, they are liable to run into bad problems. When there is no obstruction or abnormality, as determined by a veterinarian, uterine activity can be stimulated with small repeated does of pituitary, which may be continued, if necessary, every 20 to 30 minutes to maintain productive labor.

Unfortunately there has been promiscuous misuse of pituitary. It is a dangerous drug if used incorrectly. For instance, if the bitch's vagina is not fully dilated and her cervix has not opened sufficiently, an injection of pituitary to stimulate uterine contractions can be unproductive because of the closed cervix. This can result in a ruptured uterus and the death of all the puppies and of the bitch unless immediate surgery is performed to correct the rupture.

At times there is a secondary inertia (exhaustion). When

the bitch has been in labor a long time, she may become tired and stop contracting. If the contractions are not resumed, the puppies will remain in the uterus, with serious complications.

Other Causes

A heavy prenatal infestation of hookworms or roundworms can cause death. Puppies can be infected in the uterus, with the worms settling in the fetal liver and lungs.

Sometimes puppies are born with abnormalities of the heart, lungs, or other parts.

In the condition known as atresia anus, the puppy is born without an anal orifice. The puppy can be normal for a few days, and then there will be an enlargement of the abdomen due to inability to excrete waste products. In some cases surgery is possible.

Puppies are sometimes born with a constricted anal opening which causes chronic constipation. Enemas are needed, but the solution is for the veterinarian to stretch and dilate the anal muscles.

Sometimes puppies are born with a tendency for a telescoping of the bowels and twisted bowels. This is a common cause of death in puppies between 3 and 4 months of age.

NURSING

In my opinion there is no substitute for natural nursing, even though many good artificial methods have been devised. I don't believe that we can improve on nature in this respect. It has been proved time and again that puppies that have maternal feeding are usually stronger, more resistant to disease and parasites, and easier to rear than those with artificial feeding.

However, there are cases where artificial nursing is necessary, and countless thousands of puppies have been reared on artificial milk with good results. And in a large litter it is often necessary to supplement feeding if the bitch doesn't have enough milk for all the puppies, although they should be allowed to have as much natural milk as possible.

Although the suckling instinct is strong in puppies, sometimes the bitch with a first pregnancy doesn't know how to help the puppies. When they attempt to grasp the nipples, she growls at them, pushes them away, and sometimes even leaves the whelping box as they persist in their quest for milk.

The puppies should be put directly at her breast; and if she protests, she should be scolded, and then sometimes she will allow the puppies to nurse once they start.

Sometimes the bitch doesn't have enough milk to feed her brood. The veterinarian can give her certain drugs, such as pituitary injections, to stimulate the formation of milk. To produce a plentiful supply the bitch should be in good health with adequate nutrition. Nursing puppies seem to stimulate further milk production.

Sometimes a bitch has nipples that are not fully formed. Instead of being erect and conical shaped they resemble unripe raspberries, and it is difficult for a puppy to extract milk.

The nipples should be examined carefully to be sure they are opened and expelling milk properly. If a nipple is too large for the puppy, it may be necessary to massage the breast and milk it by hand so that it will not become caked and feverish.

There are puppies, such as cleft-palate puppies, who cannot suck milk from the breast. Watch the litter carefully and make sure that the small puppies are not being pushed away by the larger puppies. Often a small puppy is pushed off into a corner, and the mother may leave it alone to perish. She seems to sense that the puppy will sicken and die, and will not attempt to nurse it.

Sometimes after a difficult whelping the bitch may be so exhausted and frantic that she displays no interest in her puppies. The puppies should be put on her breasts.

Occasionally a puppy is too small or weak to grasp a nipple by himself and we must hold him up to his mother's breast for the first day or two, until he gains the strength to keep up with the rest of the litter. If he is too weak to suck, I usually hold him to the nipple and with the other hand massage the bitch's breast, squirting the milk directly into his mouth. This life-giving milk is very much needed by the newborn puppy. Of course, if the bitch doesn't have enough milk or if the puppy can't get milk on his own, it will be necessary to resort to a baby bottle or medicine dropper with a simulated formula.

Some bitches are not reliable and would even kill their puppies if left alone with them. In these cases we have found foster mothers, or we immediately start feeding artificially. We've saved many a puppy by using a foster mother who had puppies at about the same time—not more than a week earlier or later.

A puppy is dependent on his sense of smell, and the old saying that each puppy has its own breast and will not nurse on any other is entirely untrue. A hungry puppy will nurse on the first nipple that it finds, and instinctively grasps the teat in his mouth when he comes to it.

A good rule of thumb is that a healthy and well-fed puppy is quiet. He usually eats and sleeps. If a puppy is restless and crying it means that he is hungry and not getting his food, or is sick and in need of help. In either case it needs attention.

There are some brood bitches who start milk production several days to a week before the puppies are born. These bitches produce so much that milk drips from their breasts before the babies are born. Sometimes the breasts become caked, swollen and feverish before parturition. Help is needed because infection and fever will interfere with the health of the puppies to be born.

If a bitch is in good health and receives the proper nutrition, her breast glands will automatically release a flow of milk every 3 or 4 hours.

There is a common fallacy that the bitch needs to eat her afterbirth to produce good milk. The reasoning is that the hormones present in the afterbirth are a stimulant to milk production. This has not been corroborated by scientific research. Bitches who don't eat the afterbirth are found to produce good-quality milk.

LACTATION OF THE BITCH

Herewith is a summary of the stages of lactation. There is about a 6-week lactation period in which the bitch produces milk for her young.

The 1st to the 3rd day following the birth of the puppies is the most important period because that is when the colostrum is present in the milk. The colostrum gives the puppies their much needed protection against puppyhood diseases.

"Mature" milk is formed in the 2nd and 3rd weeks following parturition.

During the 4th and 5th weeks the milk becomes more concentrated.

During the 6th week the quantity of milk decreases, and it stops soon after the puppies are weaned.

The size of the bitch and the number of puppies influence the amount of milk produced. The breed itself has no effect on the composition of the milk; all breeds are equal in quality. It should be remembered that milk varies in quality with the diet and habits of the dam, and the milk flow can be affected by emotional factors. Where a happy, contented bitch produces a lot of milk, a nervous and panicky bitch will sometimes temporarily dry up when she is frightened or harassed by strangers coming to admire her newborn babies.

CANNIBALISM

The ancient canine instinct of cannibalism has to be watched out for in some bitches during whelping and for several days after. It can be precipitated by intense pain and fright (trying to save her puppies) and is found in certain breeds and in very nervous bitches.

The brachycephalic (large-headed, short-nosed) breeds—for example, English bulldog, Boston bull—are predisposed to cannibalism. Their poor line of teeth and clumsiness in moving their mouth parts can bring about mutilation and even ingestion of their puppies while they are trying to sever the umbilical cord.

In the congenitally deaf breeds—for example, Dalmatian—there may also be trouble chewing the umbilical cord. Because the bitch cannot hear a puppy squealing in pain, she can mutilate it without realizing it. She should also be watched while she is tending to her puppies and carrying them around in her mouth because she may be hurting them and mutilating them without knowing it.

During a difficult whelping—trying to deliver a stuck puppy—bitches have been known to mutilate and eat the puppy while pulling at it to remove it from the vagina.

Certainly if a bitch shows any viciousness toward her puppies, they should be kept apart from her. If they are nursed by her, it should be done only while the owner is in close attendance.

A nervous bitch should be closely watched and all fear-provoking factors, such as noises, strangers, and too much handling of the puppies, should be kept from her.

There is a theory that cannibalism is linked to lack of certain hormones and that ingestion of the puppies satisfies the deficiency. There is no supportive conclusive evidence for this theory.

PREDICTING SURVIVAL OF NEWBORN PUPS

A favorable prediction for survival is associated with one of two growth patterns: (1) the pup should gain weight from the onset of nursing, or (2) should lose no more than 10% of the birth weight during the first two days of life and then begin and continue to gain. If puppies are weighed at birth, at 12 and 24 hours after birth, and daily thereafter for one week, trouble can be detected before actual signs of sickness. A weight loss exceeding 10% makes survival questionable without therapy such as extra feedings and antibiotics.

22 POSTNATAL CARE OF THE BITCH AND PUPPIES

THE BITCH

After the initial critical whelping period is over, the normal bitch settles down in her nest with her puppies and should require little care. If she is in good health and has an adequate diet with the proper supplements, she should produce enough milk to keep her puppies content and healthy.

It is best to avoid handling the puppies for the first 10 days or so, except when absolutely necessary. Some bitches resent their brood's being handled by anyone but themselves and will lick their puppies thoroughly after the owner has put them back in the box, trying to erase fingerprints and scent.

After the bitch has completed her whelping process, she is exhausted and relieved. I would attempt to clean her breasts with a wet cloth, and her rear legs and vagina to remove any debris the puppies might ingest. I would change the papers in her whelping box and give her some milk or broth to drink.

The Milk

The normal mother should then settle down and tend to her puppies and nurse them. Her maternal instincts should take over; a good brood bitch will lick her puppies, clean them and dry them, and produce milk for her newborn family.

Colostrum, the first milk secreted by the mammary glands, is created for only the first 6 to 12 hours after birth and possesses anti-bodies that give the puppies resistance to diseases. The nursing puppy who gets colostrum gets good early protection for a long time. Any failure in nursing colostrum lowers a puppy's resistance to disease and other environmental factors that come along. If for some reason a puppy does not receive colostrum, I advise injections of canine globulin to protect him against the ravages of puppyhood diseases.

Milk production in the bitch is largely controlled by hormones, as is the maternal instinct. An inadequate milk supply or unwillingness to nurse is usually due to a lack of these hormones that are formed at whelping time. Some bitches are stimulated in their milk production by injections of hormones, such as pituitary.

On the other hand, lactation is stimulated by suckling. The milk flow is usually adjusted to the demands of the puppies, and many a bitch has nursed 12 to 13 puppies without outside help. This is a tremendous drain on the bitch's body, and her diet has to be supplemented with all the calories, vitamins, and minerals necessary to feed the extra little creatures.

The Problem Bitch in Nursing

Sometimes the maternal instinct doesn't take over, and the bitch is indifferent to her newborn litter. This indifference can be due to a background involving poor rearing, poor feeding, lack of proper exercise, or debilitation from injury or disease. Some of these bitches are products of show-dog breeding where the sole interest is in visual points without regard to fertility, litter size, ability to whelp normally, or maternal instinct. Other bitches after whelping are exhausted, hysterical, or in a state of shock from the traumatic experience of a first litter.

A bitch who shows downright aggressiveness toward her puppies should be tranquilized and the puppies removed from her until she becomes calm; otherwise she may hurt the puppies, or even kill them, or she may even devour them. When she has calmed down—and this applies to all indifferent bitches—she should be made to lie on her side and be firmly held while the puppies are put to her breast and allowed to nurse. For some bitches this will overcome the fear of the

376

puppies, and they will then take them over. If the bitch persistently refuses to nurse her puppies, putting them to her breasts and allowing them to suckle for 15 to 20 minutes at a time is necessary for the first few days. After this time she will usually allow them to nurse by themselves.

If puppies don't nurse, the milk decreases and stops altogether within 24 hours. If for some reason the puppies are removed from a nursing bitch, or die, there has to be some help for her milk-filled breasts. Injections of hormones can help decrease the milk supply, and the breasts can be bathed with camphorated oil to help the flow decrease. The diet should be changed to a light one with little fluid and no raw red meat. The bitch should be put on laxatives to keep her bowels open and draw fluid from her body.

Foods that seem to stimulate milk production in the bitch are milk, raw meat, eggs, fish, liver, and other organ foods. A nursing bitch should be fed 4 to 6 times a day with the last feeding just before bedtime because the puppies nurse on her during the night as well as all day. Supplements of vitamins, calcium, phosphorus, and other minerals should be included in her diet. There is a tremendous drain on her blood calcium, and a deficiency will lead to eclampsia, bone deformities, faulty teeth formation, and other defects in puppies and bitch.

Nutrition during Lactation

The first week after the puppies are born, the bitch's diet should be light, consisting mainly of milk and eggs with cereal and biscuits. The bitch should not be overfed the first week, as this may cause an overproduction of milk which can lead to breast problems.

After the bitch has returned to normal and the puppies are nursing and keeping the breasts depleted, her diet should gradually be increased. She needs plenty of high-protein food, such as meat, eggs, liver, and milk. Raw meat is an excellent way of providing her with the best food for stimulating milk production, and lots of fluids should be given for the same purpose. Supplementary vitamins and minerals are of utmost importance in the bone formation of the puppies and for the bitch's well-being.

The vital time for nutrition during lactation is between the 2nd and 5th weeks. During this period the food intake has to be multiplied at least 3 times. For example, a cocker spaniel with a normal daily maintenance requirement of 1 pound will require 3 pounds a day for adequate lactation during the 2nd to 5th week.

The food-consumption peak is during the 5th week, and from this point on the puppies usually will have supplementary feedings and demand less and less mother's milk.

If the bitch seems to be producing too much milk, her intake of milk and other fluids, and of raw meats and protein-rich foods, should be reduced.

As the puppies are being weaned the bitch's diet should be increasingly lighter. By the end of 6 weeks she should be receiving fewer supplements and less food in order to help her drying process.

Behavior with Her Puppies

The first few days after whelping the bitch is reluctant to leave her puppies even to go outside to relieve her bowels and bladder, but for her general comfort and health she should be encouraged to do so. During the first 2 weeks she will not leave her puppies for more than a few moments at a time.

For the first 5 days after whelping the bitch should leave the box 4 or 5 times a day to relieve herself. After the 3rd day her outings should be for longer periods and by the end of the first week she should be having regular walks and exercise to keep her body functioning normally. Exercise also seems to stimulate lactation.

The bitch needs to be assured that her puppies will not be disturbed while she is away from them. The fewer people who see the puppies until after weaning, the better the dam will feel and the less exposure the puppies will have to disease. When it is necessary to let people see the puppies, always take the dam away from the whelping box so that she will not hurt the puppies or attack a stranger. And never, never let the neighbor children try to pick up her puppies.

A spoiled house pet may go off her feed for the first several days after her first litter. This is usually due to emotional factors (but I would check her temperature to see if fever is present). Such a spoiled pet may be tempted with her favorite delicacies.

Sometimes a bitch will vomit her food, and then her puppies will eat it. Although disgusting to watch, it is part of her ancestral instincts. She partially digests the food and then regurgitates it as a step between breast feeding and teaching the

378

puppies to eat solid food. The bitch should not be punished, and I would endorse the action by letting the mother dog wean her puppies in this manner.

Postwhelping Problems

For the first week after whelping the bitch's temperature should be taken at least once a day. Any reading above 102 degrees indicates a problem. It can be due to an infection in the uterus or to a retained afterbirth. It can also be due to an inflammation of the breasts (mastitis). Constipation or diarrhea also cause fever. The constipation is easily relieved with milk of magnesia; in severe cases an enema may be indicated. I personally advise a routine dose of milk of magnesia following parturition; it helps clean out all the debris the bitch has eaten during birth. Diarrhea is debilitating, and the bitch will refuse food and even refuse to nurse her puppies. As a preventive it is advisable to restrict her diet for the first few days.

For about a week after delivery there is a vaginal discharge, usually reddish in color, and varying in quantity from a slight drip, which is normal, to a more copious discharge, which signifies some abnormality. Most bitches will keep themselves clean by licking themselves and will keep the signs of discharge from sight. However, when there is some abnormality in the vaginal tract—either an infection in the uterus due to a retained afterbirth or a tear of the cervix—the color of the discharge will vary from normal red to brownish or purulent.

When a retained afterbirth, a mummified fetus, or a dead puppy remains in the uterus, there will be a brownish color and sometimes a blackish-green discharge and the bitch will usually show signs of being feverish and lethargic, will refuse her food and will sometimes refuse to nurse her puppies. Her temperature may rise to 103-105 degrees, and she is obviously a sick dog. A veterinarian should be consulted immediately, to save not only her life but the lives of her puppies, since her milk will be affected.

If the normal red vaginal discharge continues for more than a week, it signifies some abnormality in the vaginal tract. Upon examination the veterinarian will usually find a tear in the cervix due to some problem in delivery. Those tears heal slowly and give a continuous discharge. If they are not treated properly, they can result in scar tissue which may prevent conception in subsequent breeding.

Postwhelping Complications of the Bitch

Mastitis. This is caused by the milk not being sucked by the puppies, because of either deformed nipples or an over-production of milk. The bitch becomes restless with a high temperature and refuses to eat. The breasts are feverish and swollen, with sometimes a reddish-blue appearance.

Cold packs or hot Epsom salt applications are usually helpful in bathing the breasts, and camphorated oil will help draw out some of the inflammation.

If a breast is extremely enlarged, which usually occurs in the rear two breasts, it should be milked by hand to draw out some of the coagulated and caked milk. The mother's temperature sometimes reaches 104-105 degrees, which is usually a danger signal that an abscess is forming in the breast. A veterinarian is indicated in these cases to prevent danger to the mother and the puppies. The puppies will sometimes nurse at infected breasts, only to get the infection themselves, and this can result in death.

Eclampsia (Milk Fever). This is a condition encountered in the bitch after whelping. It is due to a lowering of the blood calcium due to exhaustion by the puppies. It is usually seen in small breeds with large litters and may occur anywhere from 1 day to 4 or 5 weeks after whelping. Occasionally it will occur prior to whelping if the bitch is very deficient in calcium and there is not enough for the developing fetuses in her uterus. To save the bitch's life, immediate treatment by a veterinarian is necessary. He will give her intravenous injections of calcium.

One of the first signs is restlessness in the bitch. Her eyes show an anxious look. Respiration is short and rapid. The mucus membranes become pale. The bitch has spasms in which her legs and body shake in a jerking motion. She may lie on her side, kicking all four feet and salivating profusely. She is subject to paralysis, collapse, foaming at the mouth, and labored breathing. Temporary relief before she reaches the veterinarian is a spot of brandy as a heart stimulant. If there is no treatment within 12 hours, she will die.

Most bitches if treated in time recover without any complications. The bitch's nursing duties should be curtailed for 2 to 3 days with no puppies nursing her (the puppies will have to be nursed by hand); then, after she is fully recovered, they can gradually be allowed to nurse for possibly half an hour at a time 2 or 3 times a day. Careful return to nursing duty is necessary because the attack can recur. The bitch should be on high doses of calcium, phosphorus, and vitamins to prevent recurrence.

Agalactia (inadequate or no milk supply). This condition can usually be detected from unthrifty puppies, hungry puppies, and overactive and crying puppies. The bitch's milk can be helped in flow by pituitary and other hormones. Increasing her diet with high-protein food and plenty of fluids will also help in milk production.

Metritis (infection of the uterus). This may occur after an extremely difficult labor, and often develops into pneumonia, which is evidenced by a rapid pulse, high temperature, drooping head, and refusal to lie down because of severe chest pains. Professional help is needed immediately to save the bitch.

Hair Loss in Lactating Bitches

Many bitches, particularly the long-haired breeds, lose much of their hair following whelping. This hair loss is usually related to diet—feeding a low-energy diet which may be adequate for the normal mature adult dog but is inadequate nutritionally for the lactating bitch. A diet ample in protein and fat may help prevent postparturition hair loss and maintain the lactating bitch in good health.

Many bitches shed a lot of hair and have a dry unsightly coat after feeding a litter of puppies. But with proper diet and worming after she is rid of her puppies, within 3 or 4 weeks the bitch will regain her girlhood beauty.

THE PUPPIES

Nursing

Watch the puppies closely for the first 48 hours to make sure that they are all nursing with strong sucking motions. Sometimes a weak or small puppy will be pushed into a corner to die, and the mother will refuse to take care of it. This puppy can be hand-fed, and he usually will catch up with his litter mates after the first week. At times there will be a tiny puppy who is too small to nurse by himself; he doesn't have the strength. He can be lifted to a nipple and some of the colostrum squirted into his mouth.

Supplementary feeding to these weak puppies should be done with either a home formula or a commercial formula, such as Borden's Esbilac. Goat's milk is strengthening to newborn puppies. When supplementary feeding is given, the puppy can be returned to the nest between feedings; the bitch will lick and clean him and keep him warm.

A weak puppy who cries constantly and appears limp and cold is in critical condition. It should immediately be removed from the litter and put in a warm box with a hot-water bottle or an electric heating pad. It should be fed every half hour with glucose or water or milk, and if necessary a drop or two of brandy for stimulation.

When a puppy refuses to nurse, or the bitch doesn't produce enough milk, it is necessary to try to teach him to nurse, and if this is impossible, he must go onto artificial feeding. Putting the puppy to the bitch's nipple and squirting milk into his mouth is a good way to start his reflexes. Usually once he tastes the warm milk he will begin to suckle and continue with pleasure.

Watch the two back breasts of the bitch, which are usually the largest and the most filled with milk. Sometimes they are too large and swollen for the puppies to nurse, and instead of being relieved, the bitch gets feverish, and an infection or an abscess occurs in the breasts. If the puppies will not nurse on the two back breasts, the breasts should be milked by hand until they are small enough for the puppies to suckle. If the litter is small, the puppies should be placed on the breasts most filled with milk. By rotating the puppies none of the breasts will get caked with excess milk production.

As determined in a recent study, one-third of breast-fed puppies are dissatisfied with mother's milk. The puppies were unduly restless and didn't thrive or grow as they should have. In such cases bottle feeding is certainly indicated for the benefit of both puppies and bitch. There are some bitches whose quality of milk and possibly even quantity is not sufficient to satisfy the growing needs of their puppies.

Care and Feeding of Orphans

There are many reasons why some puppies need individual hand feeding, and the most common occurrence is the death of the bitch. Other reasons include puppies born by Caesarean section with complications causing the bitch to be unable to nurse for the first day or two; small immature puppies too weak to suckle; the bitch's rejection of a small or weak puppy in her brood; and too large a litter.

Raising puppies by hand requires perseverance and a careful tedious technique because of the complications that can result if, for example, a puppy ingests milk too quickly or ingests too much air. There are three factors to consider in artificially raising a litter of puppies: (1) the feeding formula must simulate the bitch's milk, (2) furnishing the proper environment, and (3) furnishing proper management.

The Feeding Formula. For healthy and vigorous puppies it is necessary to simulate a formula similar in quality and quantity to mother's milk. There is a home formula which is time-proven, or there's the excellent commercially prepared formula put out by Borden—Esbilac—which meets the specific and nutritional requirements of young puppies. It is a carefully balanced blend of proteins, fats, carbohydrates, vitamins, and minerals which makes it near perfect as an alternative or supplement for bitch's milk.

The home formula is good: a can of evaporated milk, equal parts of boiled water, the yolk of an egg, a tablespoon of Karo syrup (light or dark), and a teaspoon of limewater. This can be prepared, kept refrigerated, and small amounts warmed to the correct temperature at feeding time.

There are plastic nursing bottles, either baby-doll bottles or premature-infant nipples which have anticolic nipples (usually with three holes). These prevent too much air being gulped by the puppy.

Some people feed whole goat's milk and claim excellent results.

The formula must not give indigestion or colic to the puppy, and must not produce diarrhea. If the homemade formula produces diarrhea, the Karo syrup should be eliminated, as it has some laxative qualities.

The Proper Environment. Without a doubt the most serious danger to a newborn puppy is chilling, as he has no heat-control mechanism to protect him. An incubator-type box can be fixed with either an electric heating pad or an overhead infrared bulb; or an electric bulb can be used to keep the temperature between 85 and 90 degrees for the first 5 days, at about 80 degrees for the next 2 weeks, and gradually dropping down to 70-75 degrees by the end of the 4th week. But overheating is almost as bad as chilling, and the incubator box must be well regulated. If it gets hot, the puppies will pant.

It is also advisable to separate the puppies into individual pens because in the absence of their mother's breasts they tend to suckle at each other's tails and genitals. Also, with individual compartments it is possible for the owner to check on stools and be sure there is no diarrhea or constipation. Each compartment should be lined with a clean soft diaper or folded newspaper. A diaper or towel should be pinned smoothly to the box so that the puppy cannot crawl under it and become entangled and smother.

Proper Management. Proper managemcent of the orphan puppy is guided by his regular increases in weight and the feel of his body. If he is not receiving enough fluid through the milk, he will tend to feel hidebound or dehydrated. A puppy should be round and fat.

The condition of his stool is an important guideline. Consistency and regularity indicate health, and any derangement in the consistency of bowel movements indicates some abnormality. A normal stool should be firm and yellowish in color. A normal puppy that is fed 3 to 4 times a day should have 3 to 5 movements. A good rule of thumb is a bowel movement for each time he is fed.

Feeding the Orphan. At least 3 feedings a day at 8-hour intervals are required. Some puppies will want a 4th feeding. Most people who feed every 2 hours find this quite unnecessary unless the puppies are very weak and are recovering from an illness and need extra strength. A sick or weak puppy may have to be fed every half hour or so, a few drops at a time, for maximum strength.

Most researchers agree that demand feeding is best. When the puppy is sleeping, he should not be bothered. When he wakes and begins stirring, he should be fed.

In the amount to be fed, a rule of thumb is to feed enough so that the abdomen is somewhat enlarged after feeding. The puppy should not be given all he would eat, because this would cause his abdomen to become overextended or bloated and contribute to all sorts of digestive upsets, such as colic, indigestion, and diarrhea. It is best to underfeed for the first 2 or 3 days and then bring the puppy up to full feeding by the 4th or 5th day. By this time he should be accustomed to the formula.

After 2 to 3 weeks on the formula the puppy can be

started on a high-protein instant baby cereal such as Pablum, mixed with either Esbilac or a homemade formula.

At 3 weeks the puppy can be weaned to pan feeding. A good way is to put a finger into the soupy-type mixture and let the puppy suck the finger. Puppies have to be taught to lap, and sometimes they have to be spoon-fed for a few days because they will eat solids before they will learn to eat from a bowl or pan. At this age small amounts of canned dog meat or crumbled hamburger meat can be added to the cereal and the milk formula.

From the 3rd to the 4th week puppies can lap from their pan and eat on a regular schedule in-between play and exercise.

At 4 weeks they should be completely weaned from the Esbilac or home formula and should be eating their food at the rate of 1 teaspoon per 5 pounds of body weight at each meal.

Techniques of Feeding. In feeding it is best to place the puppy on his stomach. He should never be placed on his back or the nipple or dropper inserted into his mouth while he is on his back, else he will likely inhale some of the formula, which will cause coughing and possibly a foreign-body pneumonia.

The formula should be lukewarm or tepid—with the chill taken off.

The puppy should never be fed rapidly. If ever there is milk bubbling from the puppy's nostrils, it means that the milk is being forced down his throat too fast, and he is liable to choke. Either the medicine dropper is too large or the holes in the nipple are too large, and replacement should be made.

The bottle should be held at about a 45-degree angle, and no air should be allowed to enter the puppy's mouth. Gulping air leads to indigestion.

The nipple should be tested to make sure the puppy is getting enough milk. When the bottle is held upside down, the milk should ooze slowly from the opening. If the rate of flow is not free enough, the holes can be enlarged with a red-hot needle.

After each feeding the puppy should be burped. He should be held upright against a shoulder while being rubbed and patted on the back. Burping will prevent a lot of digestive disturbances.

Urination and Defecation. For the first week of his life a young puppy relies on instinct for urination and defecation.

These functions may have to be aided by the owner. To stimulate the natural acts, after each feeding the anal and abdominal regions should be gently rubbed with a cotton swab slightly moistened with warm water or baby oil.

The puppy should not be handled any more than necessary, but when his body needs have been taken care of his skin should be gently washed with warm water after each feeding and defecation.

Constipation. Constipation usually causes a swelling of the abdomen and colicky pains. A further addition of Karo syrup or honey to the formula will have a mild laxative affect. If the bowels continue sluggish, a drop or two of mineral oil on the puppy's tongue should straighten out the complication. Unless regular defecation after each meal is maintained, bowel disorders may develop that will jeopardize the puppy's chances for survival. In severe cases a warm-water soapy enema is indicated.

Diarrhea. A loose stool can mean that the puppy is ill or is being overfed, or that the formula is too rich to suit his intestinal assimilation. At the first sign of diarrhea the formula should be diluted in half by adding more water and cutting out the Karo syrup. Kaopectate is excellent to help stop the diarrhea (½ tsp. per 5 lb. of body weight 3 times a day). If the diarrhea persists, a veterinarian should be consulted.

Grooming. Daily grooming is a necessity and should consist in wiping the puppy's eyes with a boric acid solution and gently massaging the skin, which stimulates circulation and thoroughly awakens the puppy. The best time for massage is just before feeding, while the formula is being warmed. The best way to do it is to stroke the puppy's sides and back with a soft folded diaper. It is also good to occasionally rub the puppy's skin with baby oil because of the drying effect of the incubator heat. If absolutely necessary, puppies can even be washed in warm water and rubbed dry with a soft towel or diaper.

Feeding Equipment. All feeding equipment should be thoroughly scrubbed, as disease may result from contaminated formula or unsanitary feeding equipment. Formula should be made up in small batches, for a day at a time, and then warmed as needed. A premature-baby nipple with an ordinary baby bottle is the most desirable apparatus for feeding orphan puppies.

Canine Globulin. Research has proven that certain hand-reared puppies are especially susceptible to infection and are usually more easily infested with worms than are naturally nursed puppies. I advise giving orphan puppies canine globulin within 24 hours after birth to build up their resistance to disease. They would normally have gotten this from the colostrum of their mother.

Immersion Feeding of Puppies. An alternative to bottle or syringe feeding, this is an excellent method of feeding orphan puppies and puppies of dams that cannot rear their young. This method consists of plopping the youngsters into a shallow dish or pan containing the proper formula. Some pups begin lapping immediately while others may take several days before they catch on to the idea. The dish, with sides high enough to keep them from crawling out, must not be filled to a point where they would drown. In the beginning, they have to be watched carefully so that they do not get into the habit of taking in milk through the nose. Then they have to be wiped off after every meal until they are big enough to eat the food from outside the dish.

It is important to remember that only healthy puppies should be tried on this method and their throats should be checked before attempting this procedure. If a pup has a cleft palate or an opening in the soft palate, the milk would be aspirated into the lungs and a fatal pneumonia would result. Have your veterinarian check the soundness of the throat to avoid any serious problems.

The Tube Method of Emergency Feeding. A new method of feeding newborn puppies, particularly weak or sick puppies, has come into prominence in recent years and has been enthusiastically received. This tube method must be fully understood and performed correctly, otherwise fatalities can result. It is especially life-saving for cleft-palate puppies, as the milk doesn't get into the nasal passages but is injected directly into the stomach.

Small rubber catheters are used, attached to a large hypodermic syringe which holds between 20 and 40 cubic centimeters and may be adequate for several puppies without refilling. The feeding end of the tube is inserted into the puppy's mouth and when it has gone down to about the puppy's last rib a mark is made on the tube, at the mouth, as a guide for future feeding. The tube is attached to the syringe and the formula is injected. Not only milk supplements but diluted strained baby foods can be forced through the tube.

The tube should be inserted into the puppy's mouth without forcing it and usually the puppy will swallow the tube. If

387

the tube is forced into the mouth, it may go into the windpipe, with dire results. Before the milk is given, a drop should be inserted and if the puppy coughs it means that the tube has gone down into the windpipe and should be withdrawn from the mouth immediately.

I advise the novice to get instructions from his veterinarian on how to insert the tube and on the techniques for feeding. The method takes skill, patience and dexterity but is well worth learning. For small breeds a No. 8 catheter is recommended and for larger breeds a No. 10.

Tail Docking, Dew-claw Removal, Nail Clipping

Tails should be docked 48 to 72 hours after birth. There is less pain sensation in the newborn puppy; after his tail is removed, he curls up and goes right back to sleep. The bleeding must be stopped before the puppy is put back in the litter.

Each breed has a requirement for tail length, and many a potential champion has been ruined because his tail was cut too short. When in doubt leave a longer tail; it can always be recut.

A veterinarian should do the surgery, since he will know the proper length and procedure. It will be shaped and tapered and give a satisfactory appearance.

There are quacks who use a tight rubber band at the desired tail length, and after about 4 days the tip "falls off." I don't recommend this method, as it often leaves a badly scarred tail tip.

Some breeds require front dew claws to be removed (French poodle, Sealyham, wire-haired terrier, Doberman). In all breeds, if the claws are found on the rear legs, they should by all means be removed, as they usually would cause trouble later in life. They perform no function, and many a dog has lost his eyesight by being scratched by a dew claw while playing. When dew claws are allowed to remain, they often interfere with a dog's running and cause trouble when they tear off.

Puppies' nails should be clipped at 2, 4, and 6 weeks of age to avoid scratching and injuring the mother's breasts. Any type of nail clipper can be used, and only the tips of the nails should be cut to avoid bleeding. If bleeding occurs, apply alum powder or a styptic pencil to the nail tips.

Fat and Lazy Puppies

This occurs occasionally when there is a litter of only one puppy. There is no competition so it usually eats and sleeps all the time. It is important to make this puppy exercise, before it is too late, i.e. not over 3 weeks of age. Otherwise the puppy will grow up with bad leg coordination.

Growth Rate in Puppies

In the growth of puppies little gain is made the 1st week, but weight is added rapidly during the 2nd week and thereafter. Weight gains in puppies from small litters are uniformly higher than in puppies from large litters—four or more. However, the rate of gain at this stage doesn't affect adult size. After the puppies are weaned and eating by themselves, if they are given the proper foods, they will usually gain their normal weight up to their breed standard. Puppies getting too little protein, or protein of a poor quality, may still grow normally but will be more susceptible to infections.

St. Bernards and other large breeds increase their weight 40 times in the first 6 months and 60 times in the first year of life.

Some researchers have come up with the theory that overfeeding growing puppies to make them big and healthy-looking may be doing them a disservice, because the faster growth frequently results in loss of longevity. These researchers have shown that the life span can be increased by delaying the maturity of the offspring.

Mortality in Newborn Puppies

The critical stage of the puppy's life is the 1st week. The causes of death during this 1st week involve various congenital defects, environmental defects, and injuries as a result of difficult whelpings, but the greatest number of puppy deaths are attributed to chilling and to an infectious disease known as canine herpes virus.

Chilling of Puppies. When the newborn puppy leaves the warmth and security of the dam's body, during the first few minutes his body temperature drops sharply.

During the first few days of life puppies have no shivering mechanism to regenerate heat loss when the room temperature is lower than the temperature of the nest. Consequently their body temperatures can drop quickly, and they develop cooling of all body functions.

When a puppy becomes cold, he seeks shelter. He tries to nuzzle against his mother's breast or cuddle with another puppy for warmth. If this is not possible, his body temperature drops quickly.

If the puppy remains cold for as long as 48 hours, he will fail to gain weight. However, once a cold puppy is put into a warm temperature, such as an incubator temperature of 85-110 degrees, there is a distinct increase in his temperature, and he will begin gaining weight. The body temperature begins at about 90-95 degrees for the 1st week and gradually increases up to the normal range of 100-102 degrees by the 5th to 6th week.

One of the first signs that a puppy is becoming chilled is restlessness and crying. As the puppy becomes colder a high-pitched note occurs with almost every respiration, and the respiratory rate increases about 30 per minute. A rectal thermometer will show a fall in temperature from 96 degrees down to about 70 degrees. The puppy will become cold to the touch, limp, pale-gummed, and appear in a state of death.

The puppy can sometimes be revived if quickly immersed in hot (not scalding) water, and rubbed and stimulated.

Canine Herpes Virus ("Fading Puppy Syndrome"). This is an insidious disease because the bitch appears healthy, the milk production seems adequate, and all the puppies nurse in a normal manner until just a few hours prior to their deaths.

The early signs of the disease are sudden cessation of nursing, chilling, and painful crying. Abdominal pain is a diagnostic feature which is nearly synonymous with a yellowish-green diarrhea. The cry of the puppy is pitiful (one of screaming agony) since the abdominal contents are in profuse spasms. The yellowish-green stool usually appears 3 to 4 hours before death, and then the acute abdominal pain begins, and sometimes retching and vomiting is seen. The puppies stop nursing when the crying begins, their breathing becomes labored, and they begin to gasp shortly before death. It usually affects puppies about 1 week after birth, and the puppies continue to die over a 2-week period until all the puppies in the litter are dead.

I would attempt to have the puppies treated, although success is not encouraging. Vitamin K injections are given to help prevent internal hemorrhaging. Blood-building vitamins are given to the puppies by mouth, and in a sick puppy blood transfusions are used to try to build up resistance to the infection. The puppy has to be force-fed by dropper because usually he will refuse to eat.

It is believed that puppies acquire the infection while passing through the vagina during the whelping process. It is thought to be present in the vagina and not in the uterus. The herpes virus is not in any way related to canine distemper or canine hepatitis. Usually puppies older than 3 weeks will not die but go through mild symptoms of the infection. Most deaths occur up to 14 days after birth. Post-mortem examination shows areas of hemorrhage in liver, lungs, and kidneys. At present there is no vaccine for the prevention of the disease.

Adult dogs sometimes show the disease in a mild way and recovery is uneventful, even though it is 100 per cent fatal in puppies under 2 weeks of age. The sire has not been found to transmit this disease from bitch to bitch, and if a bitch loses a litter it does not necessarily mean that she ever will again. In fact, many bitches have produced normal healthy litters the following year. However, the bitch may be a carrier and lose the litter each time she whelps. The infection may be spread from infected bitches to other bitches through either vaginal or throat secretions and is spread by direct contact between susceptible dogs. But the stud is not an intermediate carrier.

There are various theories regarding the prevention of the disease. Some breeders feel that the absence of vitamin K in dogs enables the virus to predominate. Alfalfa is the only cereal known to contain vitamin K. Wheat-germ cereal or oil is also advisable (to be given to bitches prenatally). If the bitch shows signs of a vaginal infection, by a vaginal discharge, within 2 weeks of whelping, douching with an antiseptic solution should be done at least twice a day to try to clear up the infection before the puppies arrive.

Some breeders advise the use of gamma globulin in suspected cases—given to bitches within a week before they whelp and to the puppies soon after birth to help prevent the virus infection from getting started. Gamma globulin doesn't affect an already established infection but might help prevent one from getting started. Antibiotics, such as terramycin and chloromycetin, can be used but are not especially beneficial in fighting the virus. They do help secondary infections.

Although no vaccine is available for herpes virus at present, hopefully there will be one in the near future. Some bitches who have natural immunity may transfer this immunity to their puppies through the colostrum. Maiden bitches with the first litter can usually be expected to be exposed to this virus, transmitting it to their litters.

Puppy Strangles (Mumps). Caused by staphylococci, this disease usually develops when the puppy is 4-5 weeks of age. The puppy develops a skin condition around the muzzle. It spreads to the eyes and ears and then the gland under the neck begins to swell and the puppy looks as if it has the mumps. Treatment is successful if started early.

Blood Poisoning. A bacterial infection in a dog's bloodstream, this infection can occur at 4-40 days of age and is usually derived from the bitch or the environment. The usual symptoms are crying and straining and the puppy begins to become bloated. Usually within 18 hours the puppy is dead.

The puppies should be taken from the bitch until the infection is cured; without care entire litters of puppies are lost. If the puppy does live he is likely to have kidney damage.

The only cure is preventive medicine. Always examine the bitch's vulva and the stud before breeding. A blister that resembles a cold sore may be carrying the virus which will affect the vaginal tract at the time of whelping. A human douche solution may be used on the bitch just prior to whelping.

Other Causes of Death in Puppies. There are congenital defects in puppies affecting the digestive, respiratory, and circulatory systems. Heart defects in young puppies have been shown to exist much as in human babies. If a puppy dies from a congenital defect, we must recognize it and avoid use of the breeding stock that is producing it.

There is also a congenital abnormality in the lung tissue which results in respiratory failure before death. Sometimes this abnormality can be traced to a partial failure of the lung tissue in the bitch's womb. The defect results in fetal fluid in the lungs, which brings about the early death of the puppy because of his failure to breathe properly. Such a puppy is usually born alive but dies during the first few days of life. He refuses to eat, becomes dehydrated and soon gives up the struggle for life. If it is a congenital abnormality of the lungs, no treatment is possible, but if it is caused by an infection, the veterinarian, with the use of antibiotics, can possibly control the loss.

For other congenital abnormalities which can be fatal in the first critical week, see Chapter 18.

It is critically imperative to spot a puppy in the early stages of any sickness because an hour, even minutes, can mean the difference between life and death. Some signs of sickness are:

1. Rejection by the dam. Instinct seems to tell the bitch when a puppy is sick, and she will usually push it aside to die. However, if such a puppy is discovered in time, it can possibly be saved.

2. Cessation of nursing. Whenever a puppy doesn't nurse, it means that there is trouble. If it is merely a matter of needing to be taught, this should be done, or the puppy should be reared by hand.

3. Crying. It is necessary to differentiate between a hungry puppy and a sick puppy. In either case help is needed. A quiet, sleeping puppy is a healthy one.

4. Weakness or limpness. It is easy to spot a vigorous, healthy puppy by its quick movements. In contrast a sickly puppy moves slowly and with a lot of effort.

5. Dehydration. Normally the skin of a puppy is resilient. If upon lifting the skin it doesn't bounce back into place, it indicates that the puppy's body is beng depleted of fluids. This can mean lack of sufficient intake of nourishment or excessive diarrhea, or that a disease is drying out the body.

6. Paleness in the gums is a sign of a sick puppy. A puppy's gums should be pink, or reddish-pink. When the gums are pale or white, it indicates that the puppy is malnourished because of insufficient food, disease, or parasites.

7. A dark-red or bluish tint to the skin is indicative of disease. The skin of the puppy's stomach should be a nice pink; a reddish-blue color shows that the puppy is in extreme difficulty.

8. An extremely bloated puppy may be a sick one—or one whose stomach is completely empty. Either of these conditions indicates that the puppy is in trouble. The first condition means that he is constipated or has improper elimination, which can be due to a congenital deformity at the anus. An enema is needed (or if an anal problem, surgery) to rid the animal of the impending toxin. The bloated condition may also be caused by roundworms, and the bloat will disappear after worming. If the puppy's stomach is empty, it shows that

the dam does not have enough milk, that the puppy is not getting enough milk, or that he has diarrhea which is keeping him thin.

9. Diarrhea. I would estimate that intestinal disturbances are the greatest cause of fatalities in puppies. Unless the diarrhea is checked, the puppy dehydrates and quickly dies. If there is mucus in the stools, and occasionally blood, this can be a sign of roundworms or hookworms.

Disorders of Newborn Puppies

1. Digestive trouble. One of the commonest digestive problems seen in young puppies is colicky pains after feeding, which can be due to the milk itself, too-fast feeding, or possibly an irregular bowel movement involving either diarrhea or constipation.

Colic is usually caused by infections of the bowels, such as enteritis and hepatitis. There are terrible intestinal spasms which cause the puppy to cry in a pitiful way. There is usually vomiting, and the stool is loose and fetid. Palpation of the puppy causes crying and crackling pains produced by gas in the intestines. Mild enemas and milk of magnesia are sometimes beneficial. When there is severe pain, a drop of paregoric every half hour will give relief until the painful spasms stop. In diarrhea, bismuth or Kaopectate is helpful. Sometimes constipation is due to an oversight of the bitch, who is supposed to lick the rectum of each puppy to prevent hardening of the bowels.

2. There is a nutritional anemia which causes death in 40 to 100 percent of some litters, usually when they are 10 to 13 days old. In this ailment the mucus membranes are pale. The best treatment is to prevent the ailment by keeping the bitch in good health, usually with adequate quantities of liver and iron, during gestation. If the mother tends to be anemic, her puppies will subsequently suffer from a similar affliction. This can be spotted by the veterinarian in his prenatal examination of the bitch, and he will advise proper supplements before the puppies are born.

3. Another disorder in nursing puppies is staphylococcus infections. These usually develop in puppies at least a week old, and they look like puffy blisters on the body. They are caused by staphylococcus bacteria and are usually acquired by the puppies from the mammary glands and the milk. Sometimes the bitch has an infection in her vagina, and the

subsequent vaginal discharge gets rubbed onto the skin of the puppies and causes the infection.

Although most of the time the puppies seem normal and nurse normally, the skin lesions spread from puppy to puppy. The sores should be washed thoroughly with an antiseptic soap, such as Phisohex, and an antibiotic ointment applied locally. In a severe case the puppy should be put on oral antibiotics, given by dropper, to prevent generalized blood poisoning.

If the bitch is the cause of the condition, her vaginal or mammary infection must be cleared up at the same time to prevent reinfection of the puppies.

4. There is an ailment in puppies called "navel ill" in which the navel cord becomes infected if dirt or other infection gets into it. This is why an antiseptic such as hydrogen peroxide or iodine should be applied to the umbilical cords.

5. Eye trouble. A puppy's eyes should begin to open at 7 to 10 days from birth. The lids part first at the inner corner and gradually extend to the outside. If the lids fail to open properly, it may be due to pus formation, which can be determined by running a finger over the lids. The best treatment is an antibiotic ointment, such as neomycin or bacitracin, placing a layer of ointment across the lids 2 or 3 times a day and working it in with the forefinger. This softens the lid, which then can usually be parted at the inner corner and drained. Don't attempt to force the lids open too soon, else the sensitive part of the lids can be injured. Gradually lids will open a bit more each day. If the eyes are neglected, the condition can result in loss of eyesight or impairment for life. The mother dog often will help open the eyes of her puppies by licking their faces, which stimulates the eyelids to part.

6. Prolapse of the rectum is occasionally seen in puppies with severe diarrhea. It is due to strain. The cause of the diarrhea must be stopped.

Early Instincts and Care

By the age of 2 weeks the puppies are roaming around the whelping box, snuggling up to one another, and sometimes even having friendly little fights. Their eyes begin to open, and although still fairly blind, and nearsighted, they begin getting about the box investigating the world that they have been born into. The bitch begins leaving the box for longer periods and returns to it only to nurse the puppies or to clean and possibly discipline them.

By the age of 21 days there is usually a decided change in the development of the puppies. Their senses are beginning to function, and their faculties, such as sight and hearing, are becoming more evident. This is the age for them to realize that there are human beings around them, and their relationships with humans should involve trust and confidence. It would leave a bad impression if they were mauled by children or adults—and with lots of noises to scare them.

After 3 weeks of age the puppies are in their learning period of development, and any experiences they undergo will affect their temperament later in life. The first relationships, of course, are with their litter mates, and each litter has a social arrangement in which there are bullies—the larger puppies who push the small ones around—and sometimes there is an intelligent or extra-intelligent puppy who outsmarts the other puppies by always getting to the mother's breast first, or to the food dish.

After 3 weeks of age there should be gradual weaning so that the puppies learn to eat on their own. This relieves the mother of some of her chores, which have by this time become mighty wearing on her physically. She usually begins losing weight, and her breasts are sore from the constant mauling and her puppies' sharp nails and teeth.

Any time after 3 weeks the puppies should be taught to drink fluids. If they are well fed and the bitch has lots of milk, especially in a small litter, the puppies will be more reluctant to learn to drink outside milk. A formula (see p. 383) can be used which is beneficial to their digestive tracts. Any sudden change in diet can result in diarrhea or vomiting, and this goes for a 3-week-old puppy as well as for a 15-year-old dog.

In teaching a puppy to lap milk, dip a finger into the milk and allow the puppy to suck it, gradually taking the puppy toward a shallow saucer. Invariably he will walk into the milk and make a mess; however, this is all in the process of learning how to eat.

When puppies first begin to eat on their own, they usually take very small amounts of food, so they should be fed frequently—about 6 times a day.

After 3 weeks of age the stools of the puppies should be checked at least every 2 weeks, for worm parasites at this age are deadly. Many a fine litter has died from hookworms.

Roundworms are not so dangerous but should be eliminated. If a puppy shows any worm eggs upon stool examination, he should be treated. Worms can keep the puppy unthrifty, cause digestive upsets, and in some cases lower his resistance to various diseases. At this age the animal is very fragile.

Some puppies can learn to start eating lean beef at 4 weeks of age. Rub the puppy's nose in it, and gradually he will open his mouth for it.

After 4 weeks the puppies become inquisitive and begin to investigate the whelping box and the surrounding world if they are allowed to move outside the nest. They will often begin to imitate the dam, and this is why, if the dam is a nervous one, we must take the puppies away from her after 3 weeks. As soon as they can be taught to lap milk, they should be taken away from the mother, otherwise they might assume her nervousness.

After 4 weeks of age the puppies should receive some type of serum, globulin or measles vaccine for protection.

Finally, at 6 weeks of age the puppies should be on a full diet without help from their mother.

Weaning Schedule

At 3 to 4 weeks, twice a day, feed Pablum or other cereal, from a dish. Once a day feed some type of broth—chicken or beef. Nursing by the bitch is as usual.

At 4 to 6 weeks the puppies should be fed 3 times a day with milk and cereal and possibly the addition of some dry puppy meal, in a soupy state so they can lap it up. Twice a day add more cereal and dog meal with either chicken or beef broth. The puppies will nurse as they need to, allowing the bitch to wean them gradually.

Feeding Chart for Puppies

4-6 Weeks Old

(4-6 meals a day)

Morning Meal:
    warm milk (evaporated milk preferable)
    egg
    dry cereal
        Use 1 egg to a pint of milk. Dry cereal may include Pablum, shredded wheat, corn flakes, Pep, puffed rice, puffed wheat, Post Toasties, Zwieback, rusk, or Melba-toast.

If the puppy doesn't finish the meal, the bowl should be removed in a few minutes and nothing else given until the next meal.

Noon Meal:
raw beef, chopped or ground
Other desirable meats are lamb, horseflesh, and veal. Fresh pork is allowed but never smoked meat, fried meat, or spicy meat. Don't feed excessive amounts of fat. Some puppies are allergic to horse meat with resultant diarrhea.

4 P.M. Meal:
Meat
Any of the canned foods on the market that contain meat can be substituted for straight-meat meals. Dry dog foods are also good and can be substituted for canned foods. Most dogs like dry foods flavored with milk, meat, broth, or vegetables.

Bedtime Meal:
warm milk or broth
Give this about 10 P.M., till midnight; the puppy will sleep better and quieter. If the puppy is still hungry, you can add cereal or dog food.

Vitamins and Minerals:
A growing puppy needs extra amounts of cod-liver oil and calcium to build straight bones and prevent rickets. Cod-liver oil (or substitute) and calcium should be added to the food—in liquid or powder form.
Vegetables and tidbits from the table are good supplements to the diet so long as they are mixed with dog food.
Amount to be Fed: At your discretion. Don't overload stomach. A general rule is:

Toy Breeds:
At 6 weeks of age feed ¼ cup of milk and for other meals about 1 ounce of meat. Increase milk and meats in proportion to growth.

Medium-Sized Breeds:
At 6 weeks of age feed ½ cup of milk and cereal and 4 ounces of meat.

Large Breeds:
At 6 weeks of age feed 1 cup of milk for some meals and 6 ounces of meat for other meals.

The four-meals-a-day regime is continued until the puppy is about 3 months old. Gradually cut down to 3 meals a day until 6 months of age. Feed two meals a day from 6 months to 1 year of age, etc.

Barley Water Feeding

A very helpful solution that can be used to strengthen weak and debilitated puppies is a mixture made up of barley water. It has saved many a weak puppy as well as many a weak infant. This solution is easily digestible and especially good after the puppy has had diarrhea and has become very dehydrated.

To prepare, simmer 2 ounces of pearl barley in 1 quart of water for 2 hours; strain immediately to rid mixture of lumps of barley and hulls. Honey or Karo Syrup may be added to give added strength to the patient.

Behavior Patterns of Puppies

Usually the first week is mainly eating and sleeping. Then gradually the feeding periods lessen, and the play periods become more evident. Puppies growl at one another as if to tear their litter mates apart, and at times you will even notice some sexual activity, such as copulatory movements.

After 3 weeks the puppy begins to manipulate his wobbly legs and to learn the difference between his bed and his papers. This is one of the first signs of his desire to be housebroken, and the owner can help with this training process. The puppy doesn't want to lie in his own excrement and will use a different part of the whelping box to urinate and defecate. Basically this is a clean habit, but it has to be developed and helped along.

In feeding and housebreaking, regularity must be followed. The puppy expects his food at certain times, and his intestinal tract is usually attuned to these specific times. He will develop good housebreaking habits if he can depend on being taken out with the regularity.

Socialization and Transition

Most breeders call the critical period of any puppy's life the period between the ages of 21 days and 4 months. This is in regard to the development of temperament in "socialization."

Puppies raised under kennel conditions with little human

contact up to 5 weeks of age will tend to show fear reactions in later life. However, if they are handled by humans after 5 weeks of age, this shy tendency can be averted. If they are not handled until they are 12 weeks of age, and they are timid and shy, it will be much more difficult to retrain them.

After 21 days the puppy starts to learn, and he needs daily periods of socialization with humans. He should be handled, played with, and treated as an individual. He should be picked up and fondled and learn how to adapt to humans.

If a puppy is removed from the litter for brief daily periods and given individual attention, and mild discipline, he will learn more easily to adjust to humans. When he finally leaves his litter for good, he will accept his new owner more readily and respond more easily to most of his owner's wishes.

A critical age is 5 to 6 weeks, and thereafter when the puppy goes to his new home. This is a traumatic change, and it should be as gentle a transition as possible. An unhappy puppyhood can leave a marked impression on temperament for the rest of the puppy's life.

Part Six

QUESTIONS AND ANSWERS

23 100 COMMON QUERIES

AILMENTS AND DISEASES

What is the normal temperature of a dog?

The normal temperature of the adult dog is 100-101 degrees, with 102 degrees considered a high normal, while puppies are normally 101-102 degrees. A reading over 102 degrees should be considered a fever, and a veterinarian should be consulted. A temperature below 100 degrees signifies a critically ill animal, and dramatic treatment is immediately needed to save him. (See Chap. 12, p. 202.)

Do dogs get colds or flu from humans?

Researchers have been unable to find any connection between the human cold or flu virus and any such canine viruses. However, many dogs seem to come down with colds, sore throats, and upset intestines at the same time as their human families. Since dogs are getting more human-like every day, I believe they can catch colds from their masters. But there is no proof of a canine virus causing flu in humans. Dogs can catch more diseases from humans than vice versa. (See Chap. 12, p. 191.)

Is there a safe home remedy for relieving a dog of constipation?

Yes, several. I would first try a mild laxative, such as milk of magnesia or mineral oil, in tablet or liquid form. In stubborn cases, enemas, either Fleet or warm soapy water, gives instant relief. For a dog with chronic constipation add roughage (wheat bran or vegetables) to the diet. Milk and liver are also helpful in keeping the bowels free. Don't allow an animal to become dependent on habit-forming laxatives; prevention is the answer. (See Chap. 15, p. 251.)

Is it a sign a dog is ill when he passes a lot of gas (flatulence)?

No. This is a condition peculiar to dogs on a high-meat diet. Although every breed is subject to it, boxers seem to be the most prone, possibly because they gulp their food even more than others. For treatment, a change in diet with more roughage often helps. Charcoal tablets and milk of magnesia are also alleviative.

Is distemper vaccination necessary in a house pet who has no contact with other animals?

Without exception, *every* dog should be vaccinated against the "big three" of distemper-hepatitis-leptospirosis (these are combined and immunity is received with a series of shots). (See Chap. 16, p. 291.)

Some of my friends claim their dogs got lifetime distemper shots as puppies. Why do I have to bring my dog back once a year for his?

Contrary to what was believed for years, there is no such things as lifetime vaccination for any disease, and an annual booster shot for distemper-hepatitis-leptospirosis is heartily endorsed by all veterinarians. For the original vaccination, there are several techniques, and each has its merits. (See Chap. 16, p. 291.)

At what age should a dog receive his first rabies vaccination?

According to most state laws, the puppy should be at least 4 months of age before a rabies vaccination, but if he is exposed to a rabid animal, the rabies vaccine can be given at any age. It should be repeated annually or every 3 years, depending on the type of vaccine. Prevention is the only treatment for rabies. (See Chap. 16, p. 284.)

Does frothing at the mouth mean a dog has rabies?

No, no, a thousand times no! Many an innocent dog who has frothed at the mouth because of something as simple as nausea has been destroyed because he was thought to have rabies. With rabies a dog may salivate more profusely, but hundreds of other ailments and diseases can cause frothing.

What is the proper procedure when one is bitten by a dog who may be rabid?

First, catch the dog so it can be quarantined, and then wash the wound with strong soap. If the dog stays healthy for the 14-day quarantine period, the person bitten can breathe a sigh of relief. If the dog turns out to have rabies even as late as the 14th day of quarantine, there is still plenty of time for the person bitten to take the Pasteur treatment. (See Chap. 16, p. 285-286.)

Is rabies found only in dogs?

No. Rabies occurs in all warm-blooded animals and is usually spread by wild animals. Bats are a constant source of rabies infection. Any contact with a bat should be regarded with suspicion, and professional advice should be sought. If possible, the bat should be captured and tested for rabies in a laboratory.

Is there a home remedy to relieve coughing in a dog?

If there is no infection present, pure honey will soothe the dog's throat. Also, if unsalted butter is applied to the dog's nose, he will lick it and his throat will be coated and the tissues soothed.

Do excessive thirst and constant urination indicate illness?

One of the first signs of kidney trouble (nephritis) is excessive water drinking and consequent increased urination. There is a type of diabetes which causes excessive thirst. When the symptom is present, the dog should immediately be examined by a veterinarian.

Can aspirin be given to a dog, and what is the proper dosage?

The average dog can assimilate aspirin, and it is often used to reduce fever and to relieve arthritis, rheumatism, and other painful and feverish conditions. Dogs who vomit ordinary aspirin can often tolerate buffered aspirin. The average medium-sized dog can take one aspirin (adult size: 5 grains) 3 times a day, and the dosage can be regulated to other sizes. Aspirin is a worthwhile remedy which can give a dog relief until the cause of the fever is ascertained by the veterinarian.

In a case of poisoning what is the quickest and safest way to get a dog to vomit?

Hydrogen peroxide mixed with an equal amount of water—1–2 tablespoons for each 10 pounds of body weight—will cause vomiting in about 2 minutes. If peroxide is not handy 1 or 2 teaspoons of table salt in half a cup of water can be used. When the vomiting has stopped, the dog can be given 1 to 2 teaspoons of Epsom salts to further evacuate the intestinal tract, and then he should be rushed to a veterinarian. This is not an antidote for all types of poisons, but is an effective means of emptying the stomach. (See Chap. 14.)

Is there a special way to handle a dog with a broken leg while getting him to a veterinarian?

Keep the dog as flat and quiet as possible to prevent the sharp edges of the bone from moving about and cutting the blood vessels and doing further damage to the muscles and nerves. Place a stick or other straight and rigid object against the leg so that it is both above and below the fracture, and bandage it to the leg to render it immobile. (See Chap. 13.)

404

Are there any diseases humans can get from kissing dogs?

You can catch fewer germs kissing a dog than you can a human. There are few canine germs than can be spread by kissing.

Is it true that some household cleansers are poisonous to dogs?

Yes. Dogs come in contact every day with household cleansers which can prove toxic to them if they ingest too much. Young puppies especially will lick and eat just about anything, and they are more susceptible to poisons than older dogs. It is best to be careful when using such products as certain types of waxes, furniture polishes, and disinfectants. (See Chap. 14.)

BEHAVIOR

How can a new puppy be kept from crying all night?

Until the puppy gets used to sleeping without the warmth of his mother and litter mates, a hot-water bottle or an electric heating pad may be enough to simulate their warmth. A loud-ticking alarm clock will sometimes distract a puppy from crying. If these don't work, a baby aspirin, tranquilizer, or sleeping pill is in order until he gets used to being alone. (See Chap. 2.)

Is there a best way to housebreak a puppy?

Use reward and punishment, patience and perseverance, but most of all take him out at least every two hours on schedule. This should include first thing in the morning, shortly after each meal, and just before bed at night. When he errs, he should know what he has done wrong; most dogs catch on quickly. It takes anywhere from 2 weeks to 3 months, depending on the dog's age and intelligence. (See Chap. 2, p. 45.)

Do dogs dream?

All indications are that they do. When they move their legs as if running, and whine and grunt during sleep, it is a subconscious expression of their thoughts. There is an old-folk superstition that to find out what a dog is dreaming you will soon know if you put a straw between his toes.

When should one begin training a puppy in the basic commands?

The best age to start training a puppy is as early as possible, but a 6- to 8-week-old puppy cannot be expected to immediately comprehend. After 3 months of age the commands

405

will begin sinking in, and at 6 months more intensive training can be started. The discipline for a young puppy should be gentle, as he can easily be intimidated and his confidence destroyed. (See Chap. 2, p. 62.)

Is it true that mongrels are healthier and smarter than purebreds?

No. The veterinary hospitals are filled with as many sick mongrels as purebreds. Canines are similar to the humans who master them. There are both sickly and healthy dogs as well as dumb and smart ones in both mongrels and purebreds.

Which breed is smartest and best for training?

No breed has a monopoly on brains, and it has been proved conclusively that any breed is capable of competing in obedience-training programs and contests.

Can a show dog also be a good pet?

It is a common misconception that show dogs are too nervous to be gentle, loving pets. Many champion dogs have been house pets all their lives.

Do puppies remember their mothers, and vice versa?

The mother-puppy relationship is basically instinct. Once the puppies are weaned and leave their mother, I don't believe that mothers and offspring know one another.

Why do dogs roll on manure or dead animals?

In primitive days the dog rolled in something putrid to disguise his body scent so that when hunting, his prey would not be forewarned. No amount of scolding or discipline will stop a modern dog from doing it if this is one of his habits. Unfortunately the more putrid the odor, the more such a dog seems to enjoy rolling in it.

What are some of the primitive instincts that dogs still have?

As well as the above, the burying of bones goes back to ancestral days. Another is walking in circles before lying down to sleep. And finally, when a dog is frightened by another dog, or by any animal, he will tuck his tail between his legs, cower, and sometimes lie on his back as a sign of submission.

Can a dog grieve himself sick when left in a boarding kennel or hospital?

The average dog adjusts quickly and easily to environment, and even a shy and timid dog soon relaxes with a few kind words and a pat on the head. Even a pampered pet, with a tranquilizer, will relax enough to eat and adjust to his environment. Dogs don't grieve and die of a broken heart, nor do they forget their masters even after years of separation.

Will spaying or castration affect a dog's disposition or personality?

The dog's basic personality will not be changed by the operation. The operation doesn't make the male or female mean; if anything it makes them sweeter and more affectionate. For nervous or aggressive dogs I advise the operation because it quiets them down and prevents them from reproducing puppies with these undesirable traits. (See Chap. 19.)

Which makes a better house pet, a male or a female?

Pro and con can be argued indefinitely. Either sex makes the "one and only pet in your life." The female presents problems twice a year when she is in heat, and the male has the occasional urge to visit a girl friend and is not as fastidious in his habits. (See Chap. 1, p. 35.)

Is there a right way to respond to an unfriendly dog?

Stand still, and by all means the hands should be kept still. Face him and let him evaluate your scent. Talk to him in a pleasant voice all the time he is appraising you.

COAT AND SKIN

Is there something wrong with a dog who sheds all year round?

Not if it is a house dog who curls up next to radiators. Warm air dries the skin and hair, and excessive shedding results. Such dogs need a lot of brushing and extra amounts of fats and oils in their food. (See Chap. 6.)

What can I do for a dry hair coat that sheds excessively even though the dog gets extra fat and oils?

For stubborn shedding there is a solution which is useful in counteracting a dry hair coat. The solution (1 oz. of glycerine, 8 ozs. of water, 1 tbsp. of vinegar) is rubbed into the coat, to the skin, before bathing the dog. In long-coated dogs the solution should be left on an hour before the bath. However, if nothing seems to help the dry condition, a veterinarian should be consulted, as it may be caused by an internal abnormality.

Is there a long-haired breed that does not shed?

Yes; the Kerry blue terrier and the French poodle normally don't shed.

How often should a dog be bathed?

Common sense is the best answer: when he needs it. Frequent bathing with harsh soaps removes natural oils from the skin and coat and causes excessive shedding. For an indoor pet who sleeps with his human family, I advise a bath at least every 2 weeks. An outdoor dog, during the winter, doesn't need to be bathed—only brushed and combed. But during the summer months he should be bathed and dipped for external parasites and any skin problems at least every 2 weeks. (See Chap. 6.)

Should a dog wear a sweater when outside in cold weather?

For a dog such as a toy or minature, without much hair, or any fragile dog who shivers and shakes in cold weather, I advise a sweater or blanket. A normal, healthy adult dog, used to cold weather, needs no protection. Nature has provided him with a coat well lubricated to protect him against cold, wet, and dampness. (See Chap. 6.)

Is it bad for an outdoor dog to be allowed inside occasionally during cold weather?

It is not true that if an outside dog is allowed inside for a visit and then put back outside, he will catch cold. A healthy dog quickly adjusts to varying temperatures and environments.

What is the difference between "hot spots" and "weeping mange"?

They are one and the same thing, and incidentally not a mange. They are moist skin lesions caused by fungi or bacteria which usually start as innocent pinpoint lesions and grow to the size of a grapefruit within a matter of hours. They are characterized by loss of hair, redness, moistness, and purulence. (See Chap. 6, p. 113-114.)

What can be done to avoid clipper burn?

It can be caused by a very close trim with a No. 15 or 30 blade, causing irritation along the side of the face. Another cause can be an overheated clipper. Also, when the animal moves suddenly during clipping the teeth of the blades often will cut into his face. There is a special "after-clipping" lotion for poodles' faces, and this is some other soothing lotion should be used following clipping, especially a close trim. If a sore does develop, it should be cleaned with peroxide and then a soothing ointment or lotion applied. To keep the dog from scratching or irritating the burn, a little booty can be put on the rear foot of the irritated side.

Is there a test for deafness in dogs?

Know your dog. As he approaches old age there may be a slow change in his personality and responsiveness. Where he once jumped with joy at the sound of your voice, he often may not hear you. High-pitched sounds, such as whistles, can be heard long after normal voice sounds. (See Chap. 4, p. 78.)

Do dogs see color?

No; they are color-blind and only see varying shades of black and white. They are nearsighted and rely more on their noses than on their eyes.

Does a dry warm nose mean a dog is sick and has a fever?

Not necessarily. It is misleading to feel a dog's nose to diagnose illness. The moisture and temperature of a dog's nose can be affected by temperature and humidity. A normal dog can have a warm, dry nose and a dog with a 105-degree temperature can have a cold, moist nose. For a quick appraisal one can feel the inside of a dog's ear or the bare skin of the abdomen. Any warmth in either place usually signifies a fever. However, a rectal thermometer is much more reliable.

Do dogs get cavities in their teeth?

The dog is more resistant to cavities than man, mainly because of the strong germ-killing action of the saliva and the strong enamel layer of the teeth. Cavities are rare. (See Chap. 15, p. 255.)

Is there any treatment for "pitted enamel," or "distemper teeth"?

The pitting and discoloration caused by distemper or any other serious illness in a puppy cannot be removed. The ulceration of the enamel does not affect the health of the dog, but it does usually disqualify a dog in the show ring. The condition is caused when a puppy has a serious disease during the transition between his baby and permanent teeth (when the permanent teeth are being formed). (See Chap. 15.)

What causes bad breath (halitosis) in dogs?

The commonest cause of bad breath in dogs is tartar on the teeth—a brown discoloration next to the gums. Another cause is a pyorrhea-like gum infection, or loose or infected teeth. Some dogs belch up gases which are disagreeable in odor. Many people think that when a dog has bad breath, it is a sign of worms, but this is not necessarily so.

EATING HABITS: EDIBLE AND INEDIBLE

Among commercial dog foods, is dry or canned better?

Both are nutritionally balanced for the normal dog. Certain dogs need added amounts of fats, and growing puppies, pregnant and lactating bitches, convalescing dogs, and old dogs need supplements. (See Chap. 5.)

Are table scraps frowned upon by the experts?

Indeed, no. Table scraps are an excellent addition to a commercial dog-food diet. Besides providing that little extra that most dogs appreciate, table scraps relieve the boredom of the same food day in and day out. But because the commercial products are so well-balanced, table scraps and tidbits should not form more than one-quarter of the dog's basic daily diet. (See Chap. 5.)

Is it harmful to feed a dog fatty meat?

Dogs need a moderate amount of fat. If the diet is deficient in fat, the dog will be thin and have a scaly and itchy skin and a dry hair coat. All types of animal fat are beneficial to the dog if fed in moderate amounts; and fat should be increased during the winter months.

Do all dogs need vitamin or mineral supplements?

No. The commercial dog foods supply the nutrients needed by the normal healthy adult dog. However, for growing puppies, pregnant and lactating bitches, convalescing dogs, and old dogs there is a definite need for supplementation. (See Chap. 5.)

Is it true that feeding large amounts of calcium or other minerals will cause hip dysplasia?

No; this is a widespread fallacy. Hip dysplasia is a congenital defect, and diet supplementation will not cause this abnormality.

How many meals can a dog miss without becoming ill?

I advise seeking the advice of a veterinarian after a pet has been indifferent to food and missed 2 or 3 meals. Whether an emotional or physical disturbance is the cause should be determined. (See Chap. 5.)

Is poor appetite always a sign of illness?

Not always. Many high-strung dogs are finicky about their food and a challenge to their masters in finding foods they relish. Anything that might emotionally disturb a dog, and especially jealousy, can upset the appetite. (See Chap. 5).

Are raw eggs harmful to a dog?

No. Although the egg white in its raw state is indigestible to the dog and interferes with the assimilation of certain vitamins, dogs have been eating raw eggs for thousands of years, and in force-feeding a whole egg broken into the mouth has saved the life of many a dog. If possible, it is better to feed only the yolk or to cook the egg. Some dogs are allergic to eggs and it is usually the protein of the yolk that bothers them.

Is it true that potatoes are harmful to dogs?

It is a widely-held fallacy that potatoes are harmful and/or poisonous. Potatoes and other starches are a very important part of the dog's diet and within proportion are easily digested. (See Chap 5.)

Do sweets cause worms?

No. Sweets will not harm a dog nor will they give him worms or cavities in his teeth. As with children, too many sweets will spoil his appetite for his regular meals, but the occasional sweet is very pleasing to most pets. (See Chap. 5.)

Are bones essential to a dog?

Bones are not essential for good health but provide many hours of pleasure. Certain types of bones are beneficial in that they help keep the tartar from the dog's teeth and subsequently help control halitosis. Certain bones, such as chicken, lamb, pork, and veal, can be dangerous, as they tend to splinter and can scratch and puncture the intestinal tract. (See Chap. 5.)

Are cooked bones safer for a dog?

Yes. Cooked bones are slightly safer because uncooked bones are more brittle and more likely to splinter. A pressure cooker is valuable in softening bones.

Is there some way to keep a puppy from chewing everything in the house?

Yes; provide him with plenty of teething toys to divert him. Large beef or shank bones are excellent, as well as hard-rubber toys (soft-rubber toys are taboo), and beef-hide chew sticks. Don't give him an old shoe or sock, as this could develop into a bad habit and play havoc with the family clothing budget. Keep a careful watch on exposed electric wires. (See Chap. 2.)

Do dogs need salt during hot weather?

No. Unlike humans, dogs don't need any salt supplementation; there is usually enough in the daily rations. Salt itself is nauseating to a dog. It should be entirely avoided when a dog has kidney disorders or heart disease, as it causes retention of fluid in the body.

Are there special formulas for orphan puppies?

There are some excellent commercial preparations which can be obtained from any pet shop or veterinarian. They are scientifically prepared to simulate the mother's milk. There is also an excellent home formula. (See Chap. 22.)

Is alcohol harmful to dogs?

As with humans, small amounts are not harmful, and in some emergency conditions are life-saving.

Can a dog be kept small-sized by feeding him alcohol?

Definitely not! Alcohol will have no effect on the rate of growth of a dog. Another fallacy is that by starving a bitch before the birth of her puppies and then underfeeding the puppies, toy or miniature puppies will be produced. Nothing could be more inhumane; starving a puppy produces a sickly, runty dog; heredity determines size.

Why do dogs eat grass?

Almost all dogs like the taste of fresh green grass, and when they feel the need for a laxative or an emetic, they seek out long-stemmed blades, which irritate the stomach into vomiting. In persistent cases of grass eating the dog should be checked for intestinal parasites or an intestinal infection. When a dog seems to have a craving for grass, a milk of magnesia pill sometimes works miracles, as it has an anti-acid action and is a mild laxative.

How can a dog be broken from the habit of eating his vomitus?

A dog should not be stopped from doing this. Although it is not a pretty sight, some dogs do this to predigest their food. Some bitches do it to predigest food for their puppies, making it similar to homogenized baby food. If the vomiting persists, infection or a foreign object should be suspected.

Is it normal for a dog to eat wood, stones, dirt, and other inedible things?

Some dogs chew on wood, stones, etcetera, because of a diet deficiency, out of boredom or loneliness, or out of habit. Dogs eat dirt because of a nutritional deficiency—a mineral deficiency or parasitism depriving them of certain essentials. In dogs who like to play with stones, unfortunately the caps of the teeth are often broken or chipped.

Is there some way to break a dog from eating manure?

Dogs eat horse and other animal manure because they crave the partially digested cereal grains in the manure. Also, some dogs like the taste of manure (even as some humans enjoy grasshoppers, chocolate-covered ants, fish eyes, rattlesnake meat, etc.). Try adding cereal food, such as oatmeal and corn flakes, to the diet to fill that craving.

Why does a dog eat his own feces (coprophagy)?

The exact cause is not known, but experts agree that it is a mental or dietary deficiency or a combination of both. Several theories are discussed in Chapter 11. The dog should be checked for worms, and mineral and vitamin supplements should be added to his diet.

MALE AND FEMALE

Is it possible to prevent a spayed female or a castrated male from getting fat?

In the first place, have an intelligent feeding program. Most of the time it is not how much the dogs are fed as what they are given. Most commercial dog foods are high in starches and carbohydrates and add unneeded poundage. Carbohydrates and starches should be decreased and proteins (meat, fish) should be increased. The diet should include non-fattening vegetables and other non-fattening table scraps. Also, a hormone schedule should be set up to replace the hormones lost by the operation. This is usually at regular monthly intervals and should be overseen by a veterinarian, as excessive use of hormones can be harmful to the canine body. (See Chap. 3.)

Do a male and female dog have to "tie together" to have a successful breeding?

No. Once the male ejaculates into the female, which takes only 1 to 2 minutes, if the sperm is deposited well forward in the vagina, there is a good chance of conception, even though there is no "tying together." Tying together is a natural phenomenon and one of the cruelest and most dangerous things that can be done is to throw water on them or beat them to try to separate them. They should be left alone 10-20 minutes, until they separate naturally. (See Chap. 19.)

Will close breeding, such as son to mother, daughter to father, produce abnormal offspring?

Not necessarily, and it is a common fallacy that inbreeding always produces nervous dogs. Inbreeding brings out the good

413

qualities in the blood lines, but it also brings out the undesirable qualities, which if found in both sides of the family would magnify the chances for abnormal offspring. With proper inbreeding, champions are born, while with improper inbreeding, nervous and timid dogs are produced. Inbreeding should be tried only by experienced breeders after thorough investigation of the ancestry. (See Chap. 19.)

Do dogs actually masturbate?

Yes. Male dogs become aroused by licking their genitals, riding other dogs, or mounting various household objects and the legs of humans. Female dogs in heat often mount other animals and go through the motions of intercourse until they reach orgasm. (See Chap. 11.)

OLD AGE

Is it true that the smaller breeds live longer than the larger breeds?

Yes. Longevity seems to be related to size. Larger breeds are considered quite old by the time they reach the age of 10, while the smaller breeds can live an average of 13 to 15 years.

What is the comparative age of a 10-year-old dog in terms of a human?

The old theory that 1 year of a dog's life is equivalent to 7 years in man has been abandoned. According to the presently accepted scale, a 6-month-old dog is comparable to a 10-year-old child, a 1-year-old dog to a 15-year-old teen-ager, and a 2-year-old dog to a 25-year-old human. A 10-year-old dog is comparable to a human of 56; and when he is 21 years old, the dog has reached the century mark of his human equivalent. (See Chap. 3.)

What are the danger signals in old age?

Increased respiration, which can signify heart trouble; coughing, which can indicate heart failure; fainting spells, sudden collapse, or paralysis, which indicate heart trouble or cerebral stroke. Increased thirst and excessive urination are a danger signal for nephritis; urine odor from the mouth signifies that the animal is going into uremia due to kidney failure.

How does one decide when to put a dog to sleep?

If any of the following questions can be answered in the affirmative, I would advise euthanasia: (1) Is the dog suffering great pain? (2) Is the dog suffering from an incurable disease or ailment? (3) Is the dog suffering from a disability that is preventing him from enjoying life? These questions must be evaluated and answered before making the decision to put the dog to sleep. (See Chap. 4.)

PUPPIES

Has research come up with a serum to prevent puppies from dying the first few days after birth?

In years gone by when puppies died within the 1st week of birth, death was attributed to "acid milk" in the mother. It is true that the milk of the dam can contain organisms detrimental to puppies, but it has also been discovered that there are certain diseases in puppies. "Fading" puppies' disease is caused by a virus; "septicemia of the newborn" (a blood poisoning) can be derived from an infected umbilical cord; and there are congenital defects, such as heart defect (similar to "blue" babies) and cleft palate (the puppies are unable to suck milk, and weaken and die). Digestive upsets—with diarrhea—if unattended can kill puppies within a few days. Chilling is a common environmental cause of death within the 1st week. (See Chap. 22.)

When a mother pushes a newborn puppy aside and ignores it, does this mean that the mother "knows best" that the puppy is abnormal in some way?

Instinctively a mother dog knows a sick or dying puppy and will usually push it off into a corner and allow it to die. But unless the puppy has a congenital defect which would make it a cripple for life, the puppy can and should be saved by hand raising.

What is the earliest age at which a puppy can be taken from its mother?

The earliest age is 4 weeks. That is when the puppy can learn to drink milk out of a saucer and eat solid food.

What is the best age at which to adopt a puppy?

The psychologists say that the best age is 8 to 12 weeks. For discussion see Chapter 1.

At what age is a dog considered full-grown?

In the small breeds the dog reaches full growth at 6 months. In the medium breeds full growth is at 7 to 8 months. The large breeds grow in height until they are 12 months of age; then, until they are 2 years of age, they add muscle and weight to complete their full growth.

When getting a second dog, is it best to get another male, another female, or a dog of the opposite sex?

In my opinion the second dog should always be of the opposite sex. With two males or two females there is a greater tendency for fights. Even though there are complications with dogs of opposite sex, the female can be put into a kennel during her season. Spaying the female or castrating the male is a solution if problems arise.

SEX LIFE OF THE FEMALE

How often does a bitch come into heat, and how long does the heat period last?

The normal bitch comes into heat every 6 months, and the heat period lasts 21 days, counting from the first day of bloody vaginal discharge. Some dogs don't come into heat that often, and there are dogs who come into heat every 3 or 4 months. Some dogs have "silent" heat periods, and other dogs stay in heat 4 to 5 weeks. (See Chap. 19.)

What is the correct time to breed a bitch during her heat cycle?

In general, the most likely time for ovulation is 9 to 14 days after the first sign of blood. A good rule of thumb is: a week coming into heat, a week of conception, and a week going out of heat. During the middle week the discharge becomes colorless, and the bitch shows a tendency to stand with her tail aside. (See Chap. 19.)

What is the best age at which to breed a bitch for the first time?

It is best to skip the 1st heat period and breed her on the 2nd or 3rd period. She can be bred twice in a row if she is in good health and had no complications with her first litter. However, I would then skip the next heat period before breeding her again.

At what age should breeding be terminated?

When a bitch reaches the age of 7 to 8 years, one should be cautious about breeding her and should do it only on the advice of a veterinarian. Bitches have been known to deliver puppies at 10 to 12 years of age, but this is exceptional.

At what age do bitches stop their heat periods?

There is no "change of life" in female dogs. Most bitches begin having irregular heat cycles after they are 10 to 11 years old, but it is possible for them to have heat periods until 18

416

to 20 years of age. I would not trust such a dog out by herself; she might be attacked by a "traveling salesman."

Will a bitch allow herself to be bred when she is not in season?
No, and conception cannot take place. There are exceptions; and some bitches will attempt to copulate with a male while not in season. This is a form of nymphomania; these dogs show a false heat period and enlarged vagina, but no ovulation occurs and conception cannot take place. (See Chap. 19.)

Is there a pregnancy test for dogs?
No, there is no laboratory test at the moment, such as the rabbit test for humans. The veterinarian can diagnose pregnancy from 3 to 4 weeks after conception by manual examination.

Are there birth control pills for dogs?
Yes, there are very effective birth control pills for dogs. These pills, OVABAN, if given before the heat period, will prevent the dog from coming into season and will lessen the cycle if given after the dog has come into heat. Human birth control pills are not effective in dogs. (See Chap. 19.)

Can pregnancy be avoided after an accidental mating?
Yes; there is a hormone injection which is 90-99 percent effective in preventing pregnancy if given within a week after copulation. The sooner the better! The only undesirable effect is that it prolongs the heat period for a week to 10 days.

Once a purebred bitch mates with a mongrel, is she ruined forever as a breeder of purebred dogs?
No. Once the womb expels its contents, there are no after-effects on future litters of puppies. This superstition, called telegony, is still widely believed. Subsequent purebred litters can be registered with the AKC. (See Chap. 11.)

Can a bitch conceive puppies from more than one stud during a heat period?
Yes. There can be several different fathers, and this is why there are sometimes many different-looking puppies in a litter. The female dog ovulates many eggs and can be impregnated by more than one male. Thus it is wise to keep the bitch in solitary confinement after she has been bred by the dog of the owner's choice.

Is it possible to breed a bitch who has had a false pregnancy?
Yes. Actually having a litter of puppies might help prevent future false pregnancies. If the bitch is not to be bred, and

417

has had several false pregnancies, a hysterectomy is advisable. (See Chap. 20.)

Is there an abnormality in the bitch who has an odd number of breasts?

No; there is nothing pathologically significant in an odd number of nipples. And a missing breast does not mean that the bitch will make a poor mother.

Is it possible to tell when a bitch is about to whelp?

There is a drop in her temperature (under 100 degrees) within 24 hours of delivery. She pants and becomes nervous and restless. She scratches and tears at a rug, a bedspread, or newspapers, trying to prepare a nest. Most dogs refuse food as they approach their delivery hour. House pets say close to their masters, as they want all the attention they can get during this critical period. (See Chap. 21.)

How long should a bitch be in labor before a puppy is born?

The maiden bitch with her first litter is usually in labor longer than an older and experienced dog. Generally the first puppy is born after 2 to 3 hours of labor, and then the puppies come every 10 to 15 minutes up to several hours apart. If the first puppy does not arrive within 6 hours after the commencement of labor, a veterinarian should be consulted. (See Chap. 21.)

If a caesarean operation is once necessary, will it always be necessary?

Three-quarters of the dogs who have undergone Caesarean sections have had subsequent litters by the normal process of delivery. Some breeds—for example Boston bull and English bull—are more apt to need a Caesarean operation, but once a Caesarean doesn't mean always a Caesarean.

Is there best age at which to spay a dog?

There are conflicting opinions. I advise spaying the bitch, if she is not to be bred, just before her 1st heat period—usually around 6 months of age. (See Chap. 3.)

Is there an age limit in spaying a dog?

There is no age limit, but the risk increases with age. I advise spaying a bitch as soon as her breeding days are over, as this will prevent female problems in later years and reduce the incidence of mammary tumors. (See Chap. 3.)

Can a dog in heat be spayed?

It is better not to spay the dog in heat, as spaying at this time involves some risk because of the enlarged uterus and blood vessels. But if necessary, any competent veterinary surgeon can perform the operation.

SEX LIFE OF THE MALE

At what age can a male dog be first bred?
The male dog reaches puberty anywhere from 7 to 18 months of age, depending on the size of the breed; the smaller breeds mature earlier. Any time after 6 months of age he will start giving indications of sexual maturity. When he lifts his leg to urinate, he has reached "manhood." As a rule, to allow him to gain his full masculinity, it is best not to breed a dog before he is 1 year of age.

Is it true that once a male dog is bred he is ruined as a pet?
I don't think it harms a dog to breed him occasionally. Since male dogs like lovemaking once they are exposed to it, if the dog is not to be bred on a regular basis it is wise not to start in the first place.

Will breeding a male dog calm him down?
No; this is a fallacy. He might be calmed down temporarily after a night or two on the town, but he might also start roaming from home.

What can be done with a sexually frustrated male?
If the dog constantly rides people's legs or goes around the house making love to pillows, etcetera, if discipline doesn't help, castration is indicated. This will cure all his frustrations. A castrated male dog makes an excellent pet, similar to the spayed female, as his entire life become centered on his human family. (See p. 71).

Does a dog, male or female, need a sex life?
No. Many dogs have a very happy life without experiencing sex, and without being frustrated. Many people think that their dogs need sex because of human frustrations. Females not to be bred I feel should be spayed for many reasons discussed before.

WORMS

How do dogs get worms?
Some puppies are born with worms; the fetus in the womb can become infested with roundworms or hookworms. Puppies can also become infested by swallowing worm eggs on the skin or hair of the mother as they nurse, or from feces in

the cage or run. Some worms can penetrate the pads of dog's feet. Grown dogs usually pick them up from the ground; also from mosquitoes and fleas; and from animals, such as squirrels, rabbits, and mice, that a dog might ingest while hunting. (See Chap. 17.)

When a dog rubs his tail along the ground, does it mean he has worms?

Not necessarily. Most of the time when the dog rubs his tail along the ground, he is trying to relieve his anal sacs which are impacted and enlarged. This is a signal that he should be taken to a veterinarian to have his anal glands expressed, because if the condition is allowed to progress an abscess can form in his anal glands. Sometimes tapeworms and roundworms will crawl out of the rectum and cause an itchy condition in the anal region, and to relieve himself the dog rubs his tail along the ground. But many dogs have been needlessly wormed when the real problem is impacted anal glands. (See Chap. 17.)

How often should a dog be checked for worms?

A dog under 1 year of age should be checked for worms every 2 to 3 months. As he gets older he develops an increasing amount of resistance to the effects of worms, and twice a year would be sufficient for most adult dogs to be examined for worms. In certain parts of the country, for example the South, worms are more prevalent, and more frequent worm checks are advisable. All worm medicines are poisonous to a degree, and *a dog should not be wormed unless he needs it,* that is, only after microscopic examination of the feces indicates worms.

When a dog goes off his feed and seems sickly, should he be given a worm pill?

Never, Never worm a sick dog. Many dogs have died needlessly from being given worm medicine while running a fever. Even if the dog does have worms, he must be treated for the fever and sickness before being treated for the worms. Since worm medicine has to be strong to kill worms, it can be toxic to a sick dog. When to worm the dog should be up to the veterinarian.

Can children get pinworms or other worms from dogs?

Definitely not! Dogs don't have a pinworm such as is found in children. Humans are not susceptible to contamination by dog worms. Dog parasites will not live in the human body. Extensive research has been done on the subject, and dogs have been completely exonerated. (See Chap. 17.)

Part Seven

APPENDIX:
UP-TO-DATE DEVELOPMENTS

24 NUTRITION

TASTE DISCRIMINATION

Recent scientific findings on taste preferences in dogs have unearthed some interesting facts. For instance, poodles are much more discriminating than retrievers, pointers, or setters. The least fussy of all the breeds is the beagle.

Age and sex have little, if any, effect on taste discrimination; but on the whole, smaller breeds are more finicky.

Generally, dogs do not like cold foods, nor citrus fruits, but they show a decided liking for sweets.

THE NEED FOR VITAMIN C

Contrary to popular belief and medical theory, dogs, although capable of manufacturing their own Vitamin C, do not produce all of this nutrient that they need—particularly in time of stress.

During the last few years, Vitamin C's ability to counteract and destroy viruses, bacteria, and other disease-causing toxins has been demonstrated again and again. By using massive doses of Vitamin C, many veterinarians have had outstanding success in treating a wide variety of serious illnesses in pets. There is evidence that Vitamin C can help protect pets from all sorts of infectious diseases, such as: distemper and other respiratory diseases; arthritis; kidney diseases; allergy reactions; and spinal degeneration. Vitamin C may also be helpful in alleviating pain in hip dysplasia.

Scientists recommend that all pets receive a daily maintenance dose of Vitamin C as a preventive against future problems.

25 THE AILING DOG

THE EYES

Pannus is a disease of the cornea which occurs principally in the German shepherd. It can start at puppyhood, to middle age. Over a period of months or years, a cloudiness progresses to cover the entire cornea of both eyes. Blindness may result. The cause is unknown. Treatment controls the disease but does not completely cure it.

Night Blindness is now being fought with Vitamin D and Calcium. These help only in cases of chronic inflammation of the retina, and will not help in Progressive Retinal Atrophy which is an inherited disease.

Day Blindness (Hemeralopia)

Unlike night blindness (PRA), day blindness can be detected in dogs at seven weeks of age. They bump into objects and seem to be unsure of distances. Indoors, or in a dim light, or at night, the affected dog's vision is as good as that of a normal dog. Unlike night blindness, the condition does not worsen.

It is an inherited disease. There is no cure but an affected dog may lead a restricted life in familiar surroundings.

Contact Lenses

A University of Georgia professor of veterinary medicine is using plastic lenses manufactured for human use to treat certain eye problems in dogs. Dr. Gretchen Schmidt uses the lenses as a type of protective bandage while the eyes heal from disease or injury.

FRACTURES

Electric current is now being used by orthopedic research surgeons to speed the healing of bone fractures. They claim that fractures heal twice as fast as with standard methods. The surgeons are also using chemical compounds to "cement" the ends of bones together.

HIP DYSPLASIA

Hip palpation as a technique for early determination of dysplasia can be made at 7 to 9 weeks of age, although confirmation of the diagnosis must wait until the dog is 6 to 9 months of age. Even though a dog is negative at 2 months, there is no assurance that it will not be dysplastic at one year.

"LION JAW" DISEASE

Veterinarians are seeing an increase in this disease which causes an overgrowth of the jaw bones and other bones of the head. It is seen mostly in Boston terriers, cairn terriers, Scotch terriers and West Highland white terriers. The onset of the disease occurs usually when the dog is between 4 and 7 months of age. In some cases, it develops so that the dog cannot open its mouth and must be put to sleep. Most veterinarians believe that it is due to hereditary factors with secondary infectious agents causing the fever and pain.

THE SKIN

Acne

Dr. George Muller, a noted veterinary skin specialist, has revealed some interesting facts about a skin ailment which in many ways resembles acne in humans. He calls it *Canine Acne* which begins during adolescence—when the dog is between 3 and 12 months of age, the time of sexual development. Sometimes the acne persists into adult life, especially in such predisposed breeds as boxers, English bulldogs, Great Danes, and Doberman pinschers.

The most common site of canine acne is the chin, but it also occurs around the upper and lower lips, and sometimes the lower abdomen and inside the thighs. Treatment is accompanied by shampooing, hormones, and antibiotics.

Demodectic Mange

Some veterinary dermatologists believe this type of mange is NOT contagious from one dog to another—but is an inherited disease. Dr. Muller claims that numerous tests have shown that puppies are exposed to the demodectic mite while nursing

424

their mother and may break out with the skin lesions months later. Therefore, it is important to NOT breed female dogs that have had, or have, mange. They could be carriers and pass it on to their offspring.

SNAKE BITES

Cases have been reported where high doses of Vitamin C—1,200 mg. as soon as possible and 6,000 mg. every 6 hours—have saved the lives of snake-bitten dogs.

SURGERY BY ULTRA-FREEZING

Surgical removal of tumors can be performed on dogs by cooling the area in liquid nitrogen down to $-196°$ C. The advantages of this cryosurgical treatment are that little or no pain is felt by the patient and healing is rapid and almost scarless.

ULTRA-HIGH FREQUENCY SOUND IN THERAPY

Crippled dogs are being given therapy through the use of ultra-high frequency sound as a substitute for acupuncture. Ailments that are treated in this way are arthritis, hip dysplasia, and ruptured spinal discs. Some veterinarians say that this type of therapy is more effective than the needle. And the sound treatments eliminate pain and the risk of infection.

It is also used in the removal of cataracts; examination of the heart, the brain, the eyes; and can be used to determine the size, position, and number of fetuses in pregnancy examinations.

VENEREAL TUMORS

Although not fully understood, venereal tumors are known to be sexually generated and transmitted by coitus. These tumors appear primarily on the external genitalia of both sexes and can become malignant and spread to other parts of the body. Fortunately this is not very common in the U.S. and it does respond to therapy.

DANGER SIGNS OF CANCER IN DOGS

The warning signs listed below do not necessarily indicate that the dog has cancer. They do mean that all is not well with your pet and that the animal should be taken to the veterinarian for a complete physical examination.

Skin Tumors

—any abnormal swelling or lump of tissue on or just beneath the skin. Swelling may be located anywhere on the head, body, tail or legs of the animal.

Mammary Tumors

—any firm masses under the skin located near or adjacent to the nipples of the mammary glands in the female dog. Breast tumors seem to grow faster after heat periods.

Oral Tumors

—difficulty in picking up, chewing, or swallowing food (or if pieces of food are frequently dropped out of the mouth)
—a foul odor from mouth
—swelling located on the lips or jaw
—a bloody discharge from the mouth
—one side of the nose larger than the other
—chronic nasal discharge—may be mucus, purulent or bloody, usually from one side of nostril
—nasal discharge unresponsive to antibiotic therapy
—nosebleeds

Bone Tumors

Most prevalent in large breeds such as Great Danes, St. Bernards, German Shepherds.
—sudden onset of lameness
—swelling, especially in shoulder area, knee joint, in hind leg or in carpus (wrist in human anatomy)

—bilateral, large, non-painful firm swelling in the neck region beneath the lower jaw and/or in front of the front legs

The Causes of Cancer

While the causes of cancer are largely unknown, there are certain factors such as irradiation, viruses and parasites, and exposures to various chemicals that cause certain kinds of cancer. It is also thought that certain hereditary, hormonal, congenital, traumatic and even nutritional factors can cause cancer.

Statistically, it is known that tumors develop most frequently in older dogs, so owners of mature pets should be more wary in looking for tumors. Also, tumors occur more frequently in some breeds. For instance, boxers seem to have the highest incidence of tumors of all types. As a general rule, purebred dogs tend to have a higher incidence of tumors than mixed breed dogs.

26 BREEDING

A "MORNING AFTER" PILL

This form of birth control pill could be the result of investigation by researchers. They are seeking to find an acceptable method for clinical termination of mismating. A hormone pill that gives no untoward after-effects is being thoroughly tested and may soon be available.

BRUCELLA CANIS

This bacteria which causes abortion in dogs has been found to be three and one-half times greater in stray dogs than in non-strays.

FERTILITY DRUGS

There are fertility drugs, very similar to the ones used by humans, which are increasing the sizes of litters as well as helping with problems of conception. The pills are given before breeding.

CANINE PATERNITY TEST

Scientists can now confirm or deny the previous mating of dogs by a test that has been developed in the Netherlands. By a rigid blood typing regime, the testing of a dog pedigree is possible. It is so accurate that it can even determine if the puppies in a litter were sired by more than one male.

PRENATAL WORM INFESTATION OF PUPPIES

Roundworm and hookworm larvae can be dormant in the liver of the female dog and when she becomes pregnant the larvae cross the placental barrier and invade the livers of the puppies. When the puppies are born the worms develop in the intestinal tracts.

This explains why some puppies are infested with worms at an early age, even though the bitch showed a negative examination before and during gestation.

MAMMARY TRANSMISSION OF ROUNDWORMS AND HOOKWORMS

New research shows that newborn puppies can be contaminated by their mother's milk with heavy roundworm and hookworm infestation. The larvae of the worms can lie dormant in the mammary tissue of the bitch and when she becomes pregnant the larvae get into the colostrum (the first few days of milk). Thus the puppies become infested with worms even though the mother has a negative fecal examination.

These larvae can be eliminated from the milk by filtering it before feeding it to the puppies.

THE MIRACLE OF BITCHES' MILK

It has been found by researchers that the female breast during pregnancy is saturated with antibiotics which are transferred to the newborn by way of breast milk. This is how nature gives protection against disease.

27 NEW DEVELOPMENTS

PETS AS PSYCHOTHERAPY

Sometimes pets can help the emotionally ill where drugs, electro-shock, or analysts fail.

Recent research at Ohio State Psychiatric Hospital has shown that dogs facilitated psychotherapy with mental patients who have often been the most non-responsive to traditional forms of treatment.

The experimental work started at the Psychiatric Hospital; it involved 50 patients with 20 dogs in a nine-month experiment. The patients were permitted to groom, exercise, and play with the dogs.

The psychiatrists noted that the patients' behavior changed almost from the start. They livened up. They established a bond of love with the dogs by means of which they were eventually able to begin communicating better with the doctors themselves.

ANTI-BITE DEVICE

A new transistor-radio-sized device which gives off an electronic squeal now provides the postman or the meter reader with much more protection against a snarling dog than a swift kick, a hasty retreat, or a quick prayer.

The battery-powered device emits a high frequency squeal, which hurts a dog's ears. They won't stop barking but they will usually shy away. And it does no lasting harm to the animal. The sound is nearly always inaudible to the human ear. It has proved much more acceptable than mace-like chemicals.

It has worked remarkably well in protection against dog bites except on deaf dogs!

PET MEDICAL INSURANCE PLAN

A prepaid medical plan for pets is now operational, called MEDI-PET. The plan closely parallels human health insurance plans.

While entry into the program is restricted to healthy, vaccinated animals from 16 weeks to seven years, once they are qualified, dogs and cats are covered for life or as long as the pet owner continues payment of annual premiums.

Premium fees vary from region to region and will be geared to the cost of living index for that area. An estimated average yearly contract fee of $68.00 with a $6.00 reduction for a second pet and a $5.00 reduction for the third and fourth pets.

Under the plan, routine examinations and continuous health care are provided, as well as catastrophic illness or injury.

It will allow veterinarians to make decisions on the basis of medical need and not economics.

While the Medi-plan is now being offered only in the San Francisco Bay area, national and international participation is envisioned.

NATIONAL PET IDENTIFICATION SYSTEM— ANIMALERT

All animals registered with MEDI-PET will have a 10-digit number imprinted on the hairless inner portion of the ear. The tattoo-like operation will be quick and painless and does not penetrate the cartilage of the ear.

National Pet Care sees the system as aiding in the retrieval of lost or stolen pets. A person finding an imprinted animal can dial a toll free number and locate its owner.

For a $5.00 imprint fee and a $3.00 yearly computer registry fee, anyone can enter his pet in the Animalert program.

BIRTH CONTROL FOOD

Carnation Company officials have completed field tests on a contraceptive dog food utilizing as the active agent, Mibolerone.

Conducted for more than a year and involving 300 dogs of various breeds and ages, Carnation Company feels that the tests have established the effectiveness and safety of the product.

Bitches were fed a 6½ ounce can of the contraceptive food daily. Estrous or heat period was effectively controlled without harmful side effects. With discontinuation of the food, normal cycles were resumed. And, when bred, the dogs gave birth to healthy litters.

The FDA in Washington is now in the process of approving or disapproving of its use in animals. The FDA fears that teenagers might mistakenly consider it a human contraceptive agent. However, spokesmen for Upjohn Company and Carnation Company discount the probability of poisoning by Mibolerone in human beings.

Carnation Company officials cautioned that the food will be priced at a level not tempting to budget-minded consumers.

LOW-CALORIE DOG FOOD

A new diet dog food designed for overweight and inactive adult dogs has been introduced by Ralston Purina Company.

Called "FIT & TRIM," the new product is described as being 15% lower in fat than the leading dry dog food, yet contains all the vitamins, minerals, and other nutrients necessary for maintenance of adult dogs.

Another dog food company has a canned product called "Cycle," designed to meet four different types of dogs: the puppy, the adult dog, the overweight dog, and the geriatric or senior citizen dog. It has been well received by dogs and owners alike since most people are becoming diet conscious for themselves. What is good for themselves is good for their pets.

SNAKE ANTIVENIN FOR DOGS

A specific treatment for bites of venomous snakes in dogs is now available to veterinarians. The new antivenin product aids in neutralizing venom of the pit vipers, the principal group of poisonous snakes in North America including rattlesnakes, cottonmouths, and copperheads.

Survival rate in bitten animals was 89% when they were treated within 4 hours. The rate fell to 45% when there was a time lag of 4 hours or longer.

"CATHOUSE" FOR DOGS

These are the days of many bizarre business ventures. One of the most questionable enterprises to open in New York is a "Cathouse" for dogs. The Greenwich Village establishment is exactly what the name imples, believe it or not.

For $50.00, Joe Scaggs, proprietor of the "Cathouse," will provide a male dog with a female companion in a state of artificially-induced heat. As if that isn't enough, the establishment also boasts a resident photographer who will snap candid pictures of the dogs in action.

Mr. Scaggs guarrantees complete satisfaction. If a dog can't perform, they will bring the female to his home, his own territory, where he feels more secure.

Mr. Scaggs feels his establishment is filling a need in a dog-oriented community where genuine dog lovers bring their mutts to see them have a good time.

HOW TO MAKE A DOG AGGRESSIVE

Dog psychologists and dog trainers both agree on the most common ways of making a dog mean and aggressive. They are as follows:

1) Keep him on a chain or confined in a small space.

2) Do not pay much attention to him—don't pet him—don't play with him—don't praise him.

3) Yell and punish him physically when he does something wrong.

4) Keep him by himself—no other dogs or cats to play with.

THE BRANDY AND COGNAC CURE

A halfway house for alcoholics in Bridgeport, Connecticut, has found an unusual way to "beat the bottle," through resident dogs Brandy, Ginger, Blackberry, and Cognac. Bob Ryan, director of the Guenster home, and himself a reformed alcoholic, believes that many people turn to alcohol because humans are not satisfying their emotional needs. Ryan felt that a dog would be just the medicine many residents needed to give love and affection and to ask nothing in return.

Most ex-residents of the halfway house now own a previous pet of the home and are continuing the companionship that was so generously given during their rehabilitation.

Now there is a 10-part dog intelligence test developed and published by school psychologist, Cathy Coon, who once thought her dog was the dumbest in the world. Her three-year study of more than 100 dogs showed that most owners had no accurate idea of the intelligence of their pets. On a scale of 0-10—very dumb to brilliant—the mean test score is 5.75. Purebred hounds scored the highest, with a 7.63 average. Toy poodles were worst with 4.78. Obedience school dogs were no better than unschooled dogs. Mixed breeds were about as smart as pure breeds. Neither male nor female dogs were significantly smarter. "The Dog Intelligence Test Manual," complete with test, score sheet, and findings, sells for $3.00 at pet shops and department stores.

However, don't be discouraged or dissatisfied with your pet if he doesn't score too high on this test. He still loves you and is a smart dog—no matter what the test results show.

28 NEW ORGANIZATIONS

"Hearing Ear" Dogs

AUDIO CANIS is a non-profit organization for the deaf or hard-of-hearing. All breeds and cross-breeds are used after passing an evaluation test for alertness, hearing, and sight. The deaf people work with the dogs for 15 weeks—until they and the dogs are alert to routine sounds such as telephones, doorbells, knocking, as well as out-of-the-ordinary sounds.

"Feeling Hearts" Dogs

In treating certain forms of schizophrenia, it has been found that dogs can be used successfully where human therapists have failed. "Feeling Hearts" dogs, chosen for their warmth and friendliness, are used to treat patients who do not respond to conventional therapy. These dogs serve as constant companions to these people and offer the kind of love a psychiatrically sick person needs.

Dogs and Drugs

"Beat the Drug Habit" is the slogan of CADAD—Committee to Abolish Drug Abuse in Dogs—a group of people who are trying to protect dogs from ignorant or uncaring owners. The misuse of tranquilizers and stimulants is especially noted.

Index

abdominal problems, symptoms of, 187-188, 190

abnormalities: sexual, 148-149, 167-168; chance, 322, 323-327; selectional, 322, 323

abortions, 338, 339, 340, 356, 417

abscesses, 157, 214

achondroplasia, 327

acne, 424

acquired traits, 322-323

acupuncture, 131

adjustment to humans, puppy's, 39-40, 44-45

Afghans, 37, 109

afterbirth, 362, 373; retained, 379

agalactia (inadequate or no milk supply), 381

age equivalents, man-dog, 64, 414

aggressiveness, 170-171, 174-175, 176, 432

aging, physical, 78 ff.

Airedales, 319

alcohol, effects of, on dogs, 158, 412

alkalies and acids, dangers of, 230-231

all-meat diet, 99

allergies in dogs, 157, 196-197, 234-236

alopecia, 274-275

American Kennel Club (AKC), 326, 339, 417

anal glands, purposes and problems of, 262-263

anaphylactic shock, 127, 210, 214

ancestors of dogs, 32-33, 134

anemia, 236-237, 304, 305, 306, 311; in puppies, 58

anti-motion sickness pills, 165

antibiotics, 127-128, 283, 292, 294, 295, 343, 352, 364, 391, 392, 395

anti-bite device, 429

anti-estrus compounds for birth control, 131

antifreeze poisoning, 231

antisocial tendencies, 165

antivenom, snake, 431

antu poison, 225

anxiety in dogs, 166, 178-179

appetite: loss of, 162; in puppies, 53-54, poor, 410

appetite variations as symptoms, 188

arsenic, 224

arthritis, 81-82, 119, 197, 237, 404

artificial insemination, 339

artificial respiration, 210-211, 217, 221

aspirin, 126, 404

asthma, 87, 161, 180

atresia anus, 371

automobile accidents, 209, 276

bacterial infections, 341

bad breath (halitosis), 189, 254, 409-410

bandaging, 274

barking, 160, 176

basenjis, 321, 326

basset hounds, 39

bathing, 109-110, 115, 275, 356, 407; puppies, 57; in winter, 119

435

440

441

443